Human Communication Theory

HUMAN COMMUNICATION THEORY
COMPARATIVE ESSAYS

FRANK E. X. DANCE

University of Denver

HARPER & ROW, PUBLISHERS, New York
Cambridge, Philadelphia, San Francisco,
London, Mexico City, São Paulo, Sydney

1817

Sponsoring Editor: George A. Middendorf
Project Editor: Pamela Landau
Designer: Michel Craig
Production Manager: Marion Palen
Compositor: Maryland Linotype Co.
Printer: Murray Printing Co.
Binder: Murray Printing Co.
Art Studio: Vantage Art
Cover Design: Wanda Lubelska

HUMAN COMMUNICATION THEORY Comparative Essays

Copyright © 1982 by Frank E. X. Dance

Library of Congress Cataloging in Publication Data
Main entry under title:

Human communication theory.

   Includes bibliographies.
   1. Interpersonal communication—Addresses, essays, lectures.   I. Dance, Frank E. X.
BF637.C45H85   001.54   81-20054
ISBN 0-06-041481-2   AACR2

To Carol C. Zak-Dance

Contents

Preface

Human communication theory is at one and the same time both new and old. As a disciplinary or subject concentration title, the term *human communication theory* is relatively recent. It is difficult if not impossible to find it mentioned as a programmatic label or course title prior to the 1950s. Even in the early 1950s, when one did come across the term, it often was because its use was confused with or substituted for *information theory*, which was then in the early stages of popularity and influence.

Although it is new as a label or title, human communication theory is as old as the human race in terms of its presence in the daily affairs of men and women. People have always looked for reasons underlying their communicative successes and failures—reasons that could then be used to guide their future communicative efforts. The on-going search for such reasons is an example of the pervasive reality of human communication theory. Human communication theory has also had a number of enduring concerns that have interested past scholars and still interest researchers and scholars of today. Some of these concerns include the origin and the possible species-specificity of spoken language; the nature and function of spoken language; the relationship between spoken language and thought; and the ethical use of spoken language as such use bears on the individual and upon society.

The concern with the origin of spoken language is found in the writings of the Old Testament, Plato, Aristotle, and up to the present time, where it may be found highlighted in the work of those teaching what they construe to be a form of human language to nonhuman primates. A concern with the nature and function of spoken language was shared by Herodotus, Plato, Aristotle, Aquinas, Descartes, and is today evident in the work of scholars such as Noam Chomsky and Mortimer Adler. Interest in the relationship between spoken language and thought is as popular today as it was in the past. Most of the aforementioned scholars, in addition to Augustine, Bacon, Locke, Hegel, and Darwin, were interested in how spoken language impacted upon the development and practice of mental acts. Contemporary scholars who share this concern include Fodor, Chomsky, and Searle, as well as many of the authors appearing in this volume. The ethical use of human communication, and its effect on the individual and society, was also of interest to most of the above scholars. Additionally, Sophocles and Dante focused upon language and ethics. Current ethicists, such as Bok and Burke as well as a number of human communication theorists, find ethics as it relates to human communication to be among their central concerns.

The listed concerns certainly are not meant to exhaust the human communication theory concerns that have been maintained throughout the history of Western thought. There are other matters for consideration that could be singled out, as, for example, the concern in detailing the role played by human communication in individual self-actualization and self-fulfillment, which may be traced in the work of past as well as present theorists.

Those historically and presently interested in human communication theory represent diverse traditions and disciplines. Prior to the seventeenth century, rhetoric, linguistics, philosophy, and psychology were all one discipline, which was usually labeled *rhetoric*. The liberal arts of grammar, rhetoric, and logic were all centrally concerned with human language. Today, scholars such as Mortimer Adler, Jerome Bruner, Noam Chomsky, Umberto Eco, Marshall McLuhan, Susanne Langer, George A. Miller, Walter Ong, and John Searle, as well as many other anthropologists, philosophers, psycholinguists, psychologists, sociologists, and scholars from the field of speech communication, are identified or identify themselves as human communication theorists. Disciplinary boundaries melt and merge under the heat generated by the central concerns and questions of human communication theory.

Contributions to human communication theory may be either highly specific or quite broad-ranging. Whatever the boundaries of the individual contribution, if the work was carefully and responsibly executed, then it is important when viewed as a slice of a horizontal continuum. Whether a contribution is successful or unsuccessful in the eyes of its originator or in the eyes of history, that contribution has made a difference in the development of our understanding of human communication from a theoretical perspective.

The traditional data base of human communication theory has almost always been spoken language, although this data base is altered by differing disciplinary forces. As an example, literary scholars usually study human communication in its written manifestation, and scholars from the field of mass communication usually study human communication as it is mediated by technological transmission to great numbers of listeners, readers, or viewers.

In 1967, when Dance's *Human Communication Theory: Original Essays*[1] was published, most of the materials bearing specifically on the study of human communication theory came from outside of the speech communication discipline. In that volume, speech communication was represented by the contributions of the rhetorical tradition and by a framework within which contributions from other disciplines were coordinated. In 1967, constructivism, the coordinated management of meaning, and many other of the theoretical viewpoints represented in this volume were either not yet born or were in their infancy.

When Littlejohn's *Theories of Human Communication*[2] was published in 1978, there was definitely more material traceable to contributions from speech communication scholars, but the preponderance of the theoretical materials still came from representatives of other disciplines.

In 1979, *Human Communication Theory: The History of a Paradigm* by Nancy Harper[3] was published. This book presented a viewpoint wherein the historical and modern contributions of the study of rhetoric were viewed as a manifestation of human communication theory by using a rhetorical framework to examine and discuss human communication studies across Western history. Certainly, the rhetorical approach is a significant tradition from which scholars who currently identify with the field of speech communication have made important contributions to human communication theory.

By 1981, changes were evident. Although there are still many important and intriguing contributions to human communication theory emerging from many disciplines, the discipline of speech communication now offers a number of perspectives on human communication theory. These speech communication perspectives are not all aspects of the same theory, nor are they all mutually compatible.

For the purpose of bringing together these speech communication perspectives, which are not readily accessible in the literature, this book was conceived and prepared. This volume is a presentation

[1] Dance, Frank E. X. (Ed.). *Human communication theory: Original essays*. New York: Holt, Rinehart and Winston, 1967.
[2] Littlejohn, Stephen W. *Theories of human communication*. Columbus, Ohio: Charles E. Merrill, 1978.
[3] Harper, Nancy. *Human communication theory: The history of a paradigm*. Rochelle Park, N.J.: Hayden Book Co., 1979.

for comparative purposes of a number of the most visible theories currently being proposed by scholars who are identified primarily with the academic field of speech communication. It should be emphasized that this book does not include work by all extant human communication theorists, nor does it include a consideration of all extant theories of human communication. Additionally, the book is not intended to be a survey of human communication theory but is a highly selective presentation of human communication theories from a specific disciplinary viewpoint.

The theories and contributions presented herein were chosen based upon consultation with active theorists and upon a review of the literature for the purpose of discovering those theorists who have been publishing materials that set forth a view of human communication that transcends particular settings or specific instances and are characterized by internal consistency, power, precision, range, and elegance.

The book begins with a metatheoretical overview chapter designed to establish some general metatheoretical concerns that affect all other original contributions. The specific theoretical chapters are presented in alphabetical order by name of the senior author. Since not all readers may have had the opportunity to read materials on human communication theory from outside of the speech communication discipline, a chapter is presented, after the original theory chapters, that sets forth some of the major contributions to the study of human communication theory from other disciplines. This chapter representing the work of other disciplines includes many important theoretical perspectives, such as symbolic interactionism and information theory, which are necessary to know about if the reader is interested in acquiring a broad understanding of current human communication theory.

In order to achieve some degree of uniformity in the various chapters, each contributor was provided with a protocol setting forth some possible organizational points. Knowing the substance of the protocol might assist you in organizing your own approach to the individual essays.

The presumption upon which each author was selected for inclusion was that the contributor had a theory, whether partial or grand, of human communication. Each contributed chapter was to have as its main goal the succinct presentation of the contributor's theory in such a manner that the reader would be able to understand the theory's essential aspects even though the reader may have had relatively little previous experience in the speech communication discipline.

It was suggested to the contributors that some aspects that could be discussed early in the chapter would include (a) any assumptions held by the author that, although not tested, affect the theory; (b) the phenomena(on) proper to the theory; (c) the domain of the theory; (d) any metatheoretical stance consciously in the author's mind during the theory's construction; (e) any methodological bias that informs the contributor's theory-building efforts; (f) the manner in which the theorist's methodology might have interacted with the theorist's substantive theory-building efforts; and (g) a brief outline of the major points of the theory being presented. The authors were also requested to devote a few words to what would lead to further refinement or development of the theory and of how the theory might best be tested.

The protocol also supplied a list of questions about human communication behavior that are sometimes addressed by human communication theorists. The authors were requested to look over the questions, and if they found that their theories did address some or all of the questions either implicitly or explicitly, they were to mention in their chapter the manner and/or degree in which their theories interact with the questions. The following questions were set forth:

1. What do you consider to be the primary reason for the existence of human communication, that is, it's raison d'être?
2. How, if at all, does your theory consider the role of "meaning" in human communication?
3. Does your theory consider the role of "intent" or "intentionality" in human communication?
4. Does your theory view human communication from any specific level (e.g., intrapersonal, interpersonal, etc.), or is the theory not level-bound?
5. Does your theory consider the ethical aspects of human communicative behavior?
6. Does your theory take any position concerning the role of human communication mode (spoken, written, etc.) in human communication?

Finally, the protocol requested the author to include a bibliography directing the reader to any metatheoretical, methodological, or additional content readings that would engender a better understanding of the theory being set forth.

As you read the individual contributions, you will make your own decision as to the degree to which each chapter follows the suggested protocol. Certainly, there are times when deviating from the protocol seems to have enhanced the material presented. Protocol or not, each theorist speaks independently.

Since essays in speech communication journals may follow either the style of the American Psychological Association or the Modern Language Association (depending upon the specific journal), each contributor was allowed to choose between these two styles so as to familiarize student readers with both forms of manuscript preparation.

This volume presumes an audience of scholars interested in the study of human communication theory. The scholars may come from many disciplines and may represent different levels of formal training. Regardless of the disciplinary background or training level, certain expectations, if held by the reader, are likely to be disappointed.

- The reader who expects to find a grand or overall theory will find that these essays yield theories of partial or restricted range.
- The reader who expects to find one or more completed theories will find that these theories yield points of view "in process."
- The reader who expects to find unity will find that these essays yield diversity.
- The reader who expects to find simplicity will find that these essays yield complexity.
- Those who read expecting to find polarities will find that although some are indeed present, many essays yield complementarity as well.

The characteristics of process, diversity, complexity, polarity, and complementarity seem to be among the characteristics of the subject matter of spoken language—the common phenomenon upon which many of the theories herein presented are based.

The last chapter is a summary, which seeks to discuss some of the commonalities and differences that seem to develop out of the contributions. A reader wishing to develop a list of commonalities or differences might use the protocol as an organizing structure.

If I have inadvertently missed and thus omitted some speech communication theorists who deserve to be included, I apologize.

Finally, I would like to express my appreciation to those who assisted in reviewing this book while it was being prepared. Your suggestions were pertinent and helpful. Thanks to Joseph DeVito, John Johnson, Nancy Harper, and Julia Woods.

FRANK E. X. DANCE

Human Communication Theory

METHODOLOGICAL CONSIDERATIONS IN BUILDING HUMAN COMMUNICATION THEORY

W. Barnett Pearce
Vernon E. Cronen
Linda M. Harris

Learning is a natural act, performed spontaneously, usually joyfully, but with a tremendous variety of procedures and variation in sophistication. Infants aggressively handle and taste objects, and develop concepts about themselves and the other persons, objects, and events that comprise their world. Older children and adults do the same thing but with more complex concepts (sometimes called theories) and more sophisticated techniques (sometimes called research methods). Theorists are professional knowers, and at this level of sophistication, the process of knowing is much more complex and difficult than it appears to be in the naive wonder of a child. In this chapter, we describe some inherent problems in theory-building and discuss some of the ways in which theorists have dealt with those problems. To anticipate the conclusion, these problems in knowing are particularly troublesome for a theory of human communication; there is no solution for them, but there are ways of minimizing their effects. Our purpose is to provide you with the *perspective* and *information* you need to *do* theory-building and to *critique* the theories proposed by others.

Every culture has developed a complex mythology that describes the nature of reality, the origin and structure of its own social group, and the "mystery" of life.[1] Further, every culture has developed methods for expressing and/or increasing this knowledge. In primitive societies, the socially approved methods include rituals and sympathetic magic[2] (which many modern scientists think are ignorant expressions of superstitution) as well as megalithic structures, such as Stonehenge and carvings on bone or stone[3] (which amaze modern scientists as engineering feats and as evidence of a surprisingly accurate knowledge of astronomy). Other cultures have developed quite different research methods. For example, modern Western cultures use scopes to record what the human eye cannot see, telemetry to report events where persons cannot go, and computers to store and analyze quantities of data too great for human cognitive processing.

The information or data that one learns depends on one's research methods. Although primitive cultures included some excellent astronomers who did much with lunar and solar cycles, they could not know that Jupiter had moons. It took the invention of the telescope and the careful use of it by Galileo to discover Jovian satellites, and even Galileo was limited by his instrumentation. Refinements in telescopes and spacecraft, culminating in the Pioneer missions, showed that there are really twelve moons. (Stated more accurately, the best evidence *provided by the research methods currently available* makes us believe that there are no more and no less than twelve. The human activity of devising better research methods will continue to change the solar system *as we know it*.)

The rather obvious relation between data and research methods raises a more intriguing question. Why have various cultures and researchers within given cultures developed such different research methods and thus "lived" in such different worlds? If the process of learning were *in principle unproblematic*, then naive wonder should produce accurate and reliable information that would "in-form" research methods, which in turn should provide a sufficient base for the development of theories, and the "knowers" of various ages and cultures should be able to compare notes with a high degree of agreement. However, human knowledge is characterized more by diversity than by consistency; by acrimonious conflict that by serendipitous convergence of opinion. It is sometimes hard to believe that the knowers from different cultures inhabit the same environment.

At the least, these characteristics indicate that the process of knowing is more difficult than it appears, but recent developments in philosophy and in the sciences complicate the problem even more: they show that the process of knowing is inherently confounded. Just as data are selected and sometimes created by research methods, so research methods depend on the implicit or explicit theories of the researcher; and these theories derive from the array of often-unstated assumptions about the nature of reality, of knowledge, of humankind, and so on, which we call methodologies. Persons with different methodologies get different answers because they ask different questions and because they treat different events as data.[4] For example, given the belief system of primitive culture, the idea of experimentation with the "profane" elements of chemistry and physics is unthinkable and would appear absurd if suggested by an outsider.[5] The use of quantitative methods in research is an exclusively Western phenomenon that originated with the Pythagoreans. "To non-European civilizations, the idea that numbers are the key to both wisdom and power, seems never to have occurred."[6] An Analysis of Variance statistical test, complete with a semisacred $p < 0.05$, is laughable if not unintelligible to a Buddhist, whose concept of research methods, in turn, is likely to bewilder an orthodox American social scientist.[7]

Even within a culture, the selection and interpretation of data are theory-dependent. Hanson described a hypothetical meeting of Brahe and Kepler, who planned to observe the dawn as data that would enable them to choose among the geocentric and heliocentric theories of the solar system. It did not work: at the moment the sun became visible, *both* turned to the other with a triumphant "Aha! See, I'm right!" Did they see the same thing? In one sense, yes. The retinal images, we assume, were identical, but one "saw" the sun rise above an immobile earth, and the other "saw" the earth rotate to expose an immobile sun. *Seeing that* the sun appeared did not imply that they saw it *as* the same event. Their preconceived theories caused them to interpret the same data differently.[8]

The hypothetical encounter between Brahe and Kepler illustrates a recurrent theme in the history of science. The popular mythology about the "progress" of science describes an inexorable march toward increased knowledge, with clear-minded, unbiased researchers each adding his or her contribution to an expanding ability to understand, describe, explain, and control the world. More careful histories show that this simply is not the way it works. The inherent problems of knowing bias the content of any knower's "theory."[9] Koestler's is the most readable of these histories:

> . . . I have been interested . . . in the psychological process of discovery . . . and in that converse process that blinds him toward truths which, once perceived by a seer, become so heartbreakingly obvious. . . . It looks as if, while part of their spirit was asking for more light, another part had been crying out for more darkness . . . all cosmological systems . . . reflect the unconscious prejudices, the philosophical or even political bias of their authors; and . . . no branch of science, ancient or modern, can boast freedom from metaphysical bias of one kind

or another. The progress of science is generally regarded as a kind of clean, rational advance along a straight ascending line; in fact it has followed a zig-zag course. . . . The history of cosmic theories, in particular, may without exaggeration be called a history of collective obsessions and controlled schizophrenias; and the manner in which some of the most important individual discoveries were arrived at reminds one more of a sleepwalker's performance than an electronic brain's.[10]

The problem inherent in the process of knowing concerns the relationship between the "knower" and the "known." Until recently (e.g., in the philosophy of Kant), it was usually assumed that knowers existed separately from the known, and that neither was changed by the process of knowing. Schematically, this can be represented this way:

(knowing)

knower ─────────────→ the known

where the horizontal bars indicate insulation. However, there is now reason to believe that the process should be represented this way:

(knowing)

the knower ←─────────────→ the known

indicating that the process of knowing is *not* independent of the properties of either the knower or the known. The more persons look at things that ostensibly have independent existence and that are beyond human capacity to change—for example, the stars and the solar system—the more they find that the results reflect the "face" of the observer. Koestler's history of cosmology tells at least as much about the characteristics of cosmologers as it does about the universe.

The human response to reality is constructive rather than passive. Forms of knowledge are determined not so much "from outside, by the fullness or poverty of experiences that meet the mind, as from within, by the power of conception, the wealth of formulative notions with which the mind meets experiences."[11] This understanding of the process of knowing has important implications, including the addition of a dash of skepticism to the content of any theory: "the edifice of human knowledge stands before us, not as a vast collection of sense reports, but as a structure of *facts that are symbols* and *laws that are their meanings*."[12] The human study of human communication is particularly confounded because that which is studied—for example, a communicative act—and the act of studying it are *both* human symbolic constructions that are "biased" by the underlying assumptions about humankind, knowledge, and the world.

As depicted in Figure 1, the process of knowing turns back on itself and has the properties Hofstadter described as a "strange loop":

"The 'Strange Loop' phenomenon occurs whenever, by moving upwards (or downwards) through the levels of some hierarchical system, we unexpectedly find ourselves right back where we started. . . ."[13] When the data pertain to inanimate objects, the process is complicated enough, but when the data describe acts which themselves are symbolic and meaningful, the potential for debilitating bias is very great. Theorists of human communication are particularly threatened by the recursive nature of knowing.

In Figure 1, the "highest" component consists of methodological assumptions, or the ontological and epistemic beliefs that give shape to the process of knowing. We are going against common usage in identifying these assumptions as methodologies, but with reason. The thrust of our whole argument is that these assumptions are unavoidable, and that they shape the knowing process at all levels. In fact, specifically because these assumptions are frequently out-of-awareness, their influence on theory-building and research methods is strong and potentially pernicious. The reason our use of methodology may seem strange is that it is very inconsistent with positivism, the methodology that has had the greatest influence on contemporary communication theory. Positivists deny the existence of biasing assumptions—or, better, they claim that their *methods* have absolved them from a biasing *methodology;* hence, the two terms are used interchangeably. Obviously, we disagree. These issues are discussed later; for the moment, grant us our use of the term *methodology.*

The interrelationship between knower and known implies that the data of any act of knowing does not come prepackaged and predefined. Rather, an important aspect of theory-building occurs *before* data are collected. The theorist must decide, What counts as data? This is done, consciously or not, as a movement "down" the levels identified in Figure 1. As methodological assumptions provide the frame within which theories are developed, theories in turn frame the selection or invention of research methods, and the methods determine what data are observed.

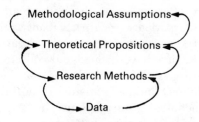

Methodological Assumptions

Theoretical Propositions

Research Methods

Data

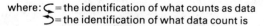

where: $\subset$ = the identification of what counts as data
$\supset$ = the identification of what data count is

Figure 1   The structure of knowing

The question, What counts as data? can be further specified as a series of decisions that any theorist must make.

• *What Is the Appropriate Unit of Analysis?* Should the researcher attend to the smallest possible units of analysis, for example, looking at phonemes, morphemes, words, or sentences? Or should the unit of analysis be more macrocosmic—messages, interacts, or episodes? For example, Chomsky uses "well-formed" sentences as the appropriate unit of analysis, while Hymes argues that the function of grammatical sentences cannot be understood without considering the episode and speech community in which they occur.[14]

• *What Is the Appropriate Unit of Observation?* Should the researcher focus on an individual's behavior, or on dyads, groups, or communities? For example, can a group be understood by studying each of its individual members, or does the group itself have a certain "thing-ness" about it? If a researcher selects aggressive acts as the unit of analysis and determines to examine 20 cases, should those cases be 20 persons, 20 dyads, 20 families, or what? The decision is not trivial, and it emerges from the theory informing the research. If aggressive behavior is theorized as an individual predisposition—a tendency each person takes to each situation—then 20 individuals are the appropriate units of observation. But if aggressive acts are theorized as components of communication systems that have particular structures, then observing 20 dyads or 20 groups might be required.

• *What Is the Appropriate Form of Data?* Should data be qualitative or quantitative? If it is quantitative, what is the most appropriate level of measurement? Sometimes the frequency with which something occurred is the best measure, but this information may be irrelevant from the perspective of other theories. Qualitative studies are similarly theory-laden and require choices. Philipsen's study, "Speaking 'Like a Man' in Teamsterville," selected one community as the unit of observation, an array of episodes as the unit of analysis, and verbal reports and his own experiences as a participant as the form of data.[15]

The process of knowing is not a simple, linear movement downward. Once the data have been defined and collected, they sometimes cause revisions in the research methods and the theory, and rejected theories or serendipitous findings sometimes cause thorough-going revisions of the methodological assumptions. In fact, the genius of the Western scientific methodology is that it has given great importance to the movement upwards from data to methodology, answering the question, "What do data count as?" This question can be further partitioned into these concerns.

• *What Does a Statistical Relationship Indicate?* Consistent with their methodologies, some scientists interpret a statistical relationship in their data that is unlikely to occur by chance as a description of the "law-like" order of reality. By refining these statistical relationships, statements describing the precise probability that event *A* will be followed by event *B* may be included in the theory. From other methodologies, some theorists have taken seriously Aristotle's discussion of multiple types of causation. For these theorists, statistical relationships mean different things, depending on which type of "cause" they hypothesize as operative in the phenomena being studied.[16]

• *What Is the Relationship Between the Data and the Theory?* In any scientific form of knowing, the data count as a test and/or a source of theory in a movement upward through the levels of Figure 1. However, the nature of the upward move differs as a function of different methodologies. From one methodology, statistical relations among data are the building blocks of theory. Theoretical statements consist of nothing more than summaries of empirical regularities; "surplus meaning" is exorcised in favor of the meaning that seeps up from observations. Another methodology describes theory as models, the properties of which can be specified well in advance of empirical research. The data provide a test of the model but are not its source.

Our purposes in this chapter are relatively modest. First, we stress the importance of differentiating between *methodology* as a cluster of basic assumptions that frame knowing per se and *methods* as a set of techniques for generating data. The fact that we can differentiate incompatible methodologies as the infrastructure of contemporary theories and research programs about human communication should serve as a strong warning to a would-be theorist or researcher. You cannot responsibly use or contribute to the literature of communication theory without analyzing the relationships among the knower's methodology, theory, and methods and that which is known, the data.

Second, we advocate and provide the basis for methodological pluralism. This perspective stands in contrast both to monism, the perspective that one methodology is correct and all others are wrong, and to ecumenicism, the perspective that all methodologies are equally correct or equally irrelevant to truth. Pluralism is the assumption that a variety of methodologies exist, with important differences among them, and that these differences comprise an array of perspectives with variable utility. Unlike ecumenicism, pluralism *acknowledges* substantive differences; unlike monism, it *celebrates* them.

Methodological pluralism is necessary precisely because the existing research programs in the social sciences have *not* been stunningly successful. Particularly when compared with the results of research in the natural sciences, communication theories have been vague, vacuous, and empirically sterile. Since the research *methods* available are varied and powerful, we suspect that the major impediment to progress has been the inability to formulate the most fertile questions or to construct the most useful integration of information in a new methodology, not the lack of sheer mass of information or the discovery of a particular, crucial datum. All theorists are surrounded by the "stuff" of human communication but have very different notions about which of it counts as data and how the data count toward a theory.

The study of human communication will probably parallel the experience of other disciplines. At some future date, a well-articulated theory will be commonly accepted by both academics and innocent civilians, and teachers in graduate seminars will find it difficult to convince their students that communication did not seem so obvious before. At present, however, we lie before the conceptual watershed, and the methodologies in the intellectual tradition apparently contain built-in blinders. The safest assumption for any theorist is that everything believed *might* be wrong and *might* preclude understanding the phenomena. In this context, the study of a variety of methodologies serves primarily to liberate theorists from a sterile blindness to the limits of their own methodology and to facilitate creativity. Methodological culture shock makes one's own assumptions seem strange and tentative, and also confers "the curious ability to look around the corners of one's own *Weltanshauung*, the ability to imagine oneself holding quite a different position."[17]

After reading this chapter, you should be able to do these things:

1. Differentiate among methodology, theory, methods, and data.
2. Identify the several methodologies that inform contemporary communication theories and research programs.
3. Explain why persons informed by different methodologies do not always agree about what counts as data.
4. Explain why persons informed by different methodologies do not always agree about what data count as.
5. Critique the fit between the methodology, theory, and research methods in particular communication theories.
6. Identify alternatives to the choices made by particular communication theorists at the level of methodology, theory, and research methods, and assess the implication of various choices.
7. Describe the means by which various methodologies deal with the recursiveness of human knowledge about humankind, and assess their relative success in avoiding dysfunctional bias.

These objectives, of course, identify important abilities for the intelligent "consumer" of communication theory. In addition, they should also facilitate the ability to do communication theory, and to do it innovatively. We recommend these exercises for those who want to try their hands at being communication theorists.

1. Take a particular communication event/situation and think about it in terms of *each* of the methodologies described in the next section. Prepare a chart with the methodologies listed across the top. Down the side, list the specific questions described above as detailed specifications of the movements up and down Figure 1: unit of analysis; unit of observation; and so on. Compare the answers generated by different methodologies, and analyze your own responses to those comparisons. What does it mean if you are dissatisfied with the answers from a particular methodology?

2. Repeat the process described above, but this time carefully pick an *array* of communication events/situations that differ in some important ways. For example, select the situations in which you feel most and least comfortable; in which you feel most in control and least in control; and so on. This will help you determine which methodologies are most able to explain a variety of events.

3. If you have persisted this far, you have probably discarded some methodologies as being hopeless and are not completely satisfied with some others. Now use a form or dialectical reasoning: take a methodology that you find appealing and systematically *change* the assumptions it makes by substituting the "opposite" assumption. For example, if the methodology implies large groups as the unit of observation, substitute individuals. How does the substitution change the theory informed by that methodology? Would you select a different array of research methods? How would you interpret the data produced by these methods? By answering these questions, you are doing communication theory.

As a communication theorist, you will find that theory-building is not an activity in which you are free to do anything you want. Every decision you make entails many consequences. For example, methodological assumptions come in clusters. If you decide that the "stuff" of reality comes in irreducible and unrelated hunks or "atoms," you cannot also assume that the phenomena you study are systematically organized—or at least you will have to be very inventive in concocting an explanation of how they can be both atomistic and systemic. Further, methodological assumptions and choice of research methods are related. If you assume that humans interpret others' behavior and respond to those interpretations, you cannot limit yourself to observations of behaviors in your research. If you do, you will be criticized as generating data that do not count as tests of your theory.

Skillful theory-builders (and users of theories) can quickly see the implications of particular decisions. They may persist in using, for example, the method of ethnography, even though it is slow and difficult, because it fits so well with the assumptions of their theory; or they will find fault with a research proposal that suggests that the factor loadings from a semantic differential (which sums across persons) be added to a Personal Construct Inventory (which assumes that each individual is unique). The best way to develop the ability to perceive the implications of decisions in theory-building is to examine the history of Western thought, where many methodologies have been offered and subjected to close scrutiny. Follow the flow of the argument in the summary of methodologies presented in the next section. You should develop an awareness of the size of various assumptions, where size is the amount of change throughout the conceptual system that would be necessitated by changing that particular part. You should also become familiar with the type of issues that must be dealt with by theorists.

A SUMMARY OF METHODOLOGIES

This section comprises much less than an intellectual history but something more than a list of the major methodologies that inform contemporary communication theories. The methodologies are listed in Table 1, with major proponents and contemporary exemplars arrayed in an approximate chronological sequence. Eastern and contemporary European thought are not included because they have thus far had relatively little influence on Anglo-American communication theories. However, these philosophies provide important sources of alternative methodological assumptions for the "dialectical" exercise described above.

The most decisive moment in the history of Western thought occurred 25 centuries ago when the Greek philosophers—unlike their Asian counterparts—made the assumption that there is a reality independent of the flux of sensory experience that can, using the right methods, be known with certainty, and that this knowledge leads to enlightenment. This assumption has provided the common element in the methodologies and the agenda for debate throughout Western civilization.

> The historical importance of the idea that disinterested science leads to purification of the soul and its ultimate liberation, can hardly be exaggerated. The Egyptians embalmed their corpses so that the soul might return to them and need not be reincarnated again; the Buddhists practiced non-attachment to escape the wheel; both attitudes were negative and socially sterile. The Pythagorean concept of harnessing science to the contemplation of the eternal . . . became a decisive factor in the making of the Western world.[18]

Table 1 METHODOLOGIES INFORMING COMMUNICATION THEORIES AND RESEARCH

METHODOLOGIES:	RATIONALISM	RATIONAL EMPIRICISM	MECHANISTIC EMPIRICISM	SKEPTICAL EMPIRICISM	POSITIVISM	CONSTRUCTIVISM	HUMAN SYSTEMS
PROPONENTS:	Plato (428/7–348/7) Descartes (1596–1650)	Aristotle (384–322)	Kepler (1571–1630) Newton (1642–1727)	Hume (1711–1776)	the Vienna Circle (1920s)	Kant (1724–1804)	von Bertalanffy, Harre
CURRENT EXEMPLARS IN COMMUNICATION:	Chomsky	Grice; Nofsinger; Sacks, et al. Dance	Feldstein; Stech; Fisher; Ellis		G. Miller; Burgoon	Goodenough; Garfinkel; Kelly; Delia	Cushman & Craig; Watzlawick; Beavin, & Jackson; Cronen & Pearce; Harris

It was in this context that the concept of theory emerged. The etymological root is *theoria,* "to behold, contemplate," and a theorist is one who gives "rapt contemplation of those fundamental principles of reality that, precisely because they are fundamental, cannot be modified by any human action."[19] For the Greeks, theoretical knowledge was pursued with religious and intellectual zeal as a means of liberation from the unreal world of sensory experience.[20] Although this concept of theory has been countered by others, it remains the often-unstated standard to which other positions are compared. A summary of the methodologies we shall review is shown in Table 2.

Rationalism

The basic assumptions of the ancient Greeks precluded them from discovering the recursiveness of human knowledge. Rather than distinguishing "between consciousness and its object . . . the knower and the known, the subjective and the objective," they differentiated between appearances and reality.[21] Appearances were characterized by being impermanent, by defects (i.e., each specific instance of a type of thing was in some ways different from all others), and by change. These attributes disqualified appearances from serious study because *theoria* was a means of personal liberation by ecstatic contemplation of and submission to the eternal, and thus, they reasoned, reality *had* to have the characteristics of unchangingness, perfection, and not being further explainable.

Plato is described as a realist because he disdained knowledge of the appearance as mere opinion and sought knowledge of the reality that lay behind them. In doing so, he established a model for rationalism, which answers the basic methodological questions, What counts as data? and What does data count as? in the following ways. *What counts as data* is reasoning, or clear, enlightened ideas. Perceptions of particular things or empirical generalizations are mere opinions that distract from knowledge. *What data counts as* is a description of reality that liberates the knower from enmeshment within the world of appearances.

For Plato, the methods for transcending appearances to get to the Forms were philosophical contemplation and dialectical reasoning. These methods produce the certainty required for theory because thought has the characteristics stipulated for reality: ". . . apart from relativity, contradiction or decay. . . . [It is] beyond, even against, the world."[22] To account for this striking isomorphism between thought and reality, Plato hypothesized a prenatal confrontation with reality. Knowledge is thus remembered rather than discovered.

Centuries later, Descartes developed a rationalism that was based

Table 2 A CLASSIFICATION OF METHODOLOGIES AND METATHEORETICAL ISSUES

	RATIONALISM	RATIONAL EMPIRICISM	MECHANISTIC EMPIRICISM	SKEPTICAL EMPIRICISM
WHAT COUNTS AS DATA?				
1. Unit of Analysis	The pure product of cognition	Reductionistic, theory neutral	Reductionistic, theory neutral	Reductionistic, but assumed to be distorted by perception
2. Unit of Observation	Irrelevant or unspecified	Individual	Individual "atoms" or "corpuscles" of mass. The relations among them are presumed to be a one-way causal force immanent in the corpuscles.	The individual event manifest in perception
3. Type of Data	Qualitative	Qualitative/Nominal	Quantitative, preferably interval or ratio level	Unspecified
HOW DO DATA COUNT?				
1. Data and Causation	Unspecified	Data reflect telic forces manifest in objects.	Data reflect nomic force manifest in corpuscles of mass.	Causation cannot be determined, only associations among observations.
2. Data and Theory	The data and theory are isomorphic.	Exemplification: data exemplify logically necessary relationships.	Data accumulate to create theory.	Unspecified

Table 2 *(Continued)*

	POSITIVISM	CONSTRUCTIVISM	HUMAN SYSTEMS
WHAT COUNTS AS DATA?			
1. Unit of Analysis	Reductionistic. The data are temporally discrete observations. Observations are not assumed to be theory-laden, as they reflect specified operational definitions.	Variable, depending on the epistemology invoked by a particular constructivist theory. Data are assumed to be theory-laden.	Holonic, reductionism is rejected. Molar units are preferred, or a combination of macro and micro units. The whole is *not* assumed to be an aggregation of parts. Data are assumed to be theory-laden.
2. Unit of Observation	The smallest individual unit is preferred.	The individual knower is the basic unit.	A variety of levels are employed. The unit of observation may be individual, dyads, groups, and so on. A combination of larger and smaller units may be employed.
3. Type of Data	Quantitative, preferably interval or ratio level	Qualitative or quantitative as appropriate	Quantitative or qualitative as appropriate.
HOW DO DATA COUNT?			
1. Data and Causation	Statistical associations are surrogates for causation. They are the legitimate substitutes for a knowledge of cause.	Statistical associations reflect cognitive processes postulated by the theorist.	Statistical associations may reflect nomic, logical, or practical forces and the interactions among these forces. Data may reflect reflexive relationships among phenomena, not just linear causal relationships.
2. Data and Theory	Knowledge "seeps up" from particular findings. These are organized into covering laws. Theory cannot advance much beyond data because theory is a summary and integration of data.	Data support or fail to support. The theorist's conception of theory can at times run well ahead of data.	Data support or fail to support aspects of the theorist's model of phenomena. Theory can at times run well ahead of data.

on "the pure, intrinsic certainty of the knowing intellect itself, needing no support beyond the luminous self-evidence of its own act of understanding."[23] Descartes believed that certain clear ideas—or intuition— were indubitable, and that if one moved carefully by deduction from one clear idea to another, "we can not only arrive . . . at *some* indubitable knowledge, but at the construction of a unified, all embracing body of such knowledge."[24]

The foremost modern rationalistic theory is Chomsky's "generative" or "transformational" linguistics; but in a sense, that is not about human communication at all. Paralleling the distinction between reality and mere appearances, Chomsky distinguished linguistic performance (what people actually say) from linguistic competence (what persons have to know to be able to use language). Chomsky is blissfully unconcerned about performance; he argues that it is the unpredictable and unaccountable result of a combination of language and the personality variables of the speaker. He further argues that language exists as a structure in the human mind quite distinct from any given act of communication. Chomsky's theory takes the form of a grammar, a set of transformations in the form of rewrite rules, which shows how simple kernel sentences can be changed to questions, conditionals, imperatives, and so on. Sentences count as data and are gathered from all available sources to test the theory. An acceptable grammar must be able to account for all and any sentences judged by native informants to be linguistically correct.[25] Sanders has attempted to apply Chomsky's program to human communication but thus far without conspicuous success.[26]

Rational Empiricism

Aristotle fully shared Plato's desire for a knowable reality, but he located that reality *within* rather than *beyond* the sensible world, and thus made rationalism empirical:

> . . . for Aristotle, the Platonic starting point, the thesis that sensible things are always in flux and there is no knowledge of them, was itself a mistake, and so the intellectual conversion away from the perceptible world to the really real of the Forms, was illusionary and unneeded. The source of certainty . . . is with us and around us in the nature of things and in the natural concordance between our own intelligence and the world.[27]

Like Plato, Aristotle assumed that the nature of reality duplicated the structure of thought. This assumption makes Aristotelian empiricism importantly different from more modern empiricisms. Observations count as data, but the data count as instances of necessary categories of entities.

True puzzlement, search for the truly unknown, and, *a fortiori*, discovery, the *advance* of knowledge, have no place whatsoever in Aristotelian science. Aristotelian method . . . is one of *exposition* of knowledge already now, not of groping forward out of new puzzles toward new solutions. That is why Aristotelian method *had* to be rejected before modern science could begin—not because Aristotle was not interested in observation; he was, but because for him the world was such and our minds were such that learning was no more than the analysis and articulation of an order already there, actually, in the forms of things themselves, and potentially in our minds, the "place of forms," suited by nature to receive them. . . . There is only the sorting out into intellectual awareness and explicit statement of what is already there. . . .[28]

The method of rational empiricism is the explication of a rational order within the array of sensible experiences. This method has great appeal to minds offended or overwhelmed by apparent inconsistency and chaos, and has a long legacy in Western thought. Medieval science was primarily Aristotelian and preoccupied with logic to an extent hard for the modern mind to comprehend. During these centuries, both the world of learning and the world of experience were perceived as fragmentary and disjointed, filled with plagues and superstitions. In striking contrast,

[logic] opened a window onto an orderly and systematic view of the world and of man's mind. The greater the decline of other sciences, the more pre-eminent appeared the orderliness of Aristotle's comprehensive picture of the workings of the human mind.

The whole process of simplification and arrangement was a revelation both of the powers of the mind, and of the orderliness which lay behind a bewildering complexity of apparently unrelated facts.[29]

Several contemporary communication theorists utilize rational empiricism. For example, Grice constructed a "logic of communication," the maxims of which explain why conversations *must* occur the way that they do. He is frankly unimpressed by "mere empirical generalizations" that document the fact that certain regularities in communication occur, arguing that the *existence* of these regularities surely does not *explain* them. Rather, he attempted to identify, using Aristotelian logic as a model, a set of categories in the human mind that makes observed patterns *necessary*.[30] Nofsinger's studies of the "demand ticket" and "indirect responses" clearly exemplify the methods of rational empiricism.[31] Transcripts or excerpts from conversations count as data, and the task of the researcher is to identify the rules that persons must follow to produce or make sense of the observed forms of communication. The hypotheses that the rules are correctly written are tested by being applied to other instances of conversation. Sacks,

Schegloff, and Jefferson's "simplest systematics" of turn taking follows the same procedure. Transcripts of conversations are inspected, and the simplest set of rules that will account for all of the observed turn taking is devised and offered as a description of how persons handle the distribution of speaking turns in conversation.[32]

It is difficult to specify how data count in rational empiricism because the structures of reality and of the mind are assumed to be isomorphic. The assumptions of this methodology make it *unthinkable* that the results of observation will in any important way force those assumptions to change. In terms of Figure 1, the process of knowing from this methodology is consistently downward, with no provision for recursive upward changes.

Mechanistic Empiricism

Newton's work as a scientist achieved an unparalleled advance in human knowledge. Pope celebrated his work in an epitaph:

> Nature and Nature's laws lay hid in night;
> God said, "Let Newton be," and all was light.

However, there is a certain inelegancy in this story. Newton's work was informed by a methodology that was soon abandoned, and he did not describe his own methods well. "In scientific discovery and formulation, Newton was a marvellous genius; as a philosopher he was uncritical, sketchy, inconsistent, even second-rate."[33]

Newton neatly reversed Aristotle's assumption that clear thinking parallels reality. Instead, he treated any reasoning as dangerously misleading. He wrote, "Whatever is not deduced from the phenomena is to be called an hypothesis, and hypotheses . . . have no place in experimental philosophy."[34] He urged scientists to shun hypotheses as they would any form of fallacious argument.[35] However, Newton agreed with Aristotle against the Rationalists that the empirical world of the appearances was "real," and ordered by knowable forces. Knowledge consisted of an ability to predict, describe, understand, and control reality, not to achieve a mystic enlightenment. He said, "Our business is with the causes of sensible events."[36] Newton believed that the world was ordered like a machine (and so physics continues to call the study of the interaction of entities "mechanics"), that laboratory experiments would discover those organizing principles, and that these principles could be best expressed in the form of mathematical relationships.

Newton summarized four Rules for Reasoning in Philosophy as a description of his methods. First is the *rule of simplicity:* "we are to admit no more causes of natural things than such as are both true and sufficient to explain their appearances . . . for nature is pleased with simplicity, and affects not the pomp of superfluous causes." Second is the *rule of causal reductionism,* or the principle of assigning the same cause to the same effects. The third rule is the *rule of generalizability.* Since Newton believed that entities were irreducible atoms, all instances of a type having the same properties, then a relationship found to hold in an experiment may be generalized to all instances of the types involved. Fourth is the *rule of empiricism:* Newton cautioned that no "law" or inference from phenomena was immune to disconfirmation by subsequent findings. This principle explicitly referred to the previous three rules, making the whole conceptual edifice subject to empirical test.

However, not even Newton followed these rules consistently, and the gap between what he *claimed* and what he *did* provides an important key for understanding subsequent intellectual history. Newton claimed to be free from any contaminating bias from methodological assumptions:

> . . . the best and safest method of philosophizing seems to be, first diligently to investigate the properties of things and establish them by experiments, and then later seek hypotheses to explain them.[37]

However, his assumption about the machine-like order of reality as well as his conceptualizations of space, time, and (to a lesser extent) mass were nonempirical and were bolstered by his avid but amateur theology. Because of his enormous scientific prestige, many people accepted his claim that he was without biasing assumptions and thus *uncritically* adopted his mechanistic empiricist methodology as well as his research methods. The continued use of the latter has forced thorough revisions in the former.

The data for mechanistic empiricism consist of observed relationships between physical phenomena, for example, the angles at which a light is cast upon and reflected by a mirror. Given Newton's methodology, these data should be descriptions of "laws," stating the exact, mathematical, and verifiable order of reality.[38] It has not turned out quite so neatly. The rule of simplicity has been undermined by demonstrations that reality is not only complex, it is *variably* complex. Hemple replaced the notion of universal laws with statements of probability, leading to "statistical-nomological" explanation,[39] and Laszlo describes the work done on systems that specify the degree of order within a particular phenomenon.[40] Further, systems theorists replace Newton's second rule, causal reductionism, with a concept of many types of causal relationships, including reciprocal causation, in which two objects each cause and are caused by the other; equifinality, in which many causes have the same effect; and multifinality, in which one cause may have many effects.[41] The third rule has also been challenged. The current view is that the generality of any given relationship must be empirically determined rather than simply assumed to be universal.[42]

The genius of Newton's method is the fourth rule, which makes all others subject to empirical tests. In terms of Figure 1, Newton's method clearly stressed the "upward" movement in which theory and methodological assumptions are revised on the basis of data. In one sense, this may be viewed as a triumph of method over methodology, a way of breaking through at least some of the problems of recursiveness in the process of knowing.

The criterial attribute of mechanistic empiricism is the assumption that there is an order or design or pattern among the events and objects of reality that can be mathematically expressed and that can be discovered by empirical experimentation and observation. The best example of mechanistic empiricism in contemporary human communication theory is a genre of research called interaction analysis. The data consist of transcripts of conversation, each message of which is coded in terms of its content, its function, or its relationship to other messages. (Some interaction analysts simply count the amount of time each person spends speaking and not speaking.[43]) These counts of time or types of message are statistically analyzed to discover patterns, for example, the "transitional probabilities" that a particular type of message will occur after or before another specified type.[44]

Skeptical Empiricism

This methodology self-destructs: it denies the possibility of a theory or of useful research methods, and there is no modern communication theory that is primarily informed by it. However, Hume's articulation of this position had important effects on other methodologies: it was a strong critique of Newton; ultimately it led to the development of logical positivism; and it awakened Kant from his "dogmatic slumbers" to develop constructivism.

In essence, Hume accepted Newton's distrust of the operation of human minds but added to that a rejection of Newton's assumption that reality is mechanistically ordered and can be positively known. Hume specified the methodology of skeptical empiricism in three principles. (1) The *Genetic Principle* restated Locke's notion that "simple ideas . . . are derived from simple impressions, which are correspondent to them, and which they exactly resemble." (2) The *Atomic Principle* declared that each percept is an irreducible unit of knowledge and is completely independent of any other percept. Reality is perceived as a string of perceptions that has no necessary connection; all ideas of cause, effect, and so on, are *complex* ideas, *not* based on a percept, and hence are illusions that can lead to the most ridiculous of ideologies. Humean skepticism consists of disbelieving anything but simple impressions. (3) The *Associative Principle* described a "gentle force" in which "nature, in a manner, [points] out to everyone those simple ideas which are most proper to be united into a complex one." While no atom of perception may *entail* another, some may *recall* others, producing some complex ideas to which Humean skepticism is only gently applied.[45]

For Hume, simple, isolated perceptions count as data, and the data count as direct perceptions of reality that can be interpreted, combined, and so on, only at the price of illusion. From this skeptical position, no science can be derived: there are no methods for acquiring knowledge other than perception of unrelated events.[46]

Positivism

In the early twentieth century, the Vienna Circle produced a methodology called logical positivism or logical empiricism, usually referred to simply as positivism. Positivism is a combination of the three empiricisms: rational, mechanistic, and skeptical.

A major purpose of positivism was to "unify" science by articulating the essential process of knowing that should be followed by all academic disciplines; this produced one of the most striking ironies in intellectual history. The positivists based their formulations of methodology on that which had been articulated by ninteenth-century physics, but by the time they wrote, the use of Newtonian *methods* had precipitated major changes in the *methodology* of physics.[47] Positivism thus is an anachronism in the physical sciences; however, when researchers in the social disciplines looked for guidance in how to do science, many of them accepted positivism as an accurate guide. The bulk of Anglo-American communication theory is primarily influenced by positivism.

The positivists assumed that the key to a unified science was recognition that knowledge could be expressed in propositions of a particular form, and that this form was the same regardless of the content of the science. A well-formed scientific proposition is expressed $Y = (f)X$, or "variable Y varies as a function of variable X," or $X \supset {}_\rho Y$, or "if variable X occurs, then (with a stipulated probability) variable Y will occur."

It is important to distinguish the "internal" structure of such propositions from the relationship the propositions as a whole have with other propositions. The internal structure consists of *variables* and *rela-*

tions among variables. Positivists accepted Newton's and Hume's distrust of reason as a source of factual knowledge about the world, and accepted Hume's argument that the nature of the relationship among variables cannot be known. According to Hume, all we can know is that Xs and Ys occur together, not that X causes Y. The key move by the positivists was in treating this as the hallmark of scientific method rather than as a refutation of the possibility of doing science. Rather than deal with the "causes of sensible events," as Newton put it, the positivists defined the *statistical correlation* between sensible events as the sufficient data for scientific method. Instead of trying to verify the illusion of causality in the mental experience of observers, scientists should simply demonstrate recurring correlations. The substance of scientific theories is *statements* that these *correlations* occurred, and this can be known with no problem.

This procedure implies a commitment to reductionism and operationalism. Reductionism is the assumption that the most useful units of analysis are the smallest, and that complex wholes may be studied as the sum of their parts. Whitehead's example is useful:[48] The process of starting a fire is studied by identifying the smallest observable events between times 1 and 5. A person is observed rubbing sticks rapidly at times 1 through 5. Smoke is observed at time 5; heat in the sticks at time 3; and an increased rubbing rate at time 2.5. Hume's critique of Newton stands. By specifying these intervening events, one *cannot* perceive cause. However, new information seems to emerge when the time span between observations is reduced. By repeating the observations with various materials and rubbing rates, statistical curves could be drawn relating rubbing rate to friction under various conditions. These curves could then be expressed as a mathematical relationship or a description of a "law."

The *objects* in scientific statements, for example, friction and heat, are defined "operationally" by specifying the operations that the scientist performs to observe them, and they have *no other* meaning or existence. "Surplus meanings," such as common-sense knowledge about events and objects, must be eliminated. For example, a cake is operationally defined by a recipe; surplus meanings such as *sweet, birthday, company coming*, and so on, are both irrelevant and dysfunctional. Trust in interpersonal relations consists of the scores recorded on a questionnaire, and nothing else.[49] The *relations* in scientific statements are defined mathematically and are compared to distributions expected to occur by chance. If Xs and Ys are found to co-occur much more often than they are likely to do unless they are somehow related, scientists may carefully and without going beyond their data state that X and Y are related with a specified probability. Thus, a "true" scientific statement is one in which every term is operationally defined and the relationship specified among terms has been demonstrated in an empirical study.[50]

Once positivists have "true" statements, they treat them logically in a manner borrowing from rationalistic empiricism. Scientific laws have the form of a major premise in an Aristotelian syllogism. Scientists *predict* events by stating the *conclusion* of syllogistic reasoning; for example, if the statement $X \supset Y$ is true, and X occurs, Y is predicted. Similarly, scientists *explain* events by stating the *major premise* of the syllogism; for example, why did Y happen? Because X had previously occurred, and if X, then Y. For positivists, explanation and prediction are the same process, started at different ends of a chain of reasoning. This is a restricted concept of "explanation" that is required by the notion that the meaning of statements is nothing more than the operations taken to observe the variables. In the positivist tradition, the methodological assumptions consist of a denial that they exist; theory comprises a logical structuring of the results of empirical observations; methods consist of operational definitions of variables (including sophisticated scaling techniques, etc.) and procedures for the statistical analysis of data. Only the results of methods count as data: "intelligence," positivists say, "is what intelligence tests measure." The data count as the sole source and content of theory.

The clearest example of positivism in contemporary human communication theory was the "attitude change" research of the 1950s and 1960s, in which attitudes were operationally defined as marks on questionnaires, and changes in these marks were statistically analyzed as a function of types of messages, types of speakers, acts done by the listeners, and so on, to the point of boredom.[51] Fishbein's strain to develop a regression equation that would name the variables that account for attitude change clearly shows the influence of positivism[52] Much of the current research on "uncertainty reduction theory"[53] and trust[54] are informed by the methodology of positivism. Skinner's theories of learning are clearly positivistic: the data are changes in behavior as a function of various reinforcement schedules, and the theory is the generalization of these relationships.[55]

Constructivism

One unexpected result of empirical studies, as noted at the beginning of this chapter, is the finding that the mind of the observer has an inherent and active role in the process of knowing. The positivists' and mechanistic empiricists' denial of having "committed a metaphysic" or of being biased by methodological assumptions is seen as wrong and dysfunctional because the effects of the knowing mind are *present* but *precluded from analysis.* For example, Rosenthal's discovery of "experimenter effects," in which the expectations of the researcher biased the results of experiments, posed a major problem for the method-centered methodology of positivism: "the experimental method is flawed in this case insofar as it uncovers facts that are constituted in the particular transaction between experimenter and subject."[56]

These empirical results were presaged by Kant's philosophy. Provoked by Hume's skepticism, Kant set himself to refute Hume's three principles. He focused on the Genetic Principle, in which Hume argued that each experience is an irreducible entity unconnected with other experiences, and that simple ideas are representations of these experiences. To the contrary, Kant argued,

> Experience is not atomic but integrated, it is integrated because it is rule-governed, it is rule-governed because it is *constituted* the experience it is by the rules I have made for it . . . nature does not simply call out to the knower information about her character and contents, but answers the questions he puts.[57]

If "mental content" or perception has been ordered by the operation of mind, the rest of Hume's position falls. The Atomic Principle is denied by the existence of the world-as-perceived as an organized structure, and the principle of association is replaced by a view of knowing as an activity involving insight, and risk and responsibility, rather than trial and error or simple temporal continuity.

From a constructivist standpoint, the meanings made by perceivers are what count as data, and these data count as evidence of the nature of the activity of minds, as a description of the "world-as-perceived" within which persons actually live, and/or as a basis for explaining and predicting a person's actions and responses to actions.

At least three types of contemporary research programs are informed by a constructivist methodology. *Ethnographies,* primarily conducted by anthropologists, assume that "speech communities" or cultures create a shared definition of themselves and their worlds, and describe the *results* of the constructive activity of mind. The most characteristic method of ethnography is participant observation, in which a person joins the culture, learns its construction of reality, and describes it. Participant observation techniques range from taking motion pictures (visual anthropology[58]) to making field notes; these are sometimes informed by an established array of topics (like Keenan's[59] use of Grice's "conversational maxims" or Hymes'[60] eight-category system summarized by the acronym SPEAKING) and sometimes are initiated with a systematic attempt to eliminate all preconceived opinions about both what the culture believes and what it values.[61] Other ethnographic techniques include componential analysis,[62] naturalistic descriptions of conversations,[63] and analyses of popular culture in films, books, folk maxims, and cautionary tales.[64] Goffman's popular descriptions of life and behavior in North America are exemplary ethnographies.[65]

Ethnomethodology is the current expression of a line of thinking deriving from Dilthay's insistence that historical interpretation, and Weber's contention that sociological explanation, must take the actor's *meanings* into account. Shutz argued that the proper object of social science is actors' subjective meanings, and Mead built a theory around the processes of symbolic interaction by which these meanings are created and, when created, guide the subsequent social actions of the persons. As expressed by Garfinkel[66] and Cicourel,[67] ethnomethodological research consists of various methods for demonstrating the interpretive procedures that people use to understand and relate to each other. The most spectacular of these methods is "garfinkeling": the tactic of demonstrating the existence of an interpretaive procedure by acting in such a way as to disrupt it and then observing the consequences. The results of ethnomethodological research are a description of the *methods* by which persons construct meanings.[68]

Contemporary *constructivists* in the social sciences focus on the *structure* of the meanings made by individuals and the *effect* of that structure on subsequent meanings and actions. Delia and his colleagues have combined Kelly's Personal Construct Theory and Werner's theory of the development of organization into a comprehensive research program that explores the accoutrements and consequences of various degrees of cognitive complexity.[69] The methods include Kelly's "repertoire grid technique" as elaborated by Bannister and Maier[70] and others, and content analysis of essays written by subjects. These methods produce quantitative scores of the complexity factors of differentiation and integration that are statistically associated with measures of other aspects of personal or social performance, such as accuracy in person perception. These statistical results, however, are interpreted quite differently from those performed by mechanistic empiricists. Rather than indices of the laws or organization of reality, they are understood to be descriptions of the ability of persons to construct reality. The studies of developmental stages of cognition by Bruner[71] and Piaget[72]—using the method of observing children in problem-solving situations—are also consistent with the constructivist methodology.

Human Systems: Emergence of a New Methodology?

Contemporary human communication theory is the arena for spirited, sometimes acerbic methodological debates. Some find in this the exhilarating prospect of creativity and progress; others, fruitless controversy that is liable to diminish the rigor of science. (Because they explicitly deny having a methodology, mechanistic empiricists and positivists tend to decry the current scene; constructivists tend to revel in it.)

Regardless of one's emotional response, the development of methodological controversy should be seen as a natural event—an event in a long series of eras during which fundamental assumptions of the then-current orthodoxy were challenged—not as a unique or cataclysmic occasion for despair. As Langer noted, all ideas are eventually exhausted, and the important question is whether the scientific community will be resourceful enough to produce a new methodology that will inform powerful new theories and productive programs of research.[73]

We believe that a new methodology is being developed, with its genesis in a wide range of related intellectual developments that undercut positivism and provide a new context for constructivism. If this methodology is used by communication theorists, the content and structure of their theories will be strikingly different from those emerging from other methodologies.

• *From Orthodox Corpuscularianism to Variated Model-Building: The Developments in Physics and the Biological Sciences.* The world view that positivists and mechanistic empiricists actually held but vociferously denied was of irreducible corpuscles of matter in a void.[74] This conceptualization, which was being abandoned about the time the Vienna Circle was developing positivism, contrasts sharply with contemporary work in physics, which is frankly cosmological, and in biology, which is systemic.

Both the content and method of contemporary physics deny the corpuscularian heritage. Einstein's theories of curved space are modeled as an elastic sheet distorted by the weights of the masses within it. Instead of the Newtonian ideal of data-then-theory, the physicists of the 1970s built theory that subsequently guided research.

> Theoretical ideas—not idle speculations, but reasonable extensions of the well established scheme—were still running ahead of experimental evidence. The color force, in particular, would not be easy to verify if the quarks were essentially coy. And before the Astronomers had fully convinced themselves that they had found black holes among the stars and in the hearts of distant galaxies, Stephen Hawkins was asking them to look for exploding black holes, for an effect that would help unify gravity and the physics of particles.[75]

The theorist who first suggested the existence of quarks waited over a decade before anyone could prove they existed. From a positivist methodology, he would never have thought of quarks; and if he had thought of them, he would not have spoken of them because—lacking any means of operationalizing observations of them—they *would not have existed in his theory.*

The biological sciences never assumed that the entities of reality are irreducible and temporally isolated.[76] With the inception of the microbe theory of disease, biologists made the assumptions that structures endure and coexist in patterned relationships through time, and that the functioning of one structure (e.g., the body of a sick person) cannot be explained without reference to other coexisting, interacting structures (e.g., a disease-producing microbe). Given these assumptions, the form of theory was that of *modeling* the structure and powers of interacting structures in either sentential or pictographic form.[77] Research methods informed by such theory utilized all the standard forms of observation and statistical analysis, but the statistical relationships were understood as evidence supporting or rejecting the scientists' model of the entities, not as a description of the laws of nature (as a mechanistic empiricist would perceive them) or as a "surrogate" for causation (as a positivist would). When the data supported a model, scientists explained what occurred in terms of the powers of the entities to act and to respond to each other.

The enterprise of model-building was systematized in General Systems Theory.[78] which undermined another tenet of positivism. Positivists were "reductionists," who believed that the smallest unit of analysis was the richest, and that larger structures were the aggregate of their parts. System theorists argued to the contrary that the variability of a system was *not* a summative function of its parts. Weiss[79] described the relationship mathematically:

$$V_s > (V_1 + V_2 + V_3 \cdots V_n)$$
where
$$V_s = \text{variance of the whole system}$$
$$V_{1-n} = \text{variance of components } 1 - n$$

Further, systems are organized hierarchically, so that the activities of any of the components cannot be understood except in the context of the whole.[80] The concept of hierarchy introduces considerations of levels of autonomy and control: principles sufficient to explain functions at a lower, simpler, level may not be adequate for the greater complexity at higher levels. Pribram found that a simple feedback loop or TOTE (test-operate-test-exit) model is sufficient to describe the function of small clusters of brain cells but is too simple to explain higher cognitive processes within the same primate brain.[81]

The implications of systems theory for the new methodology include (1) a liberation from the limiting reductionistic asssumption;

(2) a direct focus on the structures of systems per se, with the need to discover the logics by which they are organized; and (3) a reintroduction of causality as a topic for concern. The various logics of differentially complex systems not only mean that different systems can behave differently, but that the nature of the "necessity" for their behavior is of different *kinds*. Simpler organisms must do all that they can do; more complex organisms may choose among methods and among goals; and very complex organisms may have such an array of alternatives that they cannot do *all* that they *can* do. Communication theorists will probably have to deal with the simultaneous operation of *nomic force*, generated from the characteristics of entities that give them the power to act in some ways but not in others; *logical force*, generated by a calculus of the interrelationships of structures or symbols; and *practical force*, created by the planning and goal-seeking capacity of human beings.

• *From Logic to Logics: New Developments in Philosophy and Mathematics.* One of the most startling intellectual developments of the twentieth century is the rejection of the original rationalist idea that there is *a* proper and valid logic, the form of which models the correct organization of ideas. This was one of the few unquestioned and unchallenged assumptions. Even Kant believed that the content of Euclidean geometry was both obvious to the mind and a fact of nature (in his terms, a set of synthetic a priori statements), but now we have several *non*-Euclidean geometries, all of which are equally well formed (i.e., internally consistent). There is no way to determine which is "correct" because there are no formal standards for choosing among equally consistent logical systems.[82] In mathematics, Gödel was able to prove that all formal systems of logic or mathematics are inherently incomplete. There is no way *within* a system to prove the validity of a system, and if one steps *outside* the system for proof, *that* system is unproven unless one goes beyond it, and so on.[83] Modern "modal" logics provide an array of systems differing substantially from classical logic. For example, von Wright's deontic logic uses operators denoting the strength and direction of social or moral obligation rather than probability or class inclusion.[84] Brown's logic is based on the distinction between inside and outside.[85] Toulmin has argued strongly against the utility of formal systems per se and has advocated non-formal, field-dependent models of reasoning.[86]

These developments imply that the internal consistency with which statements are arranged is not a proof of their correctness or utility. Two consequences follow. First, the deductive logical pattern of explanation and prediction in positivism is stripped of any claim to special authenticity. The fact that positivists can use their logic consistently is nice but scarcely compelling, since there are any number of other alternative logics available, all of which are formally incomplete. Second, theorists are absolved from thinking in Aristotelian categories and are free to use or invent logics that are more adequate to represent the phenomena of communication. Given the advantage of hindsight, we suspect that future historians will describe the move from logic to logics in this century as a conceptual liberation equivalent to the escape from rational empiricism by the scientists of the seventeenth century.

• *Ethogeny: A New Philosophy of Science.* Harre modestly proclaims that his "ethogeny" is a new "Copernican Revolution" in the philosophy of science.[87] Ethogeny is the formulation of the developments described in the preceding subsections, the key to which, according to Harre, is the change in the role of models. In the *interpretation* of mechanistic empiricism and positivism, a theory was composed of statements of statistical relationships; and models, if any, were a sometimes useful but unnecessary luxury. Harre's "Copernican Revolution" identified the model *as* the theory, with statements of statistical relationships as sometimes useful but not essential supplements.

Harre's philosophy of science informs a very different use of research methods than does positivism. Assume that a researcher finds that statements of one type are *always* followed immediately by statements of another type—for example, questions are followed by answers. A communication theorist with a Newtonian methodology would assume that the statements—as variables—are *real,* and that the statistical relation between them is an index of some natural order. For Harre, the statistical relationship has meaning only as it informs and tests the accuracy of the models of the persons who *made* the statements. If persons are modeled as automatons, one will expect to find high correlations among their behaviors; however, if persons are modeled as somewhat autonomous, their behaviors should vary because of their natures, not necessarily as the result of intervening forces, socioeconomic conditions, and so on. This perspective leads an ethogist to treat data very differently than will a mechanistic empiricist. For a mechanistic empiricist, a close statistical relationship among, for example, human actions is considered to be evidence of a connection among *variables* (e.g., self-disclosure, credibility); for an ethogenist, it is considered to be evidence of the structure of the "powerful particular" who behaves. For a mechanistic empiricist, the inability to find close statistical relationships among variables constitutes a failure from which no inferences can be drawn; for an ethogenist who models humans as complex powerful particulars, the observed fact that persons often do *not* follow questions with answers is powerful support for the model. For mechanistic empiricists, the way to design studies is to select variables and search for statistical relationships; for ethogenists, it is to model entities and search for evidence that they have the hypothesized characteristics, which are more likely to be found in their *ability* to perform in particular ways or a variety of ways rather than their predilection to act consistently. The anomaly or exceptional case is a problem of "error variance" for mechanistic empiricists; it may be the most useful datum for ethogenists. Mechanistic empiricists construct theory by generalizing on the basis of relationships among variables; for an ethogenist, a particular sequence of behaviors may be the result of a unique interaction between two powerful particulars that informs the modeling of those particulars but that may never occur again, and thus does no violence to the theory.

The research methods of ethogeny do not differ substantially from ethnography. A variety of things may count as data, depending on the nature of the entities being studied. With automatons, the data may be observations of actions and reactions; with more autonomous entities like human beings, the data may be actors' accounts of their intentions or evaluations, their role-playing of particular situations, or their explanations of their own actions.[88] The data count as tests of the models of the particulars and/or interactions among particulars being studied.

Ethogeny comprises a new and characteristically modern methodology. Like Kant, it assumes that the knower is involved in the process of knowing, and that study of humans must take meanings into account. Unlike any previous philosophy of science, ethogeny formally includes a concept of entities differing in structure, requiring interpretations of the data depending on the degree of autonomy in the model being tested. Like Newton, Harre assumes that there is an order in the world that can be known through empirical research. Although Harre believes the world is much more complicated than Newton dreamed, both identify a search for explanations within the sensible world as basic to science. And like all theorists to date, Harre is unable to cope with the paradox involved in recursive knowing.

• *Self-Reflexivity.* The differentiation between the knower and the known has created conceptual problems that have taken a long time to understand. Hume's three principles neatly accomplished an unintended goal: they denied the possibility of a "self" to do the perceiving.

> Herein, not in his critique of causation, lies Hume's real skepticism. The self, he says, is a bundle of impressions, and . . . there is quite literally . . . nothing else for the self to be. . . . The mind is capable only of perceptions; all perceptions are separable; how shall we account for the togetherness even of that bundle of them which we may desig-

nate a "mind" or "self."? "I must plead the privilege of a skeptic, and confess that this difficulty is too hard for my understanding. I pretend not, however, to pronounce it absolutely insuperable. Others, perhaps, or myself, upon more mature reflection, may discover some hypothesis that will reconcile these contradictions."[89]

Kant's constructivism faltered at the same point. He showed that we cannot understand reality without *including* mind, but he did not show how a mind could understand itself understanding reality.

> The self as such is unknowable. All we can know . . . [is] the succession of items of awareness. . . . It makes no sense to ask Kant: *who* is knowing? . . . It makes no sense to ask Kant, how knowledge is communicated. There is for him no problem of communication, no fact of communication. There is simply mind, as active, organizing through categories, mind on its passive side receiving sensations through the media of space and time.[90]

The problem with self-reflexivity occurs when one mind, which constructs reality, attempts to know itself and/or another mind, which also constructs reality. Since the constructive processes occur at two levels, how can observers differentiate between the constructive processes of their own minds and those of the minds of others? Polanyi stated the problem in general terms by differentiating "focal" knowledge—that to which the mind is attending at a given moment—and "subsidiary" knowledge—that which is out-of-awareness but which frames or contextualizes focal knowledge. Polanyi has shown that this subsidiary knowledge—one's own constructive processes—is necessary, that it reflects one's own biases, and that it is ultimately unknowable:

> You cannot use your spectacles to scrutinize your spectacles. A theory is like a pair of spectacles; you examine things by it, and your knowledge of it lies in this very use of it. You dwell in it as you dwell in your own body and in the tools by which you amplify the powers of your body. It should be clear that someone who is said to be "testing" a theory is in fact relying, in this subsidiary and very uncritical way, upon other tacitly accepted theories and assumptions of which he cannot *in this action* be focally aware.[91]

One can move particular aspects of subsidiary knowledge to the level of focal awareness, but to do this implies a further subsidiary knowledge. Like Zeno's frog that jumped half the remaining distance to a line each time, no one can make all knowledge focal.

At least this is the way it appears if one maintains the conception of reality espoused in Whitehead and Russell's *Principia Mathematica* at the beginning of the twentieth century. Their "theory of types" clearly envisioned an Aristotelian world of discrete categories, such that no statement that *described* a class could also be a *part* of that class. By implication, any knowledge *about* knowing could not be a part of that which was known, and the Polanyian infinite regress of a necessary but unknowable subsidiary knowledge made good sense. However, this "objective" cosmology was challenged by some of the systems theories that emerged from mechanistic empiricism and that began to look for explanations of systems *within* rather than outside the systems themselves.

> . . . the primary locus of constraint and control . . . in all nonengineered living systems . . . *is the structural relations of the system itself.* . . . Constraint and control . . . lie in the hierarchical and heterarchical networks of the system itself, *both* at the level of the individual subsystem *and* at the level of the whole.
>
> This informational conception of the immanence of the locus of constraints and controls in the relations between the "partials" of an ecosystem is a conception we in the West have had to rediscover in this century, once the Newtonian energy-entity equilibrium models of social and biological reality were found wanting. . . .
>
> The notion of *external controls* has been the primary impediment to understanding systematic behavior.[92]

The use of an immanent *explanans*—"the system is its own best explanation"—is, in Aristotelian and Russellian logic, tautological and/or paradoxical, and thus useless. Given a conflict between what logic *can* do and what empirical investigations implies *must* be done, some—in the spirit of Newton—have devised new logics. Brown "solved" the problem of tautological explanation or self-referential paradox by creating a logic that simply *incorporates* self-reference as one of an array of relations among elements. His argument was simple: (1) self-referential paradoxes are not different from many common mathematical expressions, such as $\sqrt{X} = -1$; (2) these mathematical expressions were solved by simply expanding the set of numbers (positive, negative, zero) to include "imaginary" numbers; (3) logical self-reflexive paradoxes may similarly be solved by expanding the set of statements (true, false, meaningless) to include something equivalent to "imaginary" statements and (4) this solution is useful in dealing with the problem of self-reflexive paradoxes.[93] Varela suggested the operator ⌐⌐—a stylized image of a snake biting its tail—as a description of an entity that describes or denotes itself, taking the place of Brown's "imaginary" statements. Using this operator, the resultant logic becomes a calculus of logics rather than a description of reality.[94] This feature seems to be just what is needed for modeling hierarchically organized systems in which the organizational principles are different at the various levels and which include at least some levels that operate with some degree of autonomy. Brown's and Varela's logics make possible

> . . . a second-order cybernetics—a *cybernetics of cybernetics*—in order that the observer who enters the system shall be allowed to stipulate his own purpose: he is autonomous . . . the essential pillars for a theory of the observer have been worked out . . . we are now able to enter rigorously a conceptual framework which deals with observing and not only with the observed.[95]

No such cybernetics of cybernetics has been worked out thus far, but the tools seem available now, and when the task is accomplished, a problem that has vexed some of the best minds in Western philosophy will be solved.

• *Toward a New Methodology: Synthesizing Attempts.* We believe that the developments described in the paragraphs above are complementary, and may be synthesized into a new methodology strikingly different from others that have informed communication theory. Harre's ethogeny is perhaps the most complete formulation of the new methodology, although we quarrel with it in a number of places.[96] Perhaps that is the most telling point: in this time of methodological controversy, there is a large community who agree in principle on the general shape of a new set of assumptions but who are far from consensus on the details or the implications of those assumptions. On the whole, we suspect that some continuing disagreement is healthy, and that various theorists should be working on elaborating their theories and conducting their research programs rather than (only) arguing about assumptions. The proof of the new methodology will be the theories that it informs.

There are at least three theories of human communication that are consistent with the new methodology: Cushman and Craig's self-conception approach[97]; Watzlawick, Beavin, and Jackson's interactional view[98]; and the theory developed by the authors of this chapter —the coordinated management of meaning.[99]

USING AND DOING COMMUNICATION THEORY

"May you live in interesting times!" We are told that this statement is a Chinese curse. It is a curse because "interesting times" impose unique demands on those who live in them.

These are certainly interesting times for human communication theory. The original theory chapters of this book contain an array of theories informed by quite dissimilar, sometimes incompatible, methodologies. In less feverish times, students could read what each of the authors wrote and expect each to add to their understanding of communication. In these interesting times, this will not work. Communication theorists often talk about different things; and when they agree *what* to talk about, they often contradict each other. Even when they agree on a description of communication, they interpret its significance in different ways.

The primary argument of this chapter is that such differences among theorists are *not* evidence that some (or all) theorists are mentally deficient, or that some have ignored "the data," or that theorizing is an individualistic exercise in which others should not be expected to join. (These responses are all versions of methodological monism or ecumenicism.) Rather, we have shown that flatly contradictory theories may be equally reasonable, given the differing methodologies that inform them, and that the work of any theorist may be critiqued in terms of its consistency with the assumptions contained in that methodology—its boldness, its use of the strongest available methods, and so on.

In this concluding section, consider some implication of methodological pluralism for those who would use or do communication theory. First, to do good work in communication theory—or anything else—requires an unabashed commitment to a particular methodology and a determination to exploit the methods and perspectives that methodology provides. To an extent, one must "live" one's theory:

> To become a competent specialist in any branch of science is to participate with one's whole intellectual being in such a projection, to come to dwell in it and move about in it as one dwells in the familiar spatio-temporal framework which all normal human beings have in infancy and childhood built up for themselves.[100]

One characteristic of a professional in any activity is a startlingly detailed and sophisticated knowledge of the components and capabilities of the equipment, problems, and techniques required by the "reality" in-formed by that activity. Communication theory is no exception. Those committed to positivism must acquire a detailed and remarkably efficient vocabulary pertaining to research design ("I used a Solomon square"), operationalizing terms (I studied listening behavior: retention and comprehension"), and statistics ("the F was significant at point oh one, but the eta was low"). Those committed to constructivism and other methodologies have their own specialty languages no less exotic. To an outsider, these sound like deplorable jargons, but they are better understood as symptoms of shared proficiency, comparable to the technical competence of persons in athletics, construction, the military, and so on.

The extraordinarily detailed knowledge of the methodology one works with is necessary to minimize the possibility of making a mistake. Each of the levels in Figure 1 may be thought of as a lens through which theorists look at the data at one end of the process and at their own assumptions about themselves, the knowing process, and the phenomena at the other. Each lens is "polarized" or "biased" in that it facilitates the observation of some phenomena but obscures others. If the lenses are similarly aligned—that is, the methods are consistent with the theory, which is consistent with the methodology—theorists can see clearly all that is visible through those lenses. However, theorists who are not fully knowledgeable about the methodology that they use, or who attempt too shallow integrations of methods, are likely to align the lenses orthogonally. Here the multiple lens analogy breaks down. Orthogonally placed polarized lenses admit no light, and the observer quickly realizes that a mistake has been made. However, the use of incompatible concepts and methods produces data that *look* good but that are uninterpretable artifacts. For example, a theory about a curvilinear relationship between two variables will not be tested by a two-group research design: the method neatly obscures the potential for observing what is described by the theory. Further, hierarchical relationships within a system of meanings will not be studied by a second-order factor analysis, regardless of what the data show.

Commitment to a particular methodology is a necessary condition of sophisticated work, but in these "interesting" times, it is not sufficient. The second implication of methodological pluralism is an openmindedness to alternatives, an ability to see one's own commitment as an outsider and thus to evaluate the extent to which one's own methodology can deal with relevant issues. Simultaneous tentativeness and commitment seem paradoxical, but Maslow[101] and Bruner[102] both identified them as characteristics of the creative persons they studied. In communication theory, this quality of commitment is necessary for individual theorists to be creative and to provide a social/professional environment in which creativity may flourish. Grene described ambivalence—"the union of participation and withdrawal"—as the human characteristic that "creates the breathing space for human freedom and human achievement. . . . It is the transcendence of the immediate milieu, the immediate need, that characterizes human work as human."[103] This transcendence of the methodology to which one is committed is a heady experience, and is the reward of hard-working theorists who, by diligent efforts, have discovered the corners of their world and then stepped beyond them. Berger noted that this experience is the etymological meaning of *ecstasy*, from the Greek *ek* and *stasis:* standing outside oneself. "What all ecstasies have in common is breaking through the routine, every day, taken-for-granted course of our life."[104]

The social institutions of society in general and of academe in particular are not well suited to accommodate methodological pluralism. Journal selection criteria, informal networks of scholars, and hiring and tenure procedures work well to encourage commitment to and expertise in a particular methodology, but they do not accommodate persons whose work is "ecstatic" (literally, outside the system). This is nothing new: when Galileo began to publish his research (which was a primitive mechanistic empiricism), his primary opposition came not from the Church but from the rational empiricists of the universities—supposedly the centers of learning.

> The inertia of the human mind and its resistance to innovation are most clearly demonstrated not, as one might expect, by the ignorant mass . . . but by professionals with a vested interest in tradition and in monopoly of learning. Innovation is a two-fold threat to academic mediocrities: it endangers their oracular authority, and it evokes the deeper fear that their whole, laboriously constructed intellectual edifice might collapse. The academic backwoodsmen have been the curse of genius from Aristarchus to Darwin to Freud; they stretch, a solid and hostile phalanx of pedantic mediocrities, across the centuries.[105]

The twentieth century is certainly more conducive to persons who deliberately exit the system than were Galileo's contemporaries, but still, considerable skill and a modicum of courage are needed.

Despite its difficulty, methodological creativity is a prerequisite for doing communication theory. At least two problems have not been satisfactorily dealt with by any methodology: the venerable question of the one and the many, and the recursiveness of human knowledge.

Classical Greek philosophers debated about whether reality *is* one or plural; modern communication theorists grapple with the issue of whether their assumptions permit them to deal with individuals or with large groups. Positivism clearly appealed to the "law of large numbers," which permits the average behavior of groups—but not the specific behavior of any individual within the group—to be described, predicted, and explained on the basis of measurements of "central tendencies." If the scientist is interested in how an electorate will divide its votes or which government program will most effectively reduce the amount of violence in the streets, this may be sufficient. But those concerned with helping a specific individual or family break out of a dysfunctional pattern cannot gain much of value from such procedures. Kelly described the *desideratum* of those interested in particular persons as a kind of theory that employed general concepts of sufficient power so as to permit each case to stand out in its own individuality.[106]

The rival orientations toward the one and the many cut across the methodologies described in this chapter and represent a continuing, unsolved issue. Miller's research on persuasion is informed by the positivist methodology, and he has been consistently interested in the characteristics of the general population.[107] Equally influenced by positivism, Skinner aims to illuminate each specific case. For example, he demonstrated that he could elicit "superstitious" behavior from a particular pigeon.[108] In the constructivist tradition, the clinical psychologist Kelly insisted on procedures that were specific—and helpful—to individual subjects, even if the procedures did not permit generalization.[109] However, Delia and his colleagues are less interested in helping individual clients and thus have adapted constructivist techniques to describe the way persuasion works and persons develop cognitive and social skills.[110]

The issue of the one and the many also differentiates otherwise similar research that is informed by different methodologies. For example, the rules research of Nofsinger (informed by rational empiricism) assumes a homogeneous social order and thus applies to society as a whole; while the rules research of Cushman, Pearce, and Cronen (informed by human systems methodology) assumes a heterogeneous social order and applies to particular cases.[111]

Another issue with which no methodology has dealt adequately is the recursiveness of human knowledge. This is a particularly difficult problem, which we believe will require a creative response in the form of a new concept or structure of theory. Recursivity has always been a characteristic of human knowing, but sophisticated techniques for knowing had to be developed to discover it. We believe that those methodologies that can demonstrate but not account for recursivity are not adequate for human communication theory. Unfortunately, this judgment invalidates the entire array of methodologies currently available. In our opinion, some novel concept or structure of theory that will constitute a methodological revolution comparable to the work of Copernicus in cosmology, Darwin in biology, and Einstein in physics is required. We are spending our time working out the implications of grafting the self-reflexive logics developed by Brown and Varela to the ethogenic philosophy of science proposed by Harre.[112]

We believe that the next major advance in human communication theory will come as a solution to the problem of recursiveness and the issue of the one and the many. As the best procedure for achieving that advance in theory, we advocate methodological pluralism as the social/professional climate for the process of learning.

Notes

1. Joseph Campbell, *The Masks of God: Creative Mythology* (New York: Penguin, 1976). Originally published in 1959; Joseph Campbell, "Primitive Man as Metaphysician," in his *The Flight of the Wild Gander* (New York: Viking Press, 1969).

2. Ernest Becker, *Escape from Evil* (New York: Free Press, 1975), Chs. 1 and 2.

3. E. C. Krupp, ed., *In Search of Ancient Astronomics* (New York: McGraw-Hill, 1978); Alexander Marshack, *The Roots of Civilization* (New York: McGraw-Hill, 1972).

4. Susanne K. Langer, *Philosophy in a New Key: A Study in the Symbolism of Reason, Rite and Art*, 2nd ed. (New York: New American Library, 1951), pp. 15–16.

5. Mircea Eliade, *Cosmos and History: The Myth of the Eternal Return* (New York: Harper, 1959). Originally published in 1949.

6. Arthur Koestler, *The Sleepwalkers* (New York: Macmillan, 1959), p. 40.

7. I. P. Bell, "Buddhist Sociology," in *Theoretical Perspectives in Sociology*, ed. Scott G. McNall (New York: St. Martin's Press, 1979), pp. 53ff; D. T. Suzuki, "General Characteristics of Buddhism," in *Readings in Eastern Religious Thought, Volume II: Buddhism*, ed. Allie M. Frazier (Philadelphia: Westminster, 1969), pp. 70–89.

8. Norwood R. Hanson, *Patterns of Discovery* (Cambridge: Cambridge University Press, 1958).

9. Marjorie Grene, *The Knower and the Known* (Berkeley: University of California Press, 1974).

10. Koestler, pp. 14–15.

11. Langer, p. 19.

12. Langer, p. 29.

13. Richard Hofstadter, *Godel, Escher, Bach: An Eternal Golden Braid* (New York: Basic Books, 1979), p. 10.

14. Noam Chomsky, *Cartesian Linguistics: A Chapter in the History of Rationalist Thought* (New York: Harper & Row, 1966); Del Hymes, "Models of Interaction of Language and Social Life," in *Directions in Sociolinguistics: The Ethnography of Communication*, ed. J. J. Gumperz and Del Hymes (New York: Holt, Rinehart and Winston, 1972), pp. 35–71.

15. Gerry Philipsen, "Speaking 'Like a Man' in Teamsterville," *Quarterly Journal of Speech*, 61 (1975), 13–22.

16. Donald P. Cushman and W. Barnett Pearce, "Generality and Necessity in Three Types of Theory About Human Communication, with Special Attention to Rules Theory," *Human Communication Research*, 3 (1977), 344–353; Vernon E. Cronen and Leslie K. Davis, "Alternative Approaches for the Communication Theorist: Problems in the Laws-Rules-Systems Tricotomy," *Human Communication Research*, 4 (1978), 120–128.

17. Peter L. Berger, *The Precarious Vision* (Garden City, N.Y.: Doubleday, 1961), p. 17.
18. Koestler, p. 36.
19. Philip H. Rhinelander, *Is Man Incomprehensible to Man?* (Stanford, Calif.: Stanford Alumni Association, 1973), p. 47.
20. M. T. McClure, "Appearance and Reality in Greek Philosophy," *Studies in the History of Ideas* (New York: Columbia University Press, 1918), pp. 1–26.
21. McClure, p. 2.
22. Grene, p. 17.
23. Edwin Arthur Burtt, *The Metaphysical Foundations of Modern Physical Science* (New York: Harcourt Brace Jovanovich, 1927), p. 108.
24. Grene, p. 66.
25. Chomsky.
26. Robert E. Sanders and L. W. Martin, "Grammatical Rules and Explanations of Behavior," *Inquiry*, 18 (1975), 65–82.
27. Grene, p. 36.
28. Grene, p. 41.
29. R. W. Southern, *The Making of the Middle Ages* (New Haven, Conn.: Yale University Press, 1953), pp. 180–181.
30. H. P. Grice, "Logic and Conversation," in *Syntax and Semantics: Speech Acts*, ed. P. Cole and J. L. Morgan (New York: Academic Press, 1975).
31. Robert E. Nofsinger, Jr., "The Demand Ticket: A Conversational Device for Getting the Floor," *Speech Monographs*, 42 (1975), 1–9.
32. H. Sacks, E. A. Schegloff, and G. Jefferson, "A Simplest Systematics for the Organization of Turn-taking for Conversation," *Language*, 50 (1974), 696–735.
33. Burtt, p. 203.
34. Burtt, p. 214.
35. Burtt, p. 211, footnote 16.
36. Burtt, p. 208.
37. Burtt, p. 211.
38. Burtt, p. 219.
39. Carl G. Hemple, *The Philosophy of Natural Science* (Englewood Cliffs, N.J.: Prentice-Hall, 1966).
40. Ervin Laszlo, *Introduction to Systems Philosophy* (New York: Harper & Row, 1973).
41. Laszlo, passim.
42. Peter Achinstein, *Laws and Explanation* (Oxford: Oxford University Press, 1971).
43. S. Feldstein, "Temporal Patterns of Dialogue: Basic Research and Reconsiderations," in *Studies in Dyadic Communication*, ed. A. W. Siegman and B. Pope (New York: Pergamon Press, 1972), pp. 91–114.
44. Ernie L. Stech, "Sequential Structure in Human Social Communication," *Human Communication Research*, 1 (1975), 168–179.
45. Grene, passim.

46. Rom Harre and E. H. Madden, *Causal Powers* (Totowa, N.J.: Rowland and Littlefield, 1975), p. 110.

47. Arthur Koestler, *The Ghost in the Machine* (New York: Macmillan, 1967); Floyd Matson, *The Broken Image: Man, Science and Society* (Garden City, N.Y.: Doubleday, 1966).

48. Alfred North Whitehead, *Science and the Modern World* (New York: Macmillan, 1925).

49. Julian B. Rotter, "Generalized Expectancies for Interpersonal Trust," *American Psychologist*, 26 (1971), 443–452.

50. Anatol Rapoport, *Operational Philosophy: Integrating Knowledge and Action* (San Francisco: International Society for General Semantics, 1969). Originally published in 1953.

51. Carl I. Hovland, Irving L. Janis, and Harold H. Kelley, *Communication and Persuasion* (New Haven, Conn.: Yale University Press, 1953).

52. Martin Fishbein, "Behavior Theory Approach," in *Readings in Attitude Theory and Measurement*, ed. M. Fishbein (New York: John Wiley and Sons, 1967), pp. 389–400.

53. Charles Berger, R. Gardner, M. Parks, L. Schulman, and G. Miller, "Interpersonal Epistemology and Interpersonal Communication," in *Explorations in Interpersonal Communication*, ed. Gerald Miller (Beverly Hills: Sage, 1976), pp. 149–172.

54. Shirley J. Gilbert, "Empirical and Theoretical Extensions of Self-Disclosure," in *Explorations in Interpersonal Communication*, ed. Gerald Miller (Beverly Hills: Sage, 1976), pp. 197–216.

55. B. F. Skinner, *Cumulative Record: A Selection of Papers*, 3rd ed. (New York: Appleton-Century-Crofts, 1972).

56. Edward E. Sampson, "Scientific Paradigms and Social Values: Wanted —A Scientific Revolution," *Journal of Personality and Social Psychology*, 36 (1978), 1332–1343.

57. Grene, p. 135.

58. Cf. Catherine Egan, *Perspectives on Film: Ethnographic Film* (University Park, Penna: Pennsylvania State University Audio Visual Services, 1979).

59. E. O. Keenan, "The Universality of Conversational Postulates," *Language in Society*, 5 (1973), 67–80.

60. Hymes, pp. 58–65.

61. Len C. Hawes, "How Writing Is Used in Talk: A Study of Communication Logic-in-Use," *Quarterly Journal of Speech*, 62 (1976), 350–360.

62. Ward H. Goodenough, *Culture, Language and Society* (New York: Addison-Wesley, 1971).

63. Elaine M. Litton-Hawes, "A Foundation for the Study of Everyday Talk," *Communication Quarterly*, 25 (1977), 2–11.

64. Ruth Benedict, *The Chrysanthemum and the Sword* (New York: World, 1946).

65. Erving Goffman, *Encounters* (Indianapolis: Bobbs-Merrill, 1961); Erving Goffman, *Interaction Ritual: Essays on Face-to-Face Behavior* (Garden City, N.Y.: Doubleday, 1967).

66. Harold Garfinkel, *Studies in Ethnomethodology* (Englewood Cliffs, N.J.: Prentice-Hall, 1967).
67. Aaron Cicourel, *Cognitive Sociology* (New York: Free Press, 1974).
68. Cf. Lewis A. Coser, "Presidential Address: Two Methods in Search of a Substance," *American Sociological Review*, 40 (1975), 691–700; D. H. Zimmerman, "A Reply to Professor Coser," *American Sociologist*, 11 (1976), 4–13; Lewis A. Coser, "Reply to My Critics," *American Sociologist*, 11 (1976), 33–38.
69. Jesse Delia, "Change of Meaning Process in Impression Formation," *Communication Monographs*, 43 (1976), 142–157.
70. David Bannister and J. M. M. Maier, *The Evaluation of Personal Constructs* (New York: Academic Press, 1968).
71. Jerome S. Bruner, *The Relevance of Education* (New York: Norton, 1971).
72. J. H. Flavell, *The Developmental Psychology of Jean Piaget* (Princeton, N.J.: D. Van Nostrand Co., 1963).
73. Langer, passim.
74. Harre and Madden, passim.
75. Calder, p. 188.
76. Rom Harre, *The Philosophies of Science* (Oxford: Oxford University Press, 1972), passim.
77. Harre, passim.
78. Ludwig von Bertalanffy, *General Systems Theory* (New York: George Braziller, 1968).
79. P. Weiss, cited in Bertalanffy, p. 27.
80. George Miller, E. Galanter, and Karl Pribram, *Plans and the Structure of Behavior* (New York: Holt, Rinehart and Winston, 1960).
81. Karl Pribram, "Self-Consciousness and Intentionality," in *Consciousness and Self-Regulation*, Vol. 1, ed. G. E. Schwartz and D. Shapiro (New York: Plenum Press, 1976).
82. Stephen Toulmin, *The Uses of Argument* (Cambridge. Cambridge University Press, 1958).
83. Ernest Nagel and James R. Newman, *Gödel's Proof* (New York: New York University Press, 1958).
84. Georg von Wright, "Deontic Logic," *Mind*, 60 (1951), 1–15.
85. G. Spencer Brown, *Laws of Form* (New York: Julian Press, 1972).
86. Toulmin, passim.
87. Rom Harre, "The Ethogenic Approach: Theory and Practice," in *Advances in Experimental Social Psychology*, Vol. 10, ed. Leonard Berkowitz (New York: Academic Press, 1977), pp. 283–314.
88. Peter Marsh, Elisabeth Rosser, and Rom Harre, *The Rules of Disorder* (Boston: Routledge and Kegan Paul, 1978).
89. Grene, pp. 102, 109.
90. Grene, p. 142.
91. Michael Polanyi and Harry Prosch, *Meaning* (Chicago: University of Chicago Press, 1975).
92. Anthony Wilden, "Changing Frames of Order: Cybernetics and the

Machine Mundi," in *Communication and Control in Society*, ed. Klaus Krippendorf (New York: Gordon and Breach, 1979), p. 18.

93. Brown, passim.

94. Francisco J. Varela, "A Calculus for Self-Reference," *International Journal of General Systems*, 2 (1975), 5–24.

95. Heinz von Foerster, "Cybernetics of Cybernetics," in *Communication and Control in Society*, ed. Klaus Krippendorf (New York: Gordon and Breach, 1979), pp. 5–8.

96. W. Barnett Pearce, "Toward an Anthropomorphic Social Science: A Reply to Levine and to Rosser and Harre," *Journal for the Theory of Social Behaviour*, 9 (1979), 117–122.

97. Donald P. Cushman and Robert T. Craig, "Communication Systems: Interpersonal Implications," in *Explorations in Interpersonal Communication*, ed. Gerald Miller (Beverly Hills: Sage, 1976), pp. 37–58.

98. Paul Watzlawick, Janet Beavin, and Don Jackson, *Pragmatics of Human Communication* (New York: Norton, 1967).

99. Vernon E. Cronen, W. Barnett Pearce, and Linda M. Harris, "The Coordinated Management of Meaning: A Rules-Based Approach to the First Course in Interpersonal Communication," *Communication Education*, 28 (1979) 22–38; F. Barnett Pearce, Vernon E. Cronen, and Forrest Conklin, "On What to Look at When Studying Communication: A Hierarchical Model of Actors' Meanings," *Communication*, in press; Vernon E. Cronen and W. Barnett Pearce, "Logical Force: A New Concept of Necessity in Social Behavior," *Communication*, in press.

100. Grene, p. 180.

101. Abraham Maslow, *The Farther Reaches of Human Nature* (New York: Viking Press, 1971).

102. Jerome Bruner, "The Conditions of Creativity," in *Beyond the Information Given*, ed. Jeremy Anglin (New York: Norton, 1973), pp. 208–217.

103. Grene, p. 173.

104. Berger, *The Precarious Vision*, p. 96.

105. Koestler, *The Sleepwalkers*, p. 427.

106. George Kelly, *The Psychology of Personal Constructs*, 2 vols. (New York: Norton, 1955).

107. Gerald Miller and Murray Hewgill, "The Effect of Variations in Nonfluency on Audience Ratings of Source Credibility," *Quarterly Journal of Speech*, 50 (1964), 36–44.

108. Skinner, passim.

109. Kelly, passim.

110. Delia, passim.

111. William A. Donohue, Donald P. Cushman, and Robert E. Nofsinger, Jr., "Creating and Confronting Social Order: A Comparison of Rules Perspectives," *Western Journal of Speech Communication*, 44 (1980), 5–19.

112. W. Barnett Pearce and Vernon E. Cronen, *The Coordinated Management of Meaning: A Communication Theory* (New York: Praeger, in press).

THOUGHT AND TALK: "EXCUSE ME, BUT HAVE I BEEN TALKING TO MYSELF?"

Charles R. Berger
William Douglas

> Except in the rarest instances, we do not speak to others out of accident or whimsy. We speak to achieve some purpose or attain some goal.
>
> A. H. Monroe and D. Ehninger

> Social behavior is meaningful behavior. It involves an agent with certain intentions and expectations, an agent capable of deliberating and choosing from a variety of courses of action, and whose words and actions are understood by his fellows.
>
> R. Harre and P. F. Secord

> Virtually all communication is purposive.
>
> R. C. Jeffrey and O. Peterson

The central concern of this chapter is nicely illustrated by an incident involving three graduate students who were eating at our university's cafeteria. A person who was a total stranger to all three students sat down in a vacant chair next to one of them and after a moment asked, "Excuse me, but have I been talking to myself?" Further conversation revealed that the question was a serious one. The person had just finished taking doctoral qualifying examinations and was quite concerned about the outcome. While this fact can be invoked to explain the person's rather strange way of beginning the conversation, the important point of the incident is that the person entertained the possibility that her speech was not under conscious control. This rather extreme example serves to introduce the more general proposition that a considerable proportion of everyday interaction is carried out at rather low levels of self-awareness. It has frequently been pointed out that communication that occurs in nonverbal channels is generally out of the conscious control of individuals. However, the position to be explored here is that a substantial amount of *verbal interaction* in everyday situations occurs at relatively low awareness levels.

The proposition that in everyday life social interaction is conducted without full awareness is not a new one. In the early 1900s Cooley observed,

> It is true, however, that the attempt to describe the social self and to analyze the mental processes that enter into it almost unavoidably makes it appear more reflective and "self-conscious" than it usually is . . . Many people whose behavior shows that their idea of themselves is largely caught from persons they are with, are yet quite innocent of any intentional posing; it is a matter of subconscious impulse or mere suggestion.[1]

Cooley clearly argues for the position that social actors frequently have low levels of self-awareness in interaction situations, and that analysts of behavior may attribute too much conscious control of behavior to the persons they study.

More recently, Turk has raised a similar question regarding the study of small group and family interaction.[2] He asserts that in *specific relationships,* such as those involving a customer and a salesperson, people are likely to enter the interaction with clear goals in mind. In *diffuse relationships,* such as those that characterize family interaction, participants are generally not aware of specific interaction goals. Turk reminds us that psychoanalytic theory long ago advanced the notion that persons may be unaware of the goals for which they strive in social situations. Furthermore, he argues that *observers* of interactions involving diffuse relationships may be unable to identify the goals of interaction participants.

Before beginning our discussion of self-awareness and communication, there are some assumptions and issues that should be made explicit. First, the view espoused here represents neither a return to a Watsonian, radical behaviorist conception of human behavior nor an endorsement of what might be labeled a *neobehaviorist* view of human conduct. We strongly believe that cognitive processes are critical to the explanation of communication behavior; however, we also believe that it is a mistake to assume that most utterances in social interactions are the result of highly conscious thought processes. Obviously, a position that asserts that communicative behavior is frequently *not* generated by highly conscious thought processes calls into question the usefulness of the notion of "intent" in explaining communicative conduct. As we shall see, it may be difficult to speak meaningfully about intentions of actors in many everyday social interactions. Persons frequently may *not* have clear sets of interaction goals or strategies in mind before, during, or after their encounters with others.

Second, in the present view, communicative behavior may sometimes serve as a cue for the activation of expectational sequences or scripts that enable persons to proceed through interactions without paying much attention to them. Certainly, this is not the only function that communication plays in social interactions; however, it is a function that has generally been overlooked.

Third, while the present view does not focus on the issue of meaning per se, there are some implications for the concept of meaning that flow from our analysis. For example, social meaning and the concept of social expectations or scripts may be interchangeable theoretical constructs. We will not pursue this issue in this chapter, but the readers may make their own judgments on this matter as the chapter is read. Fourth, while the focus of the present chapter is on interpersonal communication contexts, we believe that the ideas presented here have implications for such areas as the consumption of mass media content and communication in formal organizations. In fact, it may be that in these two particular contexts the amount of thought that accompanies, both decoding and encoding is *less* than the amount of thought that occurs in many informal face-to-face interaction contexts.

Keeping these assumptions and issues in mind, we will now review some theory and research that addresses the relationship between self-awareness and communicative behavior. After reviewing this theory and research, we will examine their implications for the development of theories about human communication and the methods we use to study communicative behavior.

SELF-AWARENESS THEORY AND RESEARCH

Scripts and Self-Awareness

The concept of "script" is defined by Abelson in the following way: "By 'script' I mean a coherent sequence of events expected by the individual involving him either as a participant or as an observer."[3] Abelson's definition indicates three propositions that characterize the study of scripts: (1) scripts are meaningful action sequences; (2) scripts provide persons with expectations; and (3) scripts are not necessarily actor-oriented.

Scripts service an individual with information simply because the events comprising a particular script are real-world events, events that have been directly or vicariously experienced by the individual. As such, scripts tell people something about the world in which they live. However, not all event sequences can be defined as "script." While all events may indeed reveal something about a person's environment, scripts are more properly viewed as *standardized episodes*—abstract summaries of *recurring* events. Scripts are, therefore, not peopled by specific individuals but by generalized roles. For most of us, for example, the characters within our "initial interaction" script are not John, or Jack, or Liza, but, rather, a more diffuse Other. The advantage of such impersonal cognitive structures is that they provide an individual with expectations and directives regarding the appropriate behavior of self and others across a large number of situations. The disadvantage is that scripts are of little use in entirely novel situations since, by definition, no script exists for that class of events.

When an individual does witness a new event, the particular sequence of actions that occurs at that time becomes a rudimentary script for the individual and will be used by the individual when a similar situation is next encountered. This is typically the case with children for whom the cast of many scripts is not "the teacher" but "Miss Smith," not "the waiter" but "the man who served us at 'The China Garden,'" not "the best friend" but "Alan." Only through reoccurrence does the script become formalized so that classes of events rather than specific occasions can be accommodated. Furthermore, through such repetition, script theorists argue that behaviors become overlearned, so that individuals process less and less information in a conscious fashion since the person requires fewer cues to select an appropriate response. Thus, a person can be considered "thoughtful" or "aware" or "making strategic choices" only when (1) no appropriate script exists or (2) an available and appropriate script cannot reach closure because of the intrusion of unexpected action. Conversely, when events are considered by an individual to be "normal," the individual's behavior is scripted, and the individual is, therefore, not aware of his or her actions. Two studies recently reported by Langer illustrate and support this position.[4]

In the first study, requests were made of people about to use a copying machine at the City University of New York. One request was that the person wait while the confederate made five copies (small favor condition); the other, that the confederate be allowed to make 20 copies (big favor condition). Each of the requests was paired with two justifications: a placebic justification ("may I use the Xerox machine because I have to make copies?") and a realistic justification ("may I use the Xerox machine because I am in a rush?"). Ninety-three percent of those people in the small favor condition who were provided only a placebic justification granted the request (versus 60% of those given no justification and 94% of those given a realistic justification), while only 24 percent of those persons in the big favor condition given the same placebic justification allowed the confederate to make copies first (versus 24% of those given no justification and 42% of those given a realistic justification).

The second study was again designed to test the mindfulness of individual behavior. On this occasion memoranda were collected from secretaries' trash cans. The memoranda were found to be of one general form—unsigned requests. Thus, from the perspective of the secretaries, incongruent or unexpected message forms would be signed requests and any demand, be it signed or unsigned. Four memos, each with the same content (requesting or instructing the secretary to return the memo immediately to room 238—a nonexistent room) but taking a different form (signed and unsigned request and demand) were then distributed among the secretaries. Significantly, more of the secretaries who received the form of the memo congruent with past experience complied with the message, although 68 percent of all subjects returned the memorandum.

Clearly, the people in neither study can be reasonably portrayed as individuals highly aware of their actions. The explanation offered by Langer is that those subjects who consented to the experimental requests were not confronted with sufficient within-script deviance to force them into thoughtful action (either to set about constructing a new script or to "scan" for the appropriate existing script). Langer has further argued that persons frequently instantiate inappropriate scripts; particularly she has proposed that people behave *as if* skilled (they are following a "skill" script) even in chance situations. Considerable evidence supports this proposition. For example, people have been found to make causal attributions on the basis of random data and when instructed to combine base and individuating information, to consistently ignore the base data even when the validity of the specific information is doubtful.[5] Nor are these biases restricted to decisions with trivial consequences. During World War II, Londoners frequently made erroneous causal attributions for the pattern of German bombing—explanations that served as the basis for decisions regarding when and where to seek shelter. Upon later inspection, the patterns of bombing were found to approximate closely a random distribution.[6]

As has been argued, simply because people are capable of deliberation and reasoned choice is neither sufficient cause to suppose that such purposefulness is usual nor that such behavior is preferred. The view espoused here is that only under rather specific conditions can people be expected to be highly cognizant of concurrent behavior. Briefly summarized, those conditions are (1) in novel situations where, by definition, no appropriate script exists, (2) where external factors prevent completion of a script, (3) when scripted behavior becomes effortful because substantially more of the behavior is required than is usual, (4) when a discrepant outcome is experienced, or (5) where multiple scripts come into conflict so that involvement in any one script is suspended. In short, individuals will enact scripted sequences whenever those sequences are available and will continue to do so until events unusual to the script are encountered.

Public and Private Self-Consciousness

A corollary to the radical position that most behavior, private and social, is conducted outside of awareness is the suggestion that people are differentially attentive to their environment and, therefore, differentially aware of that environment.

Some persons may be frequently, even habitually, concerned with the way they appear to others and may even be preoccupied with that concern. Fenigstein, Scheier, and Buss, in fact, have argued that such self-consciousness is an enduring tendency that can be viewed as three distinct factors: public self-consciousness, private self-consciousness, and social anxiety.[7] Public self-consciousness is defined by an awareness of the self as a social object, while private self-consciousness is marked by self-reflection and a general attention to one's own thoughts, feelings, and motives. The third dimension, social anxiety, unlike public and private self-consciousness, is a measure of a person's reaction to self-examination, particularly examination of the public self. This dimension of self-consciousness is characterized by discomfort in the presence of others. The importance of the concept "self-consciousness" to the study of social behavior has been demonstrated.

Fenigstein, for example, has reported that persons high in public self-consciousness are more sensitive to rejection by a peer group than are persons low in public self-consciousness.[8] Following rejection, the high public self-conscious subjects in the study displayed less attraction and less willingness to rejoin the group than did low public self-conscious subjects. Scheier has observed that men high in private self-consciousness became more aggressive in response to an anger-arousing stimulus than did men low in private self-consciousness.[9] Thus, it seems likely that in focusing one's attention, there is some trade-off between inward- and outward-directed awareness. People simply cannot attend to all things at all times. The major premise of self-consciousness research is that people are consistently biased to adopt either a direct perspective or a metaperspective of the self. Those people who are highly private self-conscious can be expected to have a restricted knowledge of social expectations, since they are primarily concerned with their own feelings and motives, and are, therefore, potentially disposed to exhibit behavior that violates or more nearly violates public standards (in this case, aggression). Conversely, high private self-conscious persons have been shown to possess a well-differentiated view of themselves and, moreover, tend more to see themselves as causal agents in that they use more traits when describing themselves and engage in more self-attribution than do low private self-conscious individuals.[10] The suggestion that people high in private self-consciousness "know" themselves better than do people low in private self-consciousness is further supported by the positive correlation evidenced between private self-consciousness and the predictive validity of subject self-reports (of aggressive behavior).[11]

Little research has focused directly on "social anxiety." Two studies do, however, indicate that this aspect of self-consciousness also impacts upon behavior. In one study, Turner noted that social anxiety mediated the subject's sensitivity to public evaluation while, in a second study, Brockner reported that task performance was also affected by the subject's level of social anxiety.[12]

Self-Monitoring

Snyder characterized the self-monitoring individual as follows:

> The self-monitoring individual is one who, out of a concern for social appropriateness, is particularly sensitive to the expression and self-presentation of others in social situations and uses these cues as guidelines for monitoring his own self-presentation.[13]

Snyder's conceptualization of self-monitoring is, in some respects, similar to the concept of public self-consciousness discussed in the previous section. The concept of public self-consciousness emphasizes the self-awareness created by the presence of others; by contrast, self-monitoring emphasizes both the awareness dimension and the dimension of *skill* in presenting one's self as he or she wishes. These differences are supported by the findings of two studies, both of which found low positive correlations between the two measures.[14]

Snyder has developed a scale to measure self-monitoring.[15] In his initial research, he found the following differences between high and low self-monitors:

1. Peers judged high self-monitors to be better than low self-monitors at learning what is appropriate in new social situations, at having better control of their emotional expressions, and at being persons who can use this control to create the impressions they wish.
2. Theater actors scored higher in self-monitoring than did university students, while psychiatric patients scored lower than students.
3. Persons with high self-monitoring levels were better than those with low levels in expressing emotions intentionally in both verbal and nonverbal channels.

4. High self-monitors were more likely than lows to seek relevant social comparison information about their peers when involved in a self-presentation task situation.

The above differences between high and low self-monitors suggest the view that high self-monitors are more "manipulative" in social interaction situations than are low self-monitors. However, this proposition must be tempered by the finding that there was *no relationship* found between the self-monitoring scale and a scale designed to measure the extent to which persons subscribe to and behave in accordance with a Machiavellian view of humanity.[16]

Other self-monitoring studies have explored the extent to which persons behave in accordance with their beliefs. Low self-monitors' behavior is assumed to be motivated with reference to internal dispositions, while the behavior of high self-monitors is dependent upon situational cues. Given these differences, one would expect a higher degree of consistency between attitudes and behaviors of low self-monitors. Two experimental studies have demonstrated this relationship. In one of them, persons were asked to write essays in which they advocated a position at variance with their private beliefs on the issue. Amongst those persons given a choice not to write the belief-discrepant essay, individuals with low self-monitoring showed greater attitude change toward the position advocated in the essay than did individuals with high self-monitoring levels.[17] Apparently, the high self-monitoring persons could say things they did not believe without any impact upon their private beliefs. Another study found that high self-monitors changed their behavior more in response to changes in the social context of a group discussion than did low self-monitors.[18]

In another self-monitoring study, college students, who agreed to let their dating choices be determined for them by a group of researchers, were placed in a situation in which they could observe their potential dates talking with other persons in groups on a videotape.[19] The amount of time the subject looked at the videotape of the prospective date served as a measure of attention to the date. After viewing the tape, subjects were asked a series of factual questions concerning information that had been disclosed during the course of the discussions. Subjects also indicated how attractive their potential dates were and how confident they were that their prospective dates possessed certain attributes. These scales were also completed for the discussion members who were not designated as potential dates by the experimenters.

The findings of this study revealed that high self-monitors, in contrast to low self-monitors, recalled more details about their prospective dates, made more extreme and confident attributions about their anticipated dates, and were generally more attracted to their prospective dates. However, there were no differences between self-monitoring groups in terms of the actual amount of time spent looking at the videotape of the anticipated dates. High self-monitors showed superior recall of details even though they spent no more time actually viewing their anticipated dates.

The final study to be considered here examined the ways in which the social interaction of high and low self-monitors differs in ongoing interaction situations.[20] In this study, pairs of persons with similar or different levels of self-monitoring were placed in a waiting situation for five minutes. Unknown to them, their interaction during this period was videotaped. Analyses of the videotaped interactions revealed that the higher self-monitoring person within each dyad was more likely to initiate conversation. Dyads consisting of one high self-monitor and one low self-monitor showed more periods of silence during their interactions than did dyads consisting of persons with similar levels of self-monitoring. This finding supported the conclusion that dyads with one high and one low self-monitor experienced greater communication difficulties than did dyads with other combinations of self-monitoring. After the five-minute conversations, high self-monitors indicated that they generally felt more self-conscious than did the low self-monitors. Furthermore, in the dyads composed of one high and one low self-monitor, high self-monitors expressed higher levels of felt self-consciousness than did their low self-monitoring partners. Apparently, the greater communication difficulties of the high-low self-monitoring dyads were perceived to a greater extent by the high self-monitors than by the low self-monitors.

The theory and research discussed in this section indicate that persons with high levels of self-monitoring not only are more sensitive to the behavior of others in social situations but are also more likely to remember relevant information than their low self-monitoring counterparts. Moreover, high self-monitors appear to be better able to adapt their behavior to changing social situations and to be better able to present themselves in ways that they desire. If the "ideal communicator" is defined as one who is sensitive to environmental cues and uses them as guides to conduct, and one who can adapt to changing environments and control his or her self-presentation accordingly, then we might say that the high self-monitor possesses the attributes that would describe the ideal communicator.

Objective Self-Awareness

As we have seen in the previous two sections, the theory and measurement of self-consciousness and self-monitoring both assume that these are relatively enduring *traits*. By contrast, objective self-awareness theory and research rest upon the assumption that self-awareness can be increased or decreased for most individuals depending upon the presence or absence of self-reflecting stimuli in the individuals' immediate environment. Objective self-awareness theory posits two states of consciousness.[21] In the *objective state*, attention is focused upon the self as an object in the environment; when attentional focus is upon the environment, persons are said to be *subjectively self-aware*. It is further assumed that at any given moment a person is either objectively or subjectively self-aware. Movement between the two states may be rapid, but only one state can prevail at any point in time. Objective self-awareness has been experimentally induced by the use of such devices as mirrors, videotape equipment, and listening to a tape recording of one's own voice.

According to the theory, when persons are made objectively self-aware, standards by which they evaluate themselves become salient. If there are discrepancies between the standards and the ways in which the persons evaluate their current behavior, the persons are motivated to reduce the discrepancy. Alternatively, when discrepancies exist, persons may avoid the potential discomfort of negative comparisons by attending to stimuli other than themselves, thus becoming subjectively self-aware. In the initial statement of the theory, Duval and Wicklund argued that objective self-awareness is generally a noxious state, since persons can generally find some kind of shortcoming relative to a standard; however, more recently, Wicklund has conceded that the objective state need not be noxious, since persons can experience positive discrepancies at times—that is, they can do better than they expected to do.[22]

There is some evidence to support the notion that under certain conditions, objective self-awareness may lower self-evaluations.[23] In an early study, persons filled out self-esteem measures that consisted of ratings of one's ideal self and real self on the same set of scales. Persons who filled out these measures while listening to their own voices on tapes (objective self-awareness) showed greater ideal-real self-discrepancies early in their ratings than did persons who filled out the same items while listening to another person's voice (subjectively self-aware). However, even in the objectively self-aware group, ideal-real self-discrepancies decreased as the persons filled out the questionnaires. This finding was explained by suggesting that persons in the objective self-awareness group were able to divert their attention away from their tape-recorded voices as they progressed through their ratings.

Subsequent research has revealed that when persons are made objectively self-aware, they tend to use more first-person pronouns and self-descriptive terms on projective tasks like identifying pronouns in foreign languages and filling out sentence completion tests.[24] Two additional studies have shown that behavior will be more consistent with internal standards when persons are objectively self-aware. When made more self-aware by the presence of a mirror, highly punitive persons delivered more shocks than low punitive persons. The difference in shock frequency between high and low punitive persons disappeared when no mirror was present.[25] In another study, it was found that persons who filled out a test of their sociability under objective self-awareness conditions (mirror present) behaved more consistently with their test scores two days later than did persons who filled out the sociability test under subjective self-awareness conditions.[26]

In addition to the other effects, objective self-awareness appears to cause persons to attribute their outcomes more to themselves than to other factors, such as those that reside in other persons or the environment; and when persons are made self-aware. they tend to experience both positive and negative emotions more extremely than persons whose attention is not self-focused.[27] Other research has examined the impact of self-awareness upon reactions to positive and negative feedback in an interview situation. This study revealed that persons who received negative feedback from the interviewer rated the interviewer more negatively when the interview was conducted under objective self-awareness conditions (mirror present). However, inconsistent with self-awareness theory, there was no difference between the mirror and no-mirror conditions for persons who received positive feedback from the interviewer.[28]

Recent research has called into question some of the basic postulates of objective self-awareness theory. First, some evidence suggests that objective self-awareness is a noxious state only when persons focus their attention on negative discrepancies that are thought to be *permanent*. If individuals believe that the negative discrepancy they possess can be *eliminated*, objective self-awareness does not produce negative emotional responses.[29]

Second, some researchers have raised the question of whether heightened self-awareness necessarily leads one to become introspective regarding *personal standards* of conduct, as the theory suggests, or whether persons can also become aware of *social standards* regarding their performance and behavior as their levels of objective self-awareness increase.[30] Research evidence demonstrates that under some conditions, heightened self-awareness can lead persons to view themselves from a social perspective rather than from a set of internal standards.

Finally, Hull and Levy have questioned whether the basic response processes postulated by objective self-awareness theory actually take place at all.[31] According to these researchers, objective self-awareness does not necessarily lead to the activation of self-evaluative processes. They contend that heightened self-awareness leads to increased sensitivity to self-relevant cues provided by the environment. In order to predict how persons will respond to objective self-awareness, one must be able to specify in what ways various aspects of the situation are relevant to the self. Contrary to objective self-awareness theory, Hull and Levy found that objective self-awareness does not consistently result in negative self-evaluations. Also, they found that persons with higher levels of self-awareness showed higher levels of cognitive processing (memory) for terms they considered descriptive of themselves than did persons with low self-awareness levels. This evidence supports their hypothesis that increased self-awareness increases one's sensitivity to self-relevant aspects of the environment.

While there are a number of issues related to objective self-awareness theory and research that are in need of resolution, the research reviewed above strongly indicates that environmental stimuli can act to increase self-focused attention, and that self-focused attention does have an impact upon individual and social behavior. This body of theory and research is consistent with the view presented earlier that self-consciousness or self-awareness cannot be assumed to be at consistently high levels across persons or situations. The objective self-awareness research suggests that in spite of dispositional differences in self-consciousness, persons may be generally susceptible to the effects of self-reflecting stimuli in their immediate environments.

IMPLICATIONS FOR COMMUNICATION THEORY AND RESEARCH

We will now consider the implications of the theory and research discussed in the previous section for the construction of theories of human communication. In addition, we will examine the potential impact of the self-awareness issue upon some of the methods used to study human communication.

Theory Development in Communication

One clear implication that follows from the previous discussion is that theories that rest upon the assumption that persons' communicative behaviors are generally the product of deliberate planning and conscious choice are bound to provide incomplete explanations of communicative behavior. Scripted behavior is generally enacted in a mindless fashion. Furthermore, our discussion of the self-consciousness and self-monitoring research indicates that some persons may be characteristically less mindful of their communicative output than others. Finally, the objective self-awareness research suggests that certain environmental conditions may make most persons more or less mindful of their conduct. All of these research areas point to the proposition that while an individual's communicative behavior may have the *appearance* of flowing from a set of highly conscious cognitive processes, the fact may be that the individual is enacting the communicative behavior at a relatively low level of awareness. Such a situation would make explanation based upon highly complex, conscious, decision-making processes of dubious value. It cannot be assumed that "all utterances are created equal," or that the cognitive processes underlying identical utterances by two different persons are necessarily the same. For one person the verbal performance might be scripted, while for the other person the performance might be the result of highly conscious planning and calculation.

Langer has noted that a number of social psychological theories like equity theory, balance theory, and attribution theory assume that persons generally interact with high levels of awareness.[32] In view of Cooley's remarks cited earlier in this chapter, this should come as no great surprise. The persons who constructed these theories have a special interest in social behavior and as a result spend a great deal of their time thinking about the social conduct of others. As a result, some social scientists tend to overattribute mindfulness to those about whom they theorize.

The situation is little different in the discipline of communication. As we saw at the outset of this chapter, some authors conceive of most communicative acts as flowing from conscious cognitive processes. The overattribution of thoughtfulness is also apparent in theories designed to explain communicative behavior. For example, Berger and Calabrese state,

> Central to the present theory is the assumption that when strangers meet, their primary concern is one of uncertainty reduction or increasing predictability about the behavior of both themselves and others in the interaction.[33]

This view implies that when persons meet strangers for the first time, they consciously attempt to get to know the strangers. More recently, Berger has modified the statement cited above and argued that persons will attempt to reduce their uncertainties about others when the others provide rewards, behave in a deviant manner, or may be encountered in future interactions.[34] Although these limiting conditions may make the theory more "realistic," there are some additional factors that must be taken into account in order to specify when persons will become concerned with uncertainty reduction. In view of the previous discussion, we would expect persons with high levels of public self-consciousness to be more concerned with uncertainty reduction than would persons with low scores on this variable. Moreover, we would further expect that environmental conditions that give rise to objective self-awareness might lead to a heightened concern for uncertainty reduction. Finally, the usual pattern of communication followed in initial interactions in which biographical and demographic information is exchanged first and attitudinal information later might be the manifestation of a mindless enactment of a scripted sequence or a conscious attempt to elicit information from the other in order to gain some kind of advantage in the situation. Again, the communication sequence might be identical for two persons, but the cognitive processes involved in the production of that sequence would be very different— that is, script mode versus self-aware mode.

It is also possible that the self-monitoring and self-consciousness variables could make a difference in terms of how persons go about reducing uncertainty once they have decided to do so. For example, the self-monitoring research previously discussed suggested that high self-monitors pay greater attention to social comparison information made available to them before interacting with a peer. Given this finding, we might expect that in initial interaction situations, high self-monitors might be more prone to take advantage of opportunities to observe strangers unobtrusively before meeting them than might low self-monitors. Low self-monitors might approach the strangers sooner and attempt to get to know them through verbal communication only. It is also possible that there are self-monitoring differences in the strategies that are used to get to know strangers once verbal communication takes place. These hypotheses illustrate how self-monitoring and self-awareness constructs can suggest boundaries for an existing theory and add potential hypotheses for test.

Other communication perspectives in which the awareness issue becomes relevant are those that rely upon the *practical syllogism* as a way of explaining why some kinds of communication routines or episodes are initiated. Briefly, the practical syllogism as employed in the work of Cushman and Pearce states,

> A intends to bring about C.
> A considers that in order to bring about C he must do B.
> Therefore, A sets himself to do B.[35]

There are at least two ways in which to construe this syllogism. First, it could be viewed as a conscious thought process through which persons proceed before they initiate some kind of communication sequence. Second, the syllogism could be viewed as a device used by theorists to describe the way in which persons *appear* to be reasoning given their actions; that is, persons behave *as if* they were using this kind of reasoning process. In the first case, conscious thought is clearly involved, while in the second case, the syllogism is more of a heuristic device that can be used by an analyst to explain certain actions.

If the use of the practical syllogism is consistent with the spirit of the first option, we would have to conclude, on the basis of the discussion of self-awareness theory and research, that most persons spend very little of their daily lives engaging in this kind of conscious reasoning activity. In fact, Langer has argued that persons generally *prefer* to develop scripts that can be mindlessly enacted so that they can think about more important things while they go through the scripted sequence.[36] In general, if the use of the practical syllogism implies a conscious reasoning activity, we would be forced to conclude that a theory based upon this explanatory framework has extremely limited boundary conditions. Consistent with our reasoning regarding the relationships between uncertainty theory and self-awareness variables, we might expect high self-monitors and high public self-consciousness individuals to be more prone to employ conscious reasoning processes like the practical syllogism in social interaction situations. However, for persons scoring low on these variables, we would expect considerably less cognitive effort to be expanded in this direction. Of course, if the practical syllogism is used in the spirit of the second sense, then the awareness issue would not be critical. However, the discussion of the practical syllogism as presented by Cushman and Pearce appears to be consistent with the first option.

The two theories discussed above are but a small sample of those that seem to overattribute thoughtfulness and self-awareness to those in social interaction situations. It seems to us that, at a minimum, self-awareness related variables should be included as potential mediating variables in a single theory, or that theory builders should clearly specify the boundary conditions of their theories with reference to self-awareness related variables.

Methodological Implications

There are at least three methodological implications that flow from the preceding discussion. First, Langer and Newman have demonstrated that subjects who exhibit evidence of mindless behavior during a social psychological experiment are more likely to respond in accordance with the hypothesis of the study than those who exhibit signs of mindful activity.[37] In their study, they replicated the famous Asch/Kelley warm-cold experiment in which two groups of subjects were given differing introductory information about a speaker. For some the speaker was described as "warm"; for others the speaker was described as "cold." After listening to the same speaker, the two groups of subjects rated the speaker on a number of attributes, including a warm-cold scale. In addition they were asked to recall specific information given by the speaker. The findings of the Langer and Newman study indicated that persons who exhibited *less* recall (mindless) were *more* influenced by the warm-cold induction than were persons who recalled more details of the speaker's presentation (mindful). Langer and Newman suggest that when researchers plant strong environmental cues for subjects in experiments, as they frequently do, those subjects who attend to the cues and to little else are more likely to conform to experimental hypotheses than are subjects who engage in higher levels of information processing during the experiment. Thus, persons who fail to conform to experimental predictions may actually be more mindful of details of the experiment than persons who do conform to experimental hypotheses.

Second, persons are frequently asked to give self-report information as part of communication studies. For example, persons are asked to describe their feelings about others, how they communicate with others, and what kind of communication style they characteristically display in social situations. There are two possible problems with such self-report data that are raised by self-awareness research. First, the request for self-report information itself may raise objective self-awareness to levels that are rarely encountered in everyday life. Second, the processes set in motion by elevated levels of objective self-awareness—for example, awareness of ideal-real self-discrepancies—might influence other measurements in ways that distort obtained scores significantly. For example, persons might report higher levels of aggression on a self-report inventory than they actually feel they possess in everyday life situations.

A third issue that was addressed in the discussion of self-monitoring and self-consciousness research concerns the relationship between self-reports of internal states and behavior. The evidence discussed in these sections supports the proposition that self-awareness processes significantly affect the degree of consistency between the ways in which persons say they feel about an issue or about themselves and the way they will behave relative to these issues and feelings when given the chance. The accuracy and predictive value of attitude measures clearly depend upon variables related to self-awareness.

CONCLUSION

In this chapter, we have not presented a full-blown theory of communication. Rather, we have shown how a family of theoretical constructs related to scripted behavior and self-awareness is critical to the process of constructing and testing communication theory. As we pointed out earlier, in arguing for the prevalence of scripted behavior enacted at low awareness levels, we have not meant to strip human-kind of its humanity and to return to the view of persons as automatons. Rather, we have attempted to show how extant theories of communi-cation may contain unreasonable assumptions about conscious thought processes that are responsible for communicative conduct and how, by ignoring the issue of self-awareness, data gathered in communica-tion studies might be flawed. The fact that many of our face-to-face communication transactions in everyday life require little mindful activity for their successful enactment is not negative; for as A. N. Whitehead cogently argued,

> It is a profoundly erroneous truism, repeated by all copy-books and by eminent people making speeches, that we should cultivate the habit of thinking of what we are doing. The precise opposite is the case. Civilization advances by extending the number of operations which we can perform without thinking about them. Operations of thought are like cavalry charges in battle—they are strictly limited in number, they require fresh horses, and must only be made at decisive moments.[38]

Since this is a decisive moment in the development of communication as a discipline, it might be useful for more communication research-ers to begin to think about the roles that self-awareness and self-consciousness play in their research and theory-building efforts.

Notes

1. Charles H. Cooley, *Human Nature and the Social Order*, rev. ed. (New York: Charles Scribner's Sons, 1922), p. 209.
2. James L. Turk, "Power as the Achievement of Ends: A Problematic Approach in Family and Small Group Research," *Family Process*, 13 (1974), 39–52.
3. Robert P. Abelson, "Script Processing in Attitude Formation and De-cision Making," in *Cognition and Social Behavior*, ed. John S. Carroll and John W. Payne (Hillsdale, N.J.: Lawrence Erlbaum Associates, 1976), pp. 33–46.
4. Ellen J. Langer, "Rethinking the Role of Thought in Social Interaction," in *New Directions in Attribution Research*, Vol. 2, ed. John H. Harvey, William Ickes, and Robert F. Kidd (New York: John Wiley & Sons, 1978), pp. 35–58.
5. M. Hammerton, "A Case of Radical Probability Estimation," *Journal of Experimental Psychology*, 101 (1973), 252–254; Daniel Kahneman and Amos Tversky, "On the Psychology of Prediction," *Psychological Re-view*, 80 (1973), 237–251; Richard E. Nisbett and Eugene Borgida, "Attribution and the Psychology of Prediction," *Journal of Personality and Social Psychology*, 32 (1975), 932–945.

6. William Feller, *An Introduction to Probability Theory and Its Applications*, Vol. 1 (New York: John Wiley & Sons, 1968).

7. Allan Fenigstein, Michael F. Scheier, and Arnold H. Buss, "Public and Private Self Consciousness: Assessment and Theory," *Journal of Consulting and Clinical Psychology*, 43 (1975), 522–527.

8. Allan Fenigstein, *Self-Consciousness, Self-Awareness, and Rejection*, Diss. University of Texas at Austin, 1974.

9. Michael Scheier, "Self-Awareness, Self-Consciousness, and Angry Aggression," *Journal of Personality*, 44 (1976), 627–644.

10. Robert G. Turner, "Effects of Differential Request Procedures and Self-Consciousness on Trait Attributions," *Journal of Research in Personality*, 12 (1978), 431–438; David M. Buss and Michael F. Scheier, "Self-Consciousness, Self-Awareness, and Self-Attribution," *Journal of Research in Personality*, 10 (1976), 463–468.

11. Robert G. Turner, "Consistency, Self-Consciousness, and the Predictive Validity of Typical and Maximal Personality Measures," *Journal of Research in Personality*, 12 (1978), 117–132.

12. Robert G. Turner, "Self-Consciousness and Anticipatory Belief Change," *Personality and Social Psychology Bulletin*, 3 (1977), 438–441; Joel Brockner, "Self-Esteem, Self-Consciousness, and Task Performance: Replications, Extensions, and Possible Explanations," *Journal of Personality and Social Psychology*, 37 (1979), 447–461.

13. Mark Snyder, "Self-Monitoring of Expressive Behavior," *Journal of Personality and Social Psychology*, 30 (1974), 528.

14. Michael F. Scheier and Charles S. Carver, "Self-Focused Attention and the Experience of Emotion: Attraction, Repulsion, Elation, and Depression," *Journal of Personality and Social Psychology*, 35 (1977), 625–636; Allen Fenigstein, "Self-Consciousness, Self-Attention, and Social Interaction," *Journal of Personality and Social Psychology*, 37 (1979), 75–86.

15. Snyder, pp. 526–537.

16. Snyder, pp. 526–537.

17. Mark Snyder and Elizabeth D. Tanke, "Behavior and Attitude: Some People Are More Consistent Than Others," *Journal of Personality*, 44 (1976), 501–517.

18. Mark Snyder and Thomas C. Monson, "Persons, Situations, and the Control of Social Behavior," *Journal of Personality and Social Psychology*, 32 (1975), 637–644.

19. Ellen Berscheid, William Graziano, Thomas Monson, and Marshall Dermer, "Outcome Dependency: Attention, Attribution, and Attraction," *Journal of Personality and Social Psychology*, 34 (1976), 978–989.

20. William Ickes and Richard D. Barnes, "The Role of Sex and Self-Monitoring in Unstructured Dyadic Interactions," *Journal of Personality and Social Psychology*, 35 (1977), 315–330.

21. Shelley Duval and Robert A. Wicklund, *A Theory of Objective Self-Awareness* (New York: Academic Press, 1972).

22. Robert A. Wicklund, "Objective Self-Awareness," in *Advances in Experimental Social Psychology*, Vol. 8, ed. Leonard Berkowitz (New York: Academic Press, 1975).

23. William J. Ickes, Robert A. Wicklund, and C. Brian Ferris, "Objective Self-Awareness and Self-Esteem," *Journal of Experimental Social Psychology*, 9 (1973), 202–219.

24. Deborah Davis and Timothy C. Brock, "Use of First Person Pronouns as a Function of Increased Objective Self-Awareness and Performance Feedback," *Journal of Experimental Social Psychology*, 11 (1975), 381–388; Charles S. Carver and Michael F. Scheier, "Self-Focusing Effects of Dispositional Self-Consciousness, Mirror Presence, and Audience Presence," *Journal of Personality and Social Psychology*, 36 (1978), 324–332.

25. Charles S. Carver, "Physical Aggression as a Function of Objective Self-Awareness and Attitudes Toward Punishment," *Journal of Experimental Social Psychology*, 11 (1975), 510–519.

26. John B. Pryor, Frederick X. Gibbons, Robert A. Wicklund, Russell H. Fazio, and Ronald Hood, "Self-Focused Attention and Self-Report Validity," *Journal of Personality*, 45 (1977), 513–527.

27. Shelley Duval and Robert A. Wicklund, "Effects of Objective Self-Awareness on Attribution of Causality," *Journal of Experimental Social Psychology*, 9 (1973), 17–31; Scheier and Carver, pp. 625–636.

28. Fenigstein, 1979, pp. 75–86.

29. Brett N. Steenbarger and David Aderman, "Objective Self-Awareness as a Nonaversive State: Effect of Anticipating Discrepancy Reduction," *Journal of Personality*, 47 (1979), 330–339.

30. Ed Diener and Thomas K. Srull, "Self-Awareness, Psychological Perspective, and Self-Reinforcement in Relation to Personal and Social Standards," *Journal of Personality and Social Psychology*, 37 (1979), 413–423.

31. Jay G. Hull and Alan S. Levy, "The Organizational Functions of the Self: An Alternative to the Duval and Wicklund Model of Self-Awareness," *Journal of Personality and Social Psychology*, 37 (1979), 756–768.

32. Langer, pp. 35–58.

33. Charles R. Berger and Richard J. Calabrese, "Some Explorations in Initial Interaction and Beyond: Toward a Developmental Theory of Interpersonal Communication," *Human Communication Research*, 1 (1975), 99–112.

34. Charles R. Berger, "Beyond Initial Interaction: Uncertainty, Understanding, and the Development of Interpersonal Relationships," in *Language and Social Psychology*, ed. Howard Giles and Robert N. St. Clair (Oxford: Basil Blackwell, 1979).

35. Donald P. Cushman and W. Barnett Pearce, "Generality and Necessity in Three Types of Theory About Human Communication, with Special Attention to Rules Theory," *Human Communication Research*, 3 (1977), 344–353.

36. Langer, pp. 35–58.

37. Ellen J. Langer and Helen M. Newman, "The Role of Mindlessness in a Typical Social Psychological Experiment," *Personality and Social Psychology Bulletin*, 5 (1979), 295–298.

38. Alfred N. Whitehead, as cited in Langer, p. 40.

THE COORDINATED MANAGEMENT OF MEANING:

A Theory of Communication

Vernon E. Cronen
W. Barnett Pearce
Linda M. Harris

For the past several years, the three authors, with the help of their students, have been developing a theory of communication called the Coordinated Management of Meaning. What leads three otherwise sane and happy people to undertake the development of a new theory —particularly one that departs in some fundamental ways from the usual assumptions of their discipline? Obviously, there were many lines of on-going research that had not been fully exploited and that offered well-developed research procedures. Why offer a new starting point? It could be that we possess a latent streak of masochism and enjoy the epithets hurled at our early efforts, but we prefer other explanations. Before describing the central features of the theory Coordinated Management of Meaning (hereafter CMM), we want to discuss those concerns that led us to develop a new theory and that molded the kind of theory we created.

PROLEGOMENA TO A THEORY OF COMMUNICATION

The three of us began with a commitment to the view that the creation of a powerful theory of communication is one of the first priorities of modern society. The intellectual revolution of the twentieth century produced a new conception of the relationship of humankind to the social order. One of the products of this revolution was to move the concept of communication into a position of prominence unprecedented in either the Eastern or Western intellectual traditions. In the Eastern wisdom literatures, the predominant idea is that communication is a poor guide to truth. Enlightenment comes from moving beyond the false distinctions of symbolic systems. The teachings of Lao Tzu illustrate the Eastern attitude. Lao Tzu said, "He who knows speaks not, he who speaks knows not." In another place Lao Tzu said, "The Tao which can be spoken is not the true Tao."[1] He clearly repudiates the communicability of truth or the truth of anything communicated.

In contrast, Western tradition celebrates communication as a vehicle for the exchange of ideas and as a tool for dealing with reality. As a vehicle for ideas, communication is thought to be best when it does not distort ideas and when it can add effectiveness to true ideas— but, of course, the ideas are primary. Through much of Western intellectual history runs the assumption that a fundamental isomorphism exists between the form of language and thought, and the structure of reality. This assumption can be traced to the pre-Socratic philosophers' notion of *Logos,* and the assumption is explicitly articulated in the works of Aristotle. Aristotle conceived of a static universe of classes and subclasses. Classes were natural groupings of particular objects. His syllogism formalizes this classificatory mode of thought, assuming that proper syllogistic thinking must lead to truth because it reflects the natural order of things. Aristotle's concept of *nous* specified a necessary relationship between the forms of the natural order and the basic forms of thought.[2] Aristotle offered a concept of rhetoric based upon his idea of the forms of thought.

In our own century, the work of the Vienna Circle shows the same effort to make explicit the potential isomorphism of language and reality. For the adherents of the Vienna Circle, only two types of terms were useful: (1) terms that reflected either real objects in nature or sets of observable operations, and (2) terms that indicated relationships among terms of the former class. Positivism holds that true knowledge comes from making only statements limited to those two classes of terms and organizing the statements into a hypothetico-deductive system. This positivistic view was derived from Wittgenstein's famous Picture Theory of meaning, which held that the proper function of language was to convey accurate "pictures" of external reality.

It is the great contribution of recent Western thinkers to show that the traditional assumption of a natural affinity among the forms of communication, truth, and reality is both false and pernicious. The new idea of communication is that communication is a form of human action that creates social orders.

The idea that communication could be assessed by its isomorphism with proper logic was first dealt a severe blow by the development of non-Euclidian geometries. Later, in a brilliant work, Kurt Gödel showed that any well-formed mathematical system must rest on assumptions that cannot be demonstrated within that particular system.[3] In recent years, we have seen the development of formal logics based on clearly un-Aristotelian principles, notably those of Brown[4] and Varela.[5] The implication, of course, is that no formal criteria exist for choosing between equally well-formed formal systems.

This century has also seen a vigorous attack on the idea that language can mirror objects or facts in reality. This line of attack asserts that all observations are theory-laden and not neutral sense impressions.[6] The implications of these developments in logic, mathematics, and the philosophy of science for the conduct of the scientific enterprise are discussed in the article "Methodological Considerations in Building Human Communication Theory" in this volume. The implications for the study of communication itself were far-reaching. If communication could not be assessed by its isomorphism with sensible objects and formally valid relationships, what was it and how might it be assessed?

A crucial figure in the generation of our modern concept of communication is Bronislaw Malinowski. In his study of primitive tribes, he observed a high incidence of communication: in fact, primitives seemed to talk all the time. He found that this talk seemed to involve three topics. One topic was that of tasks: for example, they would talk about plans for the hunt tomorrow. Another kind of talk was magic. They would participate in rituals for the propitiation of the gods or in ceremonies designed to heal the sick, ward off evil spirits, and so on. The third kind of communication seemed to serve no function at all: they would simply sit and chatter. He called this phatic communion.

Malinowski's crucial insight was the recognition that language and each of these forms of communication were serving functions quite other than truth claims. A magical incantation, for example, from the ethnocentric position of most other anthropologists of the time, would have been interpreted as superstition and bad science, or making erroneous statements about the nature of reality. However, Malinowski understood it as the process of *creating* the reality within which the tribe lived.[7] The concept of creating reality, and not trying to describe it, then made the other types of talk intelligible. Phatic communion served no instrumental or descriptive purposes but created a sense of community.

Contemporaneously with Malinowski, the American sociologist

George Herbert Mead began to analyze communication as a process in which selves and relationships and social institutions are formed.[8] Like Malinowski, but in a different content area, he described communication as that form of action by which the social order—including answers to the questions, Who am I? Who are you? What are we doing together?—is created and sustained.

The social sciences finally overlapped with the philosophers. The later Wittgenstein, in his *Philosophical Investigations*[9] in the late 1940s and 1950s, began to analyze communication and the function of statements not as truth claims with tangible referents but as actions that people perform. Wittgenstein used the term *language games* and said that what happens when people communicate is similar to what happens when they play games with each other. Their language use has little or nothing to do with reality but a great deal to do with the definition of what they are doing together and the accomplishment of particular tasks. To paraphrase one of his illustrations: When I come into a store and ask for "the red ones in the large jar up there on the left," that statement can be demonstrated as having absolutely no connection with reality. But if it winds up that I get "the red ones" in my hand, it has served its function for me because we are playing a game in which we tacitly understand what "the red ones" means as well as "up there," "large jar," and so on. Wittgenstein's argument is that these games suffice to get things done and do not cause problems in performance or in philosophy as long as we don't try to make truth claims out of our statements.

Wittgenstein's student J. L. Austin elaborated his mentor's position. Austin discussed the extent to which the social "objects" of concern are institutional facts and not brute facts.[10] Marriage, for example, is an institutional fact. It makes no sense to ask whether a marriage ceremony is true or false—as if there were a real marriage "out there" in nature to be pictured by our actions. It does make sense to ask whether a marriage ceremony was well done according to the standards of a particular human community or a particular couple. Of course, it also makes sense to inquire into those processes through which a community or a couple constructs its concept of a well-done marriage ceremony, a concept that when formed turns back upon their actions, canalizing them in certain ways.

Today, we view ordinary communication as the locus of powerful forces through which persons cocreate, maintain, and alter social order, personal relationships, and individual identities. An adequate theory of communication must do *more* than acknowledge that the nature of communication depends on the context in which it occurs. An adequate theory must account for the creation of contexts through communication. Notice that this modern conception makes communication much more than a vehicle for thought. Communication is the process of creating the perspectives that give rise to ideas and facts. Communication is not simply one of many things that persons do in relationships; it is the process of maintaining and creating relationships.

Our commitment to this modern concept of communication has several consequences, four of which we will discuss briefly. The modern concept of communication implies for us a set of felicity conditions that should be met if that theory is to be considered well done.

The Level of Theorizing

If communication includes the process of creating contexts, then a viable theory of communication should be at a higher conceptual level than any particular context. We are dissatisfied with the current tendency to attempt low-level theories—theories of family communication, of organizational communication, of doctor-patient communication, and so on. Such efforts imply a reification of context when they take the contexts as "given." We have chosen instead to develop a general theory of interpersonal communication. The power of the theory may be assessed by the degree to which it provides insight into particular domains. This does not mean that we ignore or consider unimportant those special features that distinguish a doctor-patient context from a husband-wife context. But a theory of communication should provide insight into how to conceptualize those special features. Sound theory should possess a schema for organizing phenomena so powerful that the uniqueness of individual cases and domains is illuminated.

Unifying the Societal vs. Interpretive Foci in Social Theory

The new concept of communication requires theorists to acknowledge a reciprocal relationship between the forms of social order and people's social action. Traditionally, however, social scientists have chosen to emphasize either the individual interpretive process or the operation of social forces on individuals.

Looking first to the societal perspective, we find a common problem in the very different analyses of Durkheim and Marx. Common to both is the problem of how to explain specific instances of real social action from a macro theory of social dynamics. Keat and Urry observe that Durkheim provides inadequate analysis of how general social forces are experienced and interpreted by social actors. In their words, there is "a failure to detail the mechanisms at the level of meaning which actually cause people to behave in certain ways."[11] Althusser makes a similar criticism of Marx's structural-functional theory, noting that Marx's account of how social forces are manifest in the consciousness of the peasant is far from satisfactory.[12]

Recently, much criticism has also been directed at the interpretive paradigm. The interpretive paradigm avoids the aforementioned gap between macro and micro units of analysis by focusing strictly on methods persons use to assign meaning and decide upon action. However, recent criticism of the interpretive paradigm stresses the inadequacy of simply opting for micro analysis. Gouldner has argued that approaches like dramatism, symbolic interactionism, and ethnomethodology are unduly microscopic, for they dwell on narrow circumscribed interactions without reference to the patterns of culture that circumscribe actors' perceptions of what they can or must do.[13]

Clearly, the weaknesses of both the normative and the interpretive paradigms are serious. A theory must include an account of how cultural forces are manifest in the perceptions of persons, but it must also represent persons as social actors—not mere puppets on the strings of social forces. To put the problem in other terms, a viable rules theory has to acknowledge a mutually causal (i.e., reflexive) relationship between the social order and the forms of communication.

An Adequate Conception of Competence: Beyond Fitting In

If communication is the process of creating and maintaining context, then an adequate notion of communication competence must encompass more than individuals' ability to "fit in" with preestablished patterns of meaning and action. In contrast, Durkheim perhaps represents the paradigm case of a social theorist operating from the traditional point of view. In his classic work on suicide, Durkheim writes,

> . . . society cannot disintegrate without the individual simultaneously detaching himself from social life, without his own goals becoming predominant over the community . . . the more weakened the groups to which he belongs, the less he depends on them, the more he consequently depends on himself and recognizes no other rules of conduct than what are founded on his private interests.[14]

Durkheim is usually interpreted to mean that social integration depends on the degree to which persons follow the rules of social groups in which they belong. This view is also reflected in a variety of communication theories. Berger's Uncertainty Reduction Theory, for example, specifies that unless one follows the known pattern for initial interactions, one will be perceived as being incompetent, even mentally ill, and the possibility of creating a personal relationship will be obviated.[15] Berger's position is much like Durkheim's—the necessary consequence of extranormative performance is disintegration. But normative performance and disintegration are not the only alternatives. As our recent work has shown, people can negotiate extranormative patterns without disintegration.[16] Indeed, the goal of fitting in may be impossible, even destructive, in various situations.

In her study of a formal organization, O'Brien[17] discussed the possibility that a woman may find situations in business where there is no consensus on how to assign meanings to her actions. In that kind of situation, a woman cannot choose to "fit in"; her alternative is chaos or the ability to negotiate meanings for her actions.

The literature of clinical psychology tells us that some interpersonal systems are cruelly convoluted. The Palo Alto group has described a kind of paradoxical communication that places great stress upon the participants.[18] R. D. Laing's little book *Knots*[19] describes a variety of convoluted systems that have destructive effects for those enmeshed in them. The idea that one simply must learn to live with such systems is indeed pernicious.

However, the complexity of modern society is such that even when systems are ready formed and not ill-formed, the capacity for normative performance is not sufficient. The fact that each social unit in modern society is interdependent with a changing environment, coupled with the fact that persons who make up a specific social unit are themselves changing as a result of their participations in other systems, yields a simple conclusion: a system of meaning and action that is satisfying at one time may be highly unsatisfying at a subsequent time. We are particularly impressed by the need to reconstruct close personal relationships as partners mature and change.

Consistency with Current Knowledge About Human Functioning

A well-formed theory ought to be consistent with what we have learned about human action. Space does not permit a review of the evidence from which we have drawn; a more detailed review is available elsewhere.[20] Here we wish to offer, in propositional form, a short set of statements about human action that are well supported by the current evidence. The statements are deceptively simple and seemingly noncontroversial. Yet their acceptance imposes a set of forceful restrictions on the kind of theory that one develops.

> Proposition 1.   Human beings will create systems of meaning and order even when there are none.[21]
>
> Proposition 2.   Human beings organize meanings hierarchically.[22]
>
> Proposition 3.   Human beings organize meaning temporally.[23]

Proposition 4. Individuals' systems of meaning are to some extent ideo-syncratic.[24]

Proposition 5. The behavior of individuals is uninterpretable except in the context of larger systems.[25]

These five simple propositions suggest the kind of account that must be given for human communication.

THE COORDINATED MANAGEMENT OF MEANING: AN OVERVIEW

The central metaphor—coordinated management of meaning—is meant to be taken seriously. Before describing the details of the theory, it is important to "unpack" the terms that label it.

The Coordination Focus

CMM theory describes human actors as attempting to achieve coordination by managing the ways messages take on meaning. We want to explain the principles that make social coordination possible. Our efforts have led us to reject the notion that coorientation, or mutual understanding, is a necessary precondition for coordination.

Our own case studies have shown that some couples achieve coordinated episodes *because* they assign different meanings to certain key messages.[26] Minuchin has discussed a therapeutic technique whereby he alters patterns of family interaction by deliberately treating a message in a way he knows was *not* intended.[27] Anthropologists also report that some rituals work precisely because leaders and celebrants do not attach the same meanings to conjoint actions.[28] We have thus come to focus on coordination per se rather than upon one specific means to it. What is coordination? It may be helpful to consider this analogy: two motorists coordinate their encounter at an intersection by avoiding each other even though they inhabit different "realities." One driver is dutifully obeying the system of traffic laws that specifies which car should proceed first, while the other is spontaneously responding to the behavior of others. We think of communication as a process in which each person interprets and responds to the acts of another, monitors the sequence, and compares it to his or her desires and expectations. We have found these terms useful for describing communicative episodes: (1) *coherence*—does the emerging episode make sense to the actors? It is not necessary that each actor make the same sense of the pattern, and indeed, one person may find an episode coherent when the conversational partner does not. If both parties perceive the pattern as coherent, we can describe it as minimally coordinated; (2) *control*—does the episode seem responsive to an actor's management?; and (3) *valence*—do the actors like the product and/or process of their conjoint action? An array of patterns may occur *within* coordinated episodes. For example, conversants may perceive either a joint control over the episode or that one person exerts more control than the other. They may even perceive a joint *lack* of control, as in the case of the unwanted but repetitive patterns of action that are performed in some relationships.[29] Actors may also agree about content and locus of control in an episode but differ on the desirability of it. Such complex patterns are not at all unusual.

The Focus on Management

CMM theory is not without its value commitments. Because contexts (relationships, groups, institutions, etc.) are products of social action, a useful social theory should assist people in their management of context and meaning. The highest obligation of persons is that of taking responsibility for their parts in the cocreation, maintenance, and alteration of social orders. We are in basic agreement with Eisenstein, who says that "moral responsibility is man's awareness of his obligation to interact creatively with his fellow men without renouncing his individuality."[30] Creative interaction presupposes the ability to manage meanings. We cannot choose whether or not to manage meaning. When one responds to a greeting, one contributes to the creation of a pattern that self and others will use to establish meanings for past and future messages. We can, however, choose whether to cultivate an awareness of how our management of meaning creates patterns of order and thus accept responsibility for the reciprocal effects of these patterns on our own and others' subsequent actions.

The emancipatory value of management must sometimes supersede the concern for coherence. Watzlawick and his colleagues have shown that confusion is sometimes a necessary precondition for altering a destructive social pattern.[31]

It is not sufficient, however, to emancipate humankind from a reified view of social contexts without providing a set of conceptual tools to assist persons in the analysis of interactional systems. Consistent with our discussion of the concept of communication is denial of the Marxist position that there is a "true" social order to be discovered. Marx believed that the function of social science was to uncover the discontinuity between the outward appearance and the inner essence of things.[32] He believed that it was necessary to dereify certain concepts such as class and profit, and recognize that these concepts are the products of social interaction, not material realities. In this belief, Marx was brilliantly ahead of his time. However, Marx believed that dereification would facilitate the rooting out of "false" ideologies. Without the obstruction of false ideologies, Marx believed a society would be produced in which everyday understanding would be undistorted as people came to comprehend society accurately, and social science itself would wither away.[33] In his belief that the emancipation from falsehood would reveal a "natural" or "true" social order undistorted by erroneous ideology, Marx reveals a nineteenth-century concept of science, including social science, as the process of discovering the true organization of phenomena eminent in nature. If, however, truth tests are irrelevant to the social domain, then we cannot expect that dereification will contribute to the discovery of the true system. Rather, dereification will facilitate the on-going critique of any social systems—including socialist systems—that humankind creates.

The dual focus on the emancipatory potential of self-conscious management and the study of alternative paths to coherent, coordinated action highlights the Janus-faced character of the human condition. For human genius is manifest in both the rigorous elaboration and imaginative creation of concepts. Perhaps Gregory Bateson said it best: "rigor alone is paralytic death, but imagination alone is insanity."[34]

COMMUNICATION SYSTEMS

CMM theory conceives of individuals as systems themselves. At the same time, individuals are parts of the communication systems they create with others. The systems formed by two or more conversants cannot be explained as a simple average or aggregate of individuals' acts and abilities. However, understanding individuals is a *pre*condition for understanding transpersonal systems.

It is a basic mistake to choose between an in*tra*personal and an in*ter*personal unit of observation. The alternative is to adopt the "holonic" concept of systems espoused by Arthur Koestler. The term *holon* is derived from the Greek *holos*—whole—and the suffix—*on*—part. The notion is that a specific level of organization is simultaneously whole and part. CMM theory provides ways of modeling individuals as patterns of organized meanings, and ways of modeling these patterns as embedded within transpersonal systems. Knowledge of individuals' information-processing procedures will yield an account of persons' ability to act and the range of actions available to them in specific contexts, but will not give us the ability to predict *what* act will be performed. The structure of the transpersonal systems that individuals form specifies the contexts within which they act.

The holonic concept suggests unique features of transpersonal communication systems. Unlike more elegant cybernetic systems, human communication systems lack a single superordinate monitor extending over all parts. In communication systems, there are two or more monitors, each with very limited access to the other(s). All we know of other persons are the acts they perform. The locus of meaning is intrapersonal, while the locus of action is interpersonal.

We also observe that modern society makes the boundaries of interpersonal systems highly penetrable and ephemeral. Each human component is enmeshed in a variety of systems, each with a logic of its own. The ability to control one's degree of enmeshment in multiple, sometimes incompatible, systems is an important consideration.

Conversants' Meanings: Levels of Hierarchical Organization

CMM, like several other theories, is informed by the idea that meanings are context-dependent. While the actual number of hierarchical levels is indeterminate, we offer a useful idealization of six basic levels of meaning. These levels are shown in Figure 1.

· *Level 1. Content* level meaning describes the referential function of verbal and nonverbal communication.

Cultural Patterns (CP)
Very broad patterns of world order and humankind's relationship to that order. These patterns locate human experience in a larger conceptual framework and legitimize ways of knowing and acting.

Life Scripts (LS)
The repertories of action that make up an individual's concept of self.

Relationship (R)
Implicit agreements between persons concerning the collective "we"—who we are as a couple or family, for example.

Episodes (Ep)
Communicative routines that persons view as wholes. Episodes are comprised of reciprocal speech acts and are characterized by their constitutive and regulative rules.

Speech Acts (Sp Act)
The things that people do to each other with words and gestures. Speech acts refer to the relational level of meaning (e.g., compliments, threats, promises, etc.).

Content (Cn)
Information about anything that is communicable but containing no indication of what kind of message it is.

Figure 1   A model of hierarchically organized meanings

• *Level 2. Speech acts* are those things that one person does to another. Saying something like "You are beautiful" counts as the speech act "compliment." There are many communicative events that are better understood as performatives rather than declaratives, the meanings of which are acts rather than referents. One of Watzlawick, Beavin, and Jackson's axioms is that all messages invoke meaning on both content and relationship levels, with relational meanings comprising speech acts.[35]

• *Level 3. Episodes* are "communicative routines which communicators view as distinct wholes, separate from other types of discourse, characterized by special rules of speech and nonverbal behavior and often distinguished by clearly recognizable opening or closing sequences."[36] They appear as patterned sequences of reciprocal speech acts.

• *Level 4. Relationships* are conversants' definitions of the bonds between themselves and others. The meaning of episodes differs if contexted by the relational meaning "equal partners in love" or "a real man and his obedient spouse."

• *Level 5. Life scripts* are clusters or patterns of episodes, comprising the person's expectations for the kinds of communicative events that can and probably will occur.

• *Level 6. Cultural patterns.* There are a number of archetypal patterns persons draw upon as they aggregate episodes into relationships, relationships into life scripts, and so on. Hall, for example, discusses the pattern of face-saving in Oriental cultures and the organization of events by monochronic time in Western cultures, both of which are frames actors use to organize experience.[37]

These six levels represent an "idealization" for several reasons. First, actors do not necessarily make use of all levels of context at a particular time. Second, the model as presented makes hierarchical relationships isomorphic with part-whole relationships. In social action, this isomorphism does not always hold. In a newly developing relationship—the second date, let us say—a specific can be used as the context through which the relationship is perceived. Indeed, as contexts develop, levels of meaning may well form reflexive loops. To continue our example of persons dating, it is common for them to experience an episode as an exchange of mutual commitments and use that episode as the context through which the relationship is perceived as a close personal one. As the episode continues, the emergent view of the relationship also functions as a context for perceiving the pattern of action. A simple hierarchical relationship between levels of meaning can be expressed via Brown's contextual symbol:⌐. (For example $\frac{x}{y}$, meaning y in the context of x.) A reflexive relationship can be expressed with Varella's reflexive operator:⌐⌐. (For example,

$$\boxed{}\begin{matrix} x \\ y \end{matrix}$$

shows a reflexive relationship between x and y.) Unlike the Palo Alto Group's approach, which tends to view all reflexive relations as problematic confusions, we consider reflexive relationships as innate features of some forms of social action and not necessarily problematic.[38]

By locating hierarchies of meaning in the heads of individuals, we can explore the effects of juxtaposing different organizations of meaning in the same system. Suppose, for example, that in a marital dispute one party uses the episode as context for interpreting the relationship, while the other reverses the hierarchical order of relationship and episode. One of these persons may see the relationship as fundamentally altered, while the spouse wonders how such a "big deal" could be made of one conversation.

Finally, we invite the readers' attention to the fact that in CMM cultural patterns, or culturally stereotyped views of relationships, life scripts, and so on, *may* be represented in persons' meaning systems, thus allowing us to deal with cultural forces *as* they are manifest and *if* they are manifest in persons' meaning systems. Of course, our system is not limited to culturally shared contents. The meanings that influence actions are sometimes idiosyncratic understandings of social norms and sometimes conceptions that actors know to be their own unique creations.

Rules: A Structural and Functional Treatment

CMM is often referred to as a Rules Theory. However, our concept of rules is unique. It does not limit the concept of rules to shared meanings, and it is not based on the principles of von Wright's practical syllogism. In CMM theory, rules are organizations of cognitions. They exist in the heads of individual social actors. A special feature of the CMM approach to rules is its structural-functional description of rules, which isolates measurable relationships among the components that make up rules. Two types of rules are identified: constitutive and regulative.

· *Constitutive Rules.* Constitutive rules organize actors' hierarchies of meaning. They specify how meanings at one level of abstraction may count as meaningful at another level of abstraction. For example, "You are beautiful" counts as compliment. The sensitive reader knows, however, that "You are beautiful" in some cases counts as sarcasm or insult rather than compliment. In the episode *Playing the Dozens*, a game played by urban black youths in America, a derogatory comment about Other's mother counts as gamesmanship rather than insult, and to interpret it as an insult is to call off the episode.

The primitive form of a constitutive rule may be algebraicized as shown in Figure 2. This primitive form specifies that in a certain context, if specific antecedent conditions are satisfied, then meaning at one level of abstraction counts as meaning at another level of abstraction. For example, constitutive Rule 1 in Figure 2 should read, "In the context of the episode 'Playing the Dozens', if it is the opponent's turn, then an insult to my mother and an insult to my father both count as 'gamesmanship.'" In "Playing the Dozens", both players must share constitutive Rules 1 and 2, among others.

· *Regulative Rules.* Regulative rules guide sequential action. The form of a regulative rule may be algebraicized as shown in Figure 3. The primitive form specifies that in the context of certain forms of social action, if given antecedent conditions obtain, then there exists some degree of force for or against the performance of subsequent actions.

Primitive form of a constitutive rule:

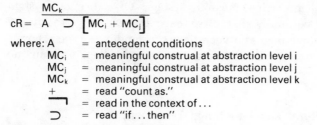

where: A = antecedent conditions
MC_i = meaningful construal at abstraction level i
MC_j = meaningful construal at abstraction level j
MC_k = meaningful construal at abstraction level k
+ = read "count as."
⌐ = read in the context of ...
⊃ = read "if ... then"

Examples of constitutive rules:

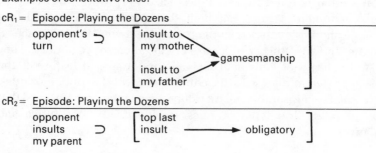

Figure 2   Constitutive rules

Primitive form of a regulative rule:

$$rR: \left[\frac{Actn_i}{A \supset (Do(Actn_i))_{1-n} \supset C} \right]$$

where: A   = antecedent message and/or conditions
Do   = deontic operator. (The deontic operators are obligatory, legitimate, prohibited, undetermined)
$\supset$ = read "if...then"
Actn   = action (a class term for social action at any level of abstraction in the hierarchy, such as episode, relationship, and so on)
i, j,...   = subscripts indicating levels of abstraction in the hierarchy, such as speech acts, episodes, and so on
C   = intended consequents

Regulative rule with levels of social action and deontic operator specified:

$$rR: \frac{Ep}{\left[A \supset (legit. (SpAct_x)) \right] \supset C}$$

Example of a regulative rule showing internalized content of a socially shared pattern of action:

$$rR_1: \frac{Episode: Playing\ the\ Dozens}{\left[\begin{array}{l} opponent \\ insults \\ own\ parent \end{array} \supset \begin{array}{l} (obligatory\ (top \\ opponents\ last \\ insult)) \end{array} \right] \supset \begin{array}{l} avoid\ losing, \\ opponent\ insults \\ back \end{array}}$$

Figure 3   Regulative rules

The primitive form further indicates that within a context of social action, if an antecedent condition is followed by specific action(s), then some consequences will follow. For example, regulative Rule 1 in Figure 3 should read, "In the episode of 'Playing the Dozens,' if the opponent insults my parent, then it is obligatory to top his or her last insult in order to avoid the consequence of losing the game." Regulatory rules are cognitive reorganizations of constitutive rules. Figure 4 shows how a regulative rule is built of constitutive rules.

The rules models of CMM contain meaningful content units at various levels of abstraction (speech acts, episodes, etc.) and structural relationships among these content units. It is important to observe that the elements of the primitive forms in Figures 2 and 3 may be simply place markers for linkages that may have various strengths in certain situations. Some rules, for example, are nonspecific as to the temporal antecedent (A) of action. In initial interaction, there seems to be a rule that obligates equal talking time at all times within the episode. The same place-making function applies to the consequent unit (C). Unlike von Wright's practical syllogism, which assumes purposive action and is thus limited in generality to task coordination

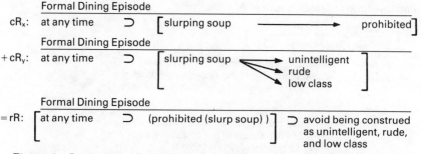

Figure 4   Derivation of regulative rule from constitutive rules

episodes, our rule structures permit us to deal with situations in which individuals may be acting ritualistically or on the basis of an inflexible self-definition with little regard to the consequences their acts will evoke.[39] Finally, we do not assume that human actors are always articulating their action to both life-scripts and elaborated episodes. Like a poor chess player, a conversant may make a choice of action contingent only upon Other's preceding act and an immediate consequent.

Rules and Measurement

Figure 5 depicts the array of linkage strengths that may be measured in any regulative rule. The various configurations of these measurements show different forms and strengths of logical force. For example,

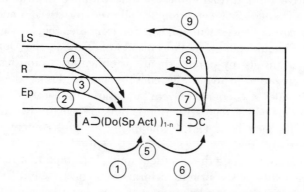

Prefigurative Forces

1. Act—antecedent linkage
2. Episode—act linkage
3. Relationship—act linkage
4. Life script—act linkage
5. Range of alternative acts

Practical Forces

6. Act—consequence linkage
7. Consequent—episode linkage
8. Consequent—master contract linkage
9. Consequent—life script linkage

Figure 5   Rule structure variables measured in recent research

the linkage of speech act to consequent can be measured by this Likert-type scale:

> I would have to perform this act regardless of what the other person would say or do next.
> strongly agree .... strongly disagree

This item measures the degree to which the choice of a speech act is predicated upon its effects or is functionally autonomous of consequences.

Within the overall logical force of regulative rules, two sets of variables can be identified: prefigurative and practical (see Figure 5). Prefigurative forces refer to the actor's conception of the episode, the meaning of prior speech acts, range of alternative actions, and other conceptions of the state of affairs, prior to action, that configure the choice of action. Practical force refers to actors' adjustment of their choices of action to anticipated consequences and to the feedback received from actions. The strength of these prefigurative and practical forces may be asymmetrical. That is, actors may feel their acts to be strongly determined by prefigurative forces, while the actors pay little attention to the consequences of the chosen acts. In this model, we break from the tradition of choosing a priori between a purposive and reactive model of the human condition, and treat prefigurative/reactive forces and practical/purposive forces as an empirically determined ratio. The utility of this measurement model has been supported in both nomothetic and case studies.[40] We have found, for example, that unwanted repetitive patterns exhibit a preponderance of prefigurative force in actors' rule structures.

Rules and Reflexivity: The Alteration of Content

We include in our measurement of rule structure linkages between consequents and levels of context. (See Figure 5, variables 7, 8, and 9.) Thus, the responses to one's acts may be represented as having influence on the maintenance or alteration of various levels of context. Considering reflexive effects of the consequences of our acts on the contexts that prefigured them produces a more dynamic conception of rule than the usual accounts. A simple listing of commonly held rules does not permit an account of the creation of social order. CMM rules are patterns of cognitions that actors create and *use*, and that they may alter or discard. In highly enigmatic episodes, one can conceive of actors "ad hoc-ing" the construction of rules, trying them out, and discarding them if they fail to facilitate the ability to manage meaning and produce coherence.

A second method of dealing with reflexivity has been developed more recently. By using the operator ⌐⌐ to represent a reflexive loop within a rule, we can identify situations where reflexive loops in the form of paradoxes set up mutually exclusive alternatives with equal force. Such a paradox is shown symbolically below:

$$\sqsupset \begin{array}{l} Ep \\ MC \end{array}$$

$$[[A_i \supset (Do(SpAct_u))] \supset C] \not\equiv [[A_k \supset (Do(SpAct_i))] \supset C]$$

where: $\not\equiv$ = exclusive disjunction

Consider the case of a couple on their third date: The male attempts to invoke an exchange of mutual commitments as he did on their last date. This time, however, his conversational partner responds with joking. The man feels that if he can assume that they have already created a close personal relationship, he should, in that context, interpret the episode as a demonstration that they are so committed to each other that they can joke about it. On the other hand, if the episode is treated as the context for defining the relationship, then the relationship would appear to be a more cool and distant one. The inability to determine whether the episode is the context for the relationship or the other way around produces alternative interpretations of what *kind* of antecedent acts the jokes are. The appropriateness of various speech acts and the kind of responses to seek must also be affected by the definition of the episode and relationship, while the reflexive relationship between episode and relationship in this case precludes establishing definitions.

Metarules

Recently, we have been exploring the idea that persons hold metarules that shape the nature of the constitutive and regulative rules used in conversation. Our speculation is that metarules (mR) are much more resistant to change than constitutive or regulative rules. Two kinds of mRs are described in CMM theory.

First, we identify A-type or authority metarules. They specify the authority behind other rules. Consider this constitutive rule:

$$cR: \quad \dfrac{\text{Episode of Conflict with Tom}}{\begin{array}{l} \text{at any} \\ \text{point} \end{array} \supset \left[\begin{array}{l} \text{"you are} \\ \text{lazy"} \end{array} \rightarrow \begin{array}{l} \text{denial} \\ \text{of love} \end{array} \right]}$$

The theorist can inquire, What is the epistemic status of this rule in the mind of the person who holds it? Does it reflect a "natural necessity"? The person may tell us that anyone who would say this is denying love because that's what such words mean—the meaning is *intrinsic* to the words themselves. We suggest that there are roughly five levels of authority that persons assign to rules:

1. *Natural necessity:* The rule is true to the nature of persons, words, or objects, and any change in it would amount to creating a false rule.
2. *Expert consensus:* Experts have found this rule to be the best guide.
3. *Community:* People like us, in our community or group, should use this certain rule.
4. *Self:* This rule reflects what is true for me—"Don't mess with my head."
5. *Negotiation:* We have jointly found it most useful to use a certain rule.

An A-type metarule can be algebraicized as shown below:

$$\text{mR}_A: \; [\text{R}_i: \; \rightarrow \text{acceptable by expert consensus}]$$

It is our suspicion that modern America's emphasis on assigning level 4 authority (self) to rules produces serious social problems. As individuals change via participation in multiple systems, it is most difficult to maintain stable relationships with others if rules for meaning and action are regarded as flowing from an inviolate self. Modern society requires that its members have the ability to trust in negotiated rules, or they are condemned to a string of very short-run relationships.

The other type of metarule we identify is the F-metarule or the metarule for form. This specifies what kinds of relationships may be reasonably obtained within constitutive or regulative rules. To illustrate, refer back to our discussions of reflexivity in rules and to our earlier discussion of how levels of meaning become reflexive during early stages of relationship development. We discussed the problem of a man on his third date with a certain woman, who responded to his invocation of "exchanging mutual commitments" with kidding or joking. At this stage of their relationship, it could not be determined whether he should regard the episode as the context for interpreting the relationship or treat the relationship as the context for interpreting the episode. Why was this situation problematic? The subject believes that if the episode "kidding responses to offers of commitment" is treated as the context, then he must interpret the relationship as "cool and distant." But if he stipulates the relationship as the higher order context and defines it as "close and committed," then he should interpret the episode as a demonstration of commitment (we are so close and committed we can even joke about it). This man's situation can be described by the following metarule:

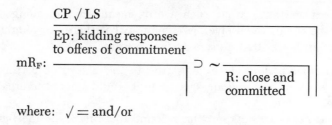

where: $\sqrt{}$ = and/or

  $\sim$ = negation

The metarule above stipulates that in light of this man's cultural pattern and/or life script, it is not possible to create rules in which an episode of kidding responses to offers of commitment forms the context for perceiving a close and committed relationship. Because of this metarule, the reflexive relationship between episode and relational levels of meaning produces a split in interpretation at the speech act level. For example,

cR: ───

offer of commitment $\supset$ [[kidding → cooling off the relationship] ⫢ [kidding → proof of commitment]]

  where: ⫢ = an exclusive disjunction

Observe, however, that this problematic disjunction of meaning is produced by an underlying metarule, not by reflexivity itself. Suppose that the episode *had* been another exchange of commitments. At this early stage of relational development, the episode is being used to interpret the relationship as much as the relationship is used to interpret the episode. But the individual believes that it *is* perfectly sensible to have an episode of exchanged commitments as the context for a close and committed relationship *and* vice versa. Thus, it does not matter whether Ep or R is the higher level context; either way "you mean so much to me ♪↘" counts as commitment.

Reflexive loops are designated in CMM as *in*transitive if reversing the hierarchical order of two levels of meaning changes the interpretation of one or both levels. These intransitive relationships that cause problems in the assignment of meaning and choice of action we call strange loops: ⌷[8]. Loops that permit the reversal of hierarchical perspective without affecting the meaning or action we call charmed loops: ⌷♥.[41] Analysis of persons' metarules, we believe, is a more fruitful way of dealing with paradox and reflexivity than is offered by the Russellian tradition, in which all "confusions" of hierarchical levels are treated as problematic conditions in need of repair.[42]

The Logic of Interpersonal Systems

The characteristics of the interpersonal system are determined by the nature of the "fit" between the individual rule systems. As in any system, the whole is not the simple sum of its parts. In human systems, this fact makes coordination of theoretical interest.

Social behavior is constrained by the interpersonal rule system. The most obvious feature of the temporal flow of communication is this: each person's behavior is both the antecedent and consequent of the other's. Given the structure of rules, alternation produces a "logic" of behavior in which an act by one person is interpreted by the constitutive rules of the other as the antecedent condition of a regulative rule. The regulative rule guides the selection of a next act in the context of expected consequences; constitutive rules describe the way to enact the next act; and so on. Figure 6 depicts the form of the logic. The amount of "logical force" impelling particular acts is a function of the structure of individual rules and the symmetry in content and structure between two intrapersonal rule systems.

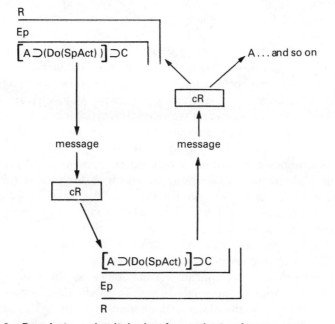

Figure 6   Regulative rules linked to form a logic of conversation

The perceptive reader will notice that the logic by which human communication systems function differs significantly from the logic of natural systems. While natural systems are open to information and energy, they are closed to changes in the logic of their operation. Human communication systems are open to changes in the logic governing the interaction of the human holons. These changes may occur in both the content of rules and in the structural relationships shown in Figure 5.

The logic of action and meaning produced by the conjoining of persons' rule systems may be studied in a variety of ways. In addition to studies of actual interactions, the implications of variation in the structure of rules for the functioning of a transpersonal system can be studied by game and computer simulations.[43]

The Assessment of Communication Competence

Most models of competence define competence as the ability of persons to learn and enact the rules of an extant system. Thus, these models emphasize knowledge of cultural skills like turn-taking or topic shifting, or they stress actors' ability to work within the extant meaning of a system through empathy, accurate listening, or understanding Other's intentions. Models of competence with such emphases do not address the problems of a reflexive relationship between modes of communication and social systems. They ignore the creative aspect of communication.

The complexity of modern society has altered the social requirements for communicative ability in ways more fundamental and drastic than have been commonly acknowledged. Specifically, there has been a *structural* change in the relationship between the social order and communication ability, such that *normal* functioning in modern society requires a type of communication ability that is *abnormally* sophisticated in any other society. However, neither formal educational institutions nor informal socialization processes have yet developed to disseminate widely the communication abilities required by modern societies. If we assume that there will be some "evolutionary" processes, we may expect that those who survive will ultimately acquire the requisite skills. In the meantime, there are many "casualties" of modernity: persons who suffer stress because they are unable to cope with the characteristics of modern society.

Harris defines communication competence as the ability to cocreate and comaintain the social order.[44] This definition focuses on the context-relevance of the skills and attributes of an individual: any particular skill may be functional or dysfunctional depending upon the requirements of the system. From this perspective, the possession or lack of particular skills is an inappropriate means of differentiating "levels" of competence. However, individuals can be assessed as more or less competent based on the comparison of their abilities with the requirements imposed by a particular social system.

The system-dependence of any "skill" is well illustrated by Harris's case study of one family's paradoxical logic.[45] The couple had studied humanistic communication skills, and both had internalized this rule: in the context of an episode of conflict, if Other discloses an aspect of self-identity, then it is obligatory to confirm the worth of that aspect of Other's identity. However, in the context of their long-term cycles of emotional buildup and conflict, the effect of these confirming messages was to lock the system in place. Both partners declared that the aspect of their own behaviors that their respective spouses found troublesome was a reflection of Self's core identity. This obligated the spouse to confirm that aspect of self as acceptable and deserving of respect. The result was to create this paradox: "we can't change but we must change."

Harris identifies three levels of competence.[46] *Minimal* competence exists when the individual's abilities are in some way less than those required by a particular system, for example, by lacking a particular skill or by being insufficiently differentiated. Such persons are "outside" the social system and unable to move effectively within it. *Satisfactory* competence exists when the individual is "enmeshed" within the system by a close fit between the abilities of that individual and the system's requirements. Such persons are well socialized and can move comfortably within but not outside the system. *Optimal* competence exists when an individual's abilities are greater than and subsume the requirements of a system. These individuals may choose whether to move easily within a system or for their own purposes to act in ways inconsistent with it.

The requisite abilities for participation in a homogeneous social system are acquired by modeling and successful socialization. Satisfactory competence is achieved by enmeshment in the system, and communication or adaptive problems are solved by becoming increasingly enmeshed within or dependent upon the system. In modern society—heterogenous, complex, reflexively self-aware of the human agency of its institutions—the structure of the social systems has changed in such a way that "satisfactory competence" is often impossible. The diversity of family interaction systems forces many couples to negotiate new patterns of interaction and new conceptions of their relationship unlike either person's family of origin.[47] The enmeshment of both partners in multiple systems fosters change in the self-concepts and value preferences of both of them. Thus, patterns of interaction that were mutually satisfying at one stage of close relationship may be unsatisfying to one or both partners at a subsequent time.

The desire for close personal relations with a partner who can step *outside* traditional interaction patterns is recognized by recent research into modern equal-partner marriage styles. "The unique feature of this marriage form," says Scanzoni, "is that nothing is nonnegotiable. Unlike in other marriage forms where certain things are prearranged, all issues are open to bargaining."[48] Creating an equal partner relationship of course requires finding a partner who is capable of negotiating new patterns of relationship and who is not enmeshed in preestablished social roles.

A recent study by Harris, Cronen, and Lesch[49] lends empirical support to the claim that young people prefer interactions with those who show an ability to deviate deliberately from traditional patterns.

The skills required to negotiate new patterns are not simply those required to "fit in." Harris discusses some of the skills of optimal competence.[50] In the domain of "assignment of meaning" to another's messages, minimal competence is reflected in mistaking the meanings of another's messages, and satisfactory competence is reflected in mutual understanding. Optimal competence, however, would entail the ability to treat knowingly a message in such a way that is inconsistent with Other's intent in order to alter a destructive pattern of talk. Another skill Harris discusses is the ability to treat an episode playfully. The ability to introduce an element of play into an otherwise serious episode can help persons to distance themselves from the episode so that they can obtain control over it, thus avoiding overenmeshment.

As stated previously, satisfactory competence is often impossible in modern society. For research and policy, the implications of modernity are that the symptoms of minimal competence should be expected to increase. These include frustrations, confusion, retardation, inefficiency, and stress-related pathologies. For pedagogy, the implication is that instruction should be designed to inculcate optimal rather than satisfactory competence.

While we have given much attention to creative social action, we do not wish to leave the impression that creative change is an individual responsibility or achievement. Only conjoint action can produce change. For example, change can be produced when a satisfactorily competent person can mirror the creative actions of another. However, some social systems may make certain changes difficult if not impossible. Some social systems seem to acculturate members into rules like this:

   cR: In the context of episode X, at any point in the episode, any action
       not currently known to be legitimate or obligatory counts as impudent and insulting.

What individuals need is sufficient skill to analyze a system that contains a rule like the one above so that they can make an informed decision about the degree of enmeshment they want in such a system.[51]

SUMMARY

We have not attempted in this short chapter to provide a review of the research that supports the CMM theory. A review is available elsewhere,[52] as is an in-depth treatment of logical force as a mode of causal explanation.[53] Instead, we have tried to convey a sense of the concerns that have guided our work. We have attempted to develop a theory that is consistent with modern developments in both the philosophy and science of humankind. We are very much concerned that our work be regarded as more than an interesting intellectual exercise. We hope that the concept we are developing can give people a perspective from which to analyze their own actions and the social systems in which they participate. Consider the problems inherent in developing critical tools for the modern age. Our tools must be sufficient for a society in which people know that they are responsible for the systems of meaning and action they create, and also know that their identities are contexted by their own creations. The modern condition leaves us not with absolute standards of judgment but with the uncomfortable admonition to value both rigor and imagination. How do we decide between rigorously extending the implications of a system and attempting to alter it? We offer no easy answers. But we do believe that we can offer an analytic schema for dealing with the logic of systems that encompasses their temporal, hierarchical, and reflexive features. Moreover, the schema provides a way of measuring the forces operating within a logic of conversation. CMM theory also proposes a new system-based concept of competence that generates a new perspective on the nature and value of communication skills.

We have applied this theory to a number of content domains: family communication,[54] family violence,[55] organizational communication,[56] and intercultural communication.[57] Thus far we have been satisfied with its ability to illuminate the complexities of human action and to meet accepted standards of empirical verification.

We do not present CMM theory as a fully elaborated position needing only extension to additional content domains. We offer it as a departure point. We invite the reader to examine critically the concept of humankind upon which the theory rests and to examine the evidence offered in its behalf. You are invited to challenge it, extend it, and argue for changes, if such are needed.

We take very seriously the view that communication is a process through which persons create, maintain, and alter social order, relationships, and identities. In consequence of this view, we see no more pressing business than the development of apparatuses that emancipate humankind from the seemingly inexorable force of events. Our theory should be assessed in that context.

Notes

1. Lao Tzu, *Tao te Ching,* trans. Gia-Fu Feng and Jane English (New York: Vantage, 1972).
2. Marjorie Grene, *The Knower and the Known* (Berkeley: University of California Press, 1974).
3. Ernest Nagel and J. R. Newman, *Gödel's Proof* (New York: New York University Press, 1958).
4. G. Spencer Brown, *Laws of Form* (New York: Bantam Books, 1972).
5. Francisco J. Varela, "A Calculus for Self-Reference," *International Journal of General Systems,* 2 (1975), 5–24.
6. Norwood R. Hansen, *Patterns of Discovery* (Cambridge: Cambridge University Press, 1958).
7. Bronislaw Malinowski, "The Problem of Meaning in Primitive Languages," in C. K. Ogden and I. A. Richards, *The Meaning of Meaning* (New York: Harcourt, Brace and Co., 1923), pp. 296–336.
8. George Herbert Mead, *Mind Self, and Society* (Chicago: University of Chicago Press, 1934); Peter Berger and Thomas Luckman, *The Social Construction of Reality* (Garden City, N.Y.: Doubleday, 1966).
9. Ludwig Wittgenstein, *Philosophical Investigations* (New York: Macmillan, 1953).
10. J. L. Austin, *How to Do Things with Words* (Oxford: Oxford University Press, 1955).
11. Russell Keat and John Urry, *Social Theory as Science* (London: Routledge and Kegan Paul, 1955), pp. 88–89.
12. L. Althusser, *For Marx* (New York: Pantheon, 1969).
13. W. A. Gouldner, *The Coming Crisis in Western Sociology* (New York: Basic Books, 1970), p. 382.
14. Emil Durkheim, *Suicide: A Study in Sociology* (London: Routledge and Kegan Paul, 1952), p. 209.
15. Charles R. Berger, Royce R. Gardner, Glen W. Clatterbuck, and Linda S. Schulman, "Perceptions of Information Sequencing in Relationship Development." Paper presented to the International Communication Association Annual Convention, 1975.
16. Linda M. Harris, "Communication Competence: An Argument for a Systemic View." Paper presented at the International Communication Association Annual Convention, 1979; Linda M. Harris, Vernon E. Cronen, and William E. Lesch, "Social Actors and Their Relationship to the Social Order: A Test of Two Theoretical Views." Paper presented to the International Communication Association Annual Convention, 1980.
17. Charlene M. O'Brien, "A Rules-Based Approach to Communication in a Formal Organization," Diss. University of Massachusetts, 1978.

18. Paul Watzlawick, Janet H. Beavin, and Don D. Jackson, *The Pragmatics of Human Communication* (New York: Norton, 1967).
19. R. D. Laing, *Knots* (New York: Vintage Books, 1970).
20. W. Barnett Pearce, Vernon E. Cronen, and Forest Conklin, "What to Look at When Analyzing Communication: A Hierarchical Model of Actors' Meanings," *Communication* 5 (1979), 179–203.
21. Paul Watzlawick, *How Real Is Real?* (New York: Vintage Books, 1976), pp. 48–54; Don D. Delaney, "The Place of Hypotheses and Intensions," in *Behavior and Awareness*, ed. C. W. Eriksen (Durham, N.C.: Duke University Press, 1962), pp. 102–129.
22. Ragar Rommetviet and E. A. Carswell, eds., *Social Context of Messages* (New York: Academic Press, 1971); W. Barnett Pearce and Forest Conklin, "A Model of Hierarchical Meanings in Coherent Conversation and a Study of Indirect Responses," *Communication Monographs*, 46 (1976), 75–87.
23. Robert C. Shank and Robert P. Abelson, *Scripts, Plans, Goals, and Understanding* (Hillsdale, N.J.: Lawrence Erlbaum Associates, 1977).
24. See the work of the Constructivists: for example, Barbara J. O'Keefe, "The Theoretical Commitments of Constructivism." Paper presented to the Seminar on Constructivism, Speech Communication Association Annual Convention, 1978. For an introduction to Constructivism, see George A. Kelly, *A Theory of Personality* (New York: Norton, 1963).
25. See the work of Don D. Jackson and the Palo Alto Group: for example, Don D. Jackson, "The Question of Family Homeostasis," *The Psychiatric Quarterly Supplement*, Part 1, 31 (1957), 79–90. For a simple simulation that demonstrates the concept, see W. Barnett Pearce and Vernon E. Cronen, *Communication, Action and Meaning: The Creation of Social Realities* (New York: Praeger, in press).
26. Linda M. Harris, Vernon E. Cronen, and Sheila McNamee, "An Empirical Case Study of Communication Episodes." Paper presented to the Theory and Methodology Workshop, National Council on Family Relations Annual Convention, 1979.
27. Salvador Minuchin, *Families and Family Therapy* (Cambridge, Mass.: Harvard University Press, 1974).
28. Joseph Campbell, *The Masks of God: Primitive Mythology* (New York: Viking Press, 1959).
29. Vernon E. Cronen, W. Barnett Pearce, and Lonna Snavely, "A Theory of Rule-Structure and Types of Episodes, and a Study of Perceived Enmeshment in Unwanted Repetitive Patterns (URPs)," in *Communication Yearbook III*, ed. Dan Nimmo (New Brunswick, N.J.: Transaction Press, 1979), pp. 225–240.
30. Ira Eisenstein, "Religious Alternatives for the Contemporary Jew," *Reconstructionist*, 65 (1980), 9.
31. Watzlawick, pp. 27–42.
32. Keat and Urry, pp. 194–195.
33. G. A. Cohen, "Marx and the Withering Away of Social Science," *Philosophy and Public Affairs*, 1 (1972), 182–203.
34. Gregory Bateson, *Mind and Nature: A Necessary Unity* (New York: E. P. Dutton, 1979), p. 219.

35. Watzlawick, Beavin, and Jackson, Ch. 1.
36. John H. Gumperz, "Introduction," in *Directions in Sociolinguistics: The Ethnography of Communication,* ed. J. J. Gumperz and D. Humes (New York: Holt, Rinehart and Winston, 1972), p. 17.
37. Edward T. Hall, *Beyond Culture* (Garden City, N.Y.: Anchor, 1977).
38. Vernon E. Cronen, Kenneth M. Johnson, John Lannamann, and W. Barnett Pearce, "Paradoxes, Double-Binds, and Reflexive Loops: A Comparison of Two Theoretical Perspectives and a Suggested Methodology." Paper accepted for presentation to the Theory and Methodology Workshop, National Council on Family Relations Annual Convention, 1980.
39. Cronen, Pearce, and Snavely: Harris, Cronen, and McNamee.
40. Cronen, Pearce, and Snavely; Harris, Cronen, and McNamee; W. Barnett Pearce, Vernon E. Cronen, Kenneth Johnson, Greg Jones, and Robert Raymond, "The Structure of Communication Rules and the Form of Conversation: An Experimental Simulation," *The Western Journal of Speech Communication,* 44 (1980), 20–34; Vernon E. Cronen, Eugene Kaczka, W. B. Pearce, and Mark Pawlik, "The Structure of Interpersonal Rules for Meaning and Action: A Computer Simulation of 'Logical Force' in Communication," *Proceeding of the 1978 Simulation Conference* (Washington, D.C.: National Bureau of Standards, 1979).
41. Cronen, Johnson, Lannamann, and Pearce.
42. Alfred North Whitehead and Bertrand Russell, *Principia Mathematica,* Vol. 1, 2nd ed. (Cambridge: Cambridge University Press, 1910), p. 37; Watzlawick, Beavin, and Jackson; Paul Watzlawick, John Weakland, and Richard Fisch, *Change: Principles of Problem Formation and Problem Resolution* (New York: Norton, 1974); Gregory Bateson, "Theory of Play and Fantasy," *Steps to an Ecology of Mind* (New York: Ballantine Books, 1972), pp. 177–193; Kenneth Johnson, "Reflexivity, Communication, and Social Structure: A Theory of Reflexive Loops in Conversation with Implications for Human Emancipation," Diss. in process, University of Massachusetts.
43. Pearce, Cronen, Johnson, Jones, and Raymond; Cronen, Kaczka, Pearce, and Pawlik.
44. Harris, "Communication Competence: An Argument for a Systemic View."
45. Linda M. Harris, "Analysis of a Paradoxical Logic: A Case Study," *Family Process,* 19 (1980), 19–34.
46. Harris, "Communication Competence: An Argument for a Systemic View"; Linda M. Harris, "Communication Competence: Empirical Tests of a Systemic Model," Diss. University of Massachusetts, 1979.
47. Minuchin.
48. John Scanzoni, "A Historical Perspective on Husband-Wife Bargaining Power and Marital Dissolution," in *Divorce and Separation: Context, Causes, and Consequences,* ed. G. Levinger and O. C. Moles (New York: Basic Books, 1979), p. 31.
49. Harris, Cronen, and Lesch.
50. Harris, "Communication Competence: Empirical Tests of a Systemic Model."

51. Harris, "Communication Competence: Empirical Tests of a Systemic Model"; W. Barnett Pearce, "The Context of Change and the Change of Contexts: Reflections on the Requirements for Successful Communication in Modern Society." Paper presented at the Speech Communication Association Annual Convention, 1978.

52. W. Barnett Pearce and Vernon E. Cronen, *Communication Action, and Meaning: The Creation of Social Realities.*

53. Vernon E. Cronen and W. Barnett Pearce, "Logical Force in Interpersonal Communication: A New Concept of 'Necessity' in Social Behavior," *Communication* (in press).

54. Harris, "Analysis of a Paradoxical Logic: A Case Study"; Harris, Cronen, and McNamee.

55. Linda M. Harris, "Power, Impotence, and Physical Violence." Paper presented to the Eastern Communication Association Annual Convention, 1980.

56. Linda M. Harris and Vernon E. Cronen, "A Rules-Based Model for the Analysis and Evaluation of Organizational Communication," *Communication Quarterly*, 27 (1979), 12–28.

57. Marsha H. Stanback and W. Barnett Pearce, "Dissimulation: An Analysis of a Form of Intercultural Communication." Paper presented to International Communication Association Annual Convention, 1980; W. Barnett Pearce and Linda M. Harris, "Optimizing the Acculturation Process: Perspectives from a Theory of Communication Competence." Paper presented to the Society for Intercultural Education, Training and Research Annual Conference, 1980.

A RULES THEORY OF INTERPERSONAL RELATIONSHIPS

Donald P. Cushman
Barry Valentinsen
David Dietrich

Human communication processes can be examined scientifically from a variety of theoretical perspectives. Three theoretical orientations of proven utility are the causal, systems, and rules perspectives. Each of these orientations is useful because each provides scientists with (1) a model for the explanation, prediction, and control of phenomena that is both general and necessary[1]; (2) a model for the construction and verification of distinct types of relationships[2]; and (3) paradigmatic exemplars of theories that shed differential light on human communication processes.[3]

The unique insights that a rules perspective can provide into human communication processes were first articulated for our discipline by Cushman and his associates in 1972, when they argued that

> Communication is an activity which gains meaning and significance from consensually shared rules. What is transmitted in communication is structure or information, but not all experiences from which we extract information are communication experiences. Communication requires in addition that at least two individuals attempt to take one another into account by developing and utilizing communication rules

to guide and constitute the significance of their communicative acts. These rules guide the choices made in decoding and encoding messages. Such rules are social, human creations subject to change and recreation. As a discipline, communication should make the explication of such rules a central concern, for they provide communication with its defining characteristic and knit together into a coherent and theoretic whole insights from transactionalism, co-orientation, symbolic interaction, and cybernetics.[4]

Since 1972, several diverse research programs aimed at clarifying[5] and redeeming these claims[6] have emerged within our discipline.

This essay reflects the cumulative efforts of one research program, namely that of Cushman and his associates, to explicate and illustrate the unique potential of a rules perspective for the creation of a rules theory of interpersonal relationships. Our analysis will be divided into three parts: (1) an explanation of the unique assumptions that underlie this rules perspective and a discussion of the implications such assumptions have for creating and verifying rules theories; (2) an explication of the self-concept as a cybernetic control system for the rules that govern and guide human communicative action; and (3) a delineation of the communication rules that direct the formation of two types of interpersonal relationships.

RULES—THEORETIC ASSUMPTIONS

It is an ancient view that the exercise of personal choice is restricted when individuals are limited to the only particular means that exist to secure a specific outcome. This view has been the basis for numerous accounts of individual conduct and social organization, and it is at the heart of the opposition of pragmatism to idealism. It is unequivocally the first principle of rhetorical and communication theory from the time of Aristotle to the present. The most visible, modern expression of the intentionalist position and related issues is action theory. The action theory tradition centers on a conception of humans as creatures of freedom and choice, who are typically engaged in intentional, goal-directed behavior and are capable of acting rather than merely being acted upon. The viability of a rules theory of human communication rooted in action theory depends upon a series of assumptions.

The Motion-Action Assumption

First, it is assumed that human behavior can be divided into two classes of activity: stimulus-response activities governed by causal necessity, and intentional and choice-oriented responses governed by practical necessity. The former behaviors are habitual and are termed *movements,* while the latter are evaluative and are termed *actions.* Action theorists restrict their domain of inquiry to those realms of human behavior in which persons have some degree of choice among alternatives, are able to critique their performance, can exercise self-monitoring capacities, and can respond to practical or normative forces. Fay and Moon summarize as follows:

> According to this distinction, actions differ from mere movements in that they are intentional and rule governed: they are performed in order to achieve a particular purpose, and in conformity to some rules. These purposes and rules constitute what we shall call the "semantic dimension" of human behavior—its symbolic or expressive aspect. An action, then, is not simply a physical occurrence, but has a certain intentional content which specifies what sort of an action it is, and which can be grasped only in terms of the system of meanings in which the action is performed. A given movement counts as a vote, a signal, a salute or an attempt to reach something, only against the background of a set of applicable rules and conventions and the purposes of the actors involved.[7]

A consensus seems to exist among action theorists that to attribute or ascribe the quality of action to a human behavior is to claim that some agent is the author or cause of the behavior which was brought about. Several important implications regarding the nature of scientific inquiry from within an action-theoretic perspective follow from this first assumption. These implications center on the nature, structure, and verification of action-theoretic explanations.

Action theory requires an explanation of human behavior in terms of the intentional link between an agent's perceptions, thoughts, and behavior so that the agent's perceptions and thoughts explain why the behavior occurred. Charles Taylor elaborates:

> Explanation in terms of purpose therefore involved taking into account the conceptual forms through which agents understand and come to grips with their world. That people think of their environment in certain concepts, that is, use certain modes of classification is an element in accounting for what they do. Indeed, it can be said to define what they do. For if we think of actions as defined by the purposes or intentions which inform them, then we cannot understand man's action without knowing the concepts in which they form their intentions.[8]

The structure for explaining human behavior within an action-theoretic perspective is the practical syllogism in which the conclusions follow from the premises with practical rather than causal or logical necessity.[9]

A *intends* to bring about B;
A *considers* that he cannot bring B unless he does C;
A *sets himself* to do C.

When cast in this structure, intentional reasoning is termed a *first-person practical syllogism*. Its distinctive feature is that it is formulated from an actor's point of view, explaining what an actor *considers practically necessary* for the fulfillment of his intention and indicating that an actor *sets* himself to do what is practically necessary to fulfill the intention. Note that even if an actor's perceptions of what he must do are in error, the first-person, practical syllogism is still a valid explanation of *why* he set himself to do what he did. Action theorists argue that the practical syllogism provides the humanities and social sciences with "something long missing from their methodology: an explanatory model in its own right which is a definite alternative to the subsumption-theoretic covering law model."[10]

While the practical syllogism does appear to offer at least one advantage as an explanatory device—its uniqueness—it also has two very serious disadvantages: it is nonpredictive and nonverifiable. The practical syllogism can be constructed only after the occurrence of an event. The explanatory force is thus *ex post acto*. In addition, the practical force that exists between promises and conclusion can be verified only through the testimony of the actor. Thus, no intersubjective source of verification exists. We shall address one method for resolving these problems under our third assumption.

The Information Processing-Coordination Assumption

Second, action theory assumes that there exist two classes of human actions: those in which an agent's choice among alternative courses of action and efforts to achieve a goal does not require the cooperation of others and those that do require such cooperation, in which case communication becomes a necessary stage in goal attainment. The former are termed *information processing situations* and function to regulate human perception and thought with regard to some goal, while the latter are termed *coordination situations* and function to regulate consensus among agents with regard to the cooperative achievement of a goal.[11] Action theorists with a communication orientation restrict their domain of scientific inquiry to coordination situations. Why? Because it is only within the domain of coordination situations that human action requires the transfer of symbolic information or communication to facilitate goal-directed behavior. Cushman and Pearce summarize as follows:

> . . . (1) there exists a class of human action which involves conjoint, combined, and associated behavior; (2) that the transfer of symbolic information facilitates such behavior; (3) that the transfer of symbolic information requires the interaction of sources, messages, and receivers guided and governed by communication rules; and (4) that the communication rules form general and specific patterns which provide

the basis for explanation, prediction, and control of communication behavior.[12]

Several important implications regarding the nature of scientific inquiry into human communication processes from within an action theoretic perspective follow from this second assumption. These implications involve a conceptualization of the function, structure, and processes of human communication in coordination situations.

One instance of a coordination task that requires the cooperation of others for goal attainment—and is thus governed and guided by communication rules—is the traditional marriage ceremony. The goal of such a ceremony is to unite a couple in matrimony. In order to attain such a goal, each participant must engage in various sequences of verbal behavior, which, according to the rules, constitute a verbal commitment. When these verbal episodes are sequenced in a certain way in the appropriate situation, they count as a marriage contract. The *function* of human communication in such a context is to regulate the consensus needed to coordinate behavior. The *structure* of human communication is the content and procedural rules involved in regulating consensus. The *process* of human communication entails the adaptation of the rules involved in regulating consensus to the task at hand.[13]

The Creative-Standardized Usage Assumption

Third, it is assumed that there are two classes of coordination situations: those in which the interactants attempt through negotiation to generate the rules that will form the basis of episodic sequences in coordinated goal attainment, and those in which some generative mechanism, which has provided such rules, already exists. The former are termed *creative* situations and do not allow for the explanation, prediction, and control of human behaviors in terms of antecedent conditions; the latter are termed *standardized* situations and do allow for the creation and verification of human communication theories within a traditional measurement model of antecedent conditions.[14] While human communication theories could be developed to explain either creative or standardized interactions, only the latter theories will allow for the explanations to predict and verify rules theories antecedent to the interaction. Communication theorists who seek to develop rules theories that employ traditional measurement thus restrict their domain of inquiry to human actions aimed at coordination within standardized situations. These rules theorists seek to locate as a basis for theory-building a coordination task that generates a standardized system of rule-governed, symbol-meaning associations that are relatively persistent because the participants engaged in some task have found the system particularly useful for coordinating their activities.[15]

A standardized usage or system of rule-governed, symbol-meaning associations has several important characteristics. First, such a usage is organized and made meaningful for those who employ it by a shared *class* of intentions. When two or more interactants employ a standardized usage, they are indicating to each other their decision to participate in the class of intentional acts. Second, because such a standardized usage involves mutual cooperation in coordinated goal attainment, each of the participants holds the other(s) to a common set of expectations and responsibilities regarding what their communicative actions mean. Deviations from these expectations require that the participants involved either provide a satisfactory account for their deviation,[16] adjust their behavior in conformity with the rule, or suffer the punishment invoked by the other(s) involved in the co-ordination task.[17] Third, the usage allows each individual involved to select sequences of communicative acts that reflect the individual's variable commitment to the class of intentions involved. Interactants thus reveal the variable strength of the practical force that caused them to participate in the coordination task.

Several important implications regarding the nature of scientific inquiry within an action-theoretic perspective follow from this third assumption. These implications indicate how one constructs and veri-fies a rules theory that aspires to explanation, prediction, and control while employing traditional empirical research methodology.

The first problem created by the attempt to verify a rules theory is how one can empirically separate rule-governed from causally de-termined patterns of behavior. When human communication patterns constitute a rule, they do so because such behaviors are consciously coordinated through mutual dependence upon one another. A rule exists when—and only when—two (or more) people do the same thing under certain conditions because both expect each other to behave in a certain way, and each is aware of the other's expectation. Thus, a pattern of behavior becomes empirically verifiable as rule-governed when mutual expectation of what constitutes appropriate behavior serves as a standard to judge and evaluate conduct, which one now has the *right* to expect. Habits are descriptive of human behavior; rules are evaluative of such behaviors and are thus moni-tored by those employing the rule.

In order for empirical research to have theoretical import within this rules perspective, Cushman and Pearce argue that first,

> . . . such research must locate tasks which require coordination because such tasks serve as the generative mechanism for communication rules which take the form of standardized usages and episodic sequences.

Next, a researcher must define and measure the generality and necessity of the standardized usage and its various episodic sequences. Finally, we outline three forms which the practical syllogism may take in modeling the generality and necessity of episodic sequences.[18]

Each of these is a necessary condition for rules research to have theoretic import. Collectively, they represent the sufficient condition for such an outcome because all human actions necessarily involve rules; all actions requiring coordination with others necessarily involve communication and communication rules; and all standardized coordination situations necessarily involve stable communication rules that are carefully monitored in order to avoid deviations and are thus intersubjectively verifiable.

When researchers follow the aforementioned procedure in constructing and verifying rules theories of human communication processes, then they automatically correct the previously mentioned problems of ad hoc explanation and nonverifiability inherent in the first-person practical syllogism. Cushman and his associates have made three changes in the practical syllogism in order to make the explanatory model predictive and verifiable. First, the major premise of the practical syllogism has been changed from an individual intention to a class of verifiable intentional situations—task coordination situations. Second, rule influence is conceptualized as the effect of a powerful rule-generating mechanism that exerts influence on minor premises selection of standardized usages by the actors. Third, the categorical logic of practical necessity has been changed to the variable logic of practical force.[19]

Cushman and his associates thus provide a theoretical perspective on the human communication processes with a unique explanatory model that can employ a traditional measurement model for predicting and verifying human behavior. In so doing, Cushman and his associates limit their domain for scientific inquiry to human actions involving coordination tasks for which standardized usages already exist. While this domain may at first appear to be unduly restrictive,[20] considerable evidence exists that such a domain includes many important social interactions.[21]

Having examined in some detail the assumptions that underlie the rules-theoretic approach of Cushman and his associates, we are now in a position to examine their methodological procedures for conceptualizing and operationalizing human action.

SELF-CONCEPT AS A CYBERNETIC CONTROL SYSTEM FOR HUMAN ACTION

Human actions that take place within a standardized coordination situation require common intentions, an established set of rules for the cooperative achievement of those intentions, and a procedure for manifesting the variable practical force the actors feel for participating in the coordination task. If rules theories of human communication processes seek the explanation, prediction, and control of individual behaviors in such situations, then we are in need of an empirically verifiable construct in terms of which to investigate the link between an individual's perceptions, thoughts, and behaviors. Such a construct will provide a theoretical representation of the conceptual forms through which actors understand and come to grips with the world. We believe that the self-concept provides just such an empirically verifiable construct. Our analysis of why and how the self-concept has the theoretical status of a cybernetic control system for human action in standardized coordination situations will be developed in three stages. First, we will explore the nature, function, and scope of the self-concept, and indicate the manner in which it organizes human action. Next, we will explore the self-concept as a cybernetic control system. Finally, we shall review briefly the empirical research that grounds our conceptualization.

The Nature of the Self-Concept

The self-concept traditionally has been viewed as the information individuals have regarding the relationship of objects or groups of objects to themselves.[22] Individuals moving in their environments are confronted by persons, places, things, or concepts. If they are to commit themselves to any actions toward those objects, individuals must perform two tasks. First, they must determine what the objects of their experiences are by associating them with and differentiating them from other objects they have experienced. Second, they must determine the relationship of the objects or groups of objects to themselves in terms of appropriate actions in appropriate circumstances. Their knowledge of what objects are and how they should act toward them are products of information based on past experiences. This does not mean that in their experiential fields individuals have only object relationships that include the self as one of the objects. The statement "Aristotle is dead," for example, provides information about Aristotle without conveying anything about one's self.

On the other hand, such statements as "I am tall," "I am a good Democrat," and "I am a good teacher and therefore must have my papers graded on time" do provide information about one's self, and therefore, would be part of the self-concept. Following Thompson, we will divide all such self-object relationships into three classes.[23] First, statements such as "I am tall" designate relationships pertaining to what an individual *is;* that is, such statements name or label an individual's attributes. These statements form the *identity self.* Second, other self-object declarations, such as *good*, describe how one feels about one's self, or one's feelings of self-satisfaction. These statements, then, form the *evaluative self*. Finally, a third type of self-object relationship exists. The statement "I am a good teacher and therefore must have my papers graded on time," in addition to providing information for identifying and evaluating the self, prescribes an appropriate behavior to be performed in regard to the self-object relationship and constitutes the *behavioral self*. Consequently, the behavioral self can be represented as a set of imperatives for action—rules governing an individual's behavior with respect to relevant objects in a situation.

The relationships that comprise the self-concept are important in at least three ways. First, the information an individual gleans as a result of an encounter with one object will apply to all other objects the individual places in the same *class*. An individual can thus make an inference about his or her relationship to an object without encountering that object. One need only encounter another object that one categorizes with the first. Second, such self-concept structures provide individuals with *expectations* about the nature of those objects they believe to be subsumed under associated rules. The self-concept thus directs perception, causing an individual to notice certain characteristics of an object and to react to an object on the basis of those characteristics. Third, as the self-concept develops, it provides the individual with *preconceived plans* of action. A self-object relationship constitutes a ready-made format for processing experience and initiating action. With such a system, a person is prepared to cope with the future and make sense out of the past. Hence, we regard the self-concept as an organized set of structures that defines the relationship of objects to individuals and that is capable of governing and directing human action. Furthermore, the self-concept, as an organized set of structures, provides the rationale for choice in the form of a valanced repertory of alternative plans of action.

The Self-Concept as a Cybernetic Control System

We regard the self-concept as the coordinator and initiator of the positive and negative feedback systems in the services of goal-seeking and systematic change. We do not, however, suggest that the process by which an individual forms and executes all acts is completely determined prior to performing a particular act. Mead's definition of the act is congruent with our view. The act, Mead asserts, encompasses a complete span of intention, with its initial point as an impulse and its terminator in some objective reaction of another which completes the impulse. Between initiation and termination, the individual is in the process of constructing, organizing, and reorganizing plans for action on the basis of environmental cues.[24]

An individual's judgment that a new approach to some situation is useful and worth pursuing requires a previous organizational pattern for comparison purposes. The self-concept provides the previous pattern and the information needed to recognize the implications of the new pattern. Thus, the self-concept is a necessary constituent in the positive feedback system. The new organization and pattern being pursued will also be represented in the self-concept as a new rule, or pattern for action in specified situations. Similarly, when the individual has a fixed goal and is in the process of pursuing a standardized pattern of coordinated behavior in order to obtain that goal, the self-concept provides the pattern of information needed for a negative feedback system to monitor behavior in accordance with previously established rules for goal attainment. When action is initiated in the external world, the actor will engage in a process of feedback evaluation to determine the goodness-of-fit between belief about the appropriate choice and progress toward attainment of the actor's purpose. Although this evaluation will be warped by the subjectivity of perception and interpretation, it will still typically allow for changes in subsequent actions and, more significantly, a modification of the current ongoing strategy. As such, human action is more than a simple negative feedback mechanism blindly tracing environmental variation or changes in internal reference signals. It certainly incorporates negative feedback to assure attainment of goals, but it also includes positive feedback to alter the goals themselves.

The self-concept is thus conceptualized as the amount of information an individual has regarding his or her relationship to objects. This information contains identity, evaluative, and behavioral aspects. The internal organization of the self-concept may remain stable or be modified by an individual's interaction with others and the environment. When Cushman and his associates restrict their domain of inquiry to communication behaviors involving human actions in coordination situations that are governed and guided by standardized rules, they are restricting the portions of the self-concept they seek to measure in three ways. First, they are attempting to measure a stable rather than a dynamic class of self-concept rules. Second, these rules are held in common by all those involved in the coordination tasks and thus are intersubjectively verifiable through measurement. Third, deviations from this stable set of rules is internally monitored and corrected by those involved in the coordination task. Thus, deviations from the rules are also intersubjectively verifiable.

Empirical Support

If the self-concept serves as a cybernetic control system for the rules that govern and guide human communicative action, then we would expect empirical research employing self-concept measures to reveal a necessary and substantial relationship between such measures and essential communicative functions. More specifically, we would expect the structure and strength of individual self-concepts to exert a necessary and substantial influence on message comprehension, message adaptation, and message effectiveness in controlling our own and other's behaviors. Our review of the research literature will attempt to demonstrate that such relationships have been found to exist. In addition, we hope to demonstrate that the rules that govern and guide human action can be scientifically measured since they are manifested in the self-concept as identity, evaluative, and behavioral relationships between the individual and the objects in the former's experiental field. Further, we shall demonstrate that those measures can be made antecedent to an individual's subsequent behavior.

The research literature that pertains to the theoretical relationship between self-concept and essential communication functions involves considerable variation in measurement procedures utilized by investigators, who differ widely in theoretical orientations and the meanings they attach to the specific constructs they are attempting to study.[25] However, despite such diversity, there is a fundamental commonality. All such studies depend on measures that differentiate, from an actor's point of view, the objects or attributes of objects that constitute that actor's experiental field. Such measures are here termed *self-concept measures*. These measures normally make three distinctions. First, some measures principally employ nominal scales to locate the set of objects or attributes of objects in an actor's experiental field. Such measures delineate the *scope* of an actor's self-concept. Second, other measures principally employ ordinal scales to locate the hierarchical ordering of objects or attributes of objects in an actor's experiental field. These measures delineate the *depth* of an actor's self-concept. Finally, still other measures employ interval and ratio scales to locate the distance between self, objects, and attributes of objects in an actor's experiental field. Such measures delineate the *configuration* of an actor's self-concept.

The most frequently used *nominal scales* are Kuhn and McPartland's Twenty Question Statement Test and Long, Ziller, and Henderson's Social Symbolic Task—measures that attempt to delineate the *scope* of the self-concept or field of perceptual objects. Typical *ordinal scales* are Kelly's Rep Test and Fitt's Tennessee Self-Concept Scale, which attempt to measure the *depth* of the self-concept or the degree of cognitive differentiation within categories of objects. Representative of *interval and ratio scales* are Osgood, Suci, and Tannenbaum's Semantic Differential Scale and Woelfel's Galileo System, which measure the *configuration* of the self-concept or the distances between self and objects.[25]

Message Comprehensive Studies

Several researchers have employed self-concept measures to examine the cognitive bases of optimal receptivity to interpersonal interactions. Couch, along with Landfield and Nawes, demonstrated that the *scope* of self-concept differentiation is related to an individual's encoding skill.[26] Triandis, Delia and Clark, and Hull and Levy showed that the depth of self-concept differentiation is related to social perspective-taking skill.[27] Newcomb, Zajone, and Carr demonstrated that the *configuration* of self-concept differentiation is related to encoding skill.[28] In addition, Glanzer and Clark; and O'Keefe, Delia, and O'Keefe found that accuracy of information recall during and after an interaction was a function of the scope and depth of an individual's self-concept.[29] Delia and his associates persistently found that scope and depth of cognitive complexity account for between 16 percent and 54 percent of the variation in social-perspective-taking skills of adults.[30] The information an individual has regarding his or her relationship to objects influences that individual's capacity to correctly encode the messages of others.

Message Adaptation Studies

Delia and his associates employed cognitive measures to investigate the relationship between social-perspective taking and the creation of listener-adapted messages. Delia and Clark found that making communication-relevant attributions of a listener's characteristics is a necessary but not sufficient condition for communication adaptation.[31] Such adaptations were directly related to the scope and depth of an individual's cognitive constructs. Applegate and Delia report on four studies investigating the degree of association between the scope and depth of interpersonal construct systems of adults and person-centered communication. They found the level of cognitive differentiation to account for 25 percent of the variation in person-centered communication and 17 percent of the variation in their rationale for the response.[32] Applegate and Delia; and Delia, Kline, and Burleson showed that construct abstractness accounted for 25 percent of the variation in person-centered communication.[33] Finally, O'Keefe and Delia demonstrated a necessary relationship between cognitive complexity and the number of communication appeals, with the latter accounting for 49 percent of the variation in the former. Also, construct comprehensiveness accounted for 49 percent of the variation in level of justification of message strategies in the same study.[34] Delia and his associates found that social-perspective taking accounts for between 16 percent and 58 percent of the variation in listener-adapted messages.[35] The degree to which an individual can accurately understand others influences that individual's capacity to adapt messages to the communication-relevant dimensions of others.

Message Effectiveness

Several researchers have employed self-concept and message-adaptation measures to explore message effectiveness in influencing attitudes and behaviors. Triandis demonstrated an independent and substantial relationship between encoding and message-adaptation skills on communication effectiveness. He found that each process accounted for substantial variation in the attitude change of a receiver.[36] Carr found that both the configuration of encoders' cognitive differentiation and their message-adaptation skills related to changes in the behavior of psychiatric patients, students, and voters.[37] Finally, Thompson reviewed literature providing support for the relationship between self-concept strength and such message-effectiveness behaviors as (1) overcoming anxiety, (2) attempting to control others, and (3) achieving communication consensus. Fitts and Dobson; and Harris found strength of self-concept to be negatively related to communication anxiety so that between 25 percent and 50 percent of the variation in communication anxiety was accounted for by a weak self-concept.[38] McFarland conducted two studies aimed at investigating the relationship between strength of self-concept and attempts at control. Strength of self-concept accounted for between 4 percent and 16 percent of the variation in communication attempts to control others.[39] Cardillo examined the relationship between self-concept and communication success in achieving consensus. He found that strength of self-concept accounts for 16 percent of the variation in achieved agreement and 25 percent of the variation in both achieved understanding and realization.[40] An individual's message-adaptation skills and the degree to which that individual can accurately understand others influence message effectiveness in coordinated goal attainment.

Our review of the research suggests several important conclusions. First, a necessary relationship exists between scope, depth, and configuration of the self-concept and message comprehension. Second, a substantial and necessary relationship exists between message comprehension and message adaptation. Finally, a necessary relationship exists between both message comprehension, message adaptation, and communicator effectiveness, as measured by attitude and behavioral change.

Taken collectively, this research suggests that the rules that govern and guide human action are manifest in the self-concept as scientifically measurable relationships between the individual and the objects in his or her experiential field. Further, these scientific measures can be antecedent to the individual's participating in a coordination situation and can be employed to explain, predict, and control that individual's subsequent communication behavior, attitude change, and behavioral change. We are now in a position to examine the development and validation of such a theory for the formation of interpersonal relationships.

A RULES THEORY OF INTERPERSONAL RELATIONSHIP FORMATION

When rules theorists restrict the scientific inquiry into human communication processes to human actions involving coordination tasks that are governed and guided by standardized rules, it becomes necessary to locate the recurrent coordination tasks that are governed by such rules in order to develop human communication theories. In the past, Cushman and his associates have attempted to delimit the broad and recurrent tasks within a given culture for which coordination and standardized communication rules are required.[41] One such coordination task is grounded in the premise that all individuals, if they are going to undertake actions, must determine who they are and how they relate to or want to relate to the others in their environment. Then in communication, individuals describe, assert, and propose their preferred relationship to others: I love you, I have you, I want to be your friend, I can persuade you to go to the movies, I hope they let me go swimming with them. These descriptions, assertions, and proposals are then accepted, questioned, or denied by others in communication. In this manner, individuals learn who they are and what they can and cannot do. Only then can an individual develop intentions and means for fulfilling those intentions. The process of obtaining such information involves the development, presentation, and validation of one's personal identity and one's identity, evaluative, and behavioral self-concept. Cushman and his associates term this process *interpersonal communication.*[42]

Functionally speaking, interpersonal communication systems are systems of interaction that regulate consensus with respect to individuals' self-concepts. The *structure* of an interpersonal communication system is given by the standardized code and network rules that guide how and where we can obtain consensus in regard to preferred self-object relationships. The typical *processes* of interpersonal communication systems involve the development, presentation, and validation of self-concept. In interpersonal interaction, an individual proposes identities for self and others. These proposed conceptions are accepted and/or rejected by others through a kind of tacit negotiation. Through such a process individuals learn what they can do and who they can be in the presence of others, thereby creating a relationship that is responsible both to the individual and to those in the relationship.[43] One would thus postulate that reciprocal self-concept support serves as a necessary basis for establishing any interpersonal relationship. Further, one would expect different types of self-concept support to lead to different types of interpersonal relationships (e.g., friend, mate, lover) and different degrees of self-concept support to reflect different gradations of interpersonal relationships (e.g., acquaintance, friend, best friend). Our attempt to verify those expectations will be divided into three parts: (1) an explication of perceived self-concept support as a central message variable in interpersonal attraction, (2) an explication of the standardized rules that guide the formation of a friend relationship, and (3) an explication of the standardized rules that guide the formation of a mate relationship.

Perceived Self-Concept Support as a Message Variable

Since the self-concept consists of an individual's perceptions regarding his or her relationship to objects, *perceived self-concept support* consists of one individual attempting to manifest symbolically support for another individual's specific relationships to objects. Such support is contingent upon a recognition of the unique scope, depth, and configuration of another's self-concept and the knowledge of the specific communication rules that govern and guide how one creates messages conveying such support. Five dimensions appear significant for the creation of messages that convey self-concept support. We may focus on an individual's identity, evaluative, or behavioral self-object relationships. In addition, we may manifest support for an individual's real or ideal self. A real self-concept involves an individual's actual self-object relationship, in contrast to an ideal self-concept, which consists of relationships to which an individual aspires. Messages that seek to manipulate self-concept support must employ one or more of these dimensions of self-object relationships in attempting to make another individual perceive self-concept support. In later sections of this paper, we will attempt to demonstrate how different combinations of these dimensions of self-concept will be instrumental in establishing different types of interpersonal relationships.

In a critical and comprehensive review of the research on self-concept, Ruth Wylie provides strong support for the importance of perceived self-concept as a message variable for creating interpersonal attraction. She begins by reviewing in detail 34 studies that demonstrate a significant main effect for manipulated self-regard or perceived self-concept support on interpersonal attraction.[44] Next, Wylie reviews three bodies of literature dealing with actual self-concept similarity and attraction, assumed self-concept similarity and attraction, and the interactive effect of actual and assured self-concept similarity on interpersonal attraction. A review of 31 studies exploring the relationship of actual similarities between the self-concepts of two individuals and interpersonal attraction provided no support for such a relationship.[45] In contrast, her review of 20 studies exploring the relationship between an individual's assumed self-concept similarities with others and interpersonal attraction to those others revealed a significant positive relationship. In each of these studies, assumed self-concept similarities were manipulated via communication.[46] Finally, five studies that compared the effects of actual and assumed self-concept similarity on interpersonal attraction were examined. Wylie concludes,

> In each instance, actual interpersonal similarity of self-description was *not* related to interpersonal attraction, whereas subjects' assumption of similarity between own and others' characteristics *were* significantly related to interpersonal attraction.[47]

It is noteworthy that several of these studies demonstrate that perceived self-concept support is a manipulable message variable, that the quantity and type of perceived self-concept support in a message is controllable, and that such manipulations retain their quantitative and qualitative effect for at least six months.

Considering the above evidence, three conclusions seem to be warranted. First, manipulated self-regard and assumed self-concept similarity, both of which are instances of perceived self-concept support, exert a *positive main effect* influence on interpersonal attraction. Second, actual self-concept similarity does *not* affect this relationship. Third, perceived self-concept support is a message variable that is manipulatable in terms of both its focus and intensity, which are sustained in their effects for extended periods of time. We are now in a position to examine the relationship between different types and quantities of self-concept support and the establishment of different types and degrees of interpersonal relationships.

The Friendship Formation Process

In an attempt to isolate empirically the underlying dimensions that uniquely define friend relationships, La Gaipa employed a two-stage analysis. First, he distinguished four different levels of friendship: best friend, close friend, good friend, and social acquaintance. Second, in a study involving 2361 college students from the United States and Canada, he uncovered the major "friendship themes" at each level. The friendship themes rated as most essential across all friendship levels were *authenticity,* or openness and honesty in regard to the relationship, and *helping behavior,* or the provisions of positive social and psychological support for another.[48] Crawford found similar results when he cited *trust* and *helping behaviors,* or social and psychological support, to be the most dominant elements of friendship in a sample of 306 middle-aged couples.[49] Gibbs undertook a study to determine the orthogonality of friendship dimensions across age levels. Three factors emerged: (1) *intimacy/assistance,* (2) *status,* and (3) *power.* The *intimacy/assistance* factor was found to be by far the most important across all age levels.[50] Cushman, Valentinsen, and Brenner found that support for ideal and real self is the major factor in friendship, with such support dividing itself into two friendship roles: confidant and companion. A confidant is someone who respects or supports an individual's evaluative self-object relationships, while a companion is someone who supports an individual's behavioral self-object relationships.[51]

While a clear pattern emerges from the literature—honesty/trust and social/psychological support are the underlying dimensions involved in friendship—the process by which one selects a friend has been far from clear until recently. It now appears possible to explicate the communication principles involved in friendship formation and growth by examining a three-step filtering process involved in determining an individual's field of available, approachable, and reciprocal friends.

• *Field of Availables.* Although one meets an indeterminately large number of people in a lifetime, several biological and social forces interact to constrain causally and normatively our field of available encounters. Such causal forces as birth and death rates, as well as the age and sex distribution of a population, serve to limit the field of availables.[52] Similarly, normative forces such as a population's social, educational, religious, and economic structures, as well as its socialization processes and role-distribution patterns, serve to further restrict encounters.[53] The process of communicative interaction in the field of availables and the principles governing these interactions have already been well delineated by Berger and Duck, and their respective associates, in their investigations of initial social interactions.[54] It only needs to be stressed here that those investigations show the communication rules governing such interactions to be standardized and general to individuals.

• *Field of Approachables.* Within one's field of availables will exist a subset of individuals who, as a result of initial interaction, are found to be desirable enough to approach for the purpose of initiating an interpersonal friendship. This subset of people constitutes one's field of approachables. Three normative variables delimit this field of approachables and thus form the basis for the interpersonal interaction rules that govern and guide the friendship initiation process. The first two variables specify the individual perceptions that form the antecedent conditions for generating messages aimed at establishing a friend relationship. The value of these antecedent perceptions is determined by the information an individual obtains in initial interaction with the field of availables. The third variable specifies the self-object relationships that a message must support in order to be perceived by a receiver as self-concept support.

1. The greater an individual's *perceived* relationship between attributes of one's ideal self-concept and the perceived attributes of another's real self-concept, the greater the likelihood that communication will be initiated.

2. The greater an individual's *perceived* likelihood that the other will accept an offer of friendship, the greater the likelihood that communication will be initiated.

3. The more frequently an individual provides messages that support some positive identity, evaluative, or behavioral self-object relationships of another's self-concept, the greater the likelihood that the other individual will perceive those messages as an attempt to initiate a friend relationship.

Thompson and Nishimura provide empirical support for our first interpersonal interaction rule when they examined the process of friendship formation in three male and five female same-sex dyads. They discovered a significant relationship between an individual's ideal self-concept and the perceived real self-concept of a friend, while no such relationship was found in nonfriends.[55] Similarly, Lundy, in a sample of 136 opposite-sex friends, found that friends' real self-concepts were viewed as having the subjects' ideal self-concept qualities, even when those qualities were stereotypically associated with the opposite sex.[56] Elman, Press, and Rosenkrantz replicated the above results in a sample of 110 sophomore college students.[57] In a sample of 90 female college students, McKenna found that friends resemble each other significantly less than they resemble the subjects' ideal selves.[58]

With regard to our second interpersonal interaction rule, when Laumann reported the results of 1271 case studies of same- and opposite-sex friends in Detroit, Michigan, he found that while 54.2 percent of the initiated relationships were not reciprocated, all the initiators acted on the assumption that their efforts would be.[59]

Finally, Cushman, Valentinsen, and Brenner provide support for our third interaction rule when they examine the effect on individuals of messages that provide perceived self-concept support for identity, evaluative, or behavioral self-object relationship. Such support is viewed by the receiver as the initiation of a friend relationship.[60]

• *Field of Reciprocals.* As Laumann clearly indicates, not all attempts to establish relationships are reciprocated. Rather, within one's field of approachables there exists a subset of individuals who will make up a list of actual friends—one's field of reciprocals. Two normative variables delimit the field of reciprocals and underlie the interpersonal interaction rules that guide the process of friendship growth.

1. The greater an individual's perceived accuracy with regard to the relationship between one's ideal and another's real self-concept, the greater the likelihood that a friend relationship will grow.

2. The greater the reciprocated perceived self-concept support, the greater the likelihood of a friend relationship.

The first interpersonal interaction rule finds support in the work of Duck, who reports that he examined the accuracy of 40 student teachers with regard to inferring same- and opposite-sex friends' personal constructs. He found significant differences between the accuracy scores of friends and those of nominal pairs. This study suggests that as confirmation of real-ideal similarity increases, so does one's accuracy.[61]

In support of the second interpersonal interaction rule, we have the research of Bailey, Finney, and Helm, who undertook a study to explore the relationship between perceived self-concept support and friendship in a sample of 50 same-sex student dyads. They found that perceived self-concept support related positively for both long-term friends (approximately six years), explaining 63 percent of the variation in interpersonal attraction, and short-term friends (six months), explaining 25 percent of the variation in interpersonal attraction. Furthermore, the difference between these scores was found to be a significant factor connoting a *relationship between friendship duration and the perceived extent of self-concept support.*[62] One year later Bailey, Digiacomo, and Zinser replicated the results found in the previous study when they explored the same relationship in 20 pairs of same-sex, long-acquaintance males and females, and 12 pairs of same-sex short-acquaintance males and females. They found that perceived self-concept support correlated positively for both long-term friends— 49 percent of variation in degree of interpersonal attraction among males and 73 percent among females—and short-term friends—25 percent among males and 49 percent among females.[63] A study by Bailey, Finney, and Bailey (1974) reported similar results.[64]

Now that we have delineated the interpersonal rules that serve as antecedents for the initiation and growth of friendship relations, we shall explore these same processes with respect to mates.

Mate Formation Process

Following Karp, Jackson, and Lester, we shall employ the term *mate* to denote any opposite-sex relationship for which one clears the field of competitors.[65] Such relationships normally involve a major proportion of the individuals who are engaged, cohabitating, or married. Pam, Plutchik, and Conte undertook a study designed to locate differences between the roles of mate, friend, and date. Their results indicate that mates differ from the other two types of relationships in the degree to which physical attraction, perception of an ideal mate, and reciprocated affection enter into the relationship.[66] We shall explore the process of mate selection through utilization of the same three-stage filtering process employed in friendship formation.

• *Field of Availables.* In addition to the previously discussed causal and normative forces that constrained the field of available friends, mates are further constrained by the marriage role, the divorce rate, and the number of individuals whose mates die.[67]

• *Field of Approachables.* Within one's field of availables, there exists a subset of individuals whom one finds desirable and would consider approaching in order to initiate an interpersonal relationship as mates. This subset constitutes one's field of approachables. Five normative variables define one's field of approachables and thus form the basis for the interpersonal interaction rules which govern and guide the initiation process.

1. The greater an individual's perceptions that an opposite-sex other is physically attractive, the greater the likelihood of initiating communication aimed at establishing a mate relationship.

2. The greater an individual's perceptions that an opposite-sex other's real-self relates to one's ideal-self for a mate, the greater the likelihood of initiating communication aimed at establishing a mate relationship.

3. The greater an individual's perception that the male's real-ideal self-concept discrepancy is small, the greater the likelihood of initiating communication aimed at establishing a mate relationship.

4. The greater an individual's perception that an opposite-sex other is likely to accept one's offer of a relationship, the greater the likelihood of initiating communication aimed at establishing a mate relationship.

5. The more frequently an individual provides messages that (a) manifest self-concept support for an opposite-sex other's physical attractiveness; (b) characterize that other as relating to the individual's ideal-mate; and (c) indicate a perceived lack of discrepancy between the mate's real and ideal self, the greater the likelihood that the other individual will perceive those messages as an attempt to initiate a mate relationship.

Common sense and numerous studies support our first interpersonal interaction rule. Cavior and Boblett explored the differential role played by physical attractiveness in dating vs. married couples. They found that physical attractiveness accounted for 49 percent of the variation in interpersonal attraction within married couples and only 0.02 percent within dating couples. They concluded that physical attractiveness is considerably more important in mate selection than in dating.[68] Hill, Rubin, and Peplay explored the relationship between physical attraction and dyadic stability in 231 couples contemplating marriage. They found a positive relationship between physical attraction and relational stability among 117 couples who stayed together over a two-year period, while the role of physical attraction within 103 couples who broke up was not significant.[69] Murstein examined the relationship of physical attractiveness to marital satisfaction in 22 middle-aged couples. He found that for wives, physical attractiveness accounted for 49 percent of the variation in marital satisfaction, while for husbands it accounted for only 25 percent.[70] Studies by Berschied and Walster; Huston; and Shanteau and Nagy also attest to the importance of physical attractiveness in the initiation of a mate relationship.[71]

Bailey and Helm provide support for our second interpersonal interaction rule with their investigation of the relationship between ideal date and actual dates in a sample of 39 college couples. They stratified dating couples on three levels: occasional dating, steady, and engaged. For engaged couples, a lack of discrepancy between actual and ideal relationship was found.[72] Similar results were obtained by Murstein when he examined the relationship between conceptions of ideal spouse and the courtship progress among 98 dating dyads. His results indicate that those couples who were making good progress in courtship rated their partners significantly more similar to their conception of an ideal spouse than those making poor progress.[73] Murstein replicated the previous finding when he examined a second sample of 101 nonstudent couples.[74] Finally, Luckey investigated the actual-ideal spouse relationship in two samples of 40 less-satisfied couples. Luckey found that in the satisfied group, there was a very strong relationship between a spouse's actual and an individual's ideal self-concept, while in the least-satisfied group, there was a marked discrepancy leading to significant difficulties in the relationship.[75] Similar results can be found in Prince and Baggely; Strauss; and Luckey.[76]

Our third interpersonal interaction rule—the greater the perception that the male's ideal-real self-concept discrepancy is small, the greater the attempt to initiate a mate relationship—is supported by the work of Luckey and Murstein. In her study of 40 satisfied and 40 least-satisfied married couples, Luckey reported that marital satisfaction was strongly related to the level of discrepancy between the ideal and real self-concepts of the male partner.[77] Murstein found the same relationship in dating dyads as they approached marriage. A lack of discrepancy between the male's ideal and real self-concept was a strong predictor of courtship progress, while the same relationship was nonsignificant for females.[78]

Fourth, a plethora of evidence exists indicating that individuals will not initiate an opposite-sex relationship unless they believe it will be accepted. Shanteau and Nagy, and Huston demonstrate an interaction between likelihood of acceptance and perceived attraction in two separate samples of students.[79] Murstein finds a similar result in regard to self-concept support in separate samples of dating, engaged, and married couples.[80]

Finally, Cushman, Valentinsen, and Brenner report the results of a study that indicate that when an individual sends a message that provides perceived self-concept support for physical attractiveness, ideal mate, and lack of ideal-real self-discrepancy in the male, such support is viewed by the receiver as the attempt to initiate a mate relationship.[81]

• *Field of Reciprocals.* Within the field of approachables exist subsets of people who will reciprocate when attempts are made to initiate a a mate relationship and as such constitute one's field of reciprocals. Two normative variables influence the individuals who will decide to reciprocate an offer; these variables form the basis for two interpersonal interaction rules:

1. The greater a female's perceived lack of discrepancy between her mate's real and ideal self-concept, the greater the likelihood the relationship will grow.

2. The greater the perception that there is reciprocation of self-concept support, the greater the likelihood the relationship will grow.

In three separate samples of dating dyads, Murstein found the accuracy of female partners regarding the male's real and ideal self-concepts and the smallness of the discrepancy between the two to be positively related to courtship progress.[82] Luckey, in a study of 594 married couples, found marital satisfaction to be significantly related to the wives' accuracy regarding the husbands' self-concepts, but the converse was not found to be the case.[83] Schafer, Braito, and Bohlen explored the same relationship in 116 married couples and derived the same results.[84]

Our second interpersonal interaction rule, which states that when an individual's perceived self-concept support is reciprocated the relationship will grow in accordance with the scope and intensity of that support, is affirmed by a variety of studies. Byrne and Blaylock found a positive relationship that accounted for 49 percent of the variation between self-concept support and attraction among a sample of 36 married couples.[85] Bailey and Mettetal found that with regard to intelligence, husbands' estimates of their self-object relationships accounted for 80 percent of the variation in estimates of their spouses' perceptions of their self-concepts.[86] Luckey explored the relationship between real and ideal self-discrepancy and marital satisfaction in a sample of 594 former University of Minnesota students. He found a strong and statistically significant relationship: the smaller the discrepancy between the real and ideal self, the more satisfied the partners.[87]

In summary, what have we found? First, we have located two standardized coordination tasks: the friendship-formation process and the mate-formation process. Second, we have outlined a three-step filtering process that controls the social, psychological, and communication episodes involved in the formation of these interpersonal relationships. Third, we have located the consensual rules that these tasks generate at each stage of this filtering process. Finally, we have reported research reflecting the practical forces involved in each rule. Since we have established that the above-mentioned relationships are situations involving coordination that is governed by standardized rules, it is evident that these relationships are subject to rigorous scientific analysis from the rules perspective—a perspective that provides for explanation, prediction, and control by taking into account the practical force to which behavior is subject. Such an analysis is best modeled by the necessary mood of the practical syllogism.

A = a class of actors;
B = episodes involved in rules for approachables;
C = episodes involved in rules for reciprocals;
D = a friendship or mate relationship.
   —A intends to bring about D;
   —A knows that without episodes B and C, D will not occur;
   —A engages in episodes B and C.

Our task has been to demonstrate that reciprocal self-concept support serves as a necessary basis for establishing interpersonal relationships. Further, we have attempted to demonstrate that different types and amounts of perceived self-concept support delimit different types and strengths of interpersonal relationships.

What then can we conclude from our rather extensive journey into the character of rules theories and their utility in creating insight into human communication processes?

First, we have attempted to demonstrate that in at least one sense, human communication theory refers to that class of scientifically grounded propositions that allows for explanation, prediction, and control. Further, we have explicated one set of procedures by which rules theories of human communication processes might develop a unique explanatory model—the practical syllogism—and have employed that model for prediction and control, by limiting the domain of scientific inquiry to human actions involving coordination tasks governed and guided by standardized rules.

Second, we have attempted to demonstrate that the self-concept, when viewed as a cybernetic control system for human behavior, can serve as a measurement model for the antecedent rules that guide standardized human actions. This demonstration took the form of indicating a substantial and necessary link between cognitive measures of self-concept scope, depth and configuration, and essential communicative behaviors, as well as attitudes and behavioral change.

Finally, the practical syllogism and the self-concept were employed as an explanatory and measurement model in developing a rules theory of interpersonal relationship formation. This analysis proceeded in four stages. First, perceived self-concept support was demonstrated to be an important message variable, which could be employed in theoretically delineating types and degree of interpersonal relationships. Second, a three-stage filtering process for establishing interpersonal relationships was defined, and the rules involved in forming such specific interpersonal relationships as friend and mate were delimited. Third, a review of the research literature regarding each rule was undertaken in order to indicate the verifiability of a given rule and to delimit its degree of practical force. Finally, the appropriate mood of the practical syllogism was located for modeling the explanation provided by this rules theory of interpersonal relationship formation.

The procedures developed by Cushman and his associates for creating and verifying rules theories in standardized tasks show promise of providing insight into cultural communication processes (Woelfel, 1981), organizational communication processes (McPhee, 1978), and other interpersonal communication processes (Adler, 1978).[88]

Notes

1. D. P. Cushman and W. B. Pearce, "Generality and Necessity in Three Types of Human Communication Theory—Special Attention to Rules Theory," in *Communication Yearbook I*, ed. D. Ruben (New Brunswick, N.J.: Transaction Press, 1977), pp. 173–183.

2. D. P. Cushman, "The Rules Perspective as a Theoretical Basis for the Study of Human Communication," *Communication Quarterly*, 25, No. 1 (Winter 1977), 30–45.

3. D. P. Cushman and R. McPhee, eds., *Message-Attitude-Behavior Relationship: Theory, Methodology and Application* (New York: Academic Press, 1980).

4. D. P. Cushman and G. Whiting, "An Approach to Communication Theory: Towards Consensus on Rules," *Journal of Communication*, 22 (1972), 217–218.

5. R. E. Sanders, "The Question of a Paradigm for the Study of Speech-Using Behavior," *Quarterly Journal of Speech*, 59 (1973), 1–10; W. B. Pearce, "Consensual Rules in Interpersonal Communication: A Reply to Cushman and Whiting," *Journal of Communication*, 23 (1973), 160–168; G. McDermott, "The Literature on Classical Theory Construction," *Human Communication Research*, 2 (1975), 83–102; W. B. Pearce, "The Coordinated Management of Meaning: A Rules-Based Theory of Interpersonal Communication," in *Explorations in Interpersonal Communication*, ed. G. R. Miller (Beverly Hills: Sage, 1976), pp. 17–36; V. Cronen and K. Davis, "Alternative Approaches for the Communication Theorists—Problems in the Laws-Rules-Systems Trichotomy," *Human Communication Research*, 4 (1978), 120–128; K. Adler, "On the Falsification of Rules Theories," *Quarterly Journal of Speech*, 64 (1978), 427–438; A. Donohue, D. P. Cushman, R. Nofsinger, Jr., "Creating and Confronting Social Order: A Comparison of Rules Perspectives," *The Western Journal of Speech Communication*, 44 (1980), 519; S. Shimanoff, *Communication Rules, Theory and Research* (Beverly Hills: Sage, 1980); R. Sanders and D. P. Cushman, "Rules and Strategies in Human Communication," *Handbook of Communication*, ed. C. Arnold and J. Bowers (Boston: Allyn and Bacon, 1981).

6. G. Philipsen, "Speaking 'Like a Man' in Teamsterville: Cultural and Patterns of Role Enactment in an Urban Neighborhood," *Quarterly Journal of Speech*, 61(1975), 13–22; L. Hawes, "How Writing Is Used In Talk: A Study of Communicative Logic—In-Use," *Quarterly Journal of Speech*, 62 (1976), 350–360; R. E. Nofsinger, "Answering Questions Indirectly," *Human Communication Research*, 2 (1976), 172–181; E. L. Hawes, "A Discourse Analysis of Topic Co-Selection in Medical Interviews," Diss. Ohio State University; S. B. Shimanoff and J. C. Brunak, "Repairs in Planned and Unplanned Discourse," *Discourse Across Time and Space*, ed. E. Keenan and T. Bennett (Los Angeles: University of Southern California, 1977), pp. 123–167; J. W. Bowers, E. Normal, and R. Desmond, "Exploiting Pragmatic Rules: Devious Messages," *Human Communication Research* 3 (1977), 235–242;

T. Smith, III, "The Development of Self Through Interaction: A Test of a Communication Paradigm," Diss. Michigan State University, 1978; V. Cronen, W. B. Pearce, and L. Snavely, "A Theory of Rules-Structure and Types of Episodes, and a Study of Perceived Enmeshment in Undesired Repetitive Patterns (URP's)," in *Communication Yearbook III*, ed. B. Ruben (New Brunswick, N.J.: Transaction Press, 1979); W. B. Pearce and F. Conklin, "A Model of Hierarchical Meaning on Coherent Conversation and a Study of Indirect Responses," *Communication Monographs*, 46 (1979), 75–87; R. E. Sanders, "Principles of Relevance: A Theory of the Relationship Between Language and Communication," *Communication and Cognition*, forthcoming.

7. B. Fay and D. Moon, "What Would an Adequate Philosophy of Social Science Look Like?" *Philosophy of Social Science*, 7 (1977), 209.

8. C. Taylor, "The Explanation of Purposive Behavior," *Explanation in the Behavioral Sciences*, ed. Robert Borger and Frank Cioffi (Cambridge: Cambridge University Press, 1970), p. 60.

9. G. H. von Wright, *Explanation and Understanding* (Ithaca, N.Y.: Cornell University Press, 1971), pp. 25–27.

10. von Wright, 1971, p. 27.

11. D. P. Cushman and G. C. Whiting, "An Approach to Communication Theory: Towards Consensus on Rules," *Journal of Communication*, 22 (1972), 217–218.

12. Cushman and Pearce, 1977, p. 178.

13. D. P. Cushman and R. T. Craig, "Communication Systems: Interpersonal Implications" in *Explorations in Interpersonal Communication*, ed. Gerald R. Miller (Beverly Hills: Sage, 1976), pp. 37–58.

14. Donohue, Cushman, and Nofsinger, 1980, pp. 8–10.

15. J. N. Cappella, "Style and the Functional Prerequisites of Intentional Communicative Systems," *Philosophy and Rhetoric*, 5 (1972), 231–297.

16. M. Scott and S. Lyman, "Accounts," *American Sociological Review*, 62 (1968), 42–62.

17. W. B. Pearce and D. P. Cushman, "Research Employing the Construct Communication Rules: A Test of the Process of Explanation and Verification." Paper presented at the Speech Communication Association Convention, 1978, pp. 10–11.

18. Cushman and Pearce, 1977, pp. 180–181.

19. Adler, 1978, pp. 433–435.

20. K. Adler, "An Evaluation of the Practical Syllogism as a Model of Man for Human Communication Research," *Communication Quarterly*, 26 (1978), 8–18.

21. L. Wittgenstein, *Philosophical Investigations* (Oxford: Blackwell, 1953); J. R. Searle, *Speech Acts: An Essay in the Philosophy of Language* (Cambridge: Cambridge University Press, 1969); E. Goffman, *Behavior in Public Places: Notes on the Social Organization of Gatherings* (New York: Free Press, 1963); S. Toulmin, "Rules and Their Relevance for Understanding Human Behavior," in *Understanding Other People*, ed. T. Mischel (Oxford: Blackwell, 1974), pp. 185–215.

22. G. H. Mead, *Mind, Self and Society* (Chicago: University of Chicago Press, 1934), p. 243.
23. W. Thompson, *Correlates of the Self-Concept*, Dade Wallace Center Monographs, 6, June 1972.
24. G. H. Mead, *The Philosophy of the Act* (Chicago: University of Chicago Press, 1938).
25. M. Kuhn and T. S. McPartland, "An Empirical Investigation of Self-Attitudes," *American Sociological Review*, 19 (1954), 68–76; B. H. Long, E. H. Henderson, and R. C. Ziller, "Developmental Change in the Self-Concept During Middle Childhood," *Merrill Palmer Quarterly*, 13 (1967), 201–219; G. A. Kelly, *The Psychology of Personal Constructs* (New York: Norton, 1955); W. H. Fitts, *Manual Tennessee Department of Mental Health, Self-Concept Scale*, Nashville, Tenn.: 1965; C. E. Osgood, G. T. Suci, and P. H. Tannenbaum, *The Measurement of Meaning* (Urbana: University of Illinois, 1957); J. Woelfel and E. Fink, *The Measurement of Communication Processes; Galileo Theory and Method* (New York: Academic Press, 1980).
26. C. A. Couch, "A Study of the Relationship Between Self Views and Role-Taking Accuracy," Diss. University of Iowa, 1955; A. W. Landfield and M. M. Nawes, "Psychotherapeutic Improvement as a Function of Communicative Adaptation of Therapists' Values," *Journal of Counseling Psychology*, 2 (1964), 336–341.
27. H. C. Triandis, "Cognitive Similarity and Communication in a Dyad," *Human Relations*, 13 (1960), pp. 175–183; J. G. Delia and R. A. Clark, "Cognitive Complexity, Social Perception and the Development of Listener Adaptational Communication in Six, Eight, Ten and Twelve Year Old Boys," *Communication Monographs*, 44 (1977), 332–345; J. H. Hull and A. S. Levy, "The Organizational Function of the Self: An Alternate to the Duval and Wickland Model of Self-Awareness," *Journal of Personality and Social Psychology*, 37 (1979), 756–768.
28. T. M. Newcomb, "An Approach to the Study of Communicative Acts," *Psychological Review*, 60 (1953), 393–404; T. M. Newcomb, "The Prediction of Interpersonal Attraction," *American Psychologist*, 2 (1956), 575–586; R. B. Zajonc, "The Process of Cognitive Tuning," *Journal of Abnormal and Social Psychology*, 61 (1960), 159–167; J. E. Carr, "Differentiation as a Function of Source Characteristics and Judge's Conceptual Structure," *Journal of Personality*, 37 (1969), 378–386; J. E. Carr, "Differentiation Similarity of Patient and Therapist and the Outcomes of Psychotherapy," *Journal of Abnormal Psychology*, 76 (1970), 361–369; J. E. Carr and J. A. Whittenbaugh, "Volunteer and Non-Volunteer Characteristics in Out-Patient Population," *Journal of Abnormal Psychology*, 73 (1968), 16–21.
29. M. Glanzer and W. H. Clark, "Accuracy of Perceptual Recall: An Analysis of Organization," *Verbal Learning and Verbal Behavior*, 1 (1963), 289–299; B. O'Keefe, J. G. Delia, and D. O'Keefe, "Construct Individuality, Cognitive Complexity and Remembering of Interpersonal Impressions," *Social Behavior and Personality*, 5 (1977), 229–240.
30. B. R. Burleson, "Developmental and Individual Differences in Comfort-

Intended Message Strategies: Four Empirical Studies," Diss. University of Illinois, 1980.

31. Delia and Clark, 1977, p. 346.
32. J. L. Applegate and J. G. Delia, "Person-Centered Speech, Psychological Development, and the Context of Language Usage, ed. S. Claire and H. G. Les (Hillsdale, N.J.: Erlbaum, in press).
33. Applegate and Delia, in press; see also J. G. Delia, S. Kline, and B. R. Burleson, "The Development of Persuasive Communication Strategies in Kindergartners Through Twelfth Graders." Paper presented at the Speech Communication Association Convention, 1978.
34. B. J. O'Keefe and J. G. Delia, "Construct Comprehensiveness and Cognitive Complexity as a Production of the Number of Strategic Adaptations of Arguments and Appeals in a Persuasive Message Communication," *Communication Monographs*, 46 (1979), 231–241.
35. Burleson, 1980.
36. Triandis, 1960, p. 178.
37. Carr, 1969, 1970.
38. Fitts, 1965; J. K. Dobson, "Predictions of Individual Student Teacher Behavior in Classrooms for Emotionally Disturbed Children," Diss. University of Michigan, 1970; G. A. Harris, "Interpersonal Sensitivity in the Counselor-Client Relationship," Diss. University of Southern Mississippi, 1968.
39. G. McFarland, "Effects of Sensitivity Training Utilized as In-Service Education," Diss. George Peabody College, 1970.
40. J. P. Cardillo, "The Effects of Teaching Communication Roles on Interpersonal Perception and Self-Concept in Disturbed Marriages," Diss. George Peabody College, 1971.
41. D. P. Cushman and B. T. Florence, "The Development of Interpersonal Communication Theory," *Today's Speech*, 22 (1974), 11–15.
42. Cushman and Florence, 1974, pp. 12–13.
43. Cushman and Craig, 1976, pp. 44–45.
44. R. C. Wylie, *The Self-Concept* (Lincoln: University of Nebraska Press, 1979), p. 482.
45. Wylie, 1979, p. 528.
46. Wylie, 1979, p. 535.
47. Wylie, 1979, p. 537.
48. J. J. LaGaipa, "Testing a Multi-Dimensional Approach to Friendship," *Theory and Practice, an Interpersonal Attraction*, ed. Steve Duck (New York: Academic Press, 1977), pp. 249–271.
49. M. Crawford, "What Is a Friend," *New Society*, 42 (1977), 116–117.
50. S. Gibbs, "A Comparative Analysis of Friendship Functions in Six Age Groups of Men and Women," Diss. Wayne State University, 1977.
51. D. P. Cushman, B. Valentinsen, and D. Brenner, "An Interpersonal Communication Theory of the Friendship Formation Process." Paper submitted to the 1981 International Communication Convention.
52. A. Hacker, "Divorce a la Mode," *New York Review of Books* (May 1979), p. 23–30.
53. A. Booth, "Sex and Social Participation," *American Sociological Re-*

view, 37 (1972), 183–192; Alan Booth and Elain Hess, "Cross Sex Friendship," *Journal of Marriage and the Family,* 36 (1974), 39–47.

54. C. R. Berger and R. J. Calabrese, "Some Explorations in Initial Interaction and Beyond: Towards a Developmental Theory of Interpersonal Communication," *Human Communication Research,* 1 (1975), 99–112; S. Duck, "Interpersonal Communication in Developing Acquaintances in Explorations in Interpersonal Communication," in *Exploration in Interpersonal Communication,* ed. G. R. Miller (Beverly Hills: Sage, 1976), pp. 127–145.

55. W. Thompson and R. Nishimura, "Some Determents of Friendship," *Journal of Personality and Social Psychology,* 10 (1952), 305–314.

56. R. M. Lundy, "Self-Perception and Description of Opposite Sex Friends Sociometric Choice," *Sociometry,* 21 (1958), 238–246.

57. J. Elman, A. Press, and R. Rosenkrantz, "Sex Roles and Self-Concepts Real and Ideal," *Proceedings of the 78th Annual Convention of the American Psychological Association,* 1970, pp. 455–456.

58. Sr. H. V. McKenna, "The Relationship Between Self and Ideal Self Consistency and Friendship," M.A. Thesis, Catholic University of America, 1955.

59. E. O. Laumann, "Friends of Urban Men: An Assessment of Accuracy in Their Reporting Their Social-Economic Attributes, Mutual Choice and Attitude Agreement," *Sociometry,* 30 (1967), 54–69.

60. D. P. Cushman, B. Valentinsen, and D. Brenner, "Three Experimental Manipulations of Perceived Self-Concept Support in Interpersonal Relationships." Paper submitted to 1981 International Communication Association.

61. Laumann, 1967, p. 56.

62. R. C. Bailey, P. Finney, and B. Helm, "Self-Concept Support and Friendship," *Journal of Social Psychology,* 96 (1975), 237–243.

63. R. C. Bailey, R. J. Digiacomo, and O. Zinser, "Length of Male and Female Friendship and Perceived Intelligence in Self and Friend," *Journal of Personality Assessment,* 40 (1976), 635–640.

64. R. C. Bailey, P. Finney, and K. G. Bailey, "Level of Self-Acceptance and Perceived Intelligence in Self and Friend," *Journal of Genetic Psychology,* 124 (1974), 61–67.

65. E. S. Karp, J. H. Jackson, and D. Lester, "Ideal-Self Fulfillment in Mate Selection: A Corollary to the Complementary Need Theory of Mate Selection," *Journal of Marriage and the Family,* 33 (1971), 269–273.

66. A. Pam, R. Plutchik, and H. Conte, "Love: A Psychometric Approach," *Proceedings of the 81st Annual Convention of the American Psychological Association,* 1973, pp. 159–160.

67. Hacker, 1979, p. 29.

68. N. Cavior and P. Boblett, "Physical Attractiveness in Dating Versus Married Couples," *Proceedings of the 80th Annual Convention of the American Psychological Association,* 1972, pp. 175–176.

69. C. T. Hill, Z. Rubin and L. A. Peplay, "Breakups Before Marriage: The End of 103 Affairs," *Journal of Social Issues,* 32 (1976), 147–168.

70. B. I. Murstein, "Physical Attractiveness and Marital Choice," *Journal of Personality and Social Psychology,* 22 (1972), 8–12.
71. E. Berscheid and E. Walster, "Physical Attractiveness," *Advances in Experimental Social Psychology,* ed. L. Barkowitz (New York: Academic Press, 1974), pp. 158–183; T. L. Huston, "Ambiguity of Acceptance, Social Desirability and Dating Choices," *Journal of Experimental Social Psychology,* 9 (1973), 32–42; J. Shanteau and G. Nagy, "Probability of Acceptance in Dating Choice," *Journal of Personality and Social Psychology,* 37 (1979), 522–533.
72. R. Bailey and R. Helm, "Matrimonial Commitment and Date/Ideal Date Perceptions," *Perceptual and Motor Skills,* 39 (1974), 1356–1357.
73. B. I. Murstein, "Self Ideal-Self Discrepancy and the Choice of Marital Partners," *Journal of Consulting and Clinical Psychology,* 37 (1971), 47–52.
74. B. I. Murstein, *Who Will Marry Whom? Theories and Research in Marital Choice* (New York: Springer Publishing, 1972).
75. E. B. Luckey, "Marital Satisfaction and Congruent Self-Spouse Concepts," *Social Focus,* 39 (1960), 153–157.
76. A. J. Prince and A. R. Baggely, "Personality Variables and Ideal Mate," *Family Life Coordinator,* 12 (1963), 93–96; A. Strauss, "The Ideal and Chosen Mate," *American Journal of Sociology,* 52 (1964), 204–208; E. B. Luckey, "Marital Satisfaction and Its Association with Congruence of Perception," *Journal of Marriage and Family,* 1 (1960), 3–9.
77. E. B. Luckey, "Perceptual Congruence of Self and Family Concepts as Related to Marital Interaction," *Sociometry,* 25 (1962), 234–250.
78. B. I. Murstein, "Person Perception and Control in Progress Among Premarital Couples," *Journal of Marriage and Family,* 34 (1972), 621–627.
79. Shanteau and Nagy, 1979; Huston, 1973.
80. Murstein, 1972, 1971, 1970.
81. Cushman, Valentinsen, and Brenner, 1981.
82. Murstein, 1970, 1971, 1972.
83. Luckey, 1960.
84. R. Schafer, R. Braito, and J. Bohlen, "Self-Concept and the Reaction of Significant Others: A Comparison of Husband and Wife," *Social Inquiry,* 46 (1973), 56–57.
85. D. Byrne and B. Blaylock, "Similarity and Assumed Similarity of Attitudes Between Husbands and Wives," *Journal of Abnormal and Social Psychology,* 67 (1963), 636–640.
86. R. C. Bailey and G. W. Mettetal, "Perceived Intelligence in Marital Partners," *Social Behavior and Personality,* 5 (1977), 137–141.
87. Luckey, 1962.
88. J. Woelfel, "A Cross Cultural Study of Male-Female Roles," unpublished manuscript. R. McPhee, "A Rules Theory of Organizational Communication," Diss. Michigan State University, 1978; K. Adler, "An Empirical Test of Two Philosophically Derived Dimensions of Advice," Diss. Michigan State University, 1978.

A SPEECH THEORY OF
HUMAN COMMUNICATION

Frank E. X. Dance

The Logos is eternal
but men have not heard it
and men have heard it and not understood.

Through the Logos all things are understood
yet men do not understand
as you will see when you put acts and words to the test
I am going to propose:

One must talk about everything according to its nature,
how it comes to be and how it grows.
Men have talked about the word without paying attention
to the world or to their own minds
as if they were asleep or absent-minded.

Heraclitus (540–480 B.C.)[1]

Underlying a discipline's "way of thought," there is a set
of connected, varyingly implicit, generative propositions

Jerome S. Bruner[2]

HOLMES: What do you think of my theory?
WATSON: It is all surmise.
HOLMES: But at least it covers all the facts. When new facts come
to our knowledge which cannot be covered by it, it will be time
enough to reconsider it.

Sir Arthur Conan Doyle[3]

A provisional overall or grand theory of human communication should examine, describe, and attempt to explain (1) the origins of human communication in the species (phylogenetic origins) and in the individual (ontogenetic origins); (2) the development of human communication in the individual and in society; and (3) the functions of human communication in the individual and in society. In the course of its attempt to explain, the theory should lead to some degree of prediction and control of the phenomenon called human communication. A total theory should also aid one in understanding how the origin and development of individual human communication could affect the individual across the life span.

This speech theory of human communication assumes that human communication is a phenomenon, and that the phenomenon is observable and open to explanation and understanding. The theory addresses specifically the origins, development, functions, and effects of human communication in the individual and, indirectly, in society.

The speech theory of human communication (STHC) *suggests that the fact that human language is spoken in its normal ontogenesis and development may serve as a principal explanatory variable for the development and effects of specifically human communication.*

The theory set forth here is essentially a developmental theory focusing most strongly upon the earliest years of individual human life. Projections from early development are used to comment on individual and social effects of speech on human communication across the life span. The STHC falls short of being a total theory and is intended as a partial and developmental theory of restricted range. The theory's goal is to argue, as elegantly and parsimoniously as possible, that the fact that human language is spoken can serve in a major way to explain other important attributes of human communication.

Speech and human communication are two among a number of concepts important to the STHC. We are seeking a conceptual grasp of a complex subject matter. Concepts are the essence of conceptualization. A concept is the result of a generalizing mental operation. Once formed, a concept structures the behavioral field observed; for example, if someone suggests that deceit may be operating in a social situation, we immediately become more sensitive and observant of any social behavior that might indicate manipulativeness. For the most part, concepts are formed inductively by making numerous individual observations and then generalizing from those individual observations to arrive at a concept. Ordinarily concepts, such as "cloud" or "dog," are arrived at fairly effortlessly and with little conscious attention to the process of concept formation. More involved concepts, such as "justice," "entropy," or "communication," are usually the result of more conscious and rigorous mental operations. The concepts with which our mind is equipped play a major role in how we perceive and organize our perceptions and observations.

Terms are not concepts but are used to designate and label concepts. People may agree on concepts but be unaware of their underlying conceptual agreement because they use different names, labels, or terms for the same concept (we sometimes call the same thing by different names). For example,

> "Here, have a bite of this appetizer."
> "Ummm, that is really good! What is it?"
> "Escargot."
> "What's that?"
> "Snail."
> "Yuk!"

On the other hand, people may disagree on concepts but be unaware of doing so because they use the same name, label, or term for different concepts (we sometimes call different things by the same name). For example,

> "I like to have fun."
> "Me too."
> "Well?"
> "Get lost!"

Given the possible confusion between terms and concepts, scholars who state that they are studying speech may find, when discussing their actual research, that they are studying quite different phenomena indeed. Conversely, scholars may share a study of speech and label their research by different terms.

The rampant profusion and confusion of concepts and terms in the academic study of human communication cause repeated and frustrating difficulties. To clarify exactly what concepts are being examined, and what terms are being used to refer to specific concepts within the STHC, both a taxonomy and glossary are useful.

A glossary of terms used in the STHC appears at the end of this essay. A glossary is an alphabetical arrangement of terms and definitions relevant to a particular work, discipline, or theory. The STHC glossary is a selection of terms that are used with a particular meaning within the STHC and are arranged alphabetically.

Taxonomies are formal systems in which concepts and their accompanying terms are presented in an orderly classification according to some presumed relationship. "Taxonomies give some order to the chaos of life. They provide a framework for explaining what we see and guide our search for further meaning."[4] A taxonomy should strive to be a logically rigorous schema of terms and concepts relevant to a specific study. The taxonomy should be informed in its construction by stated principles and should demonstrate how initial terms and the concepts to which they refer lead to succeeding terms and concepts that appear in the taxonomy. Since basic concepts and their accompanying terms provide us with a way of interpreting experience from a particular point of view, a taxonomy should strive for consistency and for a commonality of reference, both of which should encourage terminological and conceptual precision. The goal of this taxonomy is to increase understanding of the component concepts of a STHC so as to enable the taxonomic users to proceed from a common terminological and conceptual base in their consideration of the theory. The taxonomy also allows for a reference point in evaluating alternate usages or taxonomies.[5]

This STHC taxonomy is the result of efforts to ascertain and organize the stimuli, observations, and judgments bearing upon the phenomenon of human communication. The efforts are then summed in a concept, and the concept is then assigned a term. The grouping is the concept, and the name, or term, is the label for the concept.[6]

The general strategy used in developing the STHC taxonomy was a movement from more diffuse to more precise conceptual control. From a logical point of view, the taxonomy is deductive, moving from the general to the specific. From a biophysiological point of view, the taxonomy follows the principle of emergent specificity, which is similar to what Werner and Kaplan identify as their "orthogenetic principle" and which involves the increasing control of ever more precise aspects of a subject matter.[7] From the point of view of information theory, the taxonomy leads to the progressive decrease of uncertainty and the corresponding increase of predictability and thus to increasing conceptual precision and control. The taxonomy's complexity follows from the subject matter: "Communication is a complex and varied process. Taxonomies reduce variety and complexity to some understandable order. Therefore the taxonomy of communication has to be complex. It either matches the field and obeys the law of requisite variety, or it fails as a taxonomy."[8]

The STHC taxonomy also tries to relate its constituent terms and concepts to Zetterberg's classification of terms into categories of "primitive" terms (with "primitive" terms further subdivided into either "minimum" or "borrowed") and "derived" terms. The results of Zetterberg's sorting operation look like this:

Zetterberg's Classification of Terms[9]

    I. *Primitive.* A small group of extralogical words which in different combinations with each other and with logical (syntactic) terms can define all other extralogical (content) terms of the theory.

        A. *Minimum.* Primitive terms unique to a given theory or academic discipline.

        B. *Borrowed.* Primitive terms shared with other theories or academic disciplines.

II. *Derived.* Terms obtained by combinations of the primitive terms and the logical words.

As Zetterberg points out, "It should be plain that a theory does not have any subject matter that can be called exclusively its own if all its primitive terms are borrowed terms from other sciences. If so, anything that it talks about can be exhaustively presented within the frameworks of theories from other sciences. On the other hand, if we have one or more terms that can properly be called minimum terms, we also have a unique subject matter. Any phenomenon, then, that has to be defined in these minimum terms is our exclusive subject matter."[10]

The discernment of primitive terms proved to be difficult. Assistance was provided by the meaning of *primitive* itself as the concern for something original rather than derived, primary rather than secondary. Historicity, or claims to earlier usage of a term, while considered, was not allowed to serve as the final arbiter as to whether a term or its accompanying concept could be considered primitive to a STHC. A primitive term to the STHC had to be a root term labeling a primitive concept, a concept that seems original, primordial, and necessary if one is to consider a theory of human communication that uses speech as a principal explanatory variable. A STHC primitive term must identify a concept from which an important reckoning or line of argument begins and which is not itself derived from another term; and by *derived* we mean it is not in itself simply a manifestation of another term or concept from a different point of view. The primitive terms of the STHC center specifically on what seems to be the essential components of the structure of the phenomena of human communication. Those terms identified as *primitive, borrowed* are shared with other theories or academic disciplines in such a manner as to make a determination of the first user uncertain or needless. Those terms taxonomically identified as *primitive, minimum* are considered to be unique to the Speech Theory of Human Communication and to those disciplines studying the subject matter of spoken language.

The taxonomy of primitive terms clarifies the phenomenon proper to the STHC as spoken language with implications also suggested for the reading/writing or symbolic gestural derivatives of speaking/hearing. The domain of this phenomenon for the STHC includes any and all instances of the occurrence of spoken language. Thus, the STHC should hold across all levels and in all contexts of spoken language.

For the STHC, the levels of spoken language include spoken language when a single individual serves as source, channel, and receiver (Level I: Intrapersonal); spoken language between individuals in a dyad or in a group small enough to allow face-to-face interaction and where the focus of the dialog is on what sets the participants apart

Table 1   A TAXONOMY OF PRIMITIVE TERMS FOR A SPEECH
THEORY OF HUMAN COMMUNICATION

TERM	CLASSIFICATION OF TERM	CONCEPTUAL DESCRIPTION
STIMULUS	Primitive, borrowed	A unit of sensory input, either internal or external, that rouses the organism, incites to action. Stimuli are necessary for information.
INFORMATION	Primitive, borrowed	A perceived selection from available stimuli, a process resulting in the reduction of uncertainty. The selection may be either accidental or purposive. Information is that which is acted upon in communication.
COMMUNICATION	Primitive, borrowed	Acting upon information. Limited to organisms. The act may take place within an organism, or between or among organisms (the organism may or may not be human). At this level neither intent nor success is implicit in the concept of communication. At this level the information communicated is constituted of sign(s).
SIGN	Primitive, borrowed	A stimulus announcing that of which it is a part, concrete, and fixed regardless of context. A subset of signs are signals that have acquired their sign characteristics through the process of pair-wise conditioning. Signs may be processed by a variety of analyzers, such as olfactory, gustatory, tactile, visual, kinesthetic/proprioceptive, and auditory. One means of stimulation of the auditory analyzer is through vocalization.
VOCALIZATION	Primitive, borrowed	The oral production of sounds by an organism that may or may not be human. Humans have available the quality of vocalization also present in other than human animals. Humans, however, in addition to the widely distributed capacity for general vocalization, have a species-specific and additional vocalization refinement termed *speech*.

Table 1   *(Continued)*

TERM	CLASSIFICATION OF TERM	CONCEPTUAL DESCRIPTION
SPEECH	Primitive, minimum	The human genetically determined, species-specific individual activity consisting of the voluntary production of phonated, articulated sound through the interaction and coordination of peripheral effector organs as a group as well as the speech-specific neural structures and pathways.[11] The human capacity for speech leads to the inception of the symbol.
SYMBOL	The classification of this term is in doubt. Arguments for both Primitive, minimum and for Primitive, borrowed may be well made.	A stimulus whose relationship with that with which it is associated is a result of the decision or arbitrary agreement of human user(s). Symbols are learned, abstract, contextually flexible, and anthroposemiotic. Symbols (which become significant symbols[12] when agreed to by more than one person) are a primary element of human language.
LANGUAGE	Primitive, borrowed	The culturally determined syntactic systematization of signs and/or symbols. When speech fuses with language, the result is spoken language.
SPOKEN LANGUAGE	Primitive, minimum	The fusion of genetically determined speech with culturally determined language. Whereas these two terms *speech* and *language* occur earlier in the taxonomy, their fusion creates a new phenomenon that is uniquely human and thus primitive and minimum to a speech theory of human communication.

Although not part of the formal taxonomy of primitive terms, some examples of derived terms may be useful.

| HUMAN COMMUNICATION | Derived | The acting upon of information by humans. The unique way in which humans act upon information so as to communicate through spoken language and its derivatives (such as writing and |

Table 1   *(Continued)*

TERM	CLASSIFICATION OF TERM	CONCEPTUAL DESCRIPTION
		symbolic gestures or gesture systems). Thus, human communication is a derived rather than a primitive term within the STHC.
SPEECH COMMUNICATION	Derived	The acting upon of information through uniquely human speech. This is another example of an important derived term composed of two primitive terms.

rather than what they have in common (Level II: Interpersonal); and spoken language when an individual is communicating to a number of other individuals in a group, the size or nature of which calls for a focusing upon what the members have in common and where there is little if any opportunity for one-on-one dialog to develop (Level III: Person-to Persons).

The levels of spoken language occur within contexts such as family, school, work setting, confrontation, conciliation, courtship, teaching, learning, and on and on. Spoken language may also be mediated by prosthetic devices such as the telephone, radio, television, computers, and so on.

The STHC is intended to be a partial theory of the phenomenon of spoken language in any and all instances of the occurrence of spoken language. At this time the STHC bears most strongly upon spoken language in its individual initiation, early maturation, and early development.

The STHC has been built purposely drawing upon and from any and all available resources and methodologies. Evidence in support of various aspects of the theory is presented if it seems apparent that the research from which the evidence is drawn bears directly upon a stated theoretical position. As long as the evidence bears directly on a theoretical statement, the disciplinary source and the chronology are considered irrelevant.

The remainder of this chapter will be devoted to setting forth the propositions of the STHC and indicating sources of support for the stated propositions. Given realistic space limitations, it is impossible to present in detail the supporting research and arguments for each proposition. However, following each proposition a brief synthesis of relevant support will be set forth along with citations as to where further detail may be found.

The chapter will conclude with implications and projected outcomes of the propositions and of the STHC, as well as with some thoughts on falsifying the theory.

PRETHEORETICAL PROPOSITIONS

Preliminary to the propositions flowing directly from the STHC there, are two pretheoretical propositions that bear upon any observations affecting a theory of human communication. These pretheoretical propositions must be taken into account if a theory of human communication is to be grounded in scientific data already available. The pretheoretical propositions are intended to be taken seriously as they constitute required grounding prior to the generation of any theory specific to human communication.

Although the requirements implied by these pretheoretical propositions may seem so formidable as to be discouraging, I am simply saying that any theory of human communication that sets forth propositions contravened by the extant findings of the physical sciences, biological sciences, social sciences, or humanities, faces serious problems. A human communication theorist must be able to take the findings of other branches of knowledge into account as those findings bear upon human communication. Even though we cannot know everything before we do anything, we must cultivate an intellectual set that calls upon us to be aware of and sensitive to the impact of other branches of knowledge upon our own endeavors as human communication theorists.

With all succeeding propositions, whether pretheoretical or theoretical, the proposition will first be stated, then the stated proposition will be followed by a succinct suggestion as to the proposition's implications together with relevant citations. For this initial presentation of the STHC, such an abbreviated style is both required by space considerations and appropriate to the theory's stage of development. Relevant citations are not always supportive of the proposition.

PRETHEORETICAL PROPOSITION I
An understanding of the animal substratum of human communication is preliminary to an explanation and understanding of what may be unique to human communication.

The evolution of communication in nonhuman animals has had and will have an impact upon the development, the present state, and the future state of the communication of humans.[1] The question of the possible species specificity of certain aspects of the communication of humans, such as spoken language, may illuminate the proper domain of the study of uniquely human communication.[2]

Selected citations relevant to 1: Adler, 1967; Ardrey, 1963; Hinde, 1971; Langer, 1967, 1972; Sebeok, 1968a, 1968b; Wilson, 1977.

Selected citations relevant to 2: Dance, 1977a, 1978; Gardner and Gardner, 1969; Hinde, 1972; Langer, 1967, 1972; Premack, 1976; Rumbaugh, 1977; Terrace, et al., 1979.

PRETHEORETICAL PROPOSITION II

An understanding of the human communication organism is preliminary to an explanation and understanding of what may be unique to human communication.

The contributions of the physical and biological sciences (e.g., anatomy, biology, genetics, neurobiology, neurology, etc.) must be considered and factored into any theory purporting to lead to a fuller understanding of human communication.[1] The contributions of the social and behavioral sciences (e.g., anthropology, linguistics, psychology, sociology, etc.) must be considered and factored into any theory purporting to lead to a fuller understanding of human communication.[2] The contributions of the humanities (history, philosophy, etc.) must be considered and factored into any theory purporting to lead to a fuller understanding of human communication.[3]

Selected citations relevant to 1: These citations are so selective as to be almost presumptuous. An interested researcher will be informed by basic texts in the natural and biological sciences. The following citations, while beyond the basic textbooks, fall short of highly advanced work. Berry, 1969; Critchley, 1970; Dance, 1967c; Luria, 1962; Milliken and Darley, 1967; Nilsson (English translation), 1974; Pavlov, 1960; Penfield and Roberts, 1959; Pribram, 1971; Rieber, 1976; *Scientific American*, special issue on the brain, September, 1979; Selnes and Whitaker, 1976; Waddington, 1957.

Selected citations relevant to 2: These citations are also noteworthy for what is left out. An interested researcher will be informed by basic texts in the social and behavioral sciences. The following citations can give but a small idea of the wealth of material available. Berelson and Steiner, 1964; Fodor, Bever, and Garrett, 1974; Lenneberg, 1967; Miller, 1967; Mowrer, 1960; Mussen, 1970; Wiemer and Palermo, 1974.

Selected citations relevant to 3: If the citation listings for 1 and 2 above seem to be presumptuous, this listing is positively foolhardy. An interested researcher will be informed by the entire body of humanistic literature (and will need three or more full lifetimes). The following citations give some indication of what is to be sampled in the pursuit of the propositional exhortation. Bronowski, 1977; Cassirer, 1953; Highet, 1950; Lao Tzu, sixth century B.C.

PROPOSITIONS OF THE SPEECH THEORY OF HUMAN COMMUNICATION

These propositions are meant to stand as general theoretical observations but are not stated in the testable form suitable to hypotheses. It is presumed that one or more hypotheses, stated in testable form, might be generated for each STHC proposition. The testing of such hypotheses is one manner by which the theory is open to falsification either in part or in whole. The claim is not made that the list of propositions constitutes the theory, but that the propositions derive from and relate to an underlying implicit and generative model.[13]

The STHC propositions are presented in what seems to be a developmental order. In certain propositions, there are more data available than in others; this will be reflected in the varying richness of propositional detail.

In building the propositional catalog, each stated proposition was required to flow directly from the STHC and to be sufficiently distinct from the propositions preceding or following. The criterion of distinctiveness meant that a proposition should not be a simple restatement of another proposition from a different viewpoint or in different terms.

STHC PROPOSITION 1
Vocalization is prior to and different from speech in humans.

The natural utterance of sounds by human neonates is not learned but is genetically determined and has much in common with the vocalization of the newborn of some other species.[1] It should be stated that owing to terminological slippage, "vocalization" and "speech" are often confused in the literature.

Selected citations relevant to 1: Lieberman, et al., 1972; Ostwald, 1963; Routhier, 1979; Winitz, 1969.

STHC PROPOSITION 2
Speech is uniquely human.

Attributes such as the development of the supralaryngeal vocal tract with the resultant bent double tube testify both to the human uniqueness of speech, as taxonomically defined in Table 1, and to the fact that speech is not an overlaid function as the concept of "overlaid function" is commonly used and understood.[1] Infant perception of speech also seems to demonstrate a uniquely human processing of speech sounds.[2] The nonhuman animal research suggests the unique position of speech in the communicative repertoire of humans.[3] There are preconceptual roots of speech.[4]

Selected citations relevant to 1: Dingwall, 1975; DuBrul, 1976, 1977; Kavanagh and Cutting, 1975; Liberman, 1973; Lieberman, 1972, 1975; Reports of the Haskins Laboratory (Studdert-Kennedy, 1979); Routhier, 1979.

Selected citations relevant to 2: Eimas, 1974; Eimas, et al., 1971, 1973; Morse, 1971, 1974; Studdert-Kennedy, 1979.

Selected citations relevant to 3: Dance, 1977a, b, c, 1978; Fouts, 1975; Gardner and Gardner, 1969; McNeill, 1975; Petitto, et al., 1979; Rumbaugh, et al., 1974; Vygotsky, 1962.

Selected citations relevant to 4: Condon and Sanders, 1974; Dance, 1967a, b, c; Langer, 1967; Luria, 1961; Pavlov, 1960; Vygotsky, 1962, 1978.

STHC PROPOSITION 3
Speech leads to the development of human conceptualization.

The infant's oral-aural experience initiates and develops the infant's sense of contrast, which is considered the root of conceptual thought and reason.[1] The oral-aural experience also leads to the lessening of subjectivity and the corresponding growth of objectivity on the part of the infant.[2] A base for decentering,[3] and the formation and augmentation of a sense of time for the individual[4] is also provided by the oral-aural speech experience. There are prespeech roots of conceptualization.[5]

Selected citations relevant to 1: Dance, 1979; Studdert-Kennedy, 1979; Thatcher and April, 1976; Winitz, 1979.

Selected citations relevant to 2: Dance, 1979; von Humboldt, 1971.

Selected citations relevant to 3: Flavell, 1968; Johnson, 1979; Vygotsky, 1962; Zak-Dance, 1979.

Selected citations relevant to 4: Albert, 1972; Hirsch, 1967; Underwood, 1976; Vyogtsky, 1978.

Selected citations relevant to 5: Bruner, et al., 1966; Bruner, 1968; Erikson, 1977; Piaget, 1962; Vygotsky, 1962.

STHC PROPOSITION 4
Language is culturally determined.

The characteristics of human language derive from the characteristics of speech, both phylogenetically and ontogenetically.[1] (Thus, this proposition is appropriate to a speech theory of human communication.) Natural languages are culturally determined and learned rather than genetically determined and developed by the child through the process of maturation alone.[2] Human languages consist of signs and symbols, syntactically arranged and capable of making references and predication.[3]

Selected citations relevant to 1: Havelock, 1967; Lenneberg, 1967; Ong, 1967; Werner and Kaplan, 1963; Harnad, Steklis, and Lancaster, 1976.

Selected citations relevant to 2: Adler, 1967; Brown, 1973; Hoijer, 1954; Hymes, 1964.

Selected citations relevant to 3: Adler, 1976; Dance, 1967a; Ferguson and Slobin, 1973; Fodor and Katz, 1964; Whatmough, 1957.

STHC PROPOSITION 5

The fusion of genetically determined speech with culturally determined language produces a qualitatively new and uniquely human phenomenon termed spoken language.

The following paragraphs trace the movement from infant use of sign to use of symbol, and then to the jointure of signs and symbols in spoken language.

The developing infant, immersed in sociocultural spoken language, begins to utter spoken language prior to its being fully constituted within the infant.[1] The infant's use of incompletely constituted spoken language, building upon the outcomes of the earlier propositions, leads the infant to shift from the use of signs to the ontogenetic formation of symbols.[2]

The spoken language symbol provides, for the individual, the foundation of grammar[3]; augments decentering[4]; and supplies the necessary conditions for individual choice and intent.[5]

Spoken language occurs on the three levels of Intrapersonal, Interpersonal, and Person-to-persons.[6] Spoken language has three functions: (1) to link the individual with the environment in a uniquely human way; (2) to develop higher mental processes; and (4) to regulate behavior.[7] Spoken language, in the individual, develops through and is sustained in two forms: (1) external spoken language and (2) inner spoken language.[8] The two forms of spoken language may serve to explain the presence of ambiguity in human communication.[9] Spoken language provides the foundation for the development of human values and human ethics in the individual.[10]

Selected citations relevant to 1: Brown, 1973; Dance, 1979; Kavanagh and Cutting, 1975; Lenneberg, 1967; McCarthy, 1954.

Selected citations relevant to 2: Berry, 1969; Dance, 1979; Kavanagh and Cutting, 1975; Lenneberg, 1967; Menyuk, 1977; Werner and Kaplan, 1963.

Selected citations relevant to 3: Brown, 1973; Dykema, 1977; Studdert-Kennedy, 1979.

Selected citations relevant to 4: Dance, 1979; Flavell, 1968; Piaget, 1955; Zak-Dance, 1979.

Selected citations relevant to 5: Bok, 1978; Burke, 1970; Chapman and Miller, 1980; Dance, 1967b, 1977c; Piaget and Inhelder, 1969; Premack, 1976.

Selected citations relevant to 6: Dance and Larson, 1972, 1976; Ruesch and Bateson, 1951.

Selected citations relevant to 7: Dance, 1967a; Dance and Larson, 1972, 1976; Hamilton, 1973; Johnson, 1979; Lasswell, 1948; Luria, 1969.

Selected citations relevant to 8: Dance and Larson, 1976; Luria, 1966, 1969; Sokolov, 1972; Vygotsky, 1962; Zivin, 1979.

Selected citations relevant to 9: Bernstein, 1976; Dance, 1977b; Empson, 1947; Oppenheimer, 1956.

Selected citations relevant to 10: Adler, 1967; Bok, 1978; Dance, 1973, 1977b and c; Thayer, 1973.

STHC PROPOSITION 6

The fact that in its normal ontogenesis and development human language is spoken serves as a principal explanatory variable for the constitution and effects of specifically human communication.

Symbols, decentering, predication, conceptualization, a sense of time, values, and ambiguity are among the unique effects of specifically human communication.[1] The spoken language attribute of human communication accounts, in a major way, for these effects.[2]

Selected citations relevant to both 1 and 2 are comprised of the totality of selected citations for propositions 1 through 5.

The propositional catalog for a Speech Theory of Human Communication reflects the underlying theory. As future efforts are made to develop the propositions more fully, it is expected that the underlying theory will become increasingly specified, accessible, and testable.

STHC PROPOSITIONAL CATALOG

PRETHEORETICAL PROPOSITIONS

    I. An understanding of the animal substatum of human communication is preliminary to an explanation and understanding of what may be unique to human communication.

    II. An understanding of the human communication organism is preliminary to an explanation and understanding of what may be unique to human communication.

PROPOSITIONS

    1. Vocalization is prior to and different from speech in humans.

    2. Speech is uniquely human.

    3. Speech leads to the development of human conceptualization.

4. Language is culturally determined.

5. The fusion of genetically determined speech with culturally determined language produces a qualitatively new and uniquely human phenomenon termed *spoken language.*

6. The fact that in its normal ontogenesis and development human language is spoken serves as a principal explanatory variable for the constitution and effects of specifically human communication.

The theory, as stated earlier, is a developmental theory focusing upon the early stages of human development of spoken language and upon the effects of spoken language on the early stages of human development. At the outset, it is important that we learn as much as possible about the organism that we are studying and about the animal history of that organism. Such information is alluded to most forcefully in the two pretheoretical propositions of the STHC. The development of human communication, of that aspect of communication most peculiarly human, takes place within a context of evolution. The place of the human individual within the evolutionary frame must be taken into consideration when seeking an understanding of any behavior that might be considered uniquely human. A theorist of human communication has a wide-ranging charge and a concomitant wide-ranging responsibility. Human communication pervades and transforms the human condition, and the study of human communication demands a rejection of parochialism. It is this demand of universality that can easily intimidate us in our theory-building efforts, but it is a commitment to universality as a goal that may make our theory-building efforts approach more closely the explication of the part played by spoken language in the human condition. The pretheoretical propositions are meant to be taken seriously but should not be used as an excuse not to do anything until everything has been done.

The first theoretical proposition holds that human infants naturally and spontaneously utter sound. This infant vocalization does not appear to be uniquely human but shares attributes with the vocalization of other primates as well as with animals outside of the primate series. Yet, this initial vocalization is necessary for the preparation of the human infant for other stages in the acquisition of spoken language and of uniquely human communication. Early vocalization, while natural and spontaneous, seems to be reflexive rather than voluntary.

The second theoretical proposition states that the human infant, through normal maturational processes, given normal social/cultural conditions, will acquire a refinement of spontaneous vocalization, a refinement termed *speech.* Rather than being an overlaid function, a function that borrows from other more primary human functions, it

is argued that human speech is uniquely human and rests upon organismic attributes and structures having as their primary purpose the
production and reception of speech. It is also suggested within this
proposition that voluntarism rather than reflexivity is an important
attribute of human speech as distinguished from human vocalization.
The proposition also bears upon the place held by speech in human
behavior prior to the development of human conceptualization.

STHC Proposition 3 argues that infant speech plays a formative,
and perhaps primary, role in the development of human conceptualization. Contrast, it is stated, is at the root of differentiation, and of higher
mental processes. The ability to discern one thing from another and
eventually to hold these two different things in relationship to each
other for simultaneous consideration develops from contrast. Contrast
is initiated in the human infant by means of the infant's oral/aural
experience, by means of the infant's speech. In addition to the inception of contrast, infant speech also entrains a movement from total
subjectivity and a total egocentrism to a reduction of subjectivity and
a corresponding increase of objectivity. Human infants, by means of
their speech, are led to an assessment of that which is outside of self
as well as that which is inside of self; this assessment enhances the
development of conceptual decentering. Infant speech, it is also propo-
sitionally argued, leads the human infant to develop a sense of time,
of temporality through the peculiarly evanescent and sequential nature
of the oral/aural utterance. The richness of STHC Proposition 3 de-
rives from the root experience under consideration but also from the
fact that more researchers have studied aspects of infant speech and
thus have provided a correspondingly rich resource from which to
draw theoretical insights.

The fourth theoretical proposition states that human language,
while dependent upon human speech, is culturally determined. The
human child acquires a natural language not by maturation but by
cultural exposure and experience. This propostion is most controversial
in its insistence upon the dependent relationship of language on speech,
both in the race and in the individual human being.

Proposition 5 is the most fully developed of the entries in the
STHC propositional catalog. Things are becoming increasingly complex as we decipher the propositional elements and implications. Building upon the results of STHC propositions 1, 2, 3, and 4, the developing
human being evidences a fusion of speech, which is genetically determined and the result of maturation, with language, which is culturally
determined and the result of experience and practice. It is this fusion
that is termed *spoken language* and that constitutes a uniquely human
behavior. Prior to the infant's own acquisition of fully constituted
spoken language (and a corresponding movement from infant to

child), the spoken language of the responding others in the infant's environment has sign attributes for the infant. In the infant's earliest practice in uttering samples of the spoken language to which the infant has been exposed, those utterances are utterances of signs rather than utterances of symbols. However, it is through such sign utterances—which flow into and through the reality of contrast, of decreased subjectivity and increased objectivity, of temporality, of the stirrings of conceptual decentering—that the human being ontogenetically constitutes symbols and manifests fully constituted spoken language. The implications of this acquisition of spoken language are profound for the human child. The birth of choice and of intent; the augmentation and enhancement of conceptual decentering; the facilitation of linking with the specifically human environment; the development of human behavior; the development of inner spoken language; and the provision of a foundation for the development of uniquely human values and ethics all flow from the manner in which spoken language transforms every aspect of the ambient of the human child.

The last of the STHC propositions, Proposition 6, is the natural result of all the preceding propositions and their effects. That human language is spoken is not a trivial fact; quite the contrary, it is an all-important fact that enables us to explain more satisfactorily the unique attributes and effects of uniquely human communication.

Even at this early stage of theoretical development, the STHC propositions may be developed into research hypotheses and then subjected to testing by appropriate methodologies. For example, STHC Proposition 3—Speech leads to the development of human conceptualization—has been partialed into hypotheses in the research of Zak-Dance and in the research of Sharpe. Zak-Dance's research hypothesis stated,

> When appropriately matched, preschool children with the oral/aural mode available to and used by them as their primary mode of human communication (as determined by their health and/or school records) will be at a higher developmental level of self-concept (as measured by scores on the Goodenough-Harris Drawing Test) than preschool children with the gestural/visual mode available to and used by them as their primary mode of human communication (as determined by their health and/or school records).[14]

Sharp's first hypothesis stated,

> Hearing subjects, whose primary mode of human communication is oral/aural, will score significantly higher on a test of analogical reasoning than will hearing impaired subjects, whose primary mode of human communication is gestural/visual.[15]

The testing of these two research hypotheses illustrates the opportunities available for falsifying part or all of the speech theory of human communication. Similar research hypotheses or alternate questions may be constructed for any item in the STHC propositional catalog. The outcome of testing such hypotheses or examining alternate questions should lead to the continual development and refinement of the theory.

Given the early stage of individual human development currently covered by the STHC propositions, other theoretical approaches to human communication, such as the constructivist perspective[16] or the coordinated management of meaning,[17] fit comfortably with the STHC as exemplars of later developmental stages.

The STHC implies that the raison d'être of human communication, rather than being primarily transactional or interactional, is primarily mentation. In the earliest stages of human development, interaction may dominate mentation so that the behavioral ratio looks something like interaction/mentation. When human communication becomes fully constituted (at about the age of 7), mentation becomes and remains paramount as the primary raison d'être of human communication, and the usual behavioral ratio then looks more like mentation/interaction. This statement is not meant to slight the importance of interaction in human communication but to highlight that one of the unique aspects of human communication, as contrasted with the communication of other than human animals, is to take thought, to ratiocinate, to engage in higher mental processes. Indeed, humans share with animals the capacity for communicative interaction—but mentation seems to be unique to human communication and to humans. Through uniquely human communication, humans first take thought and then through the communicative repertoire that humans share with other animals, humans share their thoughts with each other interactionally.[18]

Although the theory's treatment of intent in Proposition 5[5] impinges on how meaning may be constructed, it is not developed enough to be immediately helpful. The enduring and knotty question of meaning may eventually yield some of its intransigence to the STHC—but not at this time.

Theory development is challenging, exciting, and frustrating. Theory is essential for any discipline and for all subject matters. Without theory, facts are all too often both interesting and meaningless. However, theory building takes time and tolerance. It is in the progressive elaboration of theoretical propositions and hypotheses that the theory begins to shape itself. This slow process of testing and refinement simply cannot be rushed except at the greatest danger to the end product. The actual process of theory building is in itself rewarding, and it is to this theory-building process that theorists must commit their efforts; through this process, theorists should be able to find their justification and their comfort.

Mountains should be climbed with as little effort as possible and without desire. The reality of your own nature should determine the speed. If you become restless, speed up. If you become winded, slow down. You climb the mountain in an equilibrium between restlessness and exhaustion. Then, when you're no longer thinking ahead, each footstep isn't just a means to an end but a unique event in itself.

Robert M. Pirsig[19]

Notes

1. Davenport G. (Trans.). *Herakleitos and Diogenes*. Bolinas, Calif.: Grey Fox Press, 1979, Fragment 1, p. 11.
2. Bruner, J. S. *Toward a theory of instruction*. Cambridge, Mass.: Harvard University Press, 1966, 154.
3. Doyle, Sir A. C. The Yellow Face. In W. S. Baring-Gould (Ed.), *The annotated Sherlock Holmes* (Vol. I). New York: Clarkson S. Potter, 1967, p. 586.
4. Smith, A. G. The taxonomy of communication. In B. Ruben (Ed.), *Communication yearbook I*. New Brunswick, N.J.: ICA and Transaction Books, 1977, p. 79.
5. This taxonomy owes a debt to previous efforts at taxonomic construction appearing in Dance, F. E. X., & Larson, C. E. *Speech communication: Concepts and behavior*. New York: Holt, Rinehart and Winston, 1972; *The functions of human communication: A theoretical approach*, New York: Holt, Rinehart and Winston, 1976. Taxonomic revision reflects the continuing search after increasing rigor.
6. Dance, F. E. X. The "concept" of communication. *Journal of Communication*, 1970, XX, 201–210.
7. "We assume that organisms are naturally directed toward a series of transformations . . . reflecting a tendency to move from a state of relative globality and undifferentiatedness towards states of increasing differentiation and hierarchic integration." Werner, H., & Kaplan, B. *Symbol formation*. New York: John Wiley & Sons, 1963, p. 7. Professor Jesse Delia alludes to this "orthogenetic principle" in his studies dealing with a constructivist approach to understanding the phenomenon of human communication.
8. Smith, A. G. p. 82.
9. Zetterberg, H. L. *On theory and verification in sociology* (3rd ed.). Totowa, N.J.: Bedminster Press, 1965, pp. 49–52.
10. Zetterberg, H. L. pp. 50–51.
11. Sources supporting this conceptual description are numerous. Examples of such sources include DuBrul, E. L. Biomechanics of speech sounds. In S. R. Harnad, H. D. Steklis, & J. Lancaster (Eds.), *Origins and evolution of language and speech*, Annals of the N. Y. Academy of Sciences (Vol. 280), 1976; Routhier, M. E. *A critical analysis and examination of the issue of speech as an overlaid function*. Doctoral dissertation, University of Denver, 1979.

12. Mead, G. H. A behavioristic account of the significant symbol. *Journal of Philosophy*, 1922, XIX, 157–163.
13. Dubin, R. *Theory building* (rev. ed.). New York: Free Press, 1978, p. 161. Also see Zetterberg, chap. 4.
14. Zak-Dance, C. C. *The differential effects of a child's primary mode of human communication on the child's self-concept development.* Doctoral dissertation, University of Denver, 1979.
15. Sharpe, S. L. *An investigation of the relationship of primary mode of human communication to the development of complex cognition.* Doctoral dissertation, University of Denver, 1980.
16. Delia, J., O'Keefe, D., & O'Keefe, B. The Constructivist Approach to Communication. This volume. Pp. 147–191.
17. Cronen, V. E., Pearce, W. B., & Harris, L. M. The coordinated management of meaning: A rules-based approach to the first course in interpersonal communication. *Communication Education*, 1979, *28*, 22–38.
18. Dance, F. E. X. Human communication theory: A highly selective review and two commentaries. In B. Ruben (Ed.), *Communication yearbook II*, New Brunswick, N.J.: ICA and Transaction Press, 1978, pp. 7–22.
19. Pirsig, R. M. *Zen and the art of motorcycle maintenance.* New York: William Morrow and Company, 1974, p. 204.

Bibliography of Prepropositional and Propositional Citations

Adler, M. *The difference of man and the difference it makes.* New York: Holt, Rinehart and Winston, 1967.
Adler, M. *Some questions about language.* LaSalle, Ill.: Open Court, 1976.
Albert, M. L. Auditory sequencing and left cerebral dominance for language. *Neuropsychologia*, 1972, *10*(2), 245–248.
Ardrey, R. *African genesis.* New York: Del Publishing, 1963.
Berelson, B., and Steiner, G. *Human behavior: An inventory of scientific findings.* New York: Harcourt Brace Jovanovich, 1964.
Bernstein, L. *The unanswered question.* Norton Lectures. Cambridge, Mass.: Harvard University Press, 1976.
Berry, M. F. *Language disorders in children.* New York: Appleton-Century-Crofts, 1969.
Bok, Sissela. *Lying: Moral Choice in Public and Private Life.* New York: Pantheon Books, 1978.
Bronowski, J. *A sense of the future: Essays in natural philosophy.* Cambridge, Mass.: MIT Press, 1977.
Brown, R. *A first language: The early stages.* Cambridge, Mass.: Harvard University Press, 1973.
Bruner, J. S. *Process of cognitive growth: Infancy.* Worcester, Mass.: Clark University Press with Barre Pub., 1968.
Bruner, J. S., Olver, R. R., & Greenfield, P. M., et al. *Studies in cognitive growth.* New York: John Wiley & Sons, 1966.
Burke, K. *The rhetoric of religion: Studies on logology.* Berkeley, Calif.: University of California Press, 1970.

Cassirer, Ernst. *The Philosophy of Symbolic Forms: Vol 1: Language.* New Haven, Conn.: Yale University Press, 1953.

Chapman, R. S., & Miller, J. F. Analyzing language and communication in the child. In R. L. Schiefelbusch (Ed.), *Nonspeech language and communication: Analysis and intervention.* Baltimore: University Park Press, 1980.

Condon, W. S., & Sanders, L. W. Neonate movement is synchronized with adult speech: Interactional participation and language acquisition. *Science,* 1974, *183,* 99–101.

Critchley, M. *Aphasiology and other aspects of language.* London: Edward Arnold, 1970.

Dance, F. E. X. *The functions of speech communication as an integrative concept in the field of communication.* Paper presented at the Fifteenth International Convention of Communication, Genoa, Italy. A publication of the International Institute of Communication. (Genoa, Italy), 1967a.

Dance, F. E. X. (Ed.). *Human communication theory: Original essays.* New York: Holt, Rinehart and Winston, 1967b.

Dance, F. E. X. Speech communication theory of Pavlov's second signal system. *The Journal of Communication,* 1967c, *17,* 13–24.

Dance, F. E. X. Speech communication: The revealing echo. In L. Thayer (Ed.), *Communication: Ethical and moral issues.* New York: Gordon and Breach, 1973.

Dance, F. E. X. The rhetorical primate. *The Journal of Communication,* 1977a, *2,* 12–16.

Dance, F. E. X. *The roots of ambiguity.* Lecture given at Western Michigan University as a visiting scholar, October 2–4, 1977b.

Dance, F. E. X. *Speech communication and the genesis of human values.* Lecture given at Western Michigan University as a visiting scholar, October 2–4, 1977c.

Dance, F. E. X. Human communication and the communication of chimpanzees: A differential analysis. *Proceedings of the 1975 Congress for the Study of Applied Linguistics,* Hochschul Verlag GmbH, Stuttgard, W. Germany, April–May, 1978, 17–61.

Dance, F. E. X. An acoustic trigger to conceptualization. *Health Communications and Informatics,* 1979, *5,* 203–213.

Dance, F. E. X. Swift, slow, sweet, sour, adazzle, dim: What makes human communication human. *Western Journal of Speech Communication,* 1980, *44,* 60–63.

Dance, F. E. X., & Larson, C. E. *Speech communication: Concepts and behavior.* New York: Holt, Rinehart and Winston, 1972.

Dance, F. E. X., & Larson, C. E. *The functions of human communication: A theoretical approach.* New York: Holt, Rinehart and Winston, 1976.

Dingwall, W. O. The species-specificity of speech. In D. F. Dato (Ed.), *Georgetown University round table on language and linguistics 1975.* Washington, D.C.: Georgetown University Press, 1975.

Dubrul, E. L. Biomechanics of speech sounds. In S. R. Harnad, H. D.

Steklis, & J. Lancaster (Eds.), *Origins and Evolution of Language and Speech*. Annals of the New York Academy of Science, 1976, *280*.

Dubrul, E. L. Origins of speech apparatus and its reconstruction in fossils. *Brain and Language*, 1977, *4*, 365–381.

Dykema, K. W. Where our grammar came from. In V. P. Clark, P. A. Eschholz, & A. F. Rosa (Eds.), *Language: Introductory readings* (2nd ed.). New York: St. Martin's Press, 1977.

Eimas, P. D., Siqueland, E. R., Juscyk, P., & Vigorito, J. Speech perception in infants. *Science*, 1971, *171*, 303–306.

Eimas, P. D., Cooper, W. E., & Corbit, J. D. Some properties of linguistic feature detectors. *Perception and Psychophysics*, 1973, *13*, 247–252.

Eimas, P. D. Linguistic processing of speech by young infants. In R. L. Schiefelbusch & L. L. Lloyd (Eds.), *Language perspectives: Acquisition, retardation, and intervention*. Baltimore: University Park Press, 1974.

Empson, W. *Seven types of ambiguity*. New York: New Directions, 1947.

Erikson, E. H. *Toys and reason*. New York: Norton, 1977.

Ferguson, C. A., & Slobin, D. I. *Studies of child language development*. New York: Holt, Rinehart and Winston, 1973.

Flavell, J. *The development of role-taking and communication skills in children*. New York: John Wiley & Sons, 1968.

Fodor, J. A., Beuer, T. G., & Garrett, M. F. *The Psychology of Language*. New York: McGraw-Hill Book Co., 1974.

Fodor, J. A., & Katz, J. *The structure of language*. Englewood Cliffs, N.J.: Prentice-Hall, 1964.

Fouts, R. S. The development of human linguistic behavior of chimpanzees. *Great Ideas Today 1975*. Chicago: Encyclopedia Britannica Press, 1975.

Gardner, R. S., & Gardner, B. T. Teaching sign language to a chimpanzee. *Science*, 1969, *165*, 664–672.

Hamilton, L. *The development of higher mental functions through speech communication, an exploratory study*. Doctoral dissertation, University of Denver, June 1973.

Harnad, S. R., Steklis, H. D., & Lancaster, J. (Eds.). *Origins and evolution of language and speech*. New York: New York Academy of Science, 1976.

Havelock, E. *Preface to Plato*. New York: Grosset & Dunlap, 1967.

Highet, G. *The classical tradition*. New York: Oxford University Press, 1950.

Hinde, R. *Non-verbal communication*. Cambridge, Mass.: Cambridge University Press, 1972.

Hirsch, I. J. Information processing in input channels for speech and language: The significance of serial order of stimuli. In C. H. Milliken & F. L. Darley (Eds.), *Brain mechanisms and underlying speech and language*. New York: Grune & Stratton, 1967.

Hoijer, H. (Ed.). *Language in culture*. Chicago: University of Chicago Press, 1954.

Hymes, D. *Language in culture and society*. New York: Harper & Row, 1964.

Jaynes, J. *The origin of consciousness in the breakdown of the bicameral mind.* Boston: Houghton Mifflin, 1977.

Johnson, J. R. *The relationship between speech communication egocentrism and reading achievement.* Doctoral Dissertation, University of Denver, June 1978.

Johnson, S. *The development of an instrument to measure human communication functional dominance.* Doctoral dissertation, University of Denver, June 1979.

Kavanagh, J. F., & Cutting, J. C. (Eds.). *The role of speech in language.* Cambridge, Mass.: MIT Press, 1975.

Langer, S. *Mind: An essay on human feelings* (Vol. 1). Baltimore: Johns Hopkins University Press, 1967.

————. Baltimore: Johns Hopkins University Press, 1972 (Vol. 2),

Lao Tzu. *Tao Te Ching.* Trans. D. C. Lau. Harmondsworth, Eng.: Penguin Books, 1963.

Lasswell, H. D. The structure and function of communication in society. In L. Bryson (Ed.), *The communication of ideas.* New York: Harper & Row, 1948.

Lenneberg, E. *Biological foundations of language.* New York: John Wiley & Sons, 1967.

Liberman, A. M. The speech code. In G. S. Miller (Ed.), *Communication, language, and meaning.* New York: Basic Books, 1973.

Lieberman, P. *The speech of primates.* The Hague: Mouton, 1972.

Lieberman, P. *On the origins of language.* New York: Macmillan, 1975.

Lieberman, P., Harris, K. D., Wolff, P., & Russell, A. H. Newborn infant cry and non-human primate vocalizations. In P. Lieberman (Ed.), *Speech of primates,* The Hague: Mouton, 1972.

Luria, A. R. *The role of speech in the regulation of normal and abnormal behavior.* New York: Liveright, 1961.

Luria, A. R. *Higher cortical functions in man.* New York: Basic Books Inc., 1966.

Luria, A. R. Speech development and the formation of mental processes. In M. Cole & I. Maltzman (Eds.), *Handbook of contemporary soviet psychology.* New York: Basic Books, 1969.

McCarthy, D. Language development in children. In L. Carmichael (Ed.), *Manual of child psychology* (2nd ed.). New York: John Wiley & Sons, 1954.

McNeill, D. Aspects of advanced language in chimpanzees. *Great Ideas Today 1975.* Chicago: Encyclopedia Britannica Press, 1975.

Menyuk, P. *Language and maturation.* Cambridge, Mass.: MIT Press, 1977.

Miller, George A. *The Psychology of Communication.* New York: Basic Books, 1967.

Milliken, C. H., & Darley, F. (Eds.) *Brain mechanisms underlying speech and language.* New York: Grune & Stratton, 1967.

Morse, P. A. *The discrimination of speech and nonspeech stimuli in early infancy.* Doctoral dissertation, University of Connecticut, 1971.

Morse, P. A. Infant speech perception: A preliminary model and review of the literature. In R. L. Schiefelbusch & L. L. Lloyd (Eds.), *Lan-*

guage perspectives: Acquisition, retardation and intervention. Baltimore: University Park Press, 1974.

Mowrer, O. H. *Learning theory and the symbol process.* New York: John Wiley & Sons, 1960.

Mussen, P. H. (Ed.). *Carmichael's manual of child psychology* (2 vols.). New York: John Wiley & Sons, 1970.

Nilsson, L. *Behold man: A photographic essay.* Boston: Little, Brown and Company, 1974.

Ong, W. *The presence of the word.* New Haven, Conn.: Yale University Press, 1967.

Oppenheimer, R. Analogy in science. *American Psychologist* (Vol. 2), 1956.

Ostwald, P. F. The baby cry. *Soundmaking.* Springfield, Ill.: Charles C Thomas, 1963.

Pavlov, I. *Conditioned reflexes.* New York: Dover Publications, 1960.

Penfield, W., & Roberts, L. *Speech and brain mechanisms.* Princeton, N.J.: Princeton University Press, 1959.

Petitto, L. S., & Siedenberg, M. S. On the evidence for the linguistic abilities in singing apes. *Brain and Language,* 1979, 8, 162–183.

Piaget, J. *The origins of intelligence in children.* New York: International Universities Press, 1952.

Piaget, J. *The language and thought of the child.* Cleveland: The World Publishing Company, 1955.

Piaget, J., & Inhelder, B. *The psychology of the child.* New York: Basic Books, 1969.

Premack, David. *Intelligence in Ape and Man.* Hillside, N.J.: Lawrence Erlbaum Assoc. Pub., 1976.

Pribram, K. H. *Languages of the brain.* Englewood Cliffs, N.J.: Prentice-Hall, 1971.

Ruesch, J., & Bateson, G. *Communication: The social matrix of psychiatry.* New York: Norton, 1951.

Rieber, R. W. (Ed.). *The neuropsychology of language.* New York: Plenum Press, 1976.

Routhier, M. *A critical analysis and examination of the issue of speech as an overlaid function.* Doctoral dissertation, University of Denver, 1979.

Rumbaugh, D. M., et al. Lana (chimpanzee) learning language: A progress report. *Brain and Language,* 1974, 1, 205–212.

Rumbaugh, D. M. *Language learning by a chimpanzee: The Lana project.* New York: Academic Press, 1977.

Scientific American, Special issue on the brain. September, 1979.

Sebeok, T. *Animal communication: Techniques of study and results of research.* Bloomington, Ind.: Indiana University Press, 1968a.

Sebeok, T. Zoosemiotics. *American Speech.* New York: Columbia University Press, May 1968b.

Selnes, O., & Whitaker, H. Morphological and functional development of the auditory system. In R. W. Rieber (Ed.), *The neuropsychology of language.* New York: Plenum Press, 1976.

Smith, W. *The behavior of communicating: An ethological approach.* Cambridge, Mass.: Harvard University Press, 1978.

Sokolov, A. N. *Inner speech and thought.* New York: Plenum Press, 1972.

Studdert-Kennedy, M. The beginning of speech. *Haskin's laboratory status report on speech research.* April-June, 1979, SR-58, 35–64.

Terrace, H. S., Petitto, L. A., Sanders, R. J., & Bever, T. G. Can an ape create a sentence? *Science,* 1979, *206,* 891–902.

Thatcher, R. W., & April, R. S. Evoked potential correlates of semantic information processing in normals and aphasics. In R. W. Rieber (Ed.), *The neuropsychology of language.* New York: Plenum Press, 1976.

Thayer, L. (Ed.). *Communication: Ethical and moral issues.* New York: Gordon and Breach, 1973.

Tzu, Lao, *Tao te Ching* (D. C. Lau, Trans.), Baltimore, Md.: Penguin Books, 1978.

Underwood, G. *Attention and memory.* Oxford, England: Pergamon Press, 1976.

von Humboldt, W. *Linguistic Variability and Intellectual Development.* Coral Gables, Fla.: University of Miami Press, 1971.

Vygotsky, L. S. *Thought and language.* Cambridge, Mass.: MIT Press, 1962.

Vygotsky, L. S. *Mind in society: The development of higher cortical processes.* Cambridge, Mass.: Harvard University Press, 1978.

Waddington, C. H. *The strategy of the genes: A discussion of some aspects of theoretical biology.* London: George, Allen & Unwin, Ltd., 1957.

Werner, H., & Kaplan, B. *Symbol formation.* New York: John Wiley & Sons, 1963.

Whatmough, J. *Language: A modern synthesis.* New York: Mentor, 1956.

Wiemer, W. B., & Palermo, D. S. *Cognition and the symbolic process.* Hillsdale, N.J.: Lawrence Erlbaum Associates, 1974.

Wilson, E. O. *On human nature.* Cambridge, Mass.: Harvard University Press, 1977.

Winitz, H. *Articulatory acquisition and behavior.* New York: Appleton-Century-Crofts, 1969.

Zak-Dance, C. C. *The differential effects of a child's primary mode of human communication on the child's self-concept development.* Doctoral dissertation, University of Denver, June, 1979.

Zivin, G. (Ed.). *The development of self-regulation through private speech.* New York: John Wiley & Sons, 1979.

STHC GLOSSARY

anthroposemiotic. Those sign system aspects of humankind's total communicative repertoire that are exclusively human.[1]

channel. The carrier for the human communication message, such as a telephone wire or a radio signal. Prior to the message serving as an instrument of human communication, the channel must be in interface with a human modal analyzer, such as the ear or the eye.

communication. See *taxonomy.* Acting upon information. Limited to organisms. The act may take place within an organism, or between or among organisms (the organism may or may not be human). At this level neither intent nor success is implicit in the concept of communication.

deaf.   More than 75 decibel hearing loss in the better ear. Technically refers to profound deafness.

decentering.   The capacity to step outside of one's own self and to take the *conceptual* point of view of another.

egocentrism.   Being restricted to one's own point of view, either conceptually or affectively, or both.

empathy.   The capacity to identify affectively with another person.

function.   A relationship wherein one quality is so related to another quality that it is dependent on or varies with it. Function implies a necessary relationship.

human communication.   The acting upon of information by humans. For fuller definition, see taxonomy.

information.   A perceived selection from available stimuli, a process resulting in the reduction of uncertainty. The selection may be either accidental or purposive. For fuller definition, see taxonomy.

intent.   One's goals for one's own behavior. Intent may be assessed by one's ability, upon reflection, to report one's goals for one's own behavior. The ability to judge the intent of another may be assessed by one's correctness in reporting the goals of the other for the other's own behavior.

language.   The culturally determined syntactic systematization of signs and/or symbols. For fuller definition, see taxonomy.

meaning.   The assessment of the intent underlying a communicative event.

mode.   The individual operational system for the conveyance of spoken language. The modes of spoken language are tied to the organism, for example, auditory, visual, tactile, and so on. Each sender mode has a complementary receiver mode, for example, oral/aural. Between a sender mode and a receiver mode a channel may be interposed.

nonverbal.   A stimulus not dependent upon symbolic content for meaning.

nonvocal.   A stimulus produced by other than the vocal mechanism.

protosymbol.   "Though on the surface often indistinguishable from true symbols, proto symbols lack the intentional act by which a vehicular form is taken to represent a referent."[2] Susanne Langer calls a similar concept a "quasi symbol." Some dream images may be characteristic of protosymbols or quasisymbols.

purpose.   That which can be done with something. Purpose is variable, a matter of choice, and requires intent.

rhetoric.   Planned, purposive spoken language.

role.   The pattern of expectations regarding the occupant of a position.

sign.   A stimulus announcing that of which it is a part, concrete and fixed regardless of context. For a fuller definition including a definition of signals, see taxonomy.

speech.   The human genetically determined, species-specific individual activity consisting of the voluntary production of phonated, articulated sound through the interaction and coordination of peripheral effector organs as a group as well as the speech-specific neural structures and pathways. For a fuller definition, see taxonomy.

spoken language. The fusion of genetically determined speech with culturally determined language. For a fuller definition, see taxonomy.

symbol. A stimulus whose relationship with that with which it is associated is a result of the decision or arbitrary agreement of human use (users). For a fuller description, see taxonomy.

vocalization. The oral production of sounds by an organism. The organism may or may not be human. For a fuller description, see taxonomy.

zoosemiotic. Those sign system aspects of humankind's total communicative repertoire that can be shown to be the end products of evolutionary series.[3]

Glossary Footnotes

1. Sebeok, T. A. Goals and limitations of the study of animal communication. In T. A. Sebeok (Ed.), *Animal communication.* Bloomington, Ind.: Indiana University Press, 1968, p. 8.
2. Werner, H., and Kaplan, B. *Symbol formation.* New York: John Wiley & Sons, 1963, pp. 16–17.
3. Sebeok, p. 8.

THE CONSTRUCTIVIST APPROACH TO COMMUNICATION

Jesse G. Delia
Barbara J. O'Keefe
Daniel J. O'Keefe

THE CONSTRUCTIVIST APPROACH TO COMMUNICATION

The constructivist approach to communication, which we have articulated over the last several years, recognizes the important role that philosophical and conceptual analysis and argument can play in the illumination of human communication. However, the bulk of our work consists of theoretical analyses and empirical research reports on specific topics. In the present essay, we offer a summary of our general philosophical foundations, our theoretical commitments and research foci, and our methodological commitments and research practices.

PHILOSOPHICAL FOUNDATIONS

A useful place to begin a discussion of constructivism's philosophical foundations is the Brockriede's observation that in many discussions of metatheoretical and metamethodological issues in communication, analysts have not "clearly differentiated between philosophical assumptions and a theoretical orientation" (1978, p. 3). This is a point well taken. But Brockriede's distinction between theory and philosophy is subject both to qualification and to further refinement.

First, the qualification: although a useful distinction can be drawn between theory and philosophy, this should not blind one to the dependence of substantive theory on philosophic assumptions. It is just this relationship that makes criticism of the philosophical assumptions of a theory a useful enterprise; a theory based on defective assumptions, or a theory made inconsistent by inattention to its assumptions, is obviously a less-than-ideal theory. This is not to deny that for certain purposes a distinction between "theory" and "philosophy" may be useful—indeed it may be, and such a distinction shall be employed here. But one ought not take this distinction as somehow suggesting that theories are not dependent on philosophical assumptions.

Now the refinement: there are two rather different (though connected) kinds of philosophical assumptions made in a social scientific theory. Crudely put, one kind represents assumptions about the nature of *science;* and the other, assumptions about the nature of *persons.* The first sort is the kind usually identified by a phrase such as *philosophy of science.* The second does not have so convenient a label, though *philosophical anthropology* suggests itself (and will be used here).

Of course, these two kinds of philosophical assumptions are related. Science is, after, all, a human activity. Whatever one's conception of science is, it should be consistent with one's view of persons (and vice versa). For example, it would not do to think of science as necessarily based on the availability of raw uninterpreted sense-data, and then to suggest that the nature of persons is such that we have no access to such uninterpreted data.

But given this relationship between one's philosophical anthropology and one's philosophy of science, a useful distinction can still be drawn between them. The central reason for drawing the distinction is that a recognition of "fundamental assumptions about persons" as an element of any social scientific theory permits one to see broad similarities and differences among various substantive positions. It might be useful, for example, to recognize that some substantive theories see persons as fundamentally passive creatures, while others view persons as inherently active; there might be a wide variety of "active" theories, and these might not all be completely compatible with each other, but it still may be desirable to see what it is about these theories that makes them all somehow similar.

In sum, there are three different things to be distinguished: the substantive social scientific theory, that theory's basic assumptions about the nature of persons, and that theory's basic assumptions about the nature of science. As suggested above, these are often intertwined rather tightly, and one cannot always sort things neatly into these three boxes. Still, to recognize the pragmatic value of these distinctions is to have a place to start in clarifying matters.

Now we shall move on to constructivism. Constructivism is, first and foremost, a substantive theory, and we shall correspondingly reserve the term *constructivism* for that theory. But, like any social scientific theory, constructivism is based on general assumptions about the scientific enterprise (i.e., a philosophy of science) and on general assumptions about persons (i.e., a philosophical anthropology).

The place to start in sorting things out is with the general image of persons that constructivism embraces. Perhaps the phrase that best captures constructivism's philosophical anthropology is the *interpretive orientation*. The broad and general assumptions about persons contained in this interpretive orientation are shared by a number of different substantive theories (of which constructivism is only one). An interpretive philosophical anthropology suggests that persons approach reality through ongoing processes of interpretation. As Delia and Grossberg (1977, p. 36) note, from an interpretive orientation communication is seen as

> an emergent, creative activity through which human social reality is constantly being re-created, affirmed, repaired, and changed. Within interpretive social theories, persons are agents of action, not mere responders to events. Actors are capable of creative originative action, and consequently, communication is not completely bound by its past, but involves an emergent process in which social, that is to say intersubjective, reality is constituted. Interpretive views of communication recognize this creative, emergent process of the social reconstruction of reality as involving an interplay of individual interpretive processes and socially and historically constituted processes and contexts.

Now a number of different substantive theories all fall roughly within this general interpretive orientation. Examples might include Cicourel's (1974) cognitive sociology, Schutz's (1932/1967) phenomenological social theory, Kelly's (1955) personal construct theory, Blumer's (1969) symbolic interactionism, Williams' (1965) Marxist cultural theory, and our constructivist theory. These theories, though they share some broad sense interpretive beliefs, nevertheless concretize those tenets in very different ways. The point we wish to emphasize is that constructivism is only one particular interpretive theory. A major portion of our later discussion will be directed toward elaborating the concrete claims of constructivism considered as a substantive theory.

However, our theoretical perspective not only exemplifies a general philosophical anthropology but embodies a philosophy of science as well. That philosophy of science is most conveniently captured by

Suppe's (1977) term *Weltanschauungen*. Just as the interpretive philosophical anthropology underlies a number of more specific social scientific theories, so a Weltanschauungen philosophy of science represents the general assumptions that a number of more specific philosophies of science embrace. For example, Kuhn (1970), Toulmin (1972), and Hanson (1958), among others, might all be said to share a general Weltanschauungen orientation within the philosophy of science, even while they differ importantly over more specific issues. Constructivism's particular interpretation of the general Weltanschauungen philosophy of science has been discussed elsewhere (Delia, 1977b; D. O'Keefe, 1975) and will receive further treatment below. The point at present is that the Weltanschauungen philosophy of science that underpins constructivism is something distinct from constructivism itself (i.e., the substantive theory). Just as one might adopt an interpretive philosophical anthropology while rejecting constructivism's specific concretization of that general orientation, so one might adopt a Weltanschauungen philosophy of science while rejecting constructivism proper.

These distinctions may help to clarify some of the arguments that we have advanced in other papers, for we have tried to argue for the desirability of both (1) general interpretive and Weltanschauungen assumptions and (2) our specific constructivist framework. Thus, for example, Delia's (1975a) discussion of the variable-analytic stance toward research and D. O'Keefe's (1975) analysis of logical empiricism are best seen as arguments for a general Weltanschauungen philosophy of science; Delia's (1977b) discussion of the nature of science argues both for the general Weltanschauungen orientation and for a specific constructivist reading of that general orientation; and Delia and Grossberg's (1977) discussion of the nature of evidence in communication research is based on general interpretive assumptions, not specific constructivist views. By contrast, for example, Delia and Clark's (1975), and Delia and B. O'Keefe's (1979) discussion of communicative development, Applegate's (1980b) naturalistic observations of nursery school teachers' communicative strategies, S. Jackson's (1977) analysis of the perception of political candidates, D. O'Keefe's (1980b) treatment of the attitude-behavior relationship, and Applegate and Delia's (1980), and B. O'Keefe and Delia's (1979) analyses of the social-cognitive and interactional processes underlying socialization practices and communicative development all articulate and argue for specific constructivist treatments of particular empirical domains.

The following outline of the constructivist perspective, therefore, will seek to summarize both the broader methodological implications of the perspective and the more particular theoretical claims we make about communication and interaction processes. The treatment is divided into two major sections. We first discuss the theoretical commitments and research foci of constructivism considered as a substantive theoretical position, and then we turn to a discussion of the implications of our view of the research enterprise.

THEORETICAL COMMITMENTS AND RESEARCH FOCI

The Theoretical Commitments of Constructivism

This section sketches the central theoretical claims of constructivism. Consistent with the general tenets of an interpretive philosophical anthropology, constructivism sees persons as approaching the world through processes of interpretation. The interpretive schemes persons employ channelize their activity (including their communicative conduct). Behavior is organized through the application of interpretive schemes as well as strategies that translate intentions into behavioral displays. Human interaction is a process in which individual lines of action are coordinated through reciprocal recognition of communicative intent and in which actions are organized by communicative strategies; both the reciprocal recognition of communicative intent and the employment of communicative strategies depend centrally on the interpretive schemes interactants bring to bear on the world.

This constructivist view of communication is elaborated in this section through discussion of (1) interpretive processes, (2) human action, (3) human interaction, and (4) human communication.

• *Interpretive Processes.* Our conception of interpretive processes rests on our view of persons as simultaneously (a) biological entities who approach the world through the cognitive organization of experience, and (b) members of a sociocultural community.

Because persons are seen within constructivism as biological entities, their conduct is taken to originate in natural activity. This ongoing activity is directed and organized by cognitive processes: through the application of cognitive schemes, experience is segmented into meaningful units and interpreted, beliefs about the world are created and integrated, and behavior is structured and controlled.

Our conception of cognitive processes draws heavily on Kelly's (1955) theory of personal constructs. Kelly argues that persons give structure and meaning to the world through grouping events on the basis of their similarities and differences. Constructs (e.g., friendly-unfriendly, tall-short, etc.) are the contrasts that persons use to group events. Our conception of the nature and organization of systems of constructs is essentially consistent with Kelly's original formulation. Because constructs provide the basic ways of discriminating among events, we see constructs as the most basic units of cognitive organization.

But the most general units of cognitive organization are what we call "interpretive schemes." By interpretive scheme, we refer to any classification device persons use to make sense of their world. We recognize that persons employ a variety of interpretive schemes and systems that are not best described as "constructs" per se. For example, persons use balance schemes (Heider, 1958), causal schemes (e.g., Kelley, 1971), and linear ordering schemes (e.g., De Soto & Albrecht, 1968) to give order and meaning to events; and fundamental beliefs about social relations like Cicourel's (1974) "interpretive practices" or Grice's (1975) "conversational maxims" are central to the interpretation of speech and behavior. None of these important interpretive devices is easily seen as a construct (though it might be argued that they are all in some sense derived from constructs). Hence, while we see constructs as basic to the interpretation of experience, we recognize that a variety of schemes and beliefs serve the process of interpretation.

Although we define interpretive scheme as a classification device, by classification we mean something more than simply categorization. Classification of an object, persons, or event involves not only identification or recognition of same but also placement of the object, person, or event in relation to kindred objects, persons, and events. Hence, every interpretive scheme simultaneously serves the functions of identification and placement. To take an object to *be* something is to simultaneously place it in regard to its routine functions, its routine occurrence, its expected operation or behavior, and its routine surroundings. Sacks (1972) has offered an illuminating example of the operation of a particular type of interpretive scheme in his analysis of the "membership categorization device." Sacks offers, by way of illustration, these two sentences: "The baby cried. The mommy picked it up." These two sentences are heard as a coherent story, in which "it" in the second sentence is taken to refer to the baby in the first sentence. The ability to hear these two sentences as a story arises from the operation of the membership categorization device in which one sense of the term *baby* participates. If "baby" is heard as "infant human," its routine surroundings include mothers, fathers, and other family members; its routine behaviors include crying; and the routine behaviors of mothers in relation to crying babies includes picking the babies up. The membership categorization device assures that a connection will be made between "baby" and "mommy," and further supplies the background understandings that transform these two sentences into a story about a routinely occurring event involving categories of persons classified by this device. Thus, an interpretive scheme does not simply categorize events; an interpretive scheme, in its very application, places and organizes events within a larger context of meaning and expectation.

Our conception of interpretive schemes and processes reflects a structural-developmental orientation. In our view, the cognitive system develops in accord with Werner's (1957, p. 126) Orthogenetic Principle: "Wherever development occurs it proceeds from a state of relative globality and lack of differentiation to a state of increasing differentiation, articulation, and hierarchic integration." This principle suggests that through development, cognitive systems become more complex, more organized, and more abstract. In various subsystems, these general developmental axes may be reflected in more specific kinds of developmental change. Thus, for example, in the interpersonal construct subsystem (for construing other persons), increasing abstractness is reflected in the shift from concrete behavioral constructs toward psychological and motivational constructs; increasing abstractness and differentiation are reflected in a movement away from global evaluation and its domination in judgment; increasing abstractness and integration are reflected in the increasing comprehensiveness of constructs.

General and domain-specific developmental axes describe the structure and quality of interpretive processes; and in our view, the structure and quality of interpretive processes are as important as specific content in directing and organizing behavior. Thus, for example, differentiation in a construct subsystem (a structural feature of the system) is important regardless of the specific constructs employed; the comprehensiveness of constructs (a qualitative feature) is important quite apart from the specific range of situations to which those constructs apply.

We do not mean to argue that the specific content of the constructs or other interpretive schemes employed by a person is unimportant. While many aspects of communication are more closely related to structural- and qualitative-developmental features of cognitive processes than to any specific content, the reasons that a person comes to some particular interpretation or makes some particular choice ultimate depend on the particular constructs employed.

Nor do we mean to suggest that structure, quality, and content are independent in any strict sense. After all, a construct that is relatively abstract must necessarily involve a different substantive contrast than a construct that is relatively concrete. Indeed, developmental change, in transforming cognitive processes, induces *both* structural and substantive alterations in ways of interpreting the world. Our own research reflects this recognition of the interrelation of structural and substantive features. For example, Delia and B. O'Keefe (1976) reported that differentiation in the interpersonal construct system (a

structural-developmental feature) is negatively related to Machiavel-
lianism (an aspect of the content of an individual's interpersonal
orientation).

Finally, it should be emphasized that we find *systematic* (as
against particular or idiosyncratic) differences in the content of constructs to be as important as structural and qualitative developmental
differences. Such systematic individual differences in construct content,
while not tied to developmental differences in cognitive systems, are
nevertheless important to communication. Burleson (1978), for example, investigated differences in interpersonal behavior as a function
of differences in the content of construct systems—in this case, the
degree to which constructs are "relationally oriented."

Thus, our view of persons as biological entities who organize their
experience and guide their activity through cognitive organization
leads us to see interpretive processes in structural and developmental
terms. And because our view of interpretive processes is structural
and developmental, we do not seek to explain why any particular
person applied any particular construct in any particular situation or
engaged in any particular act; rather, we hope to explain the ways in
which social and situational factors and processes of development shape
the cognitive processes of the individual and make possible the organization, control, and coordination of behavior.

But our conception of interpretive schemes does not originate
solely from a view of persons as biological entities who approach the
world through the cognitive organization of experience but also from
a view of persons as members of a sociocultural community. The world
into which persons are born is a world defined by ongoing cultural
processes of social organization and interpretation. Persons develop
interpretive processes through interaction in and with this social
world.

In our view, culture is an historically evolving complex of forms
or structures for representing and acting on the world, created and
used by a human community. Cultures manifest historical continuity;
they transcend the existence of any person or set of persons. Thus,
the human communities bound together by culture are continuous
through time; both culture and community are historical processes in
which forms of social organization and interpretation are maintained
and elaborated in and through processes of social life.

Because individuals are born into a human community, they enter
a world that is already defined, interpreted, organized, and meaningful. The world the individual faces is a world of preconstituted meaning, and it is to this meaningful world that the individual must
accommodate. However, the individual does not become a member of
a culture simply through coordinating personal constructs with those
of other persons. Culture is much more than commonality or shared-

ness in interpretive processes; it is the whole evolving social organization, and conception of reality, and complex of symbolic forms employed by the human group. Individuals become a part of their culture as they become members of the community, as they occupy the places prepared for them in the ongoing process of group life, as they participate in the most basic forms of social organization, and as they come to have cognitive systems in which their most fundamental forms of cognitive representation and behavioral organization are integrated with the meanings these hold for the social group.

It should be noted that in emphasizing the intrinsically social nature of human experience, we depart substantially from Kelly's views and the views of many cognitive-developmental theorists. It is our contention that in this regard, Kelly's man-as-scientist metaphor is misleading in a subtle but centrally important way. Kelly's metaphor implies that persons derive constructs experientially, through imposing patterns on undefined events. In fact, people erect interpretive systems principally through communication with and accommodation to the meaningful, pervasive, and enduring social world into which they are born.

One additional feature of our view of interpretive processes requires clarification. In arguing that persons approach the world through processes of interpretation, we in no way mean to suggest that persons are generally or necessarily conscious of these processes. Indeed, constructivist research has quite explicitly emphasized the tacit or nonconscious nature of interpretive processes (Delia & D. O'Keefe, 1977). It is our contention that persons act in a world experienced through cognitive representation, although the processes by which the world is represented and the specific beliefs that guide action are seldom objects of conscious attention and examination.

• *Human Action.* In our view, human action is guided by context-relevant intentions and beliefs produced by schemes of interpretation. Alternative lines of action are indicated by interpretive schemes; intentions are realized in choice among alternative lines of action; and lines of action are translated into actual behavior displays through the application of action schemes. The organization of behavior toward some end or purpose creates that we call a "strategy."

A strategy, then, is the way in which an actor chooses to actualize an intention in behavior. It is a method by which the actor makes a projected line of action concrete. Of course, a line of action may be associated with multiple intentions or goals, and thus may require the operation of multiple strategies or of strategies that simultaneously realize multiple goals; and the sequential unfolding of a line of action may call for multiple strategies that realize the same goal or intention.

This conception of strategy, as a method for actualizing lines of action in behavior, in no way implies that behavior is consciously strategic in the ordinary sense. Indeed, strategies (in our usage) are methods used by actors to direct their own behavior, tacitly known and tacitly employed.

Because persons' strategic choices are based on context-relevant intentions and beliefs, human action is always situated. Since actions reflect a person's beliefs about an unfolding situation, actions are characterized by emergence. Any choice of action is based on an individual's immediate beliefs, which originate in that individual's interpretation of his or her history. The act is projected into the future, since it is designed to accomplish the individual's intentions. The choice of strategy rests on the individual's predictions about the future from events in that person's own past, and the individual's strategically organized behavior serves as an implicit test of those predictions. Present action permits validation or modification of interpretive schemes; future choices will reflect the success or failure of the present choice. In this way, every act collapses past, present, and future; and thus, every act emerges from a new past into a new future.

• *Human Interaction.* The foregoing view of human action is the foundation for our view of human interaction. We see interaction as a process in which persons coordinate their respective lines of action through the application of shared schemes for the organization and interpretation of action. Persons' actions are channelized by interpretive schemes: individuals act on the basis of their conception of what a situation is, contains, and demands; that conception is created through the application of interpretive schemes; and as a result, the interpretive scheme outlines a set of alternative courses of action an individual may follow.

It is important to recognize that two rather different kinds of interpretive devices serve the process of coordination in interaction. On the one hand, persons employ very general and abstract interpretive principles that are relevant at every point in an interactional sequence. Examples of this type of interpretive principle can be found in Cicourel's (1974) discussion of assumptions that persons must make in order to connect their knowledge of social rules with what is occurring: persons assume that present ambiguities can be clarified in terms of past or future events, and so on. Another set of general abstract interpretive principles can be found in Grice's (1975) work. He argues that talk is structured around the principle "Be cooperative" and a set of corollaries derived from this cooperative principle.

On the other hand, in contrast to these general interpretive principles, are persons who employ a kind of interpretive scheme that is only relevant for making connections among particular kinds of acts.

We use the term *organizing scheme* to refer to these more particular interpretive devices for classifying and characterizing interactional sequences (see B. O'Keefe, Delia, & D. O'Keefe, in press). The term covers a variety of interactional classification devices: general plans for speech events (e.g., the typical form of a committee meeting), adjacency pairs (sequentially linked pairs of acts, e.g., question-answer), routine procedures for accomplishing particular tasks or goals (e.g., the standard procedure a family follows in getting up and dressing in the morning), general knowledge about the organization of behavior in institutional settings [e.g., as Schank and Abelson (1977) have described it, a general script that customers follow in restaurants], and so on. As with other interpretive schemes, organizing schemes are seldom employed in full awareness. But whereas some interpretive schemes may be idiosyncratic and reflect the psychology of some particular individual, organizing schemes are necessarily social. That is, organizing schemes exist to classify acts in relation to other acts, to fit together the lines of action of independent persons. Organizing schemes are essentially coordination devices that allow one person to produce acts with recognizable implications for another person's behavior and permit persons to respond coherently and appropriately to acts that have been produced.

Organizing schemes are conceptually distinguishable from the more general interpretive devices that serve the ends of interactional coordination but cannot be employed independently of those general practices. Cicourel (1974) has made this point in arguing that the kinds of assumptions he outlines make interpretation (and coordination of behavior and interpretation) possible; particular social rules (e.g., organizing schemes) supply the content of interpretation. The dependence of organizing schemes on some more general interpretive practices is exemplified in Nofsinger's (1976) analysis of indirect answers; he shows how Grice's general cooperative principle, in conjunction with a more particular understanding that questions are followed by answers, can be used to interpret indirect answers.

Organizing schemes thus supply the sequential connections among acts in a concrete interactional stream. Such schemes are used by participants both in interpreting the behavior produced by others and in structuring the type and placement of their own actions.

The fact that individuals share schemes such as these allows them to coordinate their activities. However, to say that such schemes are shared by members of a social group in no way implies that all members' processes are identical or that coordination can only be accomplished when processes are identical. Persons can coordinate their behavior even though their interpretive processes may be dissimilar in some respects; there must, however, be sufficient similarity for the purposes of a particular interaction. For example, although an adult and a very young child have (because of differences in development) qualitatively different understandings of social interaction, they can coordinate their actions for some (but obviously not all) purposes. Two persons can engage in a form of social activity, even if each is unaware of the details of the other's role or even of much beyond his or her own limited role, provided that their understandings and actions interlock within some very general shared scheme (e.g., someone goes to the post office to mail a letter, which is then picked up by an unseen postal worker).

Shared interpretive and organizing schemes thus serve as resources for the coordination of activities, although the process of coordinating action is not given in those procedures. Coordination is achieved and interaction is given structure as participants in an interaction establish, call upon, make reference to, and orient behavior to jointly constructed interpretive schemes. Organizing procedures do not follow automatically from context but must be referenced and called out within contexts. Such schemes cannot be unambiguously applied; interactants face the task of establishing what scheme is being followed as well as organizing behavior to fit shared schemes. In short, interactional structure and coordination are not achieved through the simple application of rules but are created as participants implicitly negotiate an orderly scheme for their interaction and attempt to display their adherence to that orderly scheme.

This process of creating orderly models for action is the process of creating social structure and social reality. The coordination of behavior and interpretation serves the process of creating and maintaining the social organization and view of reality within the social group. Persons choose strategies on the basis of their beliefs about the reality in which they are engaged; in coordinating behavior, they align and realign their beliefs. Interaction is thus a process of implicit negotiation in which persons forward their views of reality with each strategic choice and in which the consequences of their choices reflect on the consensus achieved with their partners. There are multiple issues in this process of negotiating a shared reality: the character of the present situation and the selves and relationships within it, as well as the background knowledge that participants bring with them to the situation.

Thus, through social interaction individuals create and extend their shared interpretations of the world and the forms of social organization in which they participate. This ongoing process of defining reality and creating social order is the life of a sociocultural community. In this way, the continuing and historically emergent processes of human group life unfold through the everyday actions and interactions of members of a human community.

• *Human Communication.* We see human communication as a process of interaction in which the communicative intentions of participants are a focus for coordination. In communication, persons express themselves and make sense of the communicative intentions of others. Their strategies are structured and their strategic choices are guided by their own communicative intentions and the communicative intentions of their partners. In communication, action is mobilized to serve the needs of expression, and interpretation is guided by recognition of the intention to express. Of course, many different specific intentions and types of intentions direct communicative choices. At base, however, we see communication as originating in the attempt to make publicly available some private state and the organization of behavior toward that end.

Thus, in the constructivist view communication is a process that is defined not by its products or goals but by its peculiar structure of reciprocal intentions. That is, communication is a relation among persons that is characterized by the intention to express, the recognition of such intentions in others, and the organization of action and interaction around the reciprocal communicative intentions of participants.

For constructivists, interpretation is not communication, although all communication is grounded in processes of interpretation. Action is not communication, although communication always involves coordinated action and reflects the processes that organize action in general. For this reason, we see communication as involving the strategic organization of behavior. And choosing among communication strategies, like any other strategic choice, depends on the intentions and context-relevant beliefs of the actor and the processes of interpretation in which intentions and beliefs originate. Likewise, interaction is not communication, although all communication is a form of interaction and thus shares the characteristics of interaction in general. Communication is a situated activity; it is a process in which persons coordinate their behavior through the application of shared interpretive schemes; it is a process of implicit negotiation in which strategic choices reflect the emerging consensus about the reality that participants share. Communication is a special kind of relationship and a special kind of interaction in which communicative intentions become a focus for the coordination of action.

An Overview of Constructivist Research

In this section, we discuss the application of our general view of communication to a particular area of research: the role of social-cognitive processes in communication. As indicated earlier, persons rely on a variety of interpretive processes in making sense of the world. They employ various cognitive subsystems in the process of interpretation. One of these subsystems is directed at making sense of other persons; it is composed of constructs whose range of convenience is the behavioral, interpersonal, and psychological characteristics of other persons. Beliefs about the enduring characteristics of others are often crucial to interpreting their behavior. Beliefs about the communication-relevant characteristics of others guide communicative choices. The interpersonal construct system is a primary source of these beliefs and thus plays a critical role in communication. A considerable proportion of constructivist research activity, therefore, has been directed at exploring the operation of the interpersonal construct system in producing organized sets of beliefs about persons and in directing communicative choices.

· *Interpersonal Constructs and Interpersonal Impressions.* Our conception of the nature and development of the interpersonal construct system and of the process of impression formation has been explicitly discussed by Crockett (1965) and Delia (1977b). These papers also serve as a foundation for the research on communicative strategies discussed below. They reflect an evolving theoretical view, so that our current thinking departs in some respects from these original formulations. More adequate, complete, and contemporary statements can be found in Crockett (1977), and Delia and B. O'Keefe (1979).

The interpersonal construct system is employed in construing persons and generates a variety of interpersonal judgments. Interpersonal constructs are employed in representing the behavior, roles, personality characteristics, habits, attitudes, values, intentions, beliefs, and emotions of others. Such judgments are involved in representing particular persons as individuals, in erecting a general act- and situation-independent understanding of other persons.

Many theorists have argued that the impression-formation process involved in elaborating such sets of beliefs is best seen as originating in implicit theories of personality employed by perceivers. Crockett (1965) has suggested that such implicit theories are best conceptualized as systems of interpersonal constructs. Impression formation is thus seen as a process in which behavior is construed as representing stable qualities of the person; inferential links between constructs produce impressions that are elaborated beyond the information available through the immediate representation of the observed behavior. Because impressions are erected through the operation of an individual's interpersonal construct system, impressions reflect the structure, quality, and content of the perceiver's system of interpersonal constructs.

Much of our research has been directed at elaborating an understanding of interpersonal interpretive processes within the framework provided by our analysis of the nature and functioning of the interpersonal construct system. Our work has addressed a number of specific topics, including the dimensions of difference in interpersonal construct systems (e.g., Crockett, 1965; H. Jackson, 1978; Kline, 1978; B. O'Keefe & Delia, 1978); developmental changes in interpersonal constructs (e.g., Delia, Burleson, & Kline, 1979, in press; Scarlett, Press, & Crockett, 1971a, b); the role of construct system development as a factor influencing the organization of naturally formed impressions (e.g., Delia, Burleson, & Kline, in press; Delia, Clark & Switzer, 1974; Press, Scarlett, & Crockett, 1973); the role of construct system development in the organization of inconsistent information about another under conditions of simultaneous and sequential receipt of the inconsistent information (e.g., Kaplan & Crockett, 1968; Klyver, Press, Crockett, 1972; Mayo & Crockett, 1964; McMahan, 1976; Nidorf & Crockett, 1965); the relationship of the level of construct system development and the organization of impressions as influenced by such factors as (a) the extent to which the information is open to multiple interpretations (Crockett, Gonyea, & Delia, 1970), (b) the presence of basic differences in values or background between the perceiver and the stimulus person (Delia, 1972; Meltzer, Crockett, & Rosenkrantz, 1966), (c) the use of varying interpretive sets by perceivers (Crockett, Mahood, & Press, 1975; Press, Crockett, & Delia, 1975), (d) the source of information about the stimulus person (Mulligan, 1979), and (e) the existence of emotional involvement with another (Rosenbach, Crockett, & Wapner, 1973); differences in the level of social perspective-taking of individuals with varying levels of interpersonal construct system development (e.g., Hale & Delia, 1976; Sypher & O'Keefe, 1980); the importance of idiosyncratic perceptual dimensions in processing information and organizing impressions (e.g., Delia, Gonyea, & Crockett, 1971; B. O'Keefe, Delia, & D. O'Keefe, 1977); the kinds of interpersonal constructs developed by individuals with varying sorts of interpersonal values and orientations (e.g., Borden, 1979; Delia, 1974; Delia & B. O'Keefe, 1976; Sypher, Nightingale, Vielhaber, & Sypher, 1981); the nature of the interpretive processes underlying the attribution of communicator credibility (Delia, 1975b, 1976a) and the perception of public figures (e.g., Applegate, 1978b; Freeman, 1976, 1980; S. Jackson, 1977; Mihevc, 1974; Swanson, in press; Swanson & Freeman, 1975); the differential reliance of individuals varying in construct-system development upon simplifying social schemas in understanding patterns of interpersonal relationships (e.g., Delia & Crockett, 1973; Press, Crockett, & Rosenkrantz, 1969); and the kinds of interpretive practices and contextual factors influencing the formation of impressions within nonintimate interpersonal relationships (e.g., Delia, 1980a; B. O'Keefe, 1978; Rubin, 1977, 1979).

• *Interpersonal Constructs and Communicative Strategies.* In addition to investigations focused directly upon interpretive processes, a number of studies undertaken within our general framework have explored the relationship between characteristics of the interpersonal construct system and strategic features of communication (see the general analyses and discussion of Applegate & Delia, 1980; Clark & Delia, 1979; Delia & B. O'Keefe, 1979; and B. O'Keefe & Delia, in press). We have focused on the role of the interpersonal construct system, as opposed to other interpretive systems, for several reasons. The nature and functioning of the interpersonal construct system is already reasonably well understood. The interpersonal construct system is used to represent persons, and such representations are relevant to a large number of interpersonal contexts; interpersonal constructs thus guide the production of many kinds of communicative strategies.

Interpersonal construct systems are the foundation upon which individuals build repertoires of strategies for adapting actions to fit persons and their psychological processes. We recognize that not all communication is carried out within a person-oriented mode; as Applegate and Delia (1980) have pointed out, some kinds of communication are carried out (quite appropriately) in ways that involve little or no recognition of the actual persons involved or of their psychological characteristics and processes. But many situations are intrinsically person-oriented: where persons want to teach or persuade some particular person or persons; where the communication focuses on the feelings and interpersonal needs or problems of interactants; where the regulation of an individual's behavior is at issue; and so on.

Persons implicitly rely on interpersonal construct systems in generating strategies for guiding actions in such situations. Interpersonal constructs allow for the representation of communication-relevant differences among listeners; because the difference can be represented, alternative strategies for dealing with represented differences can be constructed (although as was mentioned previously, such "choices" are frequently not made reflectively). Moreover, the kind of strategies generated must be related to the quality of the contrast embodied in the construct, since the nature of the construct suggests the alternative lines along which action can develop.

While the number and quality of interpersonal constructs serve as the basis for a strategic repertoire, constructs alone generally do not produce strategies. This is true for two reasons. First, strategies do not simply adapt communication. They adapt action to serve situated intentions. The conjunction of construed differences among persons and types of intentions generates a repertoire of strategies. Second, constructing a repertoire of strategies involves assessing, either behaviorally or through processes of perspective-taking, the likely response to various courses of action. Thus, the individual must represent the communication-relevant differences and work out courses of action that will work predictably. This second factor is especially important in the case of young children, since early stages in the development of interpersonal construct systems are characterized by an inability to coordinate multiple perspectives and by relatively unsophisticated modes of perspective-taking. These limitations complicate the task of constructing alternative strategies.

Research on the relation between developments in the interpersonal construct system and persuasive communication strategies supports both the general outline and many of the specific details of this analysis. In general, developmental change in the interpersonal construct system is accompanied by an increased number and increasing sophistication of arguments and appeals in persuasive messages. Both the number of interpersonal constructs (cognitive complexity) and the quality of those constructs (e.g., their abstractness or comprehensiveness) have been found to be related to the level of perspective-taking in persuasive message strategies of children and adolescents (see, e.g., Clark & Burke, 1980; Clark & Delia, 1977; Delia & Clark, 1977; Delia, Kline, & Burleson, 1979) and of adults (see, e.g. Burke, 1979; B. O'Keefe & Delia, 1979), though the particular pattern of relationships is more complicated than this brief characterization can describe (for further discussion, see Delia, Kline, & Burleson, 1979; B. O'Keefe & Delia, 1979).

Particular support for our analysis is provided by the findings of Clark and Delia (1977) in their study of children's skill at adapting persuasive appeals to different target persons. Children who failed to represent communication-relevant differences among targets failed to adapt their messages. Of the children who represented the relevant differences, only those who were relatively developmentally advanced were also able to produce different appeals for different targets. The children who represented the difference but could not translate the difference into alternative strategies frequently predicted that unadapted appeals would fail. Thus, Clark and Delia's (1977) findings indicate that the ability to represent communication-relevant differences in targets is a necessary but not sufficient condition for the adaptation of appeals; the individual must develop a repertoire of strategies as well as a system of constructs that serve the needs of person-centered communication.

These studies have focused on persuasive communication, but other investigations have revealed relationships between construct-system development and referential (e.g., Hale, 1980; Losee, 1976; Sarver, 1976), regulative (e.g., Applegate, 1978a), feeling-centered (e.g., Applegate, 1980, in press; Borden, 1979; Burleson, 1978, 1980; Delia, Burleson, & Kline, 1979), and identity-relevant (Kline, 1980; Kline & Delia, 1980) communication. Thus, across a variety of respondents (children, adolescents, and adults), research designs (cross-sectional, longitudinal, and age-homogenous), and communicative situations (persuasive, referential, regulative, and feeling-centered), this major line of research has directly supported our analysis of the role of the interpersonal construct system in guiding communicative action.

Related research has focused on the antecedents of developments in interpersonal cognitive and communicative processes (e.g., Applegate, 1978a; Applegate & Delia, 1980; Delia, Applegate, & Jones, 1980; Delia, Burleson, & Kline, 1979; Jones, Delia, & Clark, 1979a; Sarver, 1976), situational differences in the use of communicative strategies (e.g., Applegate, 1980a, 1980b; Clark, 1979b; Kline, 1980), and differences in interpersonal cognitive and communicative abilities between social groups (e.g., Applegate, 1980b; Jones, Delia, & Clark, 1979b; Nicholson, 1976). Constructivist theoretical analyses of communicative development in childhood also have been elaborated to encompass linguistic and language-acquisition processes (e.g., Delia, 1980b; B. O'Keefe, in press; also see Werner & Kaplan, 1963); a principal focus of this theoretical work has been the transition from pre-linguistic to linguistic communication (see especially Delia, 1980b), and initial empirical work has been completed on this problem within our framework (Clark, 1980).

• *Other Foci of Constructivist Research.* Although the lines of research just outlined have received detailed consideration, constructivist research, taken as a whole, incorporates a broader range of concerns. For example, research on the role of the interpersonal construct system in generating stable impressions of persons has been extended in a series of theoretical papers and empirical investigations focusing upon individual differences in the organization of beliefs by an evaluative consistency schema (e.g., H. Jackson, 1978), interpersonal cognitive developments underlying variations in certain attitude-change processes (e.g., Brady, 1979; Brady & O'Keefe, 1980; Burleson & Fennelly, in press; D. O'Keefe & Brady, 1980; Shepherd, 1980; Yeakley, 1976), and interpersonal cognitive developments underlying differences in the variability of behavioral intentions and the strength of the attitude-behavioral intentions relationship (e.g., Delia, Crockett, Press, & O'Keefe, 1975; Delia & D. O'Keefe, 1977; D. O'Keefe, 1980b; D. O'Keefe & Delia, in press; Swanson, in press).

We have also extended our framework to encompass work on the nature and organization of social interaction processes in both children and adults. In the area of communicative development, research has been conducted on the development of control over the conversational turn system and topic management procedures (Benoit, 1979; Taylor, 1977). Work has also been conducted on individual differences in the content of adult conversations (Delia, Clark, & Switzer, 1979) and on the interpretive processes involved in the interactional accomplishment of communication (Jacobs, 1977). A general framework for the analysis of conversational interaction also has been completed recently (B. O'Keefe, Delia, & O'Keefe, 1980), and research is now being undertaken on individual differences in the management of conversational resources. Work related to the constructivist analysis of social interaction, but more closely tied to the tradition of conversational analysis, has been undertaken by Jacobs and Jackson in a series of theoretical papers and empirical analyses (e.g., S. Jackson & Jacobs, 1978, 1980; Jacobs & Jackson, 1979).

This summary of constructivist research should serve to indicate that constructivism represents a general approach to communication with applicability to a wide range of specific phenomena. That is, constructivism offers a general orientation to communication processes. Rather than developing a tightly formalized theory with all concepts and relationships among concepts specified in advance, we have sought to formulate a theoretical perspective that presents a general set of orienting assumptions and concepts, such that within that framework more specific concepts and their interrelationships can be developed and investigated. Our strategy has been to develop and incorporate, in the course of treating particular domains of empirical phenomena, those concepts necessary for the satisfactory elaboration of the general perspective.

METHODOLOGICAL COMMITMENTS AND RESEARCH PRACTICES

In this section, we turn to a discussion of some of the research and methodological commitments we embrace as a consequence of our acceptance of a Weltanschauungen philosophy of science. It is important that we consider these commitments, since constructivism has sometimes been seen as a call for radical departure from most past research practices (e.g., Becker & Hewes, 1978; Liska & Cronkhite, 1977; G. Miller & Berger, 1978). However, we have never taken this to be constructivism's thrust. When our comments addressing general theoretical and methodological issues are read in the context of constructivist research, it should be evident that constructivists endorse many of the canons of traditional research practice. In unpacking some of the implications implicit in our research practices, the following discussion is organized in two sections. We first elaborate some of the implications following from our general commitment to a Weltanschauungen orientation and then present more particular implications embedded in our specific methodological choices.

General Orientation to the Research Enterprise

Before turning to the general implications we draw from a Weltanschauungen philosophy of science, we must emphasize at the outset that such a view has not been adopted arbitrarily. It reflects our reasoned judgment that the substance of any perspective is to be found as much in its concrete research as in avowed philosophical and theoretical orientations [a view expressed in Kuhn's (1970) conclusion that a theoretical perspective is defined by its exemplary research]. More generally, it reflects our analysis of the relative defensibility of alternative conceptions of the nature of persons and of the knowledge produced in all human activities, including science (see Delia, 1977b; D. O'Keefe, 1975). If some general orientation is judged to be superior to others on the basis of the best available evidence and analysis, it seems to us silly not to adopt the more defensible view as the beginning point for theory construction and the conduct of research. Of course, a Weltanschauungen philosophy of science or an interpretive philosophical anthropology offers only the most general sort of direction to communication theorists and researchers; such broad orientations do not provide specific, concrete explanations of communication phenomena. We have publicly argued for these broad orientations, however, precisely because we think those assumptions provide the most fertile (and defensible) ground for the development of more specific theories. At the same time, we have offered constructivism's substantive theory and its methods as the particular perspective we think has the greatest promise of success for illuminating human communication. Specific theoretical formulations along with methods to translate those formulations into research are demanded if our ideas are to be elaborated through contact with the empirical world. Our aim in the present section is to suggest some of the implications for research practice of a Weltanschauungen view of science, which, if adhered to, will have the effect of altering the characteristic approach to research in our field.

Research ought to be accompanied by reflective analysis of the implicit assumptions and ordering principles underlying research questions and methods. One of the themes of constructivist critiques of traditional communication research practices concerns the utility of becoming more reflective about the kinds of research questions we asked and the methods we used to answer them. We believe that some research questions are better than others and that, in general, researchers ought to be pursuing questions that reflect the core processes pointed to by coherent conceptual perspectives (see Clark, 1979a). To get away from the "manipulate-any-variable-that-might-influence-phenomenon-X" school of research requires that one begin to become more reflective about just what kinds of conceptual perspectives are carried by the questions one asks. Moreover, any question, even if directed at core conceptual issues, may reflect commitments that go unrecognized without reflective analysis. For instance, it could be argued reasonably that much of our research to date on the development of communicative skills reflects an implicit valuing of one use of communication (the strategic, instrumental use) over other potential uses (e.g., aesthetic and world-creative uses). It has only been through becoming reflective about the kinds of assumptions carried in our decision to study communication in particular ways that this commitment has become clearly recognized.

It is sometimes suggested that adoption of a reflective stance in the conduct of research runs the risk of getting the researcher into an infinite regress in searching for beginning points (e.g., Becker & Hewes, 1978). Certainly, one implication of the constructivist perspective is that there is no bedrock of certainty from which to conduct research. However, the regress need be neither infinite nor vicious. Reflection and research are ongoing activities that interpenetrate. There is an empirical world to be learned about, even though what is learned is never wholly independent of the interpretive frameworks employed. If questions, concepts, and research tools were neutral, research could proceed with no need of reflectiveness. But, as we have argued elsewhere, the best available evidence suggests that neutral beginning points are not available. Therefore, we opt for a reflective empiricism. Such an orientation calls on the researcher to become as self-aware as possible of the ordering principles embedded in his or her questions, theoretical orientations, and research tools, while recognizing the necessity for commitment to particular points of view and methods in learning anything about the empirical world.

Research ought to be conducted so as to extend the scope and precision of substantive theoretical viewpoints. Many research projects will be designed to yield information required to deal with practical problems. However, the constructivist view of science leads to the conclusion that social problems ought not to be confused with theoretical problems. This is not to detract from the importance of research addressing practical problems, but it must also be recognized that the task of the social scientist is that of providing progressively broader and more precise accounts of the social world. Understandings of particular events cannot be separated from the network of theoretical schemes giving those events meaning, and as a consequence, research needs to be directed at extending the theoretical schemes themselves.

Thus, constructivism's answer to the question, What research strategy is most likely to eventuate in the illumination of human communication? should be clear: "The researcher should embrace that theoretical view he finds best and undertake programmatic research under its aegis" (D. O'Keefe, 1975, p. 177). "The task of the individual researcher is to develop, utilize, and defend a coherent theoretical system" (Delia, 1977a, p. 61). "Only by explicitly laying out an approach to a domain of phenomena and articulating a system of concepts consistent with the assumptions of that stance can one maximally refine ideas. . . . What is required is sustained, systematic research with the same system of concepts; ideas must continually have their scope and precision challenged and elaborated" (Delia, 1977b, pp. 82, 83). And such "coherent theoretical frameworks . . . are created by the hard work of individual researchers elaborating, refining, and defending their entire programs—assumptions, concepts, methods, and all" (Delia, 1977b, p. 83). In short, "Maximally productive research involves the systematic extension, elaboration, and defense of a theoretical framework" (D. O'Keefe, 1975, p. 177).

Consider the consequences of not following this strategy. If, instead of consistently elaborating a single theoretical perspective, the researcher designs studies without regard for the theoretical and conceptual baggage implicit in the concepts and methods used; whatever "findings" that result may resist coherent explanation precisely because the research did not start from a unified set of assumptions. As Delia (1977b) has observed, "Such an approach necessarily leaves the research enterprise fragmented since different theoretic frames typically serve to generate the conceptualization and measurement of each variable, while still other considerations lead to their hypothesized interrelations" (p. 74). We are, of course, describing the research strategy called "variable analysis" (Blumer, 1969; Delia, 1975a, 1977b). Within this strategy, theoretical considerations enter only in ad hoc ways. One theory generates the first independent variable; another, the second independent variable; some other theories generate the dependent measures; and still other theories are utilized in "explaining" the results. The issue is whether this research strategy is likely to eventuate in a conceptually coherent theoretical perspective, with a unified set of assumptions, concepts, and methods, that can be applied broadly to a wide range of communication phenomena. Obviously enough, our suggestion is that it is not.

Our recommended research strategy is explicitly derived from our Weltanschauungen assumptions, and in particular from the Weltanschauungen denial of the theoretical-observational distinctions (see Delia, 1977b, pp. 68, 82–83; D. O'Keefe, 1975, pp. 177–179). If scientific knowledge is not constructed on a foundation of theory-free "facts," then scientific research cannot be seen as simply the progressive accumulation of more and more such "facts." Instead, research must be seen as inevitably based on some set of theoretical beliefs, and hence any particular research investigation should be based on an internally consistent and coherent set of beliefs (a theory, if you will). But if one genuinely wants to examine the strength of that unified set of beliefs, then it should be subjected to programmatic empirical and conceptual examination, in a systematic research effort designed to test the theory's claims, to elaborate and refine the theory, to extend the theory to new domains.

But why not simply have individual researchers make sure that, for any given research investigation, the theoretical underpinnings for that single investigation are coherent? Why suggest that the individual researcher choose *one* theoretical framework? To be sure, if a researcher employed a different (internally coherent) theory for each different research problem, this would at least represent an important step beyond the variable-analytic orientation. But our view is that only a full-fledged commitment to a particular theory is likely to produce research that shows both the limitations and the generality of a given framework. If a researcher jumps from one internally consistent set of beliefs to another when the research problem changes, then one will never be sure of the genuine limitations of any particular theory, since no effort will have been made to push a theory as far as it will go. And no very comprehensive account of communication that offers insights into a broad range of communication phenomena is likely to be obtained for exactly the same reason.

Thus, an important implication of the Weltanschauungen philosophy of science we embrace is that theoretical approaches are best compared on the basis of their fruitfulness as perspectives for illuminating communication processes. The best evidence of such illuminatory power, of course, is to be found in empirical research. This point has been made before in our suggestion that if a single theoretical view is to be shared by most researchers in communication studies,

> it must come through a social process in which broad numbers of researchers are won to a particular orientation because of its perceived fruitfulness as a way of asking and answering questions. . . . Such allegiance will come not from general meta-theoretical arguments so

much as by the development of research exemplars. . . . As theoretical positions are advanced which generate research models that can be applied broadly to a variety of questions, adherents will be won (Delia, 1977a, p. 61).

But this should not be taken as suggesting that metatheoretical discussions of alternative philosophical foundations are without value. If (as argued above) the research strategy most likely to result in theories that illuminate communication involves the systematic defense and elaboration of a particular theoretical viewpoint, then researchers will need to choose among alternative substantive theories. And one way of increasing the rationality of that initial choice is through public discussion of the coherence and defensibility of various philosophic groundings (e.g., alternative philosophical anthropologies). If one decides, as we have, that an interpretive philosophical anthropology currently offers the greatest promise for the development of substantive theory, then one's choice of substantive theoretic perspective is constrained—and constrained rationally, for that decision is made not on the basis of whim or caprice, but on the basis of public argument and analysis. But whatever particular theoretic stance the researcher ultimately adopts, that theory must be systematically challenged through empirical research, for it is in the confrontation with the empirical world that a theory's ability to illuminate communication can be most directly assessed.

Specific Implications for Research Practice

In this section, several more specific implications of our perspective for the conduct of communication research are delineated. After discussing the importance of making methodological choices appropriate to the questions being asked and the phenomena being investigated, particular attention is directed toward the implications of our perspective regarding the importance of techniques of "free-response" data collection and analysis in communication research.

Research methods should be selected or developed that are appropriate to the research question addressed and the nature of the phenomenon under investigation. Too frequently, communication researchers, like researchers in other fields, have proceeded by attempting simply to fit established methodologies to new problems with little reflection about the fit of the methods to the phenomenon being studied. Elsewhere, we have discussed the use of standard interaction analysis methods in the study of interactional organization (B. O'Keefe, Delia, & O'Keefe, 1980) and the typically unrecognized ordering assumptions rooted in traditional scaling techniques and psychometric methods (Delia, 1977b; see also Crockett, 1977) as examples of this sort of problem.

Such arguments as these are not arguments for never using standard interaction analysis methods or for never measuring anything with scales. Indeed, even the most cursory examination of constructivist research will reveal frequent use of traditional methods. We have asked subjects to answer specific questions on specific scales whenever there has been a need to secure specific information from respondents (e.g., see Delia, 1972, 1976b; Delia, Crockett, Press, & O'Keefe, 1975). In other instances, we have developed measuring instruments through the application of standard psychometric procedures (e.g., see the development of our measure of interpersonal behavioral intentions in D. O'Keefe & Delia, in press; see also D. O'Keefe, 1980b). We also have had respondents provide ratings on specified dimensions of judgment but in reference to elicited personal beliefs concerning some target figure (e.g., Delia, Crockett, Press, & O'Keefe, 1975; Delia, 1976b). Still other research has relied upon experimental manipulations within a rote-learning task (e.g., Delia & Crockett, 1973; Press, Crockett, & Rosenkrantz, 1969). In other studies, we have used standardized measuring instruments so as to establish the continuity between our own analyses and established lines of work in the literature (e.g., Delia & B. O'Keefe, 1976).

The point is this: the major dictum of constructivist methodology is not the use of a particular class of methods but the use of methods appropriate to the question and problem at hand. What we have objected to is reliance on standard psychometric measuring instruments in cases where their own ordering principles have seemed to us to distort rather than capture the processes they purported to measure.

Our search for methods fitted to research questions and problems has meant that we have had to expand the range of methodological approaches used in our own research. An early reliance on experimental manipulations has been supplemented by descriptive studies. Moreover, while we have been able to utilize role playing and detailed interviews in much of our recent research on communicative strategies, studying interaction processes has required that we employ methods of interaction analysis (e.g., Delia, Clark, & Switzer, 1979), naturalistic observation (e.g., Clark, 1980; Jacobs, 1977; Taylor, 1977), and ethnographic analysis (e.g., Applegate, 1980b). Our recent theoretical work points toward the integration of our perspective with analyses of the sociocultural schemes framing events of communication, particularly those governing the organization of interaction (see B. O'Keefe, Delia, & O'Keefe, 1980). Consequently, we are finding it necessary to elaborate frameworks for incorporating some modes of ethnographic analysis and aspects of conversation analysis within our repertoire of routinely employed methods.

Thus, our conclusion, illustrated in our research practices, is that the communication researcher should have available every possible methodological avenue, so that methods appropriate to the question and phenomenon being investigated can be employed.

Free-response data collection techniques should be a standardly employed part of the communication researcher's methodological reper-toire. Many individuals have advanced arguments in recent years for the use of procedures to secure data preserving persons' natural struc-turings of events. Indeed, many have made much more radical plead-ings in this regard than have constructivists, though this certainly has been a major thrust of our arguments. But a number of questions may be raised about such methods; in this and the next section, we wish to discuss some of these questions.

One question concerns when structure ought to be introduced into the measurement process. Constructivists recognize that any data-collection method illuminates certain processes and leaves others inac-cessible, that one cannot escape from the imposition of structure in data collection, and that (as just suggested) one may need to elicit specific information through narrowly circumscribed questions. Thus, the issue is not whether to introduce structure, but how much to intro-duce, when to introduce it in the research process, and the ends to which it is introduced.

Our primary reason for arguing for the greater use of free-response data collection techniques is our conviction that people's beliefs and behavior have their own internal structure and that our task as social scientists is to understand that structure. As we have already indicated, occasionally one may be able to posit very specific theoretically grounded questions that justify the collection of data precoded along specified dimensions. Too often, however, precoded data have been collected in an effort to do basic descriptive work or in efforts to test propositions derived from theories that have been elaborated (or, more properly, overelaborated) without adequate empirical grounding. Too little attention has been given to finding methods that facilitate an understanding of the pregiven natural structure of the social world. Such structure can be revealed only through the application of theo-retical abstractive principles, but much can be gained by applying theoretical principles to data that are collected in ways calculated to preserve that natural structure.

Of course, even if data are collected by free-response techniques, they should be specifically relevant to the research question and the goal of the investigation. Thus, the decision to use a free-response data collection technique does not mean that one will not frame the task so that the respondent focuses on things of direct concern to the researcher. Critics of such methods sometimes imply that the use of free-response data sources involves asking only the most global and diffuse questions. And although on occasion one may ask only very general questions (e.g., "Tell me everything you know, think, and feel about this person"), usually much more specific questions will be relevant to the researcher's interest. In constructivist uses of free-response techniques, we have frequently posed questions as specific as "How are two of these three people alike and at the same time different from the third?" or "Exactly what would you say to convince your mother to let you have three or four friends over for an overnight party?" Where a specific dimension of judgment is of interest, the researcher should frame questions (whether of an open or closed nature) that focus the respondent on the question of concern.

For many research questions, free-response data are essential. It is difficult to imagine how one is to understand the structure of interpersonal impressions or the organization of social interaction without relying on sources of such data. The use of open-ended data sources, however, has advantages beyond necessity. The primary advantage is that free-response modes of data collection facilitate the preservation of persons' spontaneous natural attitude orientations by allowing them to respond in their own terms to realistic tasks—and as a consequence of preserving such orientations, more valid data are obtained.

A convenient example of the potential for greater validity through the use of free-response data sources is provided by recent research on the use of persuasive strategies. In an investigation undertaken by Miller and his colleagues (G. Miller, Boster, Roloff, & Seibold, 1977), participants were given a list of preformulated strategies (see Marwell & Schmidt, 1967) and asked to rate the likelihood of their using each strategy (for a similar approach, see Hazen & Kiesler, 1975). This is an easy data-collection method that readily accommodates powerful data reduction and analysis techniques. But in studies undertaken by our own research group concerning communicative strategies, we have favored an alternative method of having participants actually produce their messages (in writing, interviews, or natural behavioral contexts). Work comparing the two methods has been undertaken by Clark (1979b) and Burke (1979). Clark (1979b) found highly interpretable situational differences in the kinds of strategies produced in spontaneously formulated messages. The situational variable of high self-interest, for example, elicited such strategies as threats and explicit statements of blame, while a high desire to be liked led participants to construct messages typically including such approaches as positive altercasting and emphasis on the sharing of responsibility (rather than blame). However, when participants in a second study were asked to select from lists of strategies reflecting those used by respondents in the first study, the situational differences disappeared. When participants selected strategies rather than producing their own, the situational variables of self-interest and desire to be liked had little effect, for in all conditions participants tended to choose relatively complex adaptational strategies. In Burke's (1979) study, participants wrote messages persuading their roommates to take part in a study and then indicated which strategies on the G. Miller, et al. (1977) list they thought they had used. Burke found little relation between the strategies actually produced and those participants thought they had used or not used. Thus, Clark's (1979b) and Burke's (1979) findings buttress our belief that "the results obtained with actual messages are more likely to reflect the way in which phenomena operate within real situations because individuals normally engage in actual message composition but seldom are asked to reflect on what the underlying structure of these strategies might be like" (Clark, 1979, p. 61).

Some commentators have impugned the elicitation of free-response verbal reports from respondents by doubting the validity of "introspective" data. For instance, in questioning our own use of such data, Becker and Hewes (1978) cited Nisbett and Wilson's (1977) conclusion that persons are unable to report accurately on their cognitive processes (e.g., whether they change attitudes because of cognitive dissonance), the implication being that constructivist methods are "introspective." But our experience and research practice lead us to agree with Nisbett and Wilson's conclusions about the utility of introspective methods. As we have stressed, free-response data collection methods need not—and indeed seldom do—call on respondents to reflect and report on their cognitive processes. Participants are not asked to respond in a theoretical or reflective mode but rather in their natural attitude orientations. They are asked, for example, to indicate what is remembered about some event or person (not whether a particular sort of reconstructive schema is used in remembering the event or person), or to write a persuasive message (not to reflect an abstract strategic principles), or to give their impressions of another person (not to indicate whether they use a principle of evaluative consistency in organizing their beliefs about that person). It remains for the *researcher* to discover the nature of the underlying processes by introducing theoretically grounded abstractive dimensions for coding the data.

But several critics of free-response verbal report data have questioned the extent to which such codings can in fact separate theoretically meaningful variables from extraneous factors such as verbosity (e.g., Becker & Hewes, 1978; A. Miller & Wilson, 1979). Naturally, given our reliance on open-ended verbal report data, we have considered this question. But we typically code for qualitative features of constructs, messages, or interaction behaviors (see, e.g., our codings of impression organization, psychological-centeredness of regulative and feeling-centered messages, level of persuasive strategy, construct abstractness, and the like). Hence, it ought not be surprising that such measurements seldom are significantly correlated with the simple length of the response from which they are derived. For example, Borden (1979) found that the psychological-centeredness of appeals in messages intended to deal with a listener's distressed feelings correlated only 0.08 with the number of words in the message. Similarly, in Applegate's (1978a) studies, codings for construct abstractness and for psychological-centeredness of messages did not correlate significantly with independent assessment of verbal intelligence (WAIS vocabulary subscale) or verbal fluency (Thorndike, 1927). The one exception to this independence of our measures of social-cognitive and communicative development from verbal abilities and intelligence occurs among very young children; however, even among children our social-cognitive and message indices are typically found to be independent of such factors past middle childhood (see, e.g., Applegate, 1978a; Biskin & Crano, 1977; Scarlett, Press, & Crockett, 1971a). We have elsewhere commented on the theoretical importance of this as an indication of the emergence of interpersonal developments that are independent of general intellectual maturation (Delia & B. O'Keefe, 1979; Scarlett, Press, & Crockett, 1971b).

Of course, our measure of cognitive complexity (Crockett, 1965), which is based on the number of constructs a person uses in written impressions of peers, appears on the surface to be much more directly tied to verbal abilities. For example, significant correlations in the range of 0.40 to 0.60 between the number of words written in the impressions in Crockett's instrument and the complexity score derived from those impressions have been reported by several investigators (Burleson, Applegate, & Neuwirth, 1981; Delia, 1978; Powers, Jordan, & Street, 1979). But since the complexity score involves counting the number of characteristics ascribed to the persons being described one would expect that those respondents who mention a larger number of characteristics would naturally use somewhat more words to do so. And when *independent* assessments of verbal fluency, verbal intelligence, writing speed, vocabulary, intellectual achievement, and intelligence have been made, nonsignificant correlations in the range of —0.20 to 0.25 with our complexity measure have been found—with, as mentioned previously, only the theoretically explicable exception in early childhood (see e.g., Burleson, Applegate, & Neuwirth, 1981; Crockett, 1965); Delia, 1978; Delia & Crockett, 1973; Hale, 1980;

Press, Crockett, & Rosenkrantz, 1969; Rosenkrantz, 1961; Scarlett, Press, & Crockett, 1971a). Thus, we have a good deal of confidence that our cognitive-complexity measure assesses something other than "verbal fluency" or "verbosity," since respondents clearly do something more than just give words when they are asked to describe a peer.

Importantly, a variety of studies within and without our research group has demonstrated the superior reliability and validity of our free-response complexity measure as compared to Bieri's (Bieri, Atkins, Briar, Leaman, Miller, & Tripod, 1966) more popular rating-based measure (see the general review of D. O'Keefe & Sypher, in press). For example, though most of the variance in Bieri's measure is allocated to the evaluative valence of the figures being described, most of the variance in our procedure is allocated to the describer (Horsfall, 1969); that is, our measure is truly a measure of individual differences, while Bieri's rating technique reflects something quite different—though what that something is, as several commentators have remarked (e.g., Fransella & Bannister, 1977, p. 62), is not clear at present. Beyond all this, there is the enormous weight of predictive validity in support of our approach to coding impressions for cognitive complexity. If one is to call the measure an index of verbosity, then it is necessary to account for how verbosity relates not only to qualitative features of messages but also to phenomena such as differences in the patterns of errors in learning the interpersonal relationships in a group (Delia & Crockett, 1973; Press, Crockett, & Rosenkrantz, 1969), differences in the variability of ratings of behavioral intentions and the strength of the attitude-behavioral intentions relationship (D. O'Keefe, 1980b; D. O'Keefe & Delia, in press), differences in the stability of evaluative ratings in the sequential formation of an impression (Klyver, Press, & Crockett, 1972), differential modes of using motivational attributions in organizing impressions under different situational sets (Press, Crockett, & Delia, 1975), and so forth.

None of this means that every free-response data source yields more valid data than do other sources; questions about the potential contaminating effects of extraneous verbal factors, for example, might be raised about any number of indices based on free-response verbal reports. But we think that our particular use of open-ended data displays the potential greater validity that such data can provide.

Finally (and briefly), there is yet another advantage beyond validity in using free-response data. Because such data can be analyzed in alternative ways, they provide the basis for discovering phenomena and regularities not initially looked for. Clark (1979b), for example, was able to identify a wide range of strategies not contained in previously existing strategy assessment instruments such as that of Marwell and Schmidt (1967). Similarly, the richness of free-response data permits alternative codings to test rival hypotheses or to compare the validity of coding systems. For a number of reasons, then, we think that free-response data collection techniques should be made a standard part of the communication researcher's methodological repertoire.

Reliance on free-response data will necessitate the development of sophistication in construction and application of theoretically based schemes for content and structural analysis. It perhaps goes without saying that if communication researchers are to make extensive use of free-response data, they will need to develop proficiency in the theoretically grounded analysis of such data. Many seem to find the call for greater reliance on open-ended data intuitively appealing, but there is a general uneasiness about what to do once they are collected. Thus, Bronfenbrenner (1977) has characterized the social scientist's plight as being stuck between a rock and a soft place: on the one hand, rigor and reliability are wanted; but on the other, relevance and validity are desired. It is not always easy to see how one can have both.

To have both will require, among other things, that investigators become proficient at developing theoretically based systems for the structural/content analysis of open-ended data. This is, of course, not something in which most communication researchers receive much training. Systematic training, however, is essential. Learning to make useful sense of uncoded data is not something that can be gained through a quick reading of a relevant review essay. For instance, important work with free-response data has been done in programs of research such as Kohlberg's (1969) on moral reasoning, Selman's (1980) on the structure of social cognition, and Harvey's (Harvey, Hunt, & Schroder, 1961) on conceptual systems organization (an excellent introduction to such methods as applied within a developmental context is Damon, 1977). But in each of these instances, and in our own constructivist research on social cognition and communication, considerable training is required in the development of the theoretical sophistication, empirical attitude, and specific capabilities necessary to handling free-response data.

Despite the difficulty of training researchers in the analysis of open-ended data, we obviously are convinced that the effort is worthwhile. Among the reasons sustaining this belief are the following. First, training in the analysis of free-response data forces the researcher to become truly empirical. There is something important that is learned by interviewing study participants, reading their written impressions and messages, or making detailed analyses of their natural interactions that is not obtained in transposing check marks into numbers. By embarking on the analysis of free-response data, researchers would be forced (even if in small ways) to begin to develop concepts that truly articulate with the empirical domain under investigation.

Second, the analysis of free-response data also forces the researcher to become more theoretical. One may, of course, take a coding scheme and apply it to free-response data without much theoretical self-awareness. However, one result of routinely using such modes of analysis should be the researcher's increasing theoretical self-awareness of the abstractive dimensions that are included in coding schemes. As we have commented elsewhere (B. O'Keefe, Delia, & O'Keefe, 1980), interaction analysts already are beginning to give more attention to the theoretical principles embedded in their coding systems. In our own studies using free-response data, we have tried to be explicit about the abstractive principle(s) underlying our coding schemes. By being led to recognize the ways a coding scheme functions as an abstractive template, researchers can, in the process of doing research, be led to a greater understanding of their theoretical commitments.

Third, development of skills in the content and structural analysis of free-response data can create the context for a truly reflective empiricism. Theory and data are brought into intimate interaction in the process of developing a scheme to analyze a certain body of uncoded data. Of course, one ought to have relatively clear theoretical principles to guide the analysis even at the outset, but theoretical constructs have to be elaborated in concrete ways to represent the character of the data. In this way, creative elaboration of the theoretical constructs is built into the research process at its very core. One is always abstracting from the data in particular ways, but the data are always richer along the dimensions of abstraction than one's initial theoretical concepts imply (or at least, we have found this to be so). The theoretical constructs thus come to be elaborated as they are embodied in the coding system in the very process of its development and application in the context of concrete empirical problems.

The foregoing obviously is premised on the assumption that the best use of free-response data involves making explicitly defined theoretical abstractive principles the basis for coding. This is not the case with all coding systems; all too frequently, researchers focus on superficial content or lexical features of free-response data. Similarly, we have argued that interaction analysis coding systems have seldom embodied clear abstractive dimensions (B. O'Keefe, Delia, & O'Keefe, 1980). Indeed, in some of our own work, we have opted for a looser approach in an effort to expand our general understanding of the content of some empirical domain (e.g., see the study of communicative strategies in Clark, 1979b; and the more general discussion of Clark & Delia, 1979). However, in most cases, we have employed rather narrowly circumscribed systems directed at specific empirical problems (the differentiation of an interpersonal impression, the organization of inconsistency in an impression, the level of perspective-taking implied in a persuasive strategy, the psychological-centeredness of communicative appeals, etc.). In most instances, the theoretical principle has been defined so that the data could be coded along the dimension. This technique of hierarchic structural and content analysis affords at least ordinal level measurement and, thereby, establishes the basis for much more theoretically decisive analysis than would otherwise be the case.

It should be noted that analytic schemes based on theoretical abstractive principles, such as those coding systems employed in our research, do not depend for their validity upon the recovery of specific intentions and beliefs. While our theory points to the determinative role of context-specific beliefs as the basis of conduct, we have recognized that the connections of such beliefs to behavior are not given in direct, one-to-one connections between specific intentions and specific actions. Rather, we have argued that context-specific beliefs are structured by general principles of cognitive and behavioral organization and are actualized through general strategies. It typically has been these general strategies and organizing principles that have been our focus. Thus, only in special cases have we sought to make an argument in terms of specific belief-action connections (e.g., Delia, Crockett, Press, & O'Keefe, 1975; or Delia & Clark, 1977), and even in these cases, the specific belief-action connections were analyzed with reference to general processes (see the discussions in D. O'Keefe, 1980b; and Delia & B. O'Keefe, 1979). Thus, despite the understanding given our work by some (e.g., Poole & Folger, 1978), our mode of analysis is no more dependent upon recovery of the specific content of intentions than is typical of most other applications of content/structural analysis of free-response and interaction data (or, for that matter, of orthodox measurement techniques). The validity of the coding lies in the predictive/explanatory utility of the theoretical abstractive principle employed.

Of course, particular problems will sometimes lead researchers to elicit more information from respondents than might otherwise be obtained. For example, in some instances, we have directly coded messages for the qualitative level of social understanding they imply (e.g., Clark & Delia, 1976; Delia, Kline, & Burleson, 1978; Ritter, 1979), but because of the limitations of such a procedure (see Clark & Delia, 1979; D. O'Keefe, 1980a), we have opted in some studies for the elicitation of participants' rationales for their behavioral choices (e.g., Applegate & Delia, 1980; B. O'Keefe & Delia, 1979); these rationales have then been coded using theoretically relevant schemes. Analogous procedures have been followed in other work. In some instances, we have asked participants to elaborate upon their meaning for the verbal label given a particular construct (e.g., Applegate, 1978a); in other studies, we have had respondents decompose their impressions or messages into personally defined individual units and have taken these participant-generated decompositions as indices of differentiation (e.g., B. O'Keefe & Delia, 1979); in still other investigations, we have asked participants to provide ratings of their own decomposed impression units along specified dimensions such as evaluation (e.g., Delia, 1976b; Delia, Crockett, Press, & O'Keefe, 1975). Such techniques are, of course, designed to secure more valid data; but, again, the proof of the validity is not to be lodged in the "accuracy" of the judgments but in the predictive/explanatory utility of the codings. To make "accuracy" the criterion would lodge the researcher both in the hopeless task of trying to understand each participant's behavior on a case-by-case basis by reference to the content of particular intentions and in an infinite methodological regress. In general, constructivists have not found questions of accuracy very useful for just these sorts of reasons (it might be noted that we have here a methodological parallel to the problem of locating theory-free foundations for knowledge).

Finally, in considering the sorts of procedures used to elicit free-response data, it should be emphasized that care needs to be taken to recognize and control for the kinds of factors known to influence the character of data obtained by whatever procedure is employed, so that the best data possible are obtained within the limits of pragmatic constraints on time, response format, and so on. For example, in collecting free-response data that consists of verbal reports from respondents, the researcher may face decisions about whether to interview or secure written reports, whether to secure only messages or also to ask for rationales for message choices, whether to collect only constructs or also to probe the meaning behind the verbal label in which the construct is expressed, and so on. In making such choices, the researcher will, of course, be guided by the nature of the research question, the canons of accepted research practice (how to control for order effects, how to minimize anxiety in an interview, etc.), and the practical limitations surrounding the occasion of the data collection. But the researcher also will have to be guided by acquired understandings of the ordering principles embedded in the various available methods. Although they are more open than orthodox data collection methods, so-called free-response techniques are not without their own ordering principles. A large part of one's research training with free-response techniques is the development of an understanding of these principles, of just what information different methods yield. Unfortunately, much of this understanding consists of what Polanyi (1958) has called tacit knowledge, for it is typically acquired implicitly in the actual practice of research with the methods. It is for this reason, more than any other, that systematic training in such methods will be needed in graduate programs if researchers are to become proficient in their use.

Communication research should routinely involve the study of the same phenomenon under diverse conditions and with methodological triangulation. We believe that the most productive research involves the use of multiple manipulations or natural instances of some phenomenon within a single study or a series of closely related studies (for a discussion of this point of view, see Clark, 1979a). Moreover, we think it important that communication researchers begin to develop sophistication in more than one research method so that the validity of obtained results can be established through methodological triangulation. The constructivist perspective rests on the realization that one's understanding of the world cannot be separated from the conceptual schemes and methodological tools used in reaching that understanding. To learn as much as possible about the empirical world, therefore, requires that researchers do everything possible to accommodate their theoretical schemes and methods in ways that will yield understanding of the natural structure of the social world. We have argued for the use of carefully formulated abstractive systems in combination with free-response data as one viable avenue to accomplishing such theoretical and methodological accommodation.

More generally, we think that studying phenomena under diverse conditions and through methodological triangulation is the best practical means of assuring accommodation to the empirical world. The utility of this approach is represented in several dissertations completed at the University of Illinois. In one, Taylor (1977) reported his investigations of the development of the ability to manage the resources of reciprocally coordinated and coherent conversations (the turn system, topical coherence, etc.) across middle and early childhood. Taylor utilized both naturalistic observation and analysis of interaction data from structured discussion tasks. He was able to identify common developmental progressions and also to show the kinds of differences influencing the exercise of control over conversational resources in different kinds of contexts. The richness of one data source was complemented by the precision of analysis afforded by the other.

In his dissertation, Applegate (1978a; see Applegate & Delia, 1980) reported five studies using diverse approaches to the study of the relationship between the abstractness of the interpersonal construct system and the use of psychologically centered communicative appeals in regulative and interpersonal contexts. His subjects included children, college students, teacher trainees, day-care teachers, and mothers of elementary-school-aged children. The social contexts in which he studied the variables of interest to him included friendship relationships, the mother-child relationship, and the teacher-student relationship. His methods encompassed paper and pencil free-response techniques, structured interviews, and three months of naturalistic observation of the day-care teachers who had participated in one of the interview studies. He found a strong link between construct system abstractness and psychological-centeredness of message appeals in each of the four paper and pencil/interview studies (and this despite variations in the social contexts studied and differences in methods). In the naturalistic observation study, Applegate found that the role-played communication behavior of the interview was highly consistent with the participants' day-to-day communication. However, the highly context-sensitive analysis afforded by the focused naturalistic observation also provided the basis for his identification of some of the ways in which contextual factors mediated the use of psychologically centered strategies.

We think all of us, constructivists included, have too infrequently studied phenomena under diverse conditions and with complementary methodologies. One can certainly reach the conclusion that this sort of approach to research is desirable without constructivism. However, any argument for such an orientation is bolstered by such tenets of constructivism as its emphasis upon theoretically based programmatic research and its call for methods permitting accommodation to the structure of the empirical domain being studied. More than anything else, constructivism encourages those interested in the empirical social world to study it by opening themselves as fully and as self-consciously as possible to understanding its pregiven structure.

References

Applegate, J. L. *Four investigations of the relationship between social cognitive development and person-centered regulative and interpersonal communication.* Unpublished doctoral dissertation, University of Illinois at Urbana-Champaign, 1978. (a)

Applegate, J. L. *The perception of newscasters from the viewer's point of view: The significance of social contexts in understanding others.* Paper presented at the Speech Communication convention, Minneapolis, 1978. (b)

Applegate, J. L. Adaptive communication in educational contexts: A study of teachers' communicative strategies. *Communication Education*, 1980, 29, 158–170 (a).

Applegate, J. L. Person- and position-centered communication in a day care center. In N. K. Denzin (Ed.), *Studies in symbolic interaction* (Vol. 3). Greenwich, Conn.: JAI Press, 1980b.

Applegate, J. L., & Delia, J. G. Person-centered speech, psychological development, and the contexts of language usage. In R. St. Clair & H. Giles (Eds.), *The social and psychological contexts of language.* Hillsdale, N.J.: Lawrence Erlbaum Associates, 1980.

Becker, S. L., & Hewes, D. E. *The potentials and limitations of constructivism for the study of communication.* Paper presented at the Speech Communication Association convention, Minneapolis, 1978.

Benoit, P. J. *A descriptive study of coherence in naturally occurring and experimentally structured conversations of preschool children.* Unpublished doctoral dissertation, Wayne State University, 1979.

Bieri, J., Atkins, A. L., Briar, S., Leaman, R. L., Miller, H., & Tripodi, T. *Clinical and social judgment.* New York: John Wiley & Sons, 1966.

Biskin, D. S., & Crano, W. Structural organization of impressions derived from inconsistent information: A developmental study. *Genetic Psychology Monographs,* 1977, *95,* 331–348.

Blumer, H. *Symbolic interactionism: Perspective and method.* Englewood Cliffs, N.J.: Prentice-Hall, 1969.

Borden, A. W. *An investigation of the relationships among indices of social cognition, motivation, and communicative performance.* Unpublished doctoral dissertation, University of Illinois at Urbana-Champaign, 1979.

Brady, R. M. *Cognitive development and evaluative consistency: A test of attitude polarization.* Unpublished doctoral dissertation, University of Michigan, 1979.

Brady, R. M., & O'Keefe, D. J. *Schema development and attitude polarization: A curvilinear finding.* Paper presented at the Speech Communication Association convention, New York, 1980.

Brockriede, W. The research process. *Western Journal of Speech Communication,* 1978, *42,* 3–11.

Bronfenbrenner, U. Toward an experimental ecology of human development. *American Psychologist,* 1977, *32,* 513–520.

Burke, J. A. *The relationship of interpersonal cognitive development to the adaptation of persuasive strategies in adults.* Paper presented at the Central States Speech Association convention, St. Louis, 1979.

Burleson, B. R. *Relationally oriented construct system content and messages directed to an affectively distressed listener: An exploratory study.* Paper presented at the Speech Communication Association convention, Minneapolis, 1978.

Burleson, B. R. *Developmental and individual differences in comfort-intended message strategies: Four empirical investigations.* Unpublished doctoral dissertation, University of Illinois at Urbana-Champaign, 1980.

Burleson, B. R., Applegate, J. L., & Neuwirth, C. M. Is cognitive complexity loquacity? A reply to Powers, Jordan, and Street. *Human Communication Research,* 1981, *7,* 212–225.

Burleson, B. R., & Fennelly, D. A. *The effects of persuasive appeal form and cognitive complexity on children's sharing behavior. Child Study Journal,* in press.

Cicourel, A. V. *Cognitive sociology.* New York: Free Press, 1974.

Clark, R. A. Suggestions for the design of empirical communication studies. *Central States Speech Journal,* 1979, *30,* 51–66. (a)

Clark, R. A. The impact of self interest and desire for liking on selection of communicative strategies. *Communication Monographs,* 1979, *46,* 257–273. (b)

Clark, R. A. Single word usage: Two stages? *Central States Speech Journal,* 1980, *31,* 75–84.

Clark, R. A., & Burke, J. A. *Developmental changes in explanations of persuasive strategy choice in kindergarteners through twelfth-graders: A research report with discussion of pedagogical implications.* Paper presented at the Speech Communication Association convention, New York, 1980.

Clark, R. A., & Delia, J. G. The development of functional persuasive skills in childhood and early adolescence. *Child Development,* 1976, *47,* 1008–1014.

Clark, R. A., & Delia, J. G. Cognitive complexity, social perspective-taking, and functional persuasive skills in second- to ninth-grade children. *Human Communication Research,* 1977, *3,* 128–134.

Clark, R. A., Delia, & J. G. Topoi and rhetorical competence. *Quarterly Journal of Speech,* 1979, *65,* 187–206.

Crockett, W. H. Cognitive complexity and impression formation. In B. A. Maher (Ed.), *Progress in experimental personality research* (Vol. 2). New York: Academic Press, 1965.

Crockett, W. H. *Impressions and attributions: Nature, organization, and implications for action.* Paper presented at the American Psychological Association convention, 1977.

Crockett, W. H., Gonyea, A. H., & Delia, J. G. Cognitive complexity and the formation of impressions from abstract qualities or from concrete behaviors. *Proceedings of the 78th Annual Convention of the American Psychological Association,* 1970, *5,* 375–376.

Crockett, W. H., Mahood, S. M., & Press, A. N. Impressions of a speaker as a function of set to understand or to evaluate, of cognitive complexity, and of prior attitudes. *Journal of Personality,* 1975, *43,* 168–178.

Damon, W. *The social world of the child.* San Francisco: Jossey-Bass, 1977.

Delia, J. G. Dialects and the effects of stereotypes on interpersonal attraction and cognitive processes in impression formation. *Quarterly Journal of Speech,* 1972, *58,* 285–297.

Delia, J. G. Attitude toward the disclosure of self-attributions and the complexity of interpersonal constructs. *Speech Monographs,* 1974, *41,* 119–126.

Delia, J. G. *Communication research and the variable-analytic tradition.* Paper presented at the Speech Communication Association convention, Houston, 1975. (a)

Delia, J. G. Regional dialect, message acceptance, and perceptions of the speaker. *Central States Speech Journal,* 1975, *26,* 188–194. (b)

Delia, J. G. A constructivist analysis of the concept of credibility. *Quarterly Journal of Speech,* 1976, *62,* 361–375. (a)

Delia, J. G. Change of meaning processes in impression formation. *Communication Monographs,* 1976, *43,* 142–157. (b)

Delia, J. G. Alternative perspectives for the study of human communication: Critique and response. *Communication Quarterly,* 1977, *25,* 46–62. (a)

Delia, J. G. Constructivism and the study of human communication. *Quarterly Journal of Speech,* 1977, *63,* 66–83. (b)

Delia, J. G. *The research and methodological commitments of a constructivist.* Paper presented at the Speech Communication Association convention, Minneapolis, 1978.

Delia, J. G. Some tentative thoughts concerning the study of interpersonal relationships and their development. *Western Journal of Speech Communication,* 1980, *44,* 97–103. (a)

Delia, J. G. *The transition from prelinguistic to linguistic communication.* Unpublished manuscript, University of Illinois at Urbana-Champaign, 1980. (b)

Delia, J. G., Applegate, J. L., & Jones, J. L. *Person-centeredness of mothers' regulative communication strategies and individual differences in children's social cognitive and communication development.* Paper presented at the Speech Communication Association convention, New York, 1980.

Delia, J. G., Burleson, B. R., & Kline, S. L. *The development of interpersonal cognition and communicative abilities: A longitudinal analysis.* Paper presented at the Central States Speech Association convention, St. Louis, 1979.

Delia, J. G., Burleson, B. R., & Kline, S. L. The organization of naturally formed impressions in childhood and adolescence. *Journal of Genetic Psychology,* in press.

Delia, J. G., & Clark, R. A. *A constructivist approach to the development of rhetorical competence.* Paper presented at the Speech Communication Association convention, Houston, 1975.

Delia, J. G., & Clark, R. A. Cognitive complexity, social perception, and the development of listener-adapted communication in six-, eight-, ten-, and twelve-year-old boys. *Communication Monographs,* 1977, *44,* 326–345.

Delia, J. G., Clark, R. A., & Switzer, D. E. Cognitive complexity and impression formation in informal social interaction. *Speech Monographs,* 1974, *41,* 299–308.

Delia, J. G., Clark, R. A., & Switzer, D. E. The content of informal conversations as a function of interactants' interpersonal cognitive complexity. *Communication Monographs,* 1979, *46,* 274–281.

Delia, J. G., & Crockett, W. H. Social schemas, cognitive complexity, and the learning of social structures. *Journal of Personality,* 1973, *41,* 413–429.

Delia, J. G., Crockett, W. H., Press, A. N., & O'Keefe, D. J. The dependency of interpersonal evaluations on context-relevant beliefs about the other. *Speech Monographs,* 1975, *42,* 10–19.

Delia, J. G., Gonyea, A. H., & Crockett, W. H. The effects of subject-generated and normative constructs upon the formation of impressions. *British Journal of Social and Clinical Psychology*, 1971, *10*, 301–305.

Delia, J. G., & Grossberg, L. Interpretation and evidence. *Western Journal of Speech Communication*, 1977, *41*, 32–42.

Delia, J. G., Kline, S. L., & Burleson, B. R. *A constructivist analysis of communicative development in childhood and adolescence.* Paper presented at the Speech Communication Association convention, Minneapolis, 1978.

Delia, J. G., Kline, S. L., & Burleson, B. R. The development of persuasive communication strategies in kindergarteners through twelfth-graders. *Communication Monographs*, 1979, *46*, 241–256.

Delia, J. G., & O'Keefe, B. J. The interpersonal constructs of Machiavellians. *British Journal of Social and Clinical Psychology*, 1976, *15*, 435–436.

Delia, J. G., & O'Keefe, B. J. Constructivism: The development of communication in children. In E. Wartella (Ed.), *Children communicating.* Beverly Hills: Sage, 1979.

Delia, J. G., & O'Keefe, D. J. The relation of theory and analysis in explanations of belief salience: Conditioning, displacement, and constructivist accounts. *Communication Monographs*, 1977, *44*, 166–169.

De Soto, C., & Albrecht, F. Cognition and social orderings. In R. P. Abelson, E. Aronson, W. J. McGuire, T. M. Newcomb, M. J. Rosenberg, & P. H. Tannenbaum (Eds.), *Theories of cognitive consistency: A sourcebook.* Chicago: Rand McNally, 1968.

Fransella, F., & Bannister, D. *A manual for repertory grid technique.* New York: Academic Press, 1977.

Freeman, D. N. *Personal construct theory, political perception, and mass communication: The judgmental dimensions employed in the evaluation of political figures based on mass media messages.* Unpublished doctoral dissertation, University of Illinois at Urban-Champaign, 1976.

Freeman, D. N. *A constructivist approach to political candidate perception.* Paper presented at the Eastern Communication Association convention, Ocean City, Md., 1980.

Grice, H. P. Logic and conversation. In P. Cole & J. L. Morgan (Eds.), *Syntax and semantics, Vol. 3: Speech acts.* New York: Academic Press, 1975.

Hale, C. L. Cognitive complexity-simplicity as a determinant of communication effectiveness. *Communication Monographs*, 1980, *47*, 304–311.

Hale, C. L., & Delia, J. G. Cognitive complexity and social perspective-taking. *Communication Monographs*, 1976, *43*, 195–203.

Hanson, N. R. *Patterns of discovery.* Cambridge: Cambridge University Press, 1958.

Harvey, O. J., Hunt, D. E., & Schroder, H. M. *Conceptual systems and personality orgainzation.* New York: John Wiley & Sons, 1961.

Hazen, M. D., & Kiesler, S. B. Communication strategies affected by audience opposition, feedback, and persuasibility. *Speech Monographs*, 1975, *42*, 56–68.

Heider, F. *The psychology of interpersonal relations.* New York: John Wiley & Sons, 1958.

Horsfall, R. B. *A comparison of two cognitive complexity measures.* Unpublished doctoral dissertation, The Johns Hopkins University, 1969.

Jackson, H. W. *Cognitive complexity and impression formation in an organizational setting.* Unpublished doctoral dissertation, University of Illinois at Urbana-Champaign, 1978.

Jackson, S. A. *A constructivist analysis of the perception of political candidates.* Paper presented at the Speech Communication Association convention, Washington, D.C., 1977.

Jackson, S. A., & Jacobs, C. S. *Adjacency pairs and the sequential description of arguments.* Paper presented at the Speech Communication Association convention, Minneapolis, 1978.

Jackson, S. A., & Jacobs, C. S. The organization of argument in conversation: Pragmatic bases for the enthymeme. *Quarterly Journal of Speech,* 1980, 66, 251–265.

Jacobs, C. S. *The practical management of conversational meanings: Notes on the dynamics of social understandings and interactional emergence.* Paper presented at the Speech Communication Association convention, Washington, D.C. 1977.

Jacobs, C. S., & Jackson, S. A. *The social production of influence.* Paper presented at the Central States Speech Association convention, St. Louis, 1979.

Jones, J. L., Delia, J. G., & Clark, R. A. *Person-centered parental communication and the development of communication in children.* Unpublished manuscript, University of Illinois at Urbana-Champaign, 1979. (a)

Jones, J. L., Delia, J. G., & Clark, R. A. *Socio-economic status and the developmental level of second- and seventh-grade children's persuasive strategies.* Unpublished manuscript, University of Illinois at Urbana-Champaign, 1979. (b)

Kaplan, B., & Crockett, W. H. Developmental analysis of modes of resolution. In R. P. Abelson, E. Aronson, W. J. McGuire, T. M. Newcomb, M. J. Rosenberg, & P. H. Tannenbaum (Eds.), *Theories of cognitive consistency: A sourcebook.* Chicago: Rand McNally, 1968.

Kelley, H. H. Causal schemata and the attribution process. In E. E. Jones, D. E. Kanouse, H. H. Kelley, R. E. Nisbett, S. Valins, & B. Weiner (Eds.), *Attribution: Perceiving the causes of behavior.* Morristown, N.J.: General Learning Press, 1971.

Kelly. G. A. *The psychology of personal constructs* (2 vols.). New York: Norton, 1955.

Kline, S. L. *The effect of construct system development upon the situational variability of construct repertory grid ratings.* Unpublished manuscript, University of Illinois at Urbana-Champaign, 1978.

Kline, S. L. *Identity management strategies in adolescents and young adults.* Paper presented at the Speech Communication Association convention, New York, 1980.

Kline, S. L., & Delia, J. G. *Construct system development and the use of face support strategies in persuasive messages.* Unpublished manuscript, University of Illinois at Urbana-Champaign, 1980.

Klyver, N., Press, A. N., & Crockett, W. H. *Cognitive complexity and the sequential integration of inconsistent information.* Paper presented at the Eastern Psychological Association convention, 1972.

Kohlberg, L. Stage and sequence: The cognitive-developmental approach to socialization. In D. Goslin (Ed.), *Handbook of socialization theory and research.* Chicago: Rand McNally, 1969.

Kuhn, T. S. *The structure of scientific revolutions* (2nd ed.). Chicago: University of Chicago Press, 1970.

Liska, J., & Cronkhite, G. Epilogue for the apologia: On the convergent validation of epistemologies. *Western Journal of Speech Communication,* 1977, *41,* 57–65.

Losee, G. D. *An investigation of selected interpersonal and communication variables in marital relationships.* Unpublished doctoral dissertation, University of Illinois at Urbana-Champaign, 1976.

Marwell, G., & Schmidt, D. R. Dimensions of compliance-gaining behavior: An empirical analysis. *Sociometry,* 1967, *30,* 350–364.

Mayo, C. W., & Crockett, W. H. Cognitive complexity and primacy-recency effects in impression formation. *Journal of Abnormal and Social Psychology,* 1964, *68,* 335–338.

McMahan, E. M. Nonverbal communication as a function of attribution in impression formation. *Communication Monographs,* 1976, *43,* 287–294.

Meltzer, B., Crockett, W. H., & Rosenkrantz, P. S. Cognitive complexity, value congruity, and the integration of potentially incompatible information in impressions of others. *Journal of Personality and Social Psychology,* 1966, *4,* 338–343.

Mihevc, N. T. *The stability of construct subsystems in the political domain.* Unpublished doctoral dissertation, University of Illinois at Urbana-Champaign, 1974.

Miller, A., & Wilson, P. Cognitive differentiation and integration: A conceptual analysis. *Genetic Psychology Monographs,* 1979, *99,* 3–40.

Miller, G. R., & Berger, C. R. On keeping the faith in matters scientific. *Western Journal of Speech Communication,* 1978, *42,* 44–57.

Miller, G., Boster, F., Roloff, M., & Seibold, D. Compliance-gaining message strategies: A typology and some findings concerning effects of situational differences. *Communication Monographs,* 1977, *44,* 37–51.

Mulligan, M. H. *Understanding the discloser.* Unpublished doctoral dissertation, University of Michigan, 1979.

Nicholson, J. L. *The development of role-taking abilities and sociolinguistic competence in three interpersonal communication domains among Caucasian, Black, and Spanish-American fourth-, fifth-, and sixth-grade children.* Unpublished doctoral dissertation, University of Illinois at Urbana-Champaign, 1976.

Nidorf, L. J., & Crockett, W. H. Cognitive complexity and the organization of impressions of others. *Journal of Social Psychology,* 1965, *66,* 165–169.

Nisbett, R. E., & Wilson, T. D. Telling more than we can know: Verbal reports on mental processes. *Psychological Review*, 1977, *84*, 231–259.

Nofsinger, R. E., Jr. On answering questions indirectly. *Human Communication Research*, 1976, *2*, 172–181.

O'Keefe, B. J. *A longitudinal analysis of impression formation in small groups.* Unpublished manuscript, Wayne State University, 1978.

O'Keefe, B. J. Language and symbol in human life. In W. D. Brooks & D. L. Swanson (Eds.), *Speech communication: Selected readings.* Dubuque, Iowa: Wm. C. Brown, in press.

O'Keefe, B. J., & Delia, J. G. Construct comprehensiveness and cognitive complexity. *Perceptual and Motor Skills*, 1978, *46*, 548–550.

O'Keefe, B. J., & Delia, J. G. Construct comprehensiveness and cognitive complexity as predictors of the number and strategic adaptation of arguments and appeals in a persuasive message. *Communication Monographs*, 1979, *46*, 231–240.

O'Keefe, B. J., & Delia, J. G. Psychological and interactional dimensions of communicative development. In H. Giles, R. St. Clair, & M. Hewstone (Eds.), *Language and the paradigms of social psychology.* Hillsdale, N.J.: Lawrence Erlbaum Associates, in press.

O'Keefe, B. J., Delia, J. G., & O'Keefe, D. J. Construct individuality, cognitive complexity, and the formation and remembering of interpersonal impressions. *Social Behavior and Personality*, 1977, *5*, 229–240.

O'Keefe, B. J., Delia, J. G., & O'Keefe, D. J. Interaction analysis and the analysis of interactional organization. In N. K. Denzin (Ed.), *Studies in symbolic interaction* (Vol. 3). Greenwich, Conn.: JAI Press, 1980.

O'Keefe, D. J. Logical empiricism and the study of human communication. *Speech Monographs*, 1975, *42*, 169–183.

O'Keefe, D. J. *Constructivist approaches to persuasion: Research strategies and methodological choices.* Paper presented at the Eastern Communication Association convention, Ocean City, Md., 1980, (a).

O'Keefe, D. J. The relationship of attitudes and behavior: A constructivist analysis. In D. P. Cushman & R. D. McPhee (Eds.), *The message-attitude-behavior relationship: Theory, methodology, and application.* New York: Academic Press, 1980b.

O'Keefe, D. J., & Brady, R. M. Cognitive complexity and the effects of thought on attitude change. *Social Behavior and Personality*, 1980, 849–856.

O'Keefe, D. J., & Delia, J. G. *Cognitive complexity and the relationship of attitudes and behavioral intentions. Communication Monographs*, in press.

O'Keefe, D. J., & Sypher, H. E. *Cognitive complexity measures and the relationship of cognitive complexity to communication: A critical review. Human Communication Research*, in press.

Polanyi, M. *Personal knowledge: Toward a post-critical philosophy.* Chicago: University of Chicago Press, 1958.

Poole, M. S., & Folger, J. P. *Overture to interaction research: A theory of validation for interaction coding schemes.* Paper presented at the Speech Communication Association convention, Minneapolis, 1978.

Powers, W. G., Jordan, W. J., & Street, R. L. Language indices in the measurement of cognitive complexity: Is complexity loquacity? *Human Communication Research,* 1979, *6,* 69–73.

Press, A. N., Crockett, W. H., & Delia, J. G. Effects of cognitive complexity and of perceiver's set upon the organization of impressions. *Journal of Personality and Social Psychology,* 1975, *32,* 865–872.

Press, A. N., Crockett, W. H., & Rosenkrantz, P. S. Cognitive complexity and the learning of balanced and unbalanced social structures. *Journal of Personality,* 1969, *37,* 541–553.

Press, A. N., Scarlett, H. H., & Crockett, W. H. *The organization of children's descriptions: A Wernerian developmental analysis.* Paper presented at the Society for Research in Child Development meeting, 1973.

Ritter, E. M. Social perspective-taking ability, cognitive complexity, and listener-adapted communication in early and late adolescence. *Communication Monographs,* 1979, *46,* 40–51.

Rosenbach, D., Crockett, W. H., & Wapner, S. Developmental level, emotional involvement, and the resolution of inconsistency in impression formation. *Developmental Psychology,* 1973, *8,* 120–130.

Rosenkrantz, P. S. *Relationship of some conditions of presentation and cognitive differentiation to impression formation.* Unpublished doctoral dissertation, Clark University, 1961.

Rubin, R. B. The role of context in information seeking and impression formation. *Communication Monographs,* 1977, *44,* 81–90.

Rubin, R. B. The effect of context on information seeking across the span of initial interactions. *Communication Quarterly,* 1979, *27,* 13–20.

Sacks, H. On the analyzability of stories by children. In J. J. Gumperz & D. Hymes (Eds.), *Directions in sociolinguistics.* New York: Holt, Rinehart and Winston, 1972.

Sarver, J. L. *An exploratory study of the antecedents of individual differences in the second- and seventh-graders' social-cognitive and communicative performance.* Unpublished doctoral dissertation, University of Illinois at Urbana-Champaign, 1976.

Scarlett, H. H., Press, A. N., & Crockett, W. H. Children's descriptions of peers: A Wernerian developmental analysis. *Child Development,* 1971, *42,* 439–453. (a)

Scarlett, H. H., Press, A. N., & Crockett, W. H. *Children's descriptions of peers: A two-year follow-up.* Paper presented at the Society for Research in Child Development meeting, 1971. (b)

Schank, R. C., & Abelson, R. P. Scripts, plans, and knowledge. In P. N. Johnson-Laird & P. C. Wason (Eds.), *Thinking: Readings in cognitive science.* Cambridge: Cambridge University Press, 1977.

Schutz, A. [*The phenomenology of the social world*] (G. Walsh & F. Lehnert, trans.). Evanston: Northwestern University Press, 1967. (Originally published, 1932).

Selman, R. L. *The growth of interpersonal understanding: Developmental and clinical analyses.* New York: Academic Press, 1980.

Shepherd, G. J. *Differential effectiveness of persuasive strategies.* Unpublished master's thesis, Pennsylvania State University at University Park, 1980.

Suppe, F. The search for philosophic understanding of scientific theories. In F. Suppe (Ed.), *The structure of scientific theories.* Urbana: University of Illinois Press, 1977.

Swanson, D. L. A constructivist approach to political communication. In D. Nimmo & K. R. Sanders (Eds.), *Handbook of political communication.* Beverly Hills: Sage, in press.

Swanson, D. L., & Freeman, D. N. Political construct subsystems as an approach to political communication: A preliminary report. *Indiana Speech Journal,* 1975, 9, 18–23.

Sypher, H. E., Nightingale, J., Vielhaber, M., & Sypher, B. D. The interpersonal constructs of Machiavellians: A reconsideration. *British Journal of Social Psychology,* 1981, 20, 155–156.

Sypher, H. E., & O'Keefe, D. J. *The comparative validity of several cognitive complexity measures as predictors of communication-relevant abilities.* Paper presented at the International Communication Association convention, Acapulco, Mexico, 1980.

Taylor, S. A. *The acquisition of the roles of conversation: A structural-developmental perspective and methodological comparison.* Unpublished doctoral dissertation, University of Illinois at Urbana-Champaign, 1977.

Thorndike, E. L. *The measurement of intelligence.* New York: Columbia University Teachers College, 1927.

Toulmin, S. *Human understanding, Vol. 1: The collective use and evolution of concepts.* Princeton: Princeton University Press, 1972.

Werner, H. The concept of development from a comparative and organismic point of view. In D. B. Harris (Ed.), *The concept of development.* Minneapolis: University of Minnesota Press, 1957.

Werner, H., & Kaplan, B. *Symbol formation.* New York: John Wiley & Sons, 1963.

Williams, R. *The long revolution.* Middlesex, Eng.: Penguin, 1965.

Yeakley, F. R. *Persuasion in religious conversion.* Unpublished doctoral dissertation, University of Illinois at Urbana-Champaign, 1976.

THE PRAGMATIC PERSPECTIVE OF HUMAN COMMUNICATION:

A View from System Theory

B. Aubrey Fisher

Several decades ago the Japanese film *Rashomon* received overwhelming recognition throughout the world. This movie became a classic and spawned several imitations, including the American film *Outrage*, which was set in the Old West. *Outrage* relates the story of a band of outlaws who rape a woman and kill her husband. The events are told from the viewpoints of the four principal characters, who render highly disparate and contradictory accounts of the facts. Many moviegoers interpreted this film to be an illustration of the unreliability of human observations. Others believed the film documented how human perception distorts reality or, at least, selects from reality those details consistent with the observer's own beliefs and salient desires. Unfortunately, both interpretations trivialize the issue raised by the movie and fundamentally miss the point.

Rather than detail the fallibility of human observation or perception, *Rashomon* illustrates the nature of reality. Relying on common sense, we typically believe that "a reality" exists, but we also believe that our perception or interpretation of reality is subject to psychological factors and may thus be flawed. The lesson of *Rashomon* rises above common sense to a much more sophisticated treatment of multiple realities, which are created, not by an act of interpretation, but by functioning in the context of subsequent events. Reality, then, is not merely a static physical entity but a functioning event within an ongoing stream of events. Paul Watzlawick, in his provocative *How Real Is Real?* made the same point when he revealed the central thesis of his book: "Communication creates what we call reality . . . the most dangerous delusion of all is that there is only one reality. What there are, in fact, are many different versions of reality, some of which are contradictory, but all of which are the results of communication and not reflections of eternal, objective truths."[1]

The issue, then, is not how we are to interpret reality but the nature of reality created when we deal with it. This book deals with the reality of human communication. Each theorist is creating a reality of human communication by approaching it from some theoretical viewpoint. Each resulting theory is less an interpretation of communication than it is a creation of communication. Unfortunately, each of us is constrained by using communication to create a reality of communication (theory of communication, if you prefer) and, therefore, this makes the issue even more complex. But no one should read any of the chapters of this book with the hope of finding *the* theory of communication, that is, the one communication theory that is intrinsically more valid or more objective or somehow more "real" (or better) than any other.

The choice of any theoretical perspective can be made only on the basis, of the criteria established within that theory, the reality created by communicating the theory. The criteria for choosing the theory are thus often part of the theory itself. Every study of communication must eventually choose some theory in order to understand (that is, create) the reality of communication, but you delude yourself if you believe that you will make that choice on some basis of reality or validity.

In this chapter, I shall present one alternative perspective of human communication—one version of reality. This chapter comprises four major sections, the first of which details the fundamental assumptions about communication that precede the theory. The second section details the major components or phenomena of the theory, along with a key outline of the metaperspective of system theory upon which the pragmatic view of human communication rests. The third section clarifies application of this theory by relating its implications to assumptions about and concepts of communication commonly employed in other theoretical viewpoints. The final section discusses the pragmatic perspective of communication with regard to research programs and methodologies currently employed by scholars using this perspective in ongoing inquiry.

PRELIMINARY ASSUMPTIONS

Prior to developing the details of the theoretical stance itself, some assumptions concerning human communication need to be explicit. Each of these assumptions suggests some nuance of the nature of human communication, but other suggestions are also present. The first assumption identifies the phenomena of communication that are to be considered central in this pragmatic perspective. The other three assumptions specify the domain of the theory to be explicated, that is, what communication comprises when viewed from this perspective.

Functional

To say communication is functional is to say that it does something. In other words, communication is active, dynamic, consequential, intrinsically meaningful. Thus, communication comprises actions—events or occurrences. As such, the "reality" of communication exists within the time dimension. Components of communication are events that function on other events, and events are related to each other in terms of time elements. Of course, even a rudimentary knowledge of physics informs us that human beings are structural elements. That is, the human being can be felt, seen, touched, and otherwise comprehended as material form or substance. But to assume that communication is functional is to deemphasize the significance of the physical existence of humans and to place principal importance on the actions performed by human beings.

To know that humans exist or have biological substance is to know nothing about communication. But to know that humans act (that is, behave or create events) is to take the first step to viewing communication in terms of functions. Certainly not all human actions are functional or communicative. But all communicative actions are functional. In other words, humans can act without communicating, but they cannot communicate without acting. The principle of behavioral pragmatics, to be discussed later, relies on this initial assumption: communication is functional.

Pervasive

All of us use the term *communication* to refer to an everyday conversation between two people. We use the same term in reference to disseminating information throughout entire societies or cultures through newspapers, television, telephones, satellites, and so on. We even think of communicating with other planets or possibly extraterrestrial beings. The fact is that the term *communication* is employed in reference to many kinds of phenomena existing at different levels of society. Even the curricula of university departments are often organized by widely differing social levels, for example, interpersonal communication, group communication, organizational communication, and mass communication. Communication can exist across cultural (intercultural communication) or national (international communication) boundaries, as well. But that distinction, too, can exist at any level in the sense that a single American may engage in conversation with a Japanese (interpersonal communication), or that the countries of the United States of America and Japan engage in diplomatic and economic relations (mass communication).

Communication is highly pervasive. The pragmatic perspective of communication, which emphasizes the functions of actional or event phenomena, is applicable and adaptable to any sociological level. My explication of it, however, will concentrate almost exclusively on the level of interpersonal/group communication. I do not intend the domain of this theoretical view to be restricted to interpersonal phenomena, however. Several factors account for my restricted discussion. First, and probably most important, my major interests involve interpersonal/group communication, and I have applied the perspective to those phenomena in which I have the most interest. Second, nearly all the theoretical and empirical effort has been directed to interpersonal/group communication. Third, interpersonal communication is by far the most common and most practical of all communication. Last, the less abstract the sociological level, the less complex the explanation of a theory, and the more readily it is understood by the student who first encounters a new theoretical perspective.

I shall, therefore, advance the pragmatic perspective of human communication in terms of interpersonal/group communication. On the other hand, nothing in the perspective would militate against its being applied to communication at any sociological level or in any setting.

Humanistic

Communication, in the minds of many, is often associated with inanimate or mechanistic objects. Berlo[2] has written of a "communication revolution" brought about by the rapidly advancing technology, generally in electronics. Through the aid of communication satellites, we can sit in our homes and watch live television programs from China,

Iran, and even the moon—in flawless color. Home video recorders are no longer rare or an exclusive privilege of the wealthy. Electronic games allow us to communicate with our television sets; some even talk back to us. Our telephone links us to any spot in the country immediately and directly. Computers, it is said, can now talk to other computers. Yet, throughout these overt evidences of the most recent technological revolution, communication itself remains basically unchanged.

We often tend to forget that television sets, computers, newspapers, and electronic games are inherently incapable of communication. Only humans communicate, and they communicate with other humans. Every now and then, of course, we gain knowledge that other species (such as porpoises, chimpanzees, bees, orangutans) may also have some capacity for communication, but we invariably employ human communication as the standard from which to judge the capacity of other beings. And humans employ a variety of media when engaged in communication. We use speech, writing, linguistic symbols, pictures, and even electronic signals. But speech is the predominant medium, and interpersonal conversation is the predominant form of human communication.

Regardless of the mode used, human communication comprises a series of events. Writing or reading a letter is an event that transpires in time. A television newscast is an event; a conversation is an event. In other words, the communicative act occurs in time. Certainly a book, letter, drama, or picture can be observed as a form of art or literature, and appreciated aesthetically. But as communication, it performs some function and is related to other events that precede, follow, or occur simultaneously with it. Moreover, the creators and observers of those events are inevitably people. Without people, the letter or television program may continue to exist as material substance (i.e., the paper, film, or videotape), but it will perform no function and will not be considered communication without people. It is in this sense that communication is ultimately humanistic.

I do not intend to imply that communication involves an assumption about some intrinsic humanism (with any of the connotations of that word) or that people possess some internal "essence" of humanness. I assume only that communication is regarded as a human activity, an activity that is not performable by machines or other inanimate objects. Whether bees, porpoises, monkeys, or any other animals are capable of communication is also not at issue. I take no position on animal communication but, rather, ignore that issue completely. My interests, and the domain of the pragmatic perspective of communication, are restricted to *human communication*. To consider the pragmatic perspective is automatically to consider human communication.

Social

The assumptions of communication discussed thus far have consistently conceptualized the phenomena of communication as events or actions performed by human beings. Some theorists, apparently influenced by the causal rationale promulgated by the physical sciences, have demanded answers to the question, Why do humans communicate? That is, what prompts a human to perfrom a communicative action in the first place? Toward the end of determining antecedents (or potential causes) for human behavior, social scientists have been enamored of a variety of intrapersonal (within the individual person) concepts. They have created and utilized concepts, such as motivation, intent, attitude, image, belief, perception, or self, in order to understand why humans behave as they do.

The pragmatic perspective of human communication, to be discussed later in greater detail, does not deny the potential existence of intrapersonal phenomena that may precede communicative action. On the other hand, this perspective does not consider them at all significant, though possibly relevant, to a full understanding and explanation of human communication. An action, once performed, has an existence and a function of its own, regardless of the motivation or intentionality that may have precipitated that action. In fact, whether an action is motivated or intended or not, it functions as an action whose meaning can be assessed only in the context of other actions (or other events). To discover that the action was unintentional is meaningless unless the "discovery" is itself an action (a communicative event) that occurs in that content. Its innate intentionality, then, is insignificant. To create the reality of intentionality (i.e., to function as an event) is communication regardless of its antecedent intentionality, which exists inside the individual and is thus lost to communication.

Why do humans communicate? Are they innately social? Is communication instinctive? Such questions are trivial. More important is the overtly obvious fact that humans do indeed communicate. The general function of all communication, then, is to relate humans with each other. You may have seen some public service television spot announcements, sponsored by the Speech Communication Association, concerning the fourth "R" of education—"relating." That fourth "R" is synonymous with communication. The goal of any theory is to understand and explain the phenomena. The phenomena of communication are actions or events. Explaining and understanding communicative events do not then necessitate, or even render desirable, seeking some primal cause for their existence. In this way, communication is social and is its own best explanation.

One word of caution is necessary before developing the perspective for communication theory/inquiry. Any theory, if it is new, contains within it a new conceptual base. It does not provide merely a new insight or set of techniques that will be used to infer back to an earlier implicit or explicit conceptual system belonging to another theoretical perspective. Scheflen makes this same point and foreshadows the pragmatic perspective of human communication:

> Behavior has come to be observed in its own right; that is, we study its structure and do not merely make references about neurophysiological or cognitive processes. . . . The operations for synthesis require that we not concentrate on the relations of a behavior to some conceptual system about behavior, but rather that we examine the relations of one behavior to another and these to a third until we have identified all of the behavioral elements that constitute a single defined system of behavior or change.[3]

System theory and the pragmatic perspective provide a new and different conceptual base for an understanding and explanation of human communication. No inferences are made or intended about another conceptual basis for communication. To think of communication as prompted by intentions, motives, cognitions, and so on, is to employ a different conceptual basis. The pragmatic perspective provides its own conceptual basis and contains no residue, even implicitly, of another independent conceptual system.

THE THEORETICAL PERSPECTIVE

Everything that follows in this section has been said before. This section, which details the elements of system theory and the pragmatic perspective of human communication, provides only a summary of those earlier discussions. For those who desire a more thorough discussion of system theory, I direct you to Buckley,[4] who provides probably the best single sourcebook on the subject but is heavy reading; Ruben and Kim,[5] although their treatment of the variety of systems applications to communication may be confusing at first; and to my own more extensive discussions.[6] The best and most informative source for the pragmatic perspective remains Watzlawick, Beavin, and Jackson's seminal volume.[7] For additional discussions centering on specific applications of the pragmatic perspective to communication inquiry, I will be so presumptuous as to cite my own previous discussions.[8]

Elements of System Theory

As everyone probably knows, system theory is not a theory, except in the loosest sense of the term. Nor do system theorists agree on all elements or interpretations of system theory. System theory is so general (i.e., abstract) as to incorporate within its principles virtually every epistemology known to science. Often the whole of system theory is confused with other models or epistemologies (e.g., cybernetics, structural-functionalism, information theory) that are related but not, strictly speaking, central to system theory. What follows is a discussion of a few central principles of system theory that serve as the metatheory and will be applied to communication in the form of the pragmatic perspective.

· *Holism and Nonsummativity.* Perhaps the simplest definition of a system is the "all" of a thing. System theory shuns explanation by reductionistic analysis and, instead, treats such analysis as only the first step in synthesis. In everyday lingo, the whole of a system is different from (typically greater than but occasionally less than) the sum of its parts. As Watzlawick, Beavin, and Jackson indicate, "A system cannot be taken for the sum of its parts; indeed formal analysis of artificially isolated segments would destroy the very object of interest."[9] That object of interest, the focus of scientific observation, is the organizing process that binds the system's components together in a holistic and interdependent relationship. The parts of the system are less important than the connectedness of the parts.

· *Openness.* A scholar new to system theory often regards a system in dichotomous terms; either the system is open, or it is closed. But openness is not a property of a system that can be either possessed or not possessed. It is a characteristic that every system has to some degree. Since communication presupposes a social system, a communication system is always open to some degree and more nearly open than closed.

The most popular definition of openness is the free exchange of energy between the system and its environment.[10] That is, to the extent that the boundaries of a system are permeable and allow the exchange of information—what energy is to a physical system, information is to a social system—that system is said to be more nearly open than closed. More specific characteristics of openness are more informative:

1. Open systems are characterized by equifinality, and thus the state of a system at any time is relatively independent of the initial arrangement of the component parts of the system.[11]

2. Open systems are not subject to the Second Law of Thermodynamics; hence, order and organization may increase in the system. The corollary is that entropy may decrease in an open system.[12]

3. Open systems are characterized by evolutionary processes leading to increased complexity.[13]

4. Open systems are capable of self-regulation and thus are capable of adapting to internal and external change. The corollary is that open systems include both positive and negative feedback processes of varying strengths.[14]

• *Hierarchical Organization.* Visualize an infinite series of concentric circles so that every circle has a smaller circle within it, ad infinitum, and every circle is circumscribed by a larger circle, ad infinitum. Each circle represents a system nested within a suprasystem with one or more subsystems nested within it. The investigator then enters the hierarchy at some point and focuses on some systemic level for observation.

Implicit in the hierarchical organization of systems are several significant correlative assumptions. First, the communication system is a social system. Therefore, its subsystems and suprasystems are also social systems. Second, the environment of a social system (e.g., the larger social system) is created by the social system on the basis of how it functions or acts toward the environing system. Weick[15] calls this phenomenon the "enacted environment." In this sense, the "boundaries" of any system are determined solely by how the system functions. Those boundaries are permeable (i.e., the system is open) on the basis of how the system functions—not on some conception of physicalistic boundaries and a physical environment or context.

The final implication, which emanates from the first two, illustrates how scientific investigation must proceed from foreknowledge of the population of systems so that subsystems serve to define the system. Koestler advocates conceptualizing the "holon" as "a system of relations which is represented on the next higher level as a unit."[16] The individual human being, therefore, is the unit in a dyad or group. The economic system (holon) is a unit in a nation-system. Moreover, the suprasystem provides the systemic context in which the significance or meaning of the observed system can be assessed.

• *Organized Complexity.* The most precise definition of complexity is its synonym: differentiation. Social systems generally—and communication systems specifically—are highly complex systems. That complexity is exhibited in several ways. First, the openness of the system renders the system less susceptible to deterministic or linear (e.g., causal) explanations. The principle of equifinality states that the same final state or outcome may result from a variety of initial states.

A second form of complexity, particularly in a communication system, stems from the concept of systemic functioning. The focus is thus on the connectedness of the system's components at any given point in time. In this way, the data are consistently defined in terms of time elements or events, called "states" of the system. Systems progress in time from one state to another in an evolutionary pattern. To compound matters further, systems typically evolve into systems of greater differentiation and growth (e.g., Darwin's evolutionary explanation of increasing differentiation in the number of biological species) and, hence, even greater complexity.

To understand the complexity of a system is to discover its organization or order. Rapoport and Horvath[17] describe this concept of "organized complexity" as a continuum bounded by the ideal states of "organized simplicity" (a totally determinate chain of events in which each event can be accurately predicted from the preceding event) and "chaotic complexity" (a totally random chain of events in which the occurrence of no event is more probable than any other). The chain of events characterized as "organized complexity," then, is a series in which sequential patterns of events can be observed and empirically determined. (For a discussion of some empirical treatments of organized complexity in communication systems, see Fisher, Glover, and Ellis.[18])

• *Self-Regulation.* One of the characteristics of systemic openness is the ability of the system to regulate itself, to have a say in determining its own outcome. Furthermore, this capacity for self-regulation is inherent within the system. As Sorokin explains, "The functions, change, and destiny of the system are determined not only and not so much by the external circumstances (except in the case of catastrophic accidents), but by the nature of the system itself and by the relationship between its parts."[19] In this way, every communication system is largely autonomous and not often subject to forces that impinge upon it or conditions in which it finds itself.

The capacity of a system to generate its own information and create its own environment allows the system to set goals, to forecast whether it will achieve those goals, to change its functional states in order to achieve present goals, or even to change the goals established previously. Because of the self-regulating characteristic of open systems, communication (in its reality as an open system) is not subject to the traditional explanatory models of science, which are based on if-then (antecedent-consequent) hypothesis-testing and prediction. To reiterate a point made previously, to adopt the system explanation of communication is to adopt its conceptual base and not to make inferences about systemic concepts from an implicit conceptual base belonging to another theory.

The Pragmatic Perspective

To Watzlawick, Beavin, Jackson, and other psychotherapists, past and present, associated with the Mental Research Institute in Palo Alto, the pragmatic perspective is known as *the interactional view*, which serves as the title of a book of readings by Watzlawick and Weakland.[20] In psychotherapy, such a term is informative in that it emphasizes the focus of therapeutic treatment on the interactions of individuals within a social system (typically the family) rather than on the psychoanalytic treatment of a pathological problem residing within an individual. To paraphrase a remark by Janet Beavin Bavelas, who could not understand why people in communication could not grasp the full implications of the interactional view, "The interactional view is not difficult to understand. Communication occurs *between* people and not *within* them. It's as simple as that."[21]

But the term *interactional view* is equivocal and probably misleading in the field of communication. This view has no roots in, nor any similarity to, symbolic interactionism. As one who believes "communication" and "interaction" are synonymous, I find the term tautological. I have opted instead to utilize the term from Watzlawick, Beavin, and Jackson's title, and shall consistently refer to the pragmatic perspective of human communication.

· *Social System.* Watzlawick, Beavin, and Jackson quote Birdwhistell's eloquent statement of viewing communication as a holistic system:

> An individual does not communicate; he engages in or becomes part of communication. He may move, or make noises . . . but he does not communicate. In a parallel fashion, he may see, he may hear, smell, taste, or feel—but he does not communicate. In other words, he does not originate communication; he participates in it. Communication as a system, then, is not to be understood on a simple model of action and reaction, however complexly stated. As a system, it is to be comprehended on the transactional level.[22]

In other words, any understanding of communication focuses on the pragmatic and highly observable connectedness between human actions belonging to the social system *as a whole*. Actions are not expressions of an individual or an originated or transmitted message; they are states or contributions to states of a system. Their relevance to other states (actions) is thus a matter of empirical revelation.

To render communication a social phenomenon is to deemphasize the significance of the intrapersonal level of communication. Watzlawick, Beavin, and Jackson define "interactional systems" as "two or more communicants in the process of or at the level of, defining the nature of their relationship." The focus of communication inquiry, then, is "the study of the observable manifestations of relationship" and not "an inferential study of the mind."[23]

· *Behaviors.* Although the human being is the component of a social system, the person is not the unit of analysis. The person can contribute only one element to any given state of the system: behaviors. As Weick insists,

> People don't have to agree on goals to act collectively. They can pursue quite different ends for quite different reasons. All they ask of one another at these initial stages is the contribution of their action. Why that person consents to make the contribution or why that contribution is needed is secondary to the fact that the contribution is made.[24]

In other words, the relationship between members of the social system is established by and through actions, by relating to the other person. And the only device one can use to relate to another is to act toward the other. Any contribution that an individual is able to make to the social system must ultimately take the form of action—behavior. By behaving, the person is relating. It is in this sense that all communication is behavior. And since behavior has no opposition (that is, one cannot avoid behaving), then the pragmatic slogan "One cannot not communicate" is axiomatic.

• *Interaction Sequences.* To reiterate, systems are characterized as a series of states or events that occur in time. To observe a system, then, is to observe longitudinally a succession of states or events. Behaviors, of course, are inherently events. The sequence of those events, if characterized by organized complexity, contains some recognizable pattern —a sequence that recurs with some probability greater than chance. To define a relationship, members of a social system act toward each other in recognizable ways so that they enact a pattern or sequence that can be said to characterize that communicative relationship.

To discover the pattern in the indefinitely long sequence is to punctuate the sequence, that is, to organize or group the states or behaviors into meaningful (and, hence, interpretable) sequences of behaviors. The most typical method of punctuating interaction sequences is to employ the rules of empirical redundancy from information theory. The sequential pattern, then, can be punctuated by grouping or organizing the continuous stream of behaviors into patterns that recur with some regularity. The greater the redundancy (up to a point), the more information or structure exists in the pattern. And to discover sequential structure is to interpret the meaning or significance of the social system.

• *Content and Relationship Dimensions.* Every communicative act or behavior embodies two elements: data or information that can be validated as being true or false, and information about how to interpret the first kind of information or how that information is to be taken. You can provide data to someone, but you cannot do so without providing it *in some way.* Your wording, emphasis, inflection, phrasing, and so on, provide clues as to how you define your relationship with the other person. Both dimensions, originally termed by Bateson[25] the *report* and *command* aspects of language, are present in every behavior, in every communicative act.

IMPLICATIONS FOR COMMUNICATION THEORY/INQUIRY

For generations our educational system has revered the importance of analytical and critical thinking. Courses in mathematics and logic have taught us to think in physicalistic, linear, and causal terms. Some have suggested that the greatest problem in utilizing system theory is the inability to think in terms of systems—holistic and nonlinear. To realize the potential for system theory and the pragmatic perspective of human communication is to modify many of the assumptions and concepts that have been ingrained in us during a lifetime of formal and informal training.

The implications of the pragmatic perspective, which are included in the following pages, are discussed in terms of how the pragmatic perspective contrasts with the theoretical assumptions or concepts of the traditional epistemologies that we tend to believe implicitly. Without modifying the thought processes about communication, no one can employ a new theory or gain any benefit from conducting inquiry within a new perspective.

Information—Not Energy

Like any other humanistic or social science, traditional communication theory has been embedded in the epistemology of our time. We have been burdened with the assumptions of the physical sciences in developing our own theory. The most burdensome legacy from physical science has been the Second Law of Thermodynamics, which stipulates the conservation and degradation of energy. Energy, according to the Second Law, exists in a finite amount in the universe and can be transformed (as when coal is burned to produce heat) but cannot be created. This law leads to theoretical models, which emphasize linear, causal, or unidirectional explanations, and, ultimately, to predictions of the future from events or conditions in the past. "If we only knew more about why people behave as they do," says the traditionalist, "we would be able to predict human behavior."

The pragmatic perspective, however, is an epistemology of a different sort. One principal modification of existing epistemologies is the substitution of information for energy as the key factor of social systems, although energy remains central to physical systems. Watzlawick says of this new epistemology,

> Rather than basing itself on the concept of energy and unidirectional causality, it is founded on the concept of *information*, that is, of order, pattern, negentropy. . . . with information being its core element, it is concerned with the processes of communication within systems in the widest sense—and therefore also with human systems, e.g., families, large organizations, and even international relations.[26]

Substituting information for energy requires considerable rethinking. We have been trained to believe that physical evidence and sensory data are the sine qua non of observation. After all, we say, seeing is believing. We can *see* coal burning and *feel* the heat generated. But information, defined as structure or pattern among events, is not material; it is not "thinglike." According to Wilden, "Nor is the unit of survival [of a system] 'in' entities—'in' the organism or 'in' the environment—the unit of survival is in their relationship, which is nowhere. It is nowhere because it is information."[27]

We have little trouble explaining behavior by some quasiphysicalistic construct (such as motivation, attitude, or cognition). We learn something and "carry it around" with us. Hence, the explanatory force resides "in" the individual and "causes" the individual person to act; it energizes the human being into action. But information is not a "place"; it is a relationship among events, a relationship that must exist because it occurs and occurs again with a specifiable and recognizable amount of redundancy. This redundancy is called a pattern— ergo, information. In this sense, the terms *information, structure, pattern,* and *redundancy* are synonymous.

"What"/"How"/"How Come" Questions— Not "Why" Questions

The small child learns early that the most significant question to be asked of anything is "Why?" Much of our day-to-day curiosity concerns the attribution of causes to phenomena we observe. Why do people watch television shows like *Three's Company, Laverne and Shirley,* or *Angie?* Why didn't more people watch *Paper Chase?* Why do people buy a certain brand of toothpaste? Why are gas prices so high, and why was gas in such short supply?

Traditional epistemologies of communication have emphasized the "why" questions and clouded our thinking about communication process. Why does a person behave in a certain way? Why do some communicative relationships become friendly and others disintegrate? System theory argues that such questions are not only unanswerable for human communication, they are fruitless. In the first place, according to Milsum,

> The forces tending to initiate change are often effective in a *multiplicative* rather than an *additive* way, and thus it is often useless to seek the *primary cause* for a change. . . . This seeking for simple answers to complex questions can result, for example, in the finding of *scapegoats*. Second, once the growth has started, the self-sustaining nature of the process may render irrelevant even those initial forces which can be identified, that is to say, there is no point in trying to find and remove the match with which the fire was started.[28]

Milsum is discussing the difference between two forms of causality: linear and mutual. Linear causality is the more common notion of how certain causes (antecedents) produce certain effects (consequents). Mutual causality emanates from cyclical feedback sequences built into the system and that are activated by the system to treat change or deviation. The child's naughty behavior does not cause the parent's reprimand any more than the parent's reprimand creates (or causes) the child's behavior to be naughty. The negative feedback sequence that counteracts deviations is self-reflexive and serves to regulate the system. Positive feedback sequences (such as Milsum's fire analogy) amplify deviation in a snowball effect and render the initial cause irrelevant.

But what about human communication? After all, says the skeptic, people communicate for some reason; and if we find that reason or set of reasons, we will understand more fully the process of communication (that is, why people communicate). But can we ever know the answers to such "why" questions? Jackson doesn't think so:

> I. The same behavior in two people can spring from quite different interactional causes. Thus, according to the principle of equifinality, different causes may produce similar results; e.g., two different sets of family reactions may each produce a child who steals.
>
> II. Behavior is multi-determined. A child is exposed to a vast number of learning contexts, all of which help to mold behavior.[29]

Jackson's two points are recognizable as truisms of contemporary behavioral science. Reasons or causes for behavior are so complex (i.e., so differentiated) that searching for any generalizable list of reasons is quite fruitless. In addition, one person's reason to do behavior X is another person's reason to do behavior Y, and behavior X may be performed by different people for different reasons.

Asking "why" questions conceptualizes time in a linear and unidirectional manner. The present is seen as a result of the past, and the future is determined by the present. A system theorist views time as variable, reversible, and complex. The present is a container of the past and can be used to assess the past (postdiction) or to extend into the future (prediction) as change or nonchange. System theorists attend to the present as central to inquiry. Rather than asking why does this outcome result from communication, the system theorist wants to know what the communication process is and how it did in fact lead to that outcome.

In asking "what" and "how" questions, it is but a small step to the longitudinal questions regarding development ("how come" questions). How does a communicative relationship develop over time? How does it change over time? How does it remain stable? Explanation of communication is thus more retrospective and developmental than prospective and linear. We understand communication by knowing what it is, how it is performed or created, and how it comes about developmentally.

Group—Not Individual

Perhaps the most central element in system theory is the concept of holism, to treat a system as a whole. In no area is this deceptively simple notion more difficult to apply than in human communication. We talk about "interpersonal" and "group" communication; but we insist on treating the social system as a summative collection of individuals, or we extend individually based concepts to the social system. Moreover, we consistently seek to discover differences between individuals rather than to search for the integrative elements that characterize a unified social relationship. For some inexplicable reason, we insist on depicting a social relationship from the viewpoint of the individual member. For example, when a healthy social relationship is composed of individuals who are similar, we say, "Look how much they have in common." When a healthy relationship is characterized by individual differences, we say, "Opposites attract."

Communication, then, is viewed as a social process, not merely as a collection of individual contributions. Inquiry into human communication from a system perspective requires looking not *at* people but *between* them—not what individuals do when they communicate but what processes integrate individual actions. In other words, to repeat Birdwhistell's comment, "An individual does not communicate; he engages in or becomes part of communication."

Often group concepts are biased toward viewing the individual rather than the group as a whole. The concept *role* is a case in point. We typically define role as what a person is or what a person does in a group setting. Such a definition is independent of the group as a system. If role is to be an important concept to a system viewpoint, then the concept must be relationally defined. A role exists *only* as a relationship between persons. Two roles together form a relationship; without the relationship neither role can be said to exist.

Ackoff and Emery provide another example of individually biased group concepts. They distinguish between "common and analogous objectives." The common objective is a group concept in the sense that "all the members of one or two competing teams have a common objective: to beat the other team." Their objective exists precisely because of their membership on the team. But "if each member of a collection of people wants a car for himself, the members have analogous objectives"[30]—an individual bias. That is, the analogous objective is a collection of individual objectives that happen coincidentally to be the same. The fact that all members of a group have the same objective is a point of similarity among individual objectives, but it is not a common objective that belongs to the members precisely because they are members of the group.

Behaviors—Not Motivations

Closely allied with the group-individual difference is the modification of the traditional epistemology to focus on behaviors as the unit of analysis and not on factors which cause behavior, factors which typically reside within the social actor. Scheflen calls this traditional view "an expression theory of communication," in which "we locate the origins of action within the participants, calling it a motive or need or drive or intent or emotion or instinct or whatever." "With such an epistemology," writes Scheflen, "we believed that the behavior of each person was an emergence of his thoughts or motives or instinct." Scheflen goes on: "In an interaction theory, we simplistically regarded one person's behavior as the cause of the other's behavior, and vice versa."[31] Both views, the expression theory and the interaction theory, are quite contrary to a systemic view. They treat behavior as individually based, either as an inference about neurophysiological/cognitive processes or as a force exerted by one individual on another.

The pragmatic perspective of human communication regards behavior as significant in and of itself. It employs no inference about behavior as a reflection/result of an individual's motives or as a physicalistic force, or anything else. In Scheflen's words, communication inquiry is concerned with "asking what behavior means rather than asking what people mean by their behavior."[32] People behave socially in an integrated, patterned, and orderly manner. That integration can be observed and explained without resorting to any extraneous inference. Furthermore, such an inference would destroy the purpose of the inquiry.

Keep in mind, however, that behavior is a group (i.e., social) phenomenon and not merely an action performed by an individual. According to Ackoff and Emery, "Most sociologists do not observe group behavior but the behavior of individuals in groups. . . . Given that one can observe the properties of a social group without observing the properties of its members, it follows that we can also observe its behavior, since behavior is simply a change of properties over time."[33]

Some naive critics have claimed that the pragmatic perspective, ostensibly because of its emphasis on behavior, is merely another form of neobehaviorism. Such an analysis completely overlooks the emphasis on the system as the source and possessor of the behavior. Each behavior—an event—is a state of the system. The goal of inquiry, then, is to discover pattern or order in the stream of behaviors we call conversation. Behaviors are ordered with other behaviors to form an identifiable pattern. Behavioristic explanations, on the other hand, refer back to some internalized phenomenon within the organism and relate the organism's behaviors to that internalized phenomenon and, indirectly, to similar behaviors performed by the same organism in the past. No conceptualization of a social system is present in any form of behaviorism. More importantly, behaviors are not regarded as behaviors in their own right but as expressions of some cognitive/experiential process, the mediation of the organism between past and present.

To regard behaviors and integrated patterns of behaviors as the "all" of a social system is to render communication as being less "real" than we are accustomed to thinking of it. Gone are the physicalistic connections between people (e.g., channels, transmissions, receptions); gone are the physicalistic connections between people and their behaviors (e.g., motivations, cognitions, attitudes, perceptions, values, beliefs). The result is that communication is less "real," at least in the physical sense of reality. Communication as patterned behaviors (events) exists only in time. It is fleeting, transient, ephemeral, no longer "thinglike," but no less real—only less traditional.

Evolutionary Change—Not Structures

In open system theory, the concept of change is axiomatic. Nothing is more constant than change itself. An open system never *is* but is always *becoming*. Given the previous discussion concerning the nonphysical reality of communication with its emphasis on events or behaviors, one should not be surprised that semipermanent systemic structures are less vital to an explanation of human communication than the ongoing sequence itself, that is, the process.

Earlier discussions have alluded to the developmental notion of systemic functioning—evolution. Communication systems, because they exist over time, are constantly evolving. Relationships become defined, redefined, and redefined again in an evolutionary and, perhaps, cyclical pattern. Nothing remains constant, not even time. The result is an emphasis on evolution and change with a corresponding deemphasis on structures (stable points of reference, such as social norms, social institutions, social status). Jantsch notes that "an evolutionary perspective emphasizes *process* over structure. . . . It goes even further—it is interested in the *order* [i.e., pattern] *of process.* Structure then is an incidental product of interacting processes, no more solid than the grin of the Cheshire cat."[34]

At the risk of belaboring what appears to be an obvious point, I would contrast the pragmatic perspective, based on open system theory, with another systemic view of communication that places greater stress on structure. Monge's[35] discussion of system theory depicts four kinds of systems approaches to communication, but all have one thing in common: an emphasis on systemic structures. The pragmatic perspective does not exclude structural characteristics of human communication; it only considers structure to be incidental to the primary characteristic of communication—evolutionary change.

Rules—Not Axioms

Eventually, a theory will be formalized, that is, written down or placed in some form. Only one kind of formalization has been used with any regularity in scientific theory: mathematics (typically second-order predicate calculus). The formal rigor of mathematics inherently endows the theory so normalized with a lawlike, timeless quality. Clearly, communication, with its emphasis on evolutionary change, is not susceptible to formalization in the form of such universals. Any formalization must be able to account for process, change, and the ephemeral quality of time.

The concept of *rule* is the logical candidate to serve as the form for theoretical statements of the pragmatic perspective. But we must remember that a rule is purely a form of a probabilistic statement that enables one to stipulate that people behave in a specific relationship *as a rule.* That is, the rule appears to explain the communicators' behavioral patterns, although much of their behavior may not conform to that stipulated rule. Unlike a law that stipulates a universal relationship (given specified conditions) between two or more terms, a rule implies no such relationship between the terms (in this case, behaviors). The rule stipulates only that a regularity or pattern exists as the behaviors occur but not that one behavior acts upon another.

A digression is in order, at this point, so that unnecessary confusion over the concept of *rule* can be avoided. The leading proponent of rule formalization in communication, Pearce[36] uses rules as the form for his model of communication, a model that is based on aligning individuals' goals-means relationships (specifically von Wright's[37] practical syllogism). Pearce's theory is individually based and relies on in-order-to motives as the explanatory inference for communicative behavior. His use of rules is certainly valid but is in no way related to the present discussion.

Jackson provides an excellent discussion of rules within the pragmatic perspective. He writes, "*the family is a rule-governed system:* that its members behave among themselves in an organized, repetitive manner and that this patterning of behaviors can be abstracted as a governing principle of family life."[38] Jackson considers a rule to be an ordered sequence of behaviors, a communicative pattern, a "redundancy in relationships." But remember that a rule is a probabilistic sequence and functions as a defining characteristic and not as a law that governs how people behave. Jackson continues:

> Although the family-as-a-unit indulges in uncountable numbers of different specific behaviors, the whole system can be run by a relatively small set of rules governing relationships. If one can reliably infer the general rules from which a family operates, then all its complex behavior may turn out to be not only patterned but also understandable— and, as a result, perhaps predictable.[39]

Consistent with the notion that reality is created and not discovered, Jackson unequivocally describes the nature of what a rule means within the pragmatic perspective (or, for that matter, within any scientific theory):

> We cannot emphasize the rule is an inference, an abstraction—more precisely, a *metaphor* coined by the observer to cover the redundancy he observes. We say a rule is a "format of regularity imposed upon a complicated process by the investigator," thereby preserving the distinction between theoretical term and object of Nature which is also maintained by many of our more sophisticated colleagues in the natural sciences. A rule is, but for our paucity of expression, a formula for a relationship. . . .[40]

Jackson's study[41] of rules in families resulted in the discovery of the "quid pro quo"—literally, something for something. This rule could easily be expanded to include all ongoing communicative relationships. Each member in a social group contributes (i.e., behaves) something to the relationship and, in turn, receives something from another (the relationship). The focus of inquiry into rule-governed communicative relationships would thus be to discover the "something" that each communicator contributes and receives from the relationship (the "what" question) and to observe how that quid pro quo rule evolved over time (the "how come" question). Under any circumstances, according to Jackson, to observe the redundant patterns in the communicational sequence is to observe the rules that characterize and govern the communication system.

Meanings Interpreted—Not Assigned

Traditional approaches to the concept of meaning have long been associated with catchy slogans: "Meaning is perception" or "Words don't mean; people do." The image of meaning, then, is that of a person who carries a bundle of meanings around in the head and assigns them to phenomena encountered in the environment. Of course, the person has certain organizing rules (e.g., familiarity, past associations, experiences), which govern how meanings are to be assigned. But, basically, meaning is typically thought to be a process of individualized perception. Assigning a meaning to an object is thus a guiding force in determining how to act (or respond) to environmetnal stimuli.

This traditional view of meaning becomes problematic when dealing with a social system. In order to understand how two individuals may behave idiosyncratically (have different meanings), as is typical early in a relationship, but converge on common meanings in a developmental pattern, traditionalists begin to rationalize. Idiosyncratically assigned meanings somehow coincide because of the common experience of social interaction. When common meanings evolve into idiosyncratic meanings in a deteriorating relationship, traditional rationalizing becomes even more problematic. In short, the traditional view of meaning, as perceived and assigned, is quite adequate when dealing with individuals. But it is less likely to account for meaning that is social, that is, the product of a relationship, social system, or social interaction.

When attention is shifted from the person to the behaviors, the concept of meaning also shifts. Meaning, rather than being assigned and governing behavior, becomes a process of interpretation that occurs *after* the behaviors are performed. Weick explains, "Behaviors will become meaningful and attain closure when viewed retrospectively. An actor's [social life] consists of the things that are done [in the relationship] and that are reconstructed into a meaningful life. . . . The meaning of the [relationship] and of the actor's participation in it are defined solely in terms of what is done there."[42] Meaning is thus enacted, that is, comes about through punctuating sequences of actions or social interaction. But punctuating is possible only after actions have been performed. Thus, the meaning of an action is retrospectively determined. Whatever prompted or motivated the action initially is not relevant to the meaning of that action until and unless it is confirmed by subsequent actions and only after the action has been performed.

Weick also provides an example of restrospective sense-making. His example, a typical conversation, should be a familiar experience:

> You start to interact with someone, get partway through the discussion, have no idea what you're talking about, but you keep talking. One reason you keep talking is because the eventual outcome, whatever it may be, may tell you what you have been talking about all along and, by implication, what the specific puzzling talk of this very moment is "about." . . .
>
> Thus in the case of a conversation that contains abundant enactment which cannot be punctuated, more enactment is accumulated so that the odds increase that something punctuable can be found.[43]

Meaning is thus to be found in the behaviors, specifically in the sequence of behavior. And the meaning of an event (of course, every behavior is an event) can be interpreted only after the event has transpired. Even then, the meaning is interpretable only when the event is placed in the context of other events. It was not possible to interpret the meaning of the Iranian occupation of the American embassy and the holding of hostages at the time those events were taking place. One could speculate the meaning only by predicting future events (for example, World War III, increased U.S. nationalism, shift toward U.S. isolationism). But these speculations were based on future tense thinking. The meaning of an event is only adequately interpretable after it and subsequent events have occurred—in other words, retrospectively. Meanings of objects may be assigned, but meanings of events are only retrospectively interpreted.

When the focus of communication shifts from the person to behaviors, from structures to functions, then the focus of the concept of meaning shifts. Scheflen specified this shift when he advocated "asking what behavior means rather than asking what people mean by their behavior."[44] People can assign meaning for themselves, individually; but the meaning of events can only be interpreted in the context of other events after they have transpired. Meaning is thus retrospective (interpreted) in the pragmatic perspective of human communication and not prospective (assigned) as in other theoretical perspectives.

RESEARCH PROGRAMS AND METHODOLOGIES

Haley has enumerated "three factors necessary in any scientific endeavor: (1) we must have a collection of facts—observable events which either occur or do not occur, (2) we must be able to formulate those facts into patterned regularities, and (3) we must devise theories to account for those regularities."[45] During the past decade communication scholars, guided by a pragmatic perspective, have accumulated an increasing number of facts. Those empirical facts, however, emanate from disparate research programs, each of which appears to possess an idiosyncratic purpose and method. Accumulating those facts into "patterned regularities" is difficult, at best, in light of the diversity of research programs. But such accumulation is essential before we can flesh out the skeletal framework of the theoretical stance outlined in this chapter.

One such attempt to formalize some regularities in pragmatic research has been attempted. Stech[46] enumerated 4 rules, 8 propositions, and 14 hypotheses based on empirical studies in sequential conversation. Although potentially provocative, Stech's effort underscores the frustration of prematurely seeking patterned regularities within the many different research programs currently underway. More empirical facts need to be accumulated. More focus of research purposes needs to be implemented. More cumulative research needs to be undertaken before Haley's second factor can be used to assess the communication research in the pragmatic perspective. After all, only a decade ago none of the research programs was visible. More time for more results is necessary. This final section, then, does not attempt to formalize research findings so much as it provides the flavor of such research—where the pragmatic perspective is going in light of scholarly inquiry into human communication.

One of the currently popular research programs involves inquiry into the development of social relationships. How do strangers, during the course of communicating with one another, develop a friendship or some other variety of social system? Berger and Calabrese[47]—in the spirit if not squarely within the assumptions of the pragmatic perspective—have investigated the initial stages of human interaction. Fisher and Beach[48] have extended inquiry from initial interaction to include interactional cycles of relational development. Most studies in relational development have involved dyads or pairs of interactants observed from the state of initial acquaintance.

Much of the research into social relationships has involved the dimension of relational control, behaviors that function to exert or acquiesce to social control of the other person. These research programs have emphasized Bateson's[49] dimensions of symmetrical and complementary relationships. Rogers-Millar and Millar[50] have delved into the relational control interaction of marital pairs and have sought correlations of relational control interaction with other variables, particularly psychological variables of the interactants. Other research[51] has attempted to correlate the relational control functions of communication

with the functions of content-oriented interaction. Both research programs are involved in continuing investigations.

Groups have been a common target for investigation by pragmatic
researchers. Much of the group communication research[52] has involved
the historical tracing of how collectivities of individuals develop into
cohesive groups through patterned sequences of behaviors. Other research[53] has attempted to compare and contrast the interaction patterns of different kinds of groups. The goal of such a research program
is to identify a morphology of group types[54] on the basis of how members function with one another—their patterned sequences of communicative behaviors.

Research methods appropriate to inquiry within a pragmatic perspective are limited. The focus on behaviors rather than persons
requires that researchers observe the communicative actions—the behaviors—of the individual in an ongoing observation of the interaction.
An appropriate method, then, would be one that allows the researcher
to observe events as they transpire. Furthermore, such event-data must
be interpreted as events associated with other events. In other words,
the method used to analyze event-data must allow for the time variable
in both collecting and analyzing such data.

Probably the most popular method used by pragmatic researchers
is interaction analysis, the modification of behavioral units into functional categories. And the most common method of analyzing interactional data is that of Markov chains. Both the method of collecting data
(interaction analysis) and the method of analyzing event data (Markov chains) are hardly traditional methods in social scientific, let alone
communication, research. Communication researchers[55] are still learning how to use these methods appropriately and fruitfully, and they are
still discovering the nuances involved in applying these methods to
the phenomena of human communication.

Other methods, appropriate to pragmatic research, have yet to be
employed in any systematic research program. Such methods involve
discourse/conversation analysis[56] and speech-act analysis[57]. These
methods treat directly the self-reflexive nature of communication research, that is, using communication to observe communication. Perhaps future studies will utilize multiple methodologies in order to
provide the reflexive "flavor" of interaction in addition to the abstracted
patterns of behavioral sequences generated by functional categories.

CONCLUSION

It is a matter of indisputable fact that the field of human communication does not suffer from a lack of theory. This book is but another

indication of the theoretical diversity of communication. It is also indisputable that the domain of communication inquiry is far from unified by a single theory. I have earlier[58] made this observation, and I find this situation not only not harmful but symptomatic of a viable and healthy discipline. But knowing that theoretical views of communication abound is not to be any less confused as to which perspective is for you. Although the scientific community of communication scholars as a whole is characterized by a variety of theories, each individual member of that community must eventually embrace one of them and employ it in further study and inquiry.

Eventually and inevitably, you must choose one theoretical view for yourself. At that point, the question becomes, How do I go about this process of selection? Should you choose the theory that is most valid? most true? most real? I hope the earlier discussion of the nature of reality has convinced you that no "real" reality or essence of human communication is possible except that which is created. And we create a reality by communicating it. That is, every theory of communication is another level of communication—a metacommunication—and is itself a created reality. The pragmatic perspective of human communication is certainly no exception, nor is any other theory included in this book or elsewhere.

Is the field of communication theory, then, doomed to hopeless relativism and chaos? Not necessarily. Every communication theory, if it is to be useful and fruitful, must be rationally sound. One's choice of a theory should always be made on rational grounds; but rationality is not a criterion that obviates the choice of which theory is best. Indeed, more than one theory of communication will undoubtedly be intrinsically rational, and continuing fruitful results from research using each of those theories will provide further evidence of its rationality.

The choice among rational theories and using rational criteria will inevitably be made on the basis of personal and somewhat arbitrary reasons. And that choice will not necessarily reflect a rejection of another equally rational theory but will only express your preference and your own rational basis. Therefore, choose the theoretical stance that is for you. My only caution is that you choose rationally and not for the wrong reasons.

Notes

1. Paul Watzlawick, *How Real Is Real?* (New York: Random House, 1976), p. xi.
2. David K. Berlo, "The Context for Communication," in *Communication and Behavior,* eds. Gerhard J. Hanneman and William J. McEwen (Reading, Mass.: Addison-Wesley, 1975), pp. 3–20.

3. Albert E. Scheflen, *Communicational Structure: Analysis of a Psycho-Therapy Transaction* (Bloomington: Indiana Univ. Press, 1973), pp. 7–8.
4. Walter Buckley, ed., *Modern Systems Research for the Behavioral Scientist* (Chicago: Aldine, 1968).
5. Brent D. Ruben and John Y. Kim, eds., *General Systems Theory and Human Communication* (Rochelle Park, N.J.: Hayden, 1975).
6. See B. Aubrey Fisher, *Perspectives on Human Communication* (New York: Macmillan, 1978), esp. pp. 196–204; and B. Aubrey Fisher, "Information Systems: An Overview," in *Communication Yearbook 2*, ed. Brent D. Ruben (New Brunswick, N.J.: Transaction/I.C.A., 1978), pp. 81–108.
7. Paul Watzlawick, Janet H. Beavin, and Don D. Jackson, *Pragmatics of Human Communication* (New York: Norton, 1967).
8. B. Aubrey Fisher and Leonard C. Hawes, "An Interact System Model: Generating a Grounded Theory of Small Groups," *Quarterly Journal of Speech*, 57 (1971), 444–453; B. Aubrey Fisher, "Communication Study in System Perspective," in Ruben and Kim, pp. 191–206; Fisher, *Perspectives*, pp. 207–233; and B. Aubrey Fisher, G. Lloyd Drecksel, and Wayne S. Werbel, "Social Information Processing Analysis (SIPA): Coding Ongoing Human Communication," *Small Group Behavior*, 10 (1979), 3–22.
9. Watzlawick, Beavin, and Jackson, 1967, p. 125.
10. See, for example, Anatol Rapoport, "Foreword," in Buckley, p. xviii.
11. See, for example, Ludwig von Bertalanffy, *General System Theory* (New York: Braziller, 1968), p. 132.
12. See, for example, Bertalanffy, p. 150; and J. W. S. Pringle, "On the Parallel Between Learning and Evolution," in Buckley, p. 261.
13. See, for example, Pringle, pp. 262ff.
14. See, for example, Walter Buckley, "Society as a Complex Adaptive System," in Buckley, pp. 490–513; and Magorah Maruyama, "The Second Cybernetics: Deviation-Amplifying Mutual Causal Processes, American Scientist, 51 (1963), 164–179.
15. Karl E. Weick, "Enactment Processes in Organizations," in *New Directions in Organizational Behavior*, eds. B. Staw and G. Salancik (Chicago: St. Clair, 1977), pp. 267–300.
16. Arthur Koestler, "Beyond Atomism and Holism—The Concept of the Holon," in *Beyond Reductionism*, eds. A. Koestler and J. R. Smythies (London: Hutchison, 1969), p. 200.
17. A. Rapoport and W. J. Horvath, "Thoughts on Organization Theory," in Buckley, p. 73.
18. B. Aubrey Fisher, Thomas W. Glover, and Donald G. Ellis, "The Nature of Complex Communication Systems," *Communication Monographs*, 44 (1977), 444–453.
19. Pitirim Sorokin, "Causal-Functional and Logico-Meaningful Integration," in *System, Change, and Conflict*, eds. J. J. Demerath III and R. A. Peterson (New York: Free Press, 1967), p. 113.
20. Paul Watzlawick and John H. Weakland, eds., *The Interactional View* (New York: Norton, 1977).

21. Personal communication.
22. Watzlawick, Beavin, and Jackson, p. 70.
23. Watzlawick, Beavin, and Jackson, p. 121.
24. Karl E. Weick, *The Social Psychology of Organizing*, 2nd ed. (Reading, Mass.: Addison-Wesley, 1979), p. 91.
25. Gregory Bateson, "Culture Contact and Schismogenesis," *Man*, 35 (1935), 178–183.
26. Paul Watzlawick, "Introduction," in Watzlawick and Weakland, p. xii.
27. Anthony Wilden, *System and Structure* (London: Tavistock, 1972), p. 222.
28. J. H. Milsum, "The Hierarchical Basis for General Living Systems," in *Trends in General Systems Theory*, ed. George J. Klir (New York: Wiley-Interscience, 1972), p. 171.
29. Don D. Jackson, "The Study of the Family," in Watzlawick and Weakland, p. 3.
30. R. L. Ackoff and R. E. Emery, *On Purposeful Systems* (Chicago: Aldine-Atherton, 1972), p. 213.
31. Albert E. Scheflen, *How Behavior Means* (Garden City, N.Y.: Doubleday, 1974), p. 187.
32. Scheflen, *Means*, p. 183.
33. Ackoff and Emery, p. 211.
34. Erick Jantsch, *Design for Evolution* (New York: Braziller, 1975), p. xvii.
35. Peter R. Monge, "The Systems Perspective as a Theoretical Basis for the Study of Human Communication," *Communication Quarterly*, 25 (1977), 19–29.
36. See, for example, Donald P. Cushman and W. Barnett Pearce, "Generality and Necessity in Three Types of Human Communication Theory —Special Attention to Rules Theory," in *Communication Yearbook 1*, ed. Brent D. Ruben (New Brunswick, N.J.: Transaction/I.C.A., 1977), pp. 173–182.
37. George Henrik von Wright, *Explanation and Understanding* (Ithaca, N.Y.: Cornell University Press, 1971).
38. Jackson, p. 6.
39. Jackson, p. 11.
40. Jackson, p. 11.
41. See Don D. Jackson, "Family Rules: Marital Quid Pro Quo," *Archives of General Psychiatry*, 12 (1965), 589–594.
42. Weick, *Organizing*, p. 97.
43. Weick, *Organizing*, p. 200.
44. Scheflen, *Means*, p. 183.
45. Joseph Haley, "Toward a Theory of Pathological Systems," in Watzlawick and Weakland, p. 35.
46. Ernest L. Stech, "A Grammar of Conversation with a Quantitative Empirical Test," *Human Communication Research*, 5 (1979), 158–170.
47. Charles Berger and Richard Calabrese, "Some Explorations in Initial Interaction and Beyond: Toward a Developmental Theory of Inter-

personal Communication," *Human Communication Research,* 1 (1975), 99–112.

48. B. Aubrey Fisher and Wayne A. Beach, "Relational Development in Dyads: A Preliminary Report." A paper presented to the International Communication Association, Chicago, 1978.

49. Bateson.

50. See L. Edna Rogers-Millar and Frank E. Millar III, "Domineeringness and Dominance: A Transactional View," *Human Communication Research,* 5 (1979), 238–246; and John A. Courtright, Frank E. Millar, and L. Edna Rogers-Millar, "Domineeringness and Dominance: Replication and Expansion," *Communication Monographs,* 46 (1979), 179–192.

51. B. Aubrey Fisher and Wayne A. Beach, "Content and Relationship Dimensions of Communicative Behavior: An Exploratory Study," *Western Journal of Speech Communication,* 43 (1979), 201–211; and B. Aubrey Fisher, "Content and Relationship Dimensions of Communication in Decision-Making Groups," *Communication Quarterly* (in press).

52. See B. Aubrey Fisher, "Decision Emergence: Phases in Group Decision Making," *Speech Monographs,* 37 (1970), 136–149; Edward A. Mabrey, "Exploratory Analysis of a Developmental Model for Task-Oriented Small Groups," *Human Communication Research,* 2 (1975), 66–74; Donald G. Ellis and B. Aubrey Fisher, "Phases of Conflict in Small Group Development: A Markov Analysis," *Human Communication Research,* 1 (1975), 195–212; and Dorothy Lenk Krueger, "A Stochastic Analysis of Communication Development in Self-Analytic Groups," *Human Communication Research,* 5 (1979), 314–324.

53. Donald G. Ellis, "Relational Control in Two Group Systems," *Communication Monographs,* 46 (1979), 153–166; and B. Aubrey Fisher and Wayne S. Werbel, "T-Group and Therapy Group Communication: An Interaction Analysis of the Group Process," *Small Group Behavior,* 10 (1979), 475–500.

54. See Donald G. Ellis, Wayne S. Werbel, and B. Aubrey Fisher, "Toward a Systemic Organization of Groups," *Small Group Behavior,* 9 (1978), 451–469.

55. See, for example, Ernest L. Stech, "The Effect of Category System Design on Estimates of Sequential and Distributional Structure," *Central States Speech Journal,* 28 (1977), 64–69; Fisher, Glover, and Ellis; and Dean E. Hewes, "The Sequential Analysis of Social Interaction," *Quarterly Journal of Speech,* 65 (1979), 56–73.

56. See, for example, Elaine M. Litton-Hawes, "A Foundation for the Study of Everyday Talk," *Communication Quarterly,* 25 (1977), 2–11; and Robert E. Nofsinger, Jr., "A Peek at Conversational Analysis," *Communication Quarterly,* 25 (1977), 12–20.

57. See, for example, Robert Hopper and Michael Vickery, "How to Make a Point: A Speech Act Analysis of an Argument." A paper presented to Speech Communication Association, San Antonio, 1979.

58. Fisher, *Perspectives,* pp. 47–51 and 322–325.

ALL IS FOR ONE BUT ONE IS NOT FOR ALL:

A Conceptual Perspective of Interpersonal Communication

Gerald R. Miller
Michael J. Sunnafrank

In our class on communication theory, we both occasionally have had to distinguish between a *theory* of communication and a *theoretical perspective* for attacking a particular set of communication problems; the following article falls within the latter domain. By most of the criteria encountered in the treatments of theory construction found in the philosophy of science and communication theory literatures, the perspective presented in this chapter certainly cannot be labeled a formal, fully articulated theory but, rather, a loose conceptual or theoretical vantage point for dealing with certain issues in interpersonal communication and relational development. Whether this vantage point eventually will evolve into a formal theory remains to be seen. Even if it does not, however, we have found the perspective useful, for it provides a way of thinking about the processes of interpersonal communication and relational development that is not only conceptually comfortable for us but that also suggests priorities for a program of systematic research designed to shed more empirical light on these processes.

Specifically, this chapter synthesizes and extends a previously articulated position (e.g., Miller, 1975, 1978; Miller & Steinberg, 1975) regarding interpersonal communication, presents alternative strategies for exploring research questions implied by the position, and reports the findings of several recent studies conducted to pursue such questions. Frequently, papers setting forth a theoretical perspective proceed quite rigorously and didactically, as though by magic the theory suddenly had emerged full-blown. Since we believe one potential value of this chapter lies in providing readers with a sense of the communicative concerns and cognitive activities that gave rise to the perspective, we shall adopt a more informal, at times almost stream-of-consciousness style, to sketch the essentials of our perspective.

THE FUNDAMENTAL QUESTION

The theoretical perspective described herein is rooted in the question, How can the concept of *interpersonal communication* be usefully defined? Initially, interest in this question was sparked by the sudden surge of activities, in the late 1960s and early 1970s, that purportedly were linked to the study of interpersonal communication. Elsewhere, one of us has described the field's discovery of this concept:

> Currently, *interpersonal communication* is one of the darlings of the communication field, a contemporary in-vogue interest area. Manifestations of its sudden popularity are starkly apparent. In the past several years, a spate of textbooks sporting the appellation "Interpersonal Communication" have appeared on the market. Scores of courses formerly bearing such pedestrian labels as "Basic Public Speaking" or "Introduction to Communication" have trotted out a new titular bib-and-tucker containing the magic words "Interpersonal Communication." Almost everyone, it seems, can wax eloquent on the virtues of interpersonal communication, providing us with countless reminders of its importance and complexity (Miller, 1975, p. 93).

Though this assessment was written some time ago, interest in interpersonal communication has not waned; if anything, it has continued to grow. Unfortunately, until quite recently, this interest has not been matched by serious efforts to provide a rigorous, useful conceptualization of the construct. In some cases, interpersonal communication has been equated with human communication in general; for example, interpersonal communication has been defined as "communication that occurs between persons" (Applbaum, Anatol, Hays, Jenson, Porter, & Mandel, 1973, p. 33). When authors have attempted to distinguish interpersonal exchanges from other types of communicative transactions, they have usually relied on situationally bound criteria: interpersonal communication is characterized as involving a relatively small number of communicators; occurring in physically proximal, face-to-face situations; allowing the use of a maximal number of sensory channels; and permitting opportunity for immediate feedback (Miller, 1978, p. 165).

While of some utility, situational definitions suffer from at least two problems. First, the dividing line between situational contexts is arbitrary, often unclear, and always subject to the whim of the individual student of communication. Suppose, for instance, that a theorist chooses to distinguish between *interpersonal* and *small group* situations. Does this mean that members of small groups cannot have interpersonal communication relationships? Or suppose the theorist differentiates between *mass* and *interpersonal* contexts, making the absence of any mechanical, mediating communication system (e.g., telephone, radio) a necessary situational constraint for labeling a transaction interpersonal. Does this mean that close friends and lovers cannot pursue interpersonal relationships via telephone or letter? Once one begins to analyze communication situationally, the possibilities for definitional ambiguity and confusion are rampant.

Even more important, situational attempts to define interpersonal communication impose a static, nondevelopmental perspective on the communication process, rather than a dynamic, developmental viewpoint. Communication either *is* or *is not* interpersonal depending upon the situational context in which it occurs:

> If two individuals engage in eyeball-to-eyeball interaction, they are communicating interpersonally, whether they are total strangers or close friends. For the situationalist, a phatic greeting exchange between nodding acquaintances qualifies as interpersonal communication but a telephone conversation between a husband and wife does not. . . . In short, *the situational approach large ignores quantitative and qualitative changes in the nature and outcomes of a communicative transaction in the developing relationship between the communicators* (Miller, 1978, p. 166, italics added).

The italicized sentence of the preceding quotation offers a clue about the kind of conceptual perspective we will outline in this chapter. Specifically, we will focus on a developmental approach toward defining interpersonal communication. Such an approach assumes that all initial communicative transactions are, of necessity, impersonal or noninterpersonal. By "impersonal," we mean that the communicators are relating to one another as occupants of social roles rather than as persons (Peters, p. 1974), and that they are primarily concerned with common characteristics associated with these social roles and not with getting to know each other as unique personalities. If the communicators continue their relationship—that is, if they are sufficiently motivated to exert the effort to continue it, and if their interpersonal skills are tuned finely enough to permit its growth—their relationship may undergo certain qualitative changes. When such changes accompany relational development, communicative transactions become increasingly interpersonal. In other words, our perspective is dynamic in the sense that it views communication as varying on a continuum from *completely impersonal* to *completely interpersonal*, depending upon certain qualitative characteristics of the relationship, instead of defining interpersonal communication solely in terms of the situational context of the transaction.

In just a moment we will specify the kinds of qualitative changes central to our conceptual perspective. First, however, we must briefly discuss two fundamental assumptions that not only underlie our approach to interpersonal communication but also our view of human communication in general.

TWO FUNDAMENTAL ASSUMPTIONS

Our first major assumption is that the basic function of all communication is to control the environment so as to realize certain physical, economic, or social rewards from it (Miller & Steinberg, 1975, p. 62). Initially, this assumption may antagonize some readers, since it smacks of using other people by manipulating their behavior to serve selfish ends. We do not invoke the notion of *control* in this narrow, marketplace sense; rather, as we use the term, communicators have successfully controlled their environment when at least some degree of correspondence exists between their desired and their obtained outcomes. Assume, for example, that our present desired outcome is for readers to understand, after reading this paragraph, the way we are using the term *control*. To the extent such understanding occurs, we have succeeded in controlling those aspects of the environment—that is, the cognitive processes of readers—that are of immediate significance to us; to the extent that our definition of *control* remains unclear or is radically distorted, we have failed. Naturally, as is true with most everyone, we like to be understood rather than misunderstood. Hence, our desire for control can be thought of in the broadest sense as having a preference for one set of environmental outcomes over another. In most cases, it is hard to see how such preferences can be construed as manipulative or Machiavellian. Certainly, there is nothing wrong with wanting to be loved rather than hated (though admittedly, people may sometimes use morally questionable means when trying to control loving behaviors; e.g., bribery or lying), with striving to comfort others rather than exacerbating their grief, with seeking to educate people rather than confusing them, or with seeking a comfortable level of economic security rather than a life of wretched poverty. In short, control per se is neither moral nor immoral; instead, it is a staple ingredient of all communicative transactions. What often raises people's moral hackles is not control itself but rather the exercise of certain kinds of control—for example, normally, it is immoral to try to exacerbate another's grief—or the use of certain means to achieve it—for example, under most circumstances, it is morally questionable to attempt to control economic or status rewards by using ingratiation tactics.

What we have said about control also holds for the concept of using other people. In common parlance, "using others" implies a selfish, egocentric philosophy of human relations. Nevertheless, when viewed more globally, the roots of culture and civilization spring from humanity's mutual use of one another. As the ethical theorist, Marietta, Jr., puts it,

> Civil society is made possible through an interdependence of persons. To be fully human, we must use one another. To say we only use the services of other people is a meaningless nicety and is not entirely accurate. We must use the minds and bodies of other people. We begin life by using the body of a mother, and we never cease using other people. We derive most of the great satisfactions in life from letting other people use us. A refusal to accept the notion of using other people is an unjustifiable squeamishness which comes from failure to distinguish between moral and immoral uses of people (1972, pp. 232–233).

Thus, not only is the basic communicative function of control morally defensible as we have defined it, the fact that people are often used as instruments of environmental control need cause no alarm as long as these uses are morally justifiable. Indeed, only a rare person would argue that a baby's attempt to control his or her environment by crying to obtain food (an act that, at the least, involves the services and, at the most, the body of the mother) constitutes an unethical communicative act.

The second fundamental assumption stems directly from the centrality of control to our conceptual perspective; indeed, it might even be viewed as a corollary proposition. We assume that whenever people communicate with others, they make predictions about the probable consequences, or outcomes, of their messages (Miller, 1975; Miller & Steinberg, 1975). Stated differently, messagemaking is not a random activity. Instead, in seeking to control their environment, communicators purposively weigh the perceived available message alternatives (including the option of sending no verbal message) and select the one expected to produce the most favorable outcomes.

Undoubtedly, some readers will find it strange for us to assume that every message transmission entails a prediction-making process by the communicator. In certain situations, such cognitive rehearsal and anticipation are readily apparent. Important job interviews, oral examinations for advanced degrees, imminent interrogation by police officers, marriage proposals, and a host of other crucial communicative transactions are characterized by extensive rehearsals leading to overt predictions about the probable consequences of various message alternatives. Still, many of our routine exchanges with others happen spontaneously and appear to be largely devoid of conscious thought. Does it make sense to argue that predictions are made about message outcomes in such transitory encounters; for example, do individuals make predictions about the way acquaintances will respond to their greetings?

Granted, the degree of conscious involvement in prediction making may vary drastically across communicative situations. Nevertheless, predictions underlie the most casual, commonplace interactions. Typically, communicators remain blissfully unaware of the predictions they are making *until* such predictions are disconfirmed. Consider, for example, the previously mentioned, mundane transaction of exchanging greetings. Common salutations such as "Good morning" or "How are you?" seldom require much conscious cognition. Even so, prediction making is inherent in the remark, since the greeter expects to hear "Good morning" or "Fine, thank you" in return. Imagine how a greeter might react if a "How are you?" drew a response of "What's it to you?" or a 15-minute description of the person's physical or personal woes. Such rejoinders would result in considerable anxiety and uncertainty; the greeter would wonder why his or her message had produced this highly unexpected outcome. In terms of our second fundamental assumption, the incident can be translated as follows: the greeter transmitted a message that was expected to result in a particular response outcome, and the greeter's prediction of this outcome was subsequently disconfirmed.

Two points about this assumed prediction-making process merit emphasis. First, it may seem that when prediction making requires little conscious thought—in a sense, when it is viewed analogously with perception—its utility for the communication theorist is limited. To some extent, this point has merit; however, as this chapter progresses, it will become apparent that one crucial difference between impersonal and interpersonal communication relationships lies in the fact that the latter normally involve greater cognitive involvement in the prediction-making process. Second, nothing in our discussion of prediction making implies that predictions are always accurate; instead, as our far-fetched greeting exchange example suggests, erroneous prediction is a communicative commonplace. Again, as our conceptualization unfolds, it will become obvious that the potential for accurate prediction is greater in interpersonal than in impersonal communication relationships.

Unless a random decision process is assumed (and in a few instances, this assumption may be valid because of the total absence of relevant data, e.g., people frequently speculate about how they would communicate with beings from other planets), prediction making requires information. At least three kinds of information can assist communicators in predicting the probable outcomes of their messages. Since the crux of our conceptual perspective of interpersonal communication lies in the kind of information primarily employed to make predictions, we next consider these three types of information.

THREE KINDS OF INFORMATION: THE BASIS OF COMMUNICATIVE PREDICTION

Sometimes a communicator's predictions about probable message outcomes are grounded in *cultural information*. Knowledge about another person's culture—its language, dominant values, beliefs, and prevailing ideology—often permits prediction of the person's probable responses to certain messages. Returning to our previous example, greeting exchanges are principally governed by shared cultural norms; people expect others to respond to greetings in particular ways because most members of a culture share common greeting responses. Though culture is often equated with political boundaries, several cultures may thrive within a given country. Thus, many blacks within the United States share a set of greeting responses evolving from black culture. In fact, black culture has created a language of its own, some of which has been appropriated by members of the white middle-class culture. The noted author James Baldwin recently underscored this assimilative tendency when he observed, "I do not know what white Americans would sound like if there had never been any black people in the United States, but they would not sound the way they sound" (1979, p. E19).

Cultural information facilitates prediction in areas besides greeting and leave-taking. If a communicator tries to convince most groups in the United States of the virtues of determinism, heated opposition is predictable, since our society strongly emphasizes the importance of individual freedom and responsibility. Similarly, aspirants to public office in this country would be ill-advised to trumpet the superiority of Marxism or to embrace religious tenets alien to Judeo-Christian doctrine—at least if the desired outcome is election to office. So pervasive are certain cultural values that one writer (Weaver, 1953) has provided a handy list of god-words (e.g., "progress" and "science") and devil-words (e.g., "communist" and "un-American") to aid communicators who wish to base predictions on cultural information.

Upon first encountering a stranger, cultural information provides the only grounds for communicative prediction. This fact explains the uneasiness and perceived lack of control most people experience when thrust into an alien culture: they not only lack information about the individuals with whom they must communicate, they are bereft of information concerning shared cultural norms and values. In the absence of such information—which frequently includes the lack of a common language with members of the other culture—attempts to communicate proceed in a potentially hazardous, trial-and-error fashion. Often, in despair of ever achieving any semblance of control, these interlopers retreat to a cultural enclave inhabited by those who share their cultural heritage. Moreover, if they remain insulated, they may both indulge in and fall victim to cultural stereotyping, causing members of each culture to accept largely erroneous generalizations about members of the other culture.

This latter consideration underscores an important point about predictions based on cultural information: *of necessity, such predictions are based on a process of stimulus generalization, and as a result, they are subject to error when applied to individuals.* Some members of our society fail to respond conventionally to greetings (as our earlier hypothetical example implied), some are determinists, and some subscribe to Marxist ideology. Communicators such as mass media sources and candidates for national political office, who must transmit messages to large, heterogeneous audiences, recognize this fact; they tolerate a margin of individual error so as to influence the majority of their receivers. If their cultural inferences are inaccurate, they pay the penalty associated with failing to sense "the mood of the people"—this failure to exert adequate control is manifested in various ways, ranging from lagging car sales to defeat in major national elections. But when communicating with another individual, predictions derived from cultural information are either correct or totally wrong; there is no margin of tolerable error. Furthermore, when predictions about another's response to a message are based primarily on cultural information—that is when the other person is treated as a member of a cultural category rather than as an individual—the resulting communication is impersonal, not interpersonal.

Sociological information may also serve as the major basis for prediction making. Knowledge of an individual's membership groups, as well as the reference groups to which he or she aspires, permits numerous predictions about probable responses to various messages. Most members of feminist groups support abortion; most members of the American Medical Association oppose federal health plans; and most members of the Unitarian-Universalist Church favor social welfare legislation. College professors share many norms, values, and attitudes; as do students, academic administrators, and boards of regents. The list of relevant membership and reference groups is almost endless.

Indeed, sociological information probably affords the principal means for communicative prediction making in our society. The standard sales pitch of the Avon representative, the local insurance agent, the educational fund raiser, and the college fraternity or sorority—to mention but a few—relies heavily on sociological information. Messages exchanged at casual social encounters are largely based on predictions derived from sociological information; at most cocktail parties, guests are inundated with such messages. For example, at a recent meeting, we listened to another faculty member argue heatedly that security surrounding final examinations should be tightened, since "Most students will do anything for a grade." Among the student representatives at the meeting, these remarks met with resentment, with each representative taking pains to point ou that *this particular student* would not do "anything" for a grade. Hopefully, their rejoinders made the faculty member aware that his communicative predictions were heavily dominated by sociological information of questionable validity.

The preceding example reveals that sociological predictions are also arrived at by a process of stimulus generalization. The communicator tries to identify norms and values shared by most members of certain groups and then generalizes communicative predictions to other group members. Seldom do all members of a group conform to all of its norms and values: some members of feminist groups do not support abortion and some AMA members are not opposed to federal health programs. Moreover, predictive problems are compounded by multiple-group membership. People not only belong to numerous membership groups, they also aspire to many reference groups. Often, individuals encounter situations where the norms and values of two or more relevant groups conflict. Research (e.g., Charters, Jr., & Newcomb, 1958) has shown that when such conflicts exist, the individual's behavior depends upon his or her perceptions of the relative salience of the competing groups. Consequently, to use sociological information effectively, communicators must not only correctly identify the other's relevant membership and reference groups, they must know which group is most salient at a given time.

Since predictions grounded primarily in sociological information rely on group similarities, they culminate in impersonal communication. The other person is perceived not as an individual but as a bundle of role behaviors common to all members of that person's particular group. Often, of course, sociological predictions are accurate, for no one questions the powerful influence of group norms and values on individual behavior. Furthermore, sociological prediction is a vital component of many daily communicative transactions. Despite the pleas for universal intimacy voiced by some writers, it is impractical to expect everyone to get to know everyone else as individuals; enough time and human energy are simply not available. Also, as Marietta, Jr., (1972) points out, making all human relationships intimate would be ethically intolerable since doing so would invade people's privacy and solitude, as well as impose unlimited demands by others on their time. Still, there are instances when accuracy of individual predictions is vital; and in such cases, reliance on sociological information is bound to result in some errors.

Our third type of information used in prediction making differs drastically from the two types discussed previously. Though our usage is more restricted than is typically the case, we call the third type *psychological information.* Such information differs from sociological or cultural information because it directs attention to the other individual's prior learning history, particularly as it *differs* from the learning histories of other persons. Consequently, the key question becomes, *How does this individual differ from others with similar cultural and sociological backgrounds* and not What things do these people share in common? In Dance and Larson's terms, "Each participant relates to the other in terms of what sets the other apart from most other people. They take into consideration each other's individual differences in terms of the subject and the occasion" (1972, p. 56).

When psychological information provides the major grounds for inference, prediction involves a process of *stimulus discrimination,* rather than stimulus generalization. The key question facing the communicator is, How does this individual differ from other individuals with whom I have communicated? Successful prediction hinges on identifying verbal and nonverbal cues that distinguish a particular person from others of common cultural and sociological lineage. Obviously, as we have previously noted, making these discriminations is hard work; it requires more physical and psychic effort than relying on a few cultural or sociological generalizations. But when communicative outcomes are crucially important, the additional energy is justified by the potential payoff, since error can be substantially reduced —and in principle totally eliminated—by basing predictions on psychological information.

When predictions about another's message responses are based primarily on psychological information, communication is interpersonal, rather than impersonal. The primary unit of analysis shifts from the culture or group to the individual. Moreover, differences, not similarities, provide the basis for prediction. Thus, the crux of our conceptualization of interpersonal communication can be stated as follows: *when predictions about communicative outcomes are based primarily on cultural or sociological information, the communicators are engaged in impersonal communications; when predictions are based primarily on psychological information, the communicators are engaged in interpersonal communication.* When viewed transactionally, this conceptualization identifies three types of *communication relationships: impersonal,* where all communicators are basing predictions primarily on cultural or sociological information; *interpersonal,* where all communicators are basing predictions primarily on psychological information; and *mixed,* where some communicators are relying primarily on cultural or sociological information, but others are relying primarily on psychological information.

SOME RESEARCH IMPLICATIONS OF THE CONCEPTUAL PERSPECTIVE

The perspective sketched above is dynamic and developmental, since it assumes all initial communicative exchanges are highly impersonal and are governed by cultural and sociological level predictions. Under certain conditions, a relationship may evolve so as to become increasingly interpersonal; that is, as time passes, the communicators may base more and more of their predictions about message outcomes on psychological information. Note that such a pattern of relational evolution is not inevitable; under some circumstances, relationships may remain impersonal for a long and indefinite time. One potentially fruitful area of research, then, lies in identifying variables that influence relational development.

Obviously, communication itself is one such relevant variable. Typically, information to be used in making future communicative predictions is obtained by prior message exchanges with other relational parties. During initial encounters, communication exerts a powerful impact on relational development. Much interaction occurring in the beginning stages of a relationship aims at eliciting information that can facilitate prediction making. Consider the ritual of exchanging names, places of residence, occupations or academic majors, hobbies or other interests, and so on—almost mandatory first steps in communication (Berger, 1973; Calabrese, 1975). These exchanges reduce uncertainty about one another (Berger & Calabrese, 1975), and the communicators accumulate additional sociological, and perhaps even psychological, information that improves prediction about the subsequent outcomes of message alternatives. Clearly, this process of interrogation and information seeking is not fully understood, and our conceptual perspective suggests that research dealing with strategies for information acquisition merits high priority (Berger, Gardner, Parks, Schulman, & Miller, 1976).

There is a second way that communication may influence initial interaction and subsequent relational development. Often, individuals have at their disposal some cultural or sociological information about another person before any communication with that person takes place. For example, even though someone has never communicated with another person, he or she may know that the other's attitudes are similar or dissimilar to his or her own. Considerable research has shown that attitudinally similar individuals are initially perceived as more attractive than attitudinally dissimilar persons (Byrne, 1961, 1971; Clore & Baldridge, 1968; Griffitt, 1969). This fact suggests that communication between attitudinally dissimilar persons will be severely constrained, and that the communication relationship, if any, will probably remain impersonal. Suppose, however, that the very act of communicating in normative, nonthreatening ways is sufficient to ameliorate, or even eliminate, the impact of precommunication dissimilarity. If this is the case, the probability of the relationship evolving to a more interpersonal level will be increased. Later in this chapter, we shall report the findings of a study examining this possibility.

The cognitive styles of communicators undoubtedly also influence the likelihood of a relationship moving to an interpersonal level. Individuals with rigid, simplistic cognitive styles—for example, high dogmatics (Rokeach, 1960) or high authoritarians (Adorno, Frenkel-Brunswick, Levinson & Sanford, 1950)—are more likely to think habitually in terms of cultural and sociological stereotypes (Miller & Steinberg, 1975). Even if motivated to do so, such persons may find it difficult, or impossible, to make the discriminations needed to acquire psychological information. By contrast, communicators with flexible, complex cognitive styles should find it easier to practice stimulus discrimination and should therefore be more successful in acquiring and using psychological information. We later briefly discuss the results of research, conducted by several of our colleagues at Michigan State University, aimed at exploring these potential differences.

Perhaps the reader has identified other research implications of our conceptual perspective. Rather than pursuing these matters in further detail, we now turn to specific research strategies that can be helpful in investigating empirical issues derived from our conceptualization. In the course of examining these strategies, other research implications will emerge.

SOME RESEARCH STRATEGIES FOR EXAMINING THE CONCEPTUAL PERSPECTIVE

Research questions arising from our perspective can be explored using various research strategies. The strategies examined in this section are conveniently grouped into three general categories: those focusing on initial acquaintanceship between relative strangers; those examining developed relationships; and those tracing developing relationships from initial acquaintanceship to more developed stages. We will discuss some specific research strategies associated with each of these general categories and identify their implications for our conceptual perspective.

Research Strategies Focusing on Initial Acquaintanceship

Communication and its influence on relational development or attraction between individuals during initial stages of acquaintanceship have traditionally been a heavily researched area. This is largely due to the relative ease of conducting research on initial acquaintanceship, rather than to any disproportionate interest in this stage of relational development. Nevertheless, the results of these studies have implications for our developmental perspective. Additionally, this proliferation of research on the initial stages of relational development has produced several research strategies that can be usefully employed to examine this phase of relationships.

Perhaps the most popular strategy employed to examine factors that impact on relational development and/or interpersonal attraction is the "bogus stranger" method developed by Byrne (1961). Users of this technique typically give participants in their studies various items of information that purportedly describe certain characteristics of an individual who is a stranger to the participants. This information is actually manufactured by the researcher to produce the desired experimental manipulations. The participants then complete Byrne's Interpersonal Judgment Scale (1961), which contains items for obtaining an estimate of how much the participants would like the stranger and how much they would enjoy working with him or her. Researchers employing these methods have successfully isolated several variables that influence preacquaintance attraction. For example, as mentioned earlier, several studies have shown that individuals are more attracted to strangers who are portrayed as attitudinally similar than to strangers who are portrayed as attitudinally dissimilar (Byrne, 1961, 1971; Byrne, London, & Griffitt, 1968; Clore & Baldridge, 1968).

This bogus stranger research has been conducted primarily to build and to test theory. A byproduct of this theory-testing process has been the identification of several variables, including attitude similarity, which may influence interpersonal attraction and relational development in nonlaboratory settings. As we have noted, people often have some information about strangers they are likely to encounter prior to entering the stage of initial acquaintanceship. For instance, persons are often placed in situations where they know they must be interacting with a particular stranger in the near future—for example, going on a "blind" date; going for a job interview; and being assigned a new superior, subordinate, or partner in a work situation. In most of these situations, the individuals involved probably experience some anxiety owing to a shortage of information on which to base predictions about the stranger's future interaction behaviors and reactions to the individual's own communicative behaviors. If so, the individual probably attempts to gain some information about the stranger, such as his or her attitudes on topics relevant to future interactions, before the initial interaction so as to increase the ability to make predictions about the stranger's future behavior. The findings of previous bogus stranger research may well generalize to these naturally occurring situations. As noted earlier, what is not clear from research employing this strategy is how such preinteraction knowledge about a stranger combines with the cultural and sociological information typically exchanged during initial interactions to influence interpersonal attraction and relational development.

Recently, Sunnafrank (1979) examined this issue in a study dealing with the combined impact of preinteraction knowledge about a stranger's attitudinal similarity and information exchange during normative initial interactions on subsequent perceptions of interpersonal attraction. He reasoned that in situations where individuals know they will be interacting with a relative stranger concerning topics on which they either do or do not share similar attitudes with the stranger, attitude similarity will influence perceptions of interpersonal attraction because similarity affects perceived ability to predict the future interaction behaviors of the stranger. If people know they will be interacting with an attitudinally similar stranger, they typically feel they can predict that future interactions with the stranger will proceed normally and not lead to disagreements, thereby increasing perceived attraction. On the other hand, individuals paired with dissimilar strangers cannot confidently make this prediction. These individuals are likely to perceive that future interaction *may or may not* lead to disagreements, thus reducing their ability to predict and to exert control over the future interaction, thereby reducing the stranger's attractiveness. Sunnafrank also reasoned that interacting with a relative stranger in a normative, nonthreatening manner would increase the individual's ability to predict and to control future interactions with the stranger regarding topics about which they had similar or dissimilar attitudes, thereby increasing the stranger's attractiveness. Moreover, since knowing that one is going to interact with an attitudinally similar stranger would increase the stranger's predictability and his or her perceived attractiveness, increases in predictability and attraction during normative initial interactions should be minimal. Conversely, if knowing that one is going to interact with an attitudinally dissimilar stranger decreases the stranger's predictability and his or her initial attractiveness, then engaging in normative, nonthreatening initial interactions with the stranger should produce substantial increases in perceived predictability and attractiveness.

To test this reasoning, 124 student participants, who were strangers to one another, were paired on the basis of a pretest showing they were either attitudinally similar or dissimilar on two topics. The two individuals selected as partners reported at an appointed time. Upon arriving, each individual was escorted to a separate room to assure that partners would not see or communicate with each other prior to the interaction phase of the study. Both individuals then completed a dichotomous measure of their current attitudes concerning the two selected topics. They were told their responses would be shown to a stranger who would be working with them on a project involving discussion of the topics.

The experimenter next exchanged these attitude measures between the partners, who were told to examine the other's responses and to form a general impression of him or her. These procedures produced 32 attitudinally dissimilar pairs and 30 similar pairs. Fourteen of the similar and 14 of the dissimilar pairs were then allowed to meet under the guise of being participants in a separate experiment. The remaining pairs did not meet until the study was completed. The pairs who met were told they would be participating in a second study in which videotapes of conversations were being made to examine typical interaction behavior. They were asked if they would mind being videotaped, and each pair agreed to participate. They next interacted with each other for five minutes while being videotaped by hidden cameras. The participants then were told that they would work with their respective partners on the original project in just a few minutes. All participants were then asked to complete a questionnaire that included a measure of interpersonal attraction.

These procedures resulted in the following four experimental conditions: attitudinally similar/no interaction; attitudinally similar/interaction; attitudinally dissimilar/no interaction; and attitudinally dissimilar/interaction. These four conditions are displayed in Table 1.

The findings of this study (Table 1) indicated that among noninteractants, individuals were more attracted to similar partners than dissimilar partners, a result comparable to earlier findings of Byrne and his associates. Interestingly, however, no differences in attraction to similar and dissimilar partners were found among interactants. More-

Table 1   MEANS AND STANDARD DEVIATIONS FOR INTERPERSONAL ATTRACTION TOWARD SIMILAR AND DISSIMILAR INTERACTANTS AND NONINTERACTANTS

INTERACTION CONDITION	SIMILARITY CONDITION	
	SIMILAR	DISSIMILAR
Engaged in Initial Interaction	$\overline{X} = 17.54$ $s = 2.86$ $n = 28$	$\overline{X} = 16.68$ $s = 2.74$ $n = 28$
Did Not Engage in Initial Interaction	$\overline{X} = 17.16$ $s = 2.62$ $n = 32$	$\overline{X} = 13.14$ $s = 2.76$ $n = 36$

over, while dissimilar interactants were more attracted to their partners than dissimilar noninteractants, similar interactants and noninteractants did not differ on the attraction variable. In fact, the only group differing from the others on the attraction measure was the attitudinally dissimilar noninteractants, who were less attracted to their partners than all other participants.

These results indicate that the opportunity to engage in a brief, nonthreatening conversation with an attitudinally dissimilar stranger largely cancels the negative impact of dissimilarity on initial perceptions of attraction. Sunnafrank interpreted the finding as support for the position that such interactions increase the perceived ability to predict the future communicative behaviors of the stranger, thus rendering the stranger less threatening and enhancing his or her perceived attractiveness. Whether or not this interpretation is accurate, the results do suggest that initial attitude dissimilarity does not pose an insurmountable barrier against subsequent relational development. If early communicative encounters follow normative, nonthreatening patterns, the interactants may find each other increasingly more attractive, and the relationship may withstand the negative impact of initially differing attitudes.

Future research that measures the individual's perception of the predictability of relative strangers is needed to examine the validity of Sunnafrank's interpretation. However, the results of this study support the commonsense belief that communication has a powerful influence on initial, precommunicative perceptions of others. Any research strategy employed to examine acquaintanceship development among relative strangers that ignores communicative exchanges may produce results that are not generalizable to the "real" world.

Earlier, we discussed the possibility that differences in the cognitive styles of individuals could affect the ways individuals employ cultural, sociological, and psychological information in making predictions about others, which would ultimately influence their ability to develop interpersonal relationships. A study by Bundens, Shelby, and Fontes (in preparation) employed yet another research strategy to examine this possibility.

Along with several other predictions, these researchers hypothesized that high dogmatics exposed to either psychological or sociological information about a relative stranger would be less accurate in predicting future responses of the stranger than would their low-dogmatic counterparts. To test this prediction, Bundens et al. exposed students to videotapes of individuals responding to questions designed to elicit either sociological or psychological information. At the sociological level, these included such questions as "How much education have you had?" while at the psychological level, questions such as "How do love and sex differ?" were asked. After viewing the videotape, the participants completed a questionnaire that included a dogmatic measure and measures of how the participants thought the stimulus person would respond to other questions designed to elicit sociological and psychological information. These additional questions were actually asked of the stimulus persons, and their responses were included as one of the alternatives available to participants along with a number of responses manufactured by the experimenters.

Preliminary results of the study indicate that low dogmatics are not able to predict the future responses of relative strangers in this situation more accurately than high dogmatics. However, Bundens et al. report that reliability for their dogmatism measure was relatively low, suggesting that future research using different measures of dogmatism may produce the predicted differences in accuracy. Furthermore, while no differences were obtained for the dogmatism variable, the results of the study do indicate that individuals exposed to psychological information more accurately predicted the stimulus person's future responses than did individuals exposed to sociological information. This finding supports our contention that psychological information about an individual provides a better basis for prediction making than does sociological information.

One further research strategy used by numerous researchers (Berger, 1973; Berger, Gardner, Clatterbuck, & Schulman, 1976; Calabrese, 1975) has produced results supporting the position that during the initial stages of acquaintanceship, individuals are likely to discuss cultural or sociological information, rather than psychological information. These researchers typically ask participants to sort a large number of conversational topics, previously rated for their intimacy value, into different time periods during an initial conversation at which they think the topic might come up. During the very early stages of conversations, the most likely topics involve the exchange of biographical and demographical information, which appears to be cultural and sociological in nature, while more intimate, psychological information is reserved for discussion, if at all, at later points in the conversation. Moreover, several studies (Berger, Gardner, Parks, Schulman, & Miller, 1976) have shown that violations of conversational norms—that is, including excessively intimate information in early stages of the conversation—result in the norm violator being perceived as less attractive than persons who restrict themselves to biographical and demographic information. Apparently, people are uncomfortable with, and respond negatively to, individuals who "come on too strongly" at the outset of an acquaintanceship.

Numerous other research strategies have been employed to examine the initial stages of acquaintanceship between relative strangers, and these strategies could also be used to examine some of the research questions implied by our perspective. For example, content analysis of actual initial conversations could be employed to examine the level of information exchanged and the effect of differing information-seeking strategies. Experimental confederates could be paired with naive participants to manipulate some aspect of the initial interaction and to examine its impact on subsequent relational development. Since space does not permit more detailed exposition of these possibilities, we next consider several research strategies that focus on developed relationships.

Research Strategies Focusing on Developed Relationships

As noted, most prior research dealing with interpersonal attraction and relational development has concentrated on the initial stage of acquaintanceship. The difficulties of conducting research on developed and developing relationships, some of which are mentioned in the rest of this chapter, constitute a major reason for the limited research focusing on these relationships. Regardless of the difficulties surrounding research on developed and developing relationships, our dynamic, developmental view of interpersonal relationships suggests that such studies are imperative for a better understanding of relational development. In this section, we will suggest possible research strategies for examining developed relationships, while in the final section we will concentrate on developing relationships. To some extent, the distinction between "developed" and "developing" is a false one made for the sake of categorical convenience, since all maintained relationships are constantly evolving and developing.

We know of no research that has examined developed relationships from the perspective outlined in this paper. We will, therefore, concentrate on the usual method of studying developed relationships:

correlational analysis. The correlational method is relatively simple in its application; the difficulties associated with this strategy arise from interpreting its findings. In dealing with developed relationships, correlational analysis involves obtaining measures on the variables of interest from members of numerous developed relationships and correlating these measures with the measures obtained from each individual's relational partner. To ascertain the factors that differentiate developed relationships from undeveloped ones, the researcher typically compares these correlations with those obtained from random pairs of unacquainted individuals.

The correlational approach was one of the earliest strategies applied to the study of developed relationships. More than four decades ago, several researchers sought to discover the factors that contributed to relational development (Hunt, 1935; Newcomb & Svehla, 1937; Vreeland & Corey, 1935; Winslow, 1937). These investigators were among the first to report a positive relationship between attitude similarity and interpersonal attraction.

The problems of interpreting correlational findings can be illustrated by examining the results for attitude similarity and attraction produced by these early studies. One possible interpretation of the finding that friends and spouses are more attitudinally similar than random pairs of individuals is that individuals who are attitudinally similar are more likely to develop ongoing relationships than individuals who are attitudinally dissimilar. Still, it is equally plausible that during the developmental process of the relationship, the partners influence each other's attitudes so that they become more attitudinally similar. If this were the case, attitudinal similarity prior to the development of relationships could have little influence on relational development. Unfortunately, no ready means exist for assessing the relative merits of either of these interpretations when dealing with developed relationships.

Although there are problems associated with this particular strategy, certain of its strengths recommend it as a useful tool for examining our conceptual perspective of interpersonal communication. For instance, problems of interpretation are reduced when measures of relatively enduring individual characteristics are employed. It seems likely that many personality traits would be relatively unaffected by participating in a particular relationship. This possibility suggests that at least one research question implied by our perspective could be usefully pursued by correlational analysis; namely, how does cognitive style influence an individual's ability to move from impersonal to interpersonal relationships? Consider, for illustrative purposes, the dogmatism variable discussed earlier. If highly dogmatic individuals are less likely to move beyond impersonal relationships than low-dogmatic persons, high dogmatics should be less accurate in predicting how their partners in developed relationships differ from other individuals. The correlational method could test this possibility by examining differences between high and low dogmatics in their ability to predict their partners' responses to questions aimed at soliciting psychological information. If our speculation is accurate, then the correlation between predicted and actual responses should be lower for high- than for low-dogmatic individuals.

Though few recent studies on interpersonal attraction and relational development have employed correlational analysis to study developed relationships, this strategy still has a place in the study of relational development. We now turn to a strategy that assumes a central role in the study of relational development but that has received less research attention than any strategy thus far discussed: following developing relationships from initial acquaintanceship to more developed stages.

Research Strategies Focusing on Developing Relationships

Explicit in our view of the formation of interpersonal relationships is the notion that they are formed through a dynamic, developmental process. All of the research we have discussed thus far takes "snapshots" or, at best, short excerpts from this process and attempts to piece together the underlying dynamics of relational development. We will now outline a strategy that follows the process of relational development from initial acquaintanceship through later stages of relational development. Few research projects have employed this method of examining relational development, but the exceptions have added greatly to our knowledge concerning relational development (Newcomb, 1961; Sherif & Sherif, 1953). This section briefly describes the specific strategy used in an investigation conducted by Newcomb (1961)—a classic example of this longitudinal method.

In a project designed to test predictions emanating from balance theory (Newcomb, 1953), Newcomb studied the development of interpersonal relationships among two separate groups of male college students for a period of two academic years, with each group participating in one year of the study. Measures of several variables were obtained from the students prior to their participation to examine the impact of these variables on postacquaintance attraction. Included were certain personality traits, attitudes toward topics that Newcomb thought would be important to male college students, and basic values.

The participants were all new transfer students who had been persuaded to reside in one residence house for the school year and who were unacquainted with each other prior to the study.

At various points in time during the two years of the study, Newcomb took measures of several variables deemed relevant to relational development: for example, the students' perceptions of the attitudes held by other house members, multiple measures of attraction, and frequency of communication among residents.

Several of the findings of this study have particular relevance for the conceptual perspective set forth in this chapter. During the second year of the study, Newcomb found that authoritarian personality types were less accurate in estimating the attitudes held by others than were nonauthoritarians. Moreover, he found that extreme authoritarians were more likely to keep to themselves. At several points in this chapter, we have suggested that individuals with rigid, simplistic cognitive styles, such as authoritarians, will have difficulty moving from impersonal to interpersonal relationships and in discriminating between individuals at the psychological level. These findings support our speculation.

Another recurring theme of this chapter, which Newcomb examined extensively, concerns the relationship of similarity, attraction, and relational development. As we have stressed, during initial stages of a relationship, when persons are relating to one another impersonally, they should have limited information about each other's attitudes and values. If so, similarity of attitudes and values should exert little impact on attraction during initial stages of relational development. If attitude and/or value similarity influence attraction and relational development, this influence should emerge when individuals begin to exchange psychological information at later stages in the relationship. Again, Newcomb's findings support this position. During the early stage of acquaintanceship, attitude and value similarity were not related to attraction or relational development. On the other hand, similarity of attitudes and values was found to be influential in later relational encounters, with friendships tending to develop among similar individuals. Furthermore, the individuals' attitudes and values remained relatively stable over the year's time, indicating that similarity of attitudes and values leads to friendship formation rather than the converse. Evidence collected during the second year of the study suggests, however, that under certain circumstances, this relationship may not hold. During the second year, Newcomb assigned roommates who were either highly similar or dissimilar with respect to attitudes and values. In all but one case, the roommates became and remained highly attracted to one another regardless of their degree of attitude and value similarity. This finding suggests that, when situations dictate, individuals who maintain communicative relationships are likely to develop close relationships with one another despite basic dissimilarities.

The major difficulties with a longitudinal research strategy are pragmatic. Although this strategy is ideal for examining the process of relational development, it is also the most costly strategy in terms of time, energy, and money. This difficulty suggests that most researchers will often choose to examine "snapshots" of the developmental process when attempting to assemble the puzzle of interpersonal relationship formation. Hopefully, however, future research will make greater use of strategies that permit the investigator to follow relationships through time, particularly if the goal is to test hypotheses derived from the kind of conceptual perspective we have sketched in this chapter.

References

Adorno, T. W., Frenkel-Brunswik, E., Levinson, D. J., & Sanford, N. R. *The authoritarian personality.* New York: Harper, 1950.

Applbaum, R. L., Anatol, K., Hays, E. R., Jenson, O. O., Porter, R. E., & Mandel, J. E. *Fundamental concepts in human communication.* San Francisco: Canfield Press, 1973.

Baldwin, J. If black English isn't a language, then tell me, what is? *New York Times,* July 29, 1979, E19.

Berger, C. R. *The acquaintance process revisited: Explorations in initial interaction.* Paper presented at the annual convention of the Speech Communication Association, New York, November, 1973.

Berger, C. R., & Calabrese, R. J. Some explorations in initial interaction and beyond: Toward a developmental theory of interpersonal communication. *Human Communication Research,* 1975, *1,* 99–112.

Berger, C. R., Gardner, R. R., Clatterbuck, G. W., & Schulman, L. S. Perceptions of information sequencing in relationship development. *Human Communication Research,* 1976, *3,* 29–46.

Berger, C. R., Gardner, R. R., Parks, M. R., Schulman, L. S., & Miller, G. R. Interpersonal epistemology and interpersonal communication. In G. R. Miller (Ed.), *Explorations in interpersonal communication.* Beverly Hills: Sage, 1976, pp. 149–172.

Bundens, R., Shelby, J., & Fontes, N. E. Predicting a stranger's behavior: The effects of level of information, dogmatism, and sex of dyad on predictive accuracy. Department of Communication, Michigan State University, in preparation.

Byrne, D. Interpersonal attraction and attitude similarity. *Journal of Abnormal and Social Psychology,* 1961, *62,* 713–715.

Byrne, D. *The attraction paradigm.* New York: Academic Press, 1971.

Byrne, D., London, O., & Griffitt, W. The effect of topic importance and attitude similarity-dissimilarity on attraction in an intra-stranger design. *Psychonomic Science,* 1968, *11,* 303–304.

Calabrese, R. J. *The effects of privacy and probability of future interaction on interpersonal attraction patterns.* Unpublished doctoral dissertation, Department of Communication Studies, Northwestern University, 1975.

Charters, W. W., Jr., & Newcomb, T. M. Some attitudinal effects of experimentally increased salience of a membership group. In E. E. Maccoby, T. M. Newcomb, & E. L. Hartley (Eds.), *Readings in social psychology* (3rd ed). New York: Holt, 1958, pp. 276–281.

Clore, G. L., & Baldridge, B. Interpersonal attraction: The role of agreement and topic interest. *Journal of Personality and Social Psychology,* 1968, *9,* 340–346.

Dance, F. E. X., & Larson, C. E. *Speech communication: Concepts and behavior.* New York: Holt, Rinehart and Winston, 1972.

Griffitt, W. Attitude evoked anticipatory responses and attraction. *Psychonomic Science,* 1969, *14,* 153–155.

Hunt, A. A study of the relative values of certain ideals. *Journal of Abnormal and Social Psychology,* 1935, *30,* 222–228.

Marietta, D. E., Jr. On using people. *Ethics,* 1972, *82,* 232–238.

Miller, G. R. Interpersonal communication: A conceptual perspective. *Communication,* 1975, *2,* 93–105.

Miller, G. R. The current status of theory and research in interpersonal communication. *Human Communication Research,* 1978, *4,* 164–178.

Miller, G. R., & Steinberg, M. *Between people: A new analysis of interpersonal communication.* Chicago: Science Research Associates, 1975.

Newcomb, T. M. An approach to the study of communicative acts. *Psychological Review,* 1953, *60,* 393–404.

Newcomb, T. M. *The acquaintance process.* New York: Holt, Rinehart and Winston, 1961.

Newcomb, T. M., & Svehla, G. Intra-family relationships in attitudes. *Sociometry,* 1937, *1,* 180–205.

Peters, R. S. Personal understanding and personal relationships. In T. Mischel (Ed.), *Understanding other persons.* Oxford: Basil Blackwell, 1974, pp. 37–65.

Rokeach, M. *The open and closed mind.* New York: Basic Books, 1960.

Sherif, M., & Sherif, C. *Groups in harmony and tension.* New York: Harper, 1953.

Sunnafrank, M. J. *The impact of attitude similarity and initial interaction on interpersonal attraction.* Unpublished doctoral dissertation, Department of Communication, Michigan State University, 1979.

Vreeland, F. M., & Corey, S. M. A study of college friendships. *Journal of Abnormal and Social Psychology,* 1935, *30,* 229–236.

Weaver, R. M. *The ethics of rhetoric.* Chicago: Henry Regnery Co., 1953.

Winslow, C. N. A study of the extent of agreement among friends' opinions and their ability to estimate the opinions of each other. *Journal of Social Psychology,* 1937, *8,* 433–442.

AN OVERVIEW OF CONTRIBUTIONS TO HUMAN COMMUNICATION THEORY FROM OTHER DISCIPLINES

Stephen W. Littlejohn

Academic life is characterized by themes and fields. A theme is the subject, topic, or focus of the scholar; the field consists of the community of scholars who associate with a particular theme. Fields are important in academic life because scholarship is fundamentally a social activity. By this I mean that scholarship is built on the work of others and is sustained through interaction within the community. We learn our methods from other scholars, and our ideas are tested and criticized by others. Theories develop, grow, and change based on the scrutiny of colleagues within a field.

All of the authors of this volume associate primarily with the field of Speech Communication, and we share a common interest in human communication as our theme. However, human communication is also the legitimate theme of a variety of other disciplines. The study of human communication illustrates the fuzziness of traditional academic boundaries and the permeability of various fields. A field may consist of a *discipline*, or community of scholars who share a common focus that is relatively distinct from the foci of other disciplines. A *sub-discipline* is a narrower field within the confines of the broader discipline. An *interdiscipline* is a field of scholars who identify with various disciplines but share a common interest in a theme that crosses traditional boundaries.

At its best, the study of human communication constitutes an interdiscipline, in which communication processes are investigated using insights from several traditional disciplines. Figure 1 illustrates this idea. The interdiscipline is represented by a circle in the middle of the figure. Five major contributing disciplines are also represented— four by triangles and one by a rectangle. (In actuality, there are far more contributing disciplines than are represented here.) This figure illustrates that each major discipline, except Speech Communication, is concerned with subjects outside the realm of communication, but they all include themes related to it as well. All of the disciplines overlap, because some communication themes are dealt with by more than one discipline. At the same time, each has its special contribution as well. Speech Communication lies completely within the circle, since it is the only single discipline that is concerned entirely with communication as a focus. It is highly eclectic and multidisciplinary, and is therefore shown to overlap all of the others.

Any serious communication scholar must recognize that our understanding of this phenomenon stems from the work of many disciplines. Communication lies at the heart of just about all human affairs. We cannot fully probe individual behavior, social structures, political activity, artistic creation, language and culture, or a host of other human concerns without including investigations of communication processes. This is why communication is such a ubiquitous theme.

The study of communication as an interdiscipline flips the traditional scholarly coin by focusing on communication, allowing formerly focal themes to support rather than dominate theory and research. So, for example, the communication scholar might focus on interaction in groups, using earlier findings on such topics as leadership, roles, norms, and such to support our understanding of group communication. In this book, we have seen several fine examples of this kind of work.

The best interdisciplinary research and theory must recognize and integrate the narrower, disciplinary work of such fields as psychology, sociology, philosophy, and anthropology. Thus, an important stage toward an interdisciplinary view is to understand how these disciplines have approached communication and what they have produced. This kind of survey is what I have called a *multidisciplinary framework* (Littlejohn, 1978). Unlike most of the theories presented in this book, which provide integrated or singular pictures, the multidisciplinary framework attempts to piece together a composite picture of communication based on diverse work. It further attempts to bridge findings from various fields, identifying points of conceptual similarity

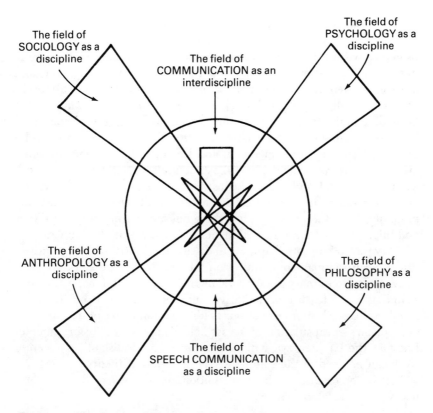

Figure 1   The Study of Human Communication

and difference. This kind of conceptualization is essential groundwork for the study of communication as an interdiscipline, and it is an important tool in allowing the scholar to understand interdisciplinary theories by placing these in perspective.

A multidisciplinary approach yields other advantages as well. It keeps our eyes open to the broad scope of communication activity. No single theory, no matter how large its domain, can provide a comprehensive picture of the process. In addition, communication is a process that can be fruitfully conceptualized in a variety of ways. No single conceptualization is necessarily best, and a fuller understanding can be obtained from conceptual shifting, which is made possible by a multidisciplinary framework. Finally, this approach guards against methodological defensiveness by recognizing multiple methods of inquiry. The full richness of communication processses simply cannot be investigated by a single method. At the same time, it is not realistic for a single discipline or subdiscipline to command the variety of methods required by a theme as big as communication.

Of course, a multidisciplinary approach presents problems as well. First, it is an immense task fraught with conceptual puzzles. For example, we must ferret out those theories that reflect most directly upon communication. This task requires considerable judgment, and any single attempt will inevitably be incomplete. (For various attempts, see Budd & Ruben, 1972; Dance, 1967; Lin, 1973; Littlejohn, 1978.) Second, a multidisciplinary framework requires a carefully conceived but broad definition or taxonomy of issues, themes, or concepts to be included. The resulting model, if too broad, will be unmanageable; and if too narrow, incomplete. Last, a multidisciplinary framework can never present an internally consistent, clear view. The scholar will encounter numerous theoretical issues and controversies. It uncovers more questions than answers, but these questions are vitally important and might never be raised within the work of single disciplines.

My purpose in this chapter is to discuss the contributions of various disciplines to human communication theory. Really, we can only sample a multidisciplinary framework in this space, but I hope that our sampling is at least representative and includes some of the most significant contributions of various fields. The following represents only one person's encapsulation of a vast field; it is necessarily incomplete. Later in the chapter, we will discuss how a multidisciplinary framework can be used in the comparative evaluation of theory.

In order to discuss the contributions of various fields, it is first necessary to develop an analytical model for our survey.

ELEMENTS OF A MULTIDISCIPLINARY FRAMEWORK

In this section, we will develop a model in which diverse theoretical contributions can be compared. This model consists of four basic elements. First, we need to classify theories according to *epistemological assumptions*. Epistemology is the study of the ways in which we come to "discover" or "create" knowledge. Behind every theory lies a set of normally tacit assumptions about knowledge. We need to raise these assumptions to a conscious level to understand theoretical similarities and differences.

Second, we will generate a *multidisciplinary definition* that will function to outline the broad limits of communication theory. This is a tricky task. Our definition must be broad enough to include the most significant contributions without denying the potential usefulness of narrower, field-specific definitions of communication.

Relying on this definition, we will next develop a set of *thematic categories* under which most of the work on communication can be placed. These categories are vitally important because they allow us to see how various aspects of communication are elaborated by different disciplines. They also suggest areas for additional research and theory.

Finally, we will list some broad *theoretical questions* that theories related to communication have addressed. Again, our questions will have to be stated rather generally to accommodate a diversity of theory.

Later in the chapter, we discuss theoretical contributions within the four elements of this model.

Epistemological Assumptions

Epistemology is that branch of philosophy that addresses the question, How do we know what we know? or, By what processes does reality come to be known? These questions can be answered only in conjunction with a cousin branch in philosophy: metaphysics, which questions the nature of reality. We do not have enough space here to uncover all of the facets of these philosophical questions, which are discussed in thousands of pages from Plato to contemporary philosophers of science (e.g., Black, 1962; Grene, 1974; Pepper, 1942; Polanyi, 1969). However, it is necessary to understand that various communication theorists see the process differently, precisely because they hold different assumptions about knowledge and reality.

For our purposes, we will divide theorists into two broad epistemological camps. It would be a serious mistake to dichotomize these camps or to suggest that there are only two clear positions on epistemological issues. So our camps are just general categories that will serve to make some comparisons as we go along. I have labelled these positions *World View I* and *World View II*. Table 1 lists some important philosophical issues on which these two world views would generally disagree.

How do these issues relate to communication theories? The first four issues deal primarily with the nature of reality and knowledge. Theories of World View I tend to specify generalizations about communication. Many of them seek covering laws, or universal explanations of communication phenomena. World View II theories, in contrast, attempt to understand everyday communication experience as lived by the individual. Generalizations, especially covering laws, are often viewed with suspicion. These theories also sometimes attempt to uncover perceptual processes behind people's behavior in everyday communication.

Issues 5, 6, and 7 deal primarily with the knower-known relationship. Communication theories of World View I tend to rely heavily on research methods adapted from the physical sciences, which assume that reality is to be observed objectively. Even human behavior is treated as an object and viewed via instrumentation. Theories from

Table 1 WORLD VIEWS

FOCUS	EPISTE-MOLOGICAL ISSUE	WORLD VIEW I	WORLD VIEW II
NATURE OF REALITY AND KNOWLEDGE	(1) To what extent is knowledge a priori?	Knowledge is discovered. It is in no way a priori.	Part of knowledge is a priori. What we know emerges from structures that are part of human existence.
	(2) To what extent is reality universal?	Reality is absolute and immutable, to be received or discovered.	Reality results from human interpretation. Reality is in flux and exists only in context.
	(3) To what extent is knowledge explicit?	Knowledge is explicit.	Most knowledge is implicit or tacit.
	(4) Where is the locus of reality?	Reality is in the world, outside the person.	Reality is in personal experience.
KNOWER-KNOWN RELATION-SHIP	(5) By what process is knowledge achieved?	Knowledge arises from sensory experience. Sensory experience results from specific, definable operations. Reality is thus discovered systematically by controlled observation of well-defined elements.	Knowledge is a perceptual process, shaped by individual human interpretation. Knowledge is a construction of the person, resulting from a transaction between knower and known.
	(6) To what extent is knowledge social?	Knowledge is discovered by the observer alone.	Knowledge is constructed by symbolic interaction in social groups.
	(7) How are humans different from or the same as non-human objects?	Humans are basically objects, controlled by the same features and operations.	Humans act with purpose and are therefore entirely different from non-human objects.
STRUCTURE OF REALITY	(8) Does knowledge consist of understanding parts or wholes?	Reality is best understood via analysis, or knowledge of parts.	Reality is best understood in terms of interrelated wholes.

Table 1 *(continued)*

FOCUS	EPISTE-MOLOGICAL ISSUE	WORLD VIEW I	WORLD VIEW II
	(9) What is the structure of reality?	Objects in reality have discernible structure and predictable, machine-like operations.	Reality is process. Its "structure" is imposed. It is most useful to understand process in terms of relations and functions.
	(10) Why do events happen?	Events are caused.	Events are part of goal-seeking processes.

the second tradition, however, rely more on individual researcher interpretation, which assumes that reality is constructed at least in part by the observer. Thus, research consists more of participant observation. It tends to be descriptive and contextualistic.

Finally, the last three issues deal with the structure of reality. Assuming that events are best understood in parts rather than wholes, World View I theories tend to conceive of communication as a linear process, and relations among elements are ascertained by hypothesis and test (hypothetico-deductive method). Contrasting theories tend to be more holistic, focusing on communication purposes.

We will return to these issues and world views when discussing specific disciplines.

A Multidisciplinary Definition of Communication

Just as no particular theory is best, there is no single correct definition of communication (for discussions of definition, see Dance, 1970; Dance & Larson, 1976). Any definition should be judged in terms of its utility for guiding research and theory within the realm being investigated. Still, it is important to come to some agreement on the general class of phenomena to be included as communication. Such a definition is especially important for this multidisciplinary framework.

For our purposes, it is better not to conceive of communication as one kind of activity. It is not a singular concept. I prefer to follow Dance (1967) in his notion that *communication* is a label for a "family of concepts." It consists of a variety of phenomena that have two common qualities.

First, communication activities are *processual*. In other words, most communication concepts involve organized sets of variables that are interrelated in complex ways. Such systems operate through time and in context. Communication events involve ongoing occurrences rather than static objects or entities.

The concept of process by itself is a necessary but not a sufficient criterion for delimiting communication. Communication processes must also involve *symbolic interaction*. People create messages by using symbols, and the exchange of messages results in mutual effect, creating interdependence. Thus, any phenomenon involving *processes of symbolic interaction* can be considered proper to include in our multidisciplinary framework.

Theoretical Themes

Within this very broad definition of communication, what theoretical themes have emerged in the disciplines? In my review of theories from various disciplines, I have encountered three types of themes. First, some theories relate to the general nature of communication as a whole, attempting to capture its essence. Relying on our definition, we can single out the themes of *process* and *symbolic interaction* in this first category.

The second type of theme deals with the central contributing processes related to communication. We have to be somewhat arbitrary in naming these processes, but the following five theme labels seem appropriate. *Coding* refers to the use of symbols to produce and receive messages. Theories dealing with language and nonverbal codes are most closely aligned with this theme. *Meaning* relates to the intricate symbol-person-referent relationship. Whereas theories related to coding deal primarily with the structure and function of symbolic forms, theories in this second theme area focus more on the origin and nature of sign processes. *Thinking* is the mental manipulation of symbols for personal adaptation in the form of conceptualization and problem solving. Thinking must be included as a communication theme because it is wedded so closely to symbolic interaction. The fourth theme in this category is *information*, or the relationship of the message to uncertainty and predictability. Finally, *persuasion* consists of change processes resulting from symbolic interaction. Obviously, these five themes are closely related; conceptual overlaps are unavoidable. The operational distinction among these will become apparent in the next section, where theoretical questions related to these themes are listed.

The third type of theme includes topics focusing on communication contexts. There are a number of valid ways to conceptualize contexts, but the theories seem to be divided rather nicely among four context themes: interpersonal, group, organization, and mass communication. It is useful to conceive of these contexts as nested levels of a hierarchy, and while it is important to recognize the overlap among these contexts, most theories in this area deal rather directly with one or another of them.

The *interpersonal context* as a theme includes primarily theories dealing with relationships, especially in dyads. *Group context* theories focus on networks and processes in task and social groups. *Organizational context* involves explanations of interrelated groups and system-wide communication concerns. *Mass context* refers to broad societal levels of interaction with special focus on media.

At this point, our multidisciplinary model looks more complete. We can now envision communication as a set of symbolic interaction processes involving coding, meaning, thinking, information, and persuasion. These processes occur in a hierarchy of four contexts. We turn now to a list of theoretical questions within these theme areas.

Theoretical Questions

It would be impossible to list every question addressed by communication theories. The following is therefore only a sampling, but I have tried to include many of the most important issues of communication theory. Also, these questions are rather broadly stated in terms that will accommodate just about any discipline.

  I. Themes related to the general nature of communication
      A. Process
          1. In what ways is communication processual?
      B. Symbolic interaction
          1. How does communication involve symbolic interaction?
 II. Themes related to central communication processes
      A. Coding
          1. What is the nature of the relationship between sign and signified?
          2. How do codes function to create messages?
          3. How is language structured?
          4. How is language produced and understood?
          5. How is language acquired?
          6. What nonverbal behaviors function as signs in communication?
          7. How are nonverbal codes structured?
          8. How are nonverbal codes acquired?
          9. How do nonverbal behaviors function?
      B. Meaning
          1. What is meaning?

2. What conditions give rise to meaning?
3. Where is the locus of meaning?
C. Thinking
  1. By what mechanisms is information processed?
  2. How does thought develop?
  3. How do humans solve problems?
D. Information
  1. What is information?
  2. How is information transmitted?
  3. In what ways does information affect people and systems?
E. Persuasion
  1. What factors in the communication source and message inhibit or facilitate change?
  2. What elements of the person change as a result of communication?
  3. What elements in the person inhibit or facilitate change?
III. Themes related to contexts of communication
A. Interpersonal context
  1. What are the elements of interpersonal relationship?
  2. What is the nature of interpersonal perception/attribution?
  3. What are the factors of attraction?
  4. What facilitates interpersonal empathy and understanding?
  5. What factors enter into conflict?
B. Group context
  1. What distinguishes a small group?
  2. How do groups affect individuals?
  3. What factors contribute to task output?
  4. What motivates group participation?
  5. What is the nature of interaction in groups?
  6. What is the nature of decision making in groups?
C. Organizational context
  1. What is the essence of organization?
  2. How does authority arise within an organization?
  3. What factors contribute to organizational success?
  4. What is the nature of decision making in organizations?
D. Mass context
  1. What are the functions of mass communication?
  2. How are information and influence disseminated in mass communication?
  3. What is the impact of media on society?

THEORETICAL CONTRIBUTIONS

The list of disciplines concerned with human communication is long indeed. Franklin Knower listed sixteen disciplines that deal with it in one form or another. Many disciplines apply the research and theory produced in other fields to content areas such as agriculture, labor, or health. Other fields, such as journalism and speech pathology, concentrate on developing communication skills or training professionals to practice in communication careers. In this chapter, we are concerned only with those disciplines that produce substantial *theory* that contributes to our understanding of communication. Four such disciplines clearly emerge as leaders: philosophy, psychology, sociology, and anthropology. Several other fields, including some interdisciplines, have also made contributions. These are grouped as follows: mathematics and engineering; English, literature, and media criticism; general semantics; general system theory; psychiatry; and management.

Overview

Table 2 presents an approximate distribution of theoretical contributions. The cells in the table indicate whether a discipline's contribution to a theoretical question lies primarily in World Views I or II, or both.

Philosophy

We have already seen that epistemology and metaphysics are important contributions of philosophy. In addition, philosophy produces important substantive thought bearing on communication, as summarized in Table 3. Four important traditions have emerged: theories of signs, ordinary language philosophy, pragmatism, and phenomenology. These traditions address primarily coding, meaning, and thinking as central processes of communication.

One of the most general theories related to coding is Morris's work in semiotic (1946, 1955, 1964). Owing a direct debt to Mead and symbolic interactionism, Morris developed a three-fold model integrating states of action, types of signs, and values. The model is quite eclectic, drawing from behavioral psychology, symbolic interactionism, and value theory. In his early work on signs, Morris took a distinctly World View I stance, but his later work shifted considerably toward the alternate view.

First Cassirer (1944, 1953, 1955, 1957) and later his protégé Langer (1942, 1967, 1972) produced interesting work on symbolic forms. Cassirer taught that predominant symbolic forms, such as language, myth, art, and science, literally shape the experience of the

Table 2 AN APPROXIMATE DISTRIBUTION OF THEORETICAL CONTRIBUTIONS

THEMATIC AREAS AND QUESTIONS	DISCIPLINES AND INTERDISCIPLINES											
	1 PHILOSOPHY	2 PSYCHOLOGY: HUMANISTIC AND CLINICAL	3 PSYCHOLOGY: BEHAVIORAL AND SOCIAL	4 PSYCHOLOGY: COGNITIVE	5 SOCIOLOGY	6 ANTHROPOLOGY AND LINGUISTICS	7 MATHEMATICS AND LINGUISTICS	8 ENGLISH, LITERATURE, AND MEDIA CRITICISM	9 GENERAL SEMANTICS	10 GENERAL SYSTEM THEORY	11 PSYCHIATRY	12 MANAGEMENT
I. PROCESS												
A. In what ways is communication processual?							II			II		
II. SYMBOLIC INTERACTION												
A. How does communication involve symbolic interaction?					II			II				
III. CODING												
A. What is the nature of the relationship between sign and signified?	II		I		II							
B. How do codes function to create messages?						II						
C. How is language structured?	II			II		I, II						
D. How is language produced and understood?			I	II		I, II						
E. How is language acquired?			I	II		I, II						

254

F. What nonverbal behaviors function as signs in communication?						I, II
G. How are nonverbal codes structured?			I			I, II
H. How are nonverbal codes acquired?			I			I, II
I. How do nonverbal behaviors function?			I			I, II

IV. MEANING

A. What is meaning?	II		I	II	II	
B. What conditions give rise to meaning?	II		I	II	II	
C. Where is the locus of meaning?	II		I	II	II	

V. THINKING

A. By what mechanisms is information processed?		II		
B. How does thought develop?		II		
C. How do humans solve problems?	II	II		

VI. INFORMATION

A. What is information?			I	I
B. How is information transmitted?			I	I
C. In what ways does information affect people and systems?				I

VII. PERSUASION

A. What factors in the communication source and message inhibit or facilitate change?		I	
B. What elements of the person change as a result of communication?	I		
C. What elements in the person inhibit or facilitate change?	I		

Table 2 *(Continued)*

THEMATIC AREAS AND QUESTIONS	PHILOSOPHY	PSYCHOLOGY: HUMANISTIC AND CLINICAL	PSYCHOLOGY: BEHAVIORAL AND SOCIAL	PSYCHOLOGY: COGNITIVE	SOCIOLOGY	ANTHROPOLOGY AND LINGUISTICS	MATHEMATICS AND LINGUISTICS	ENGLISH, LITERATURE, AND MEDIA CRITICISM	GENERAL SEMANTICS	GENERAL SYSTEM THEORY	PSYCHIATRY	MANAGEMENT
	1	2	3	4	5	6	7	8	9	10	11	12
VIII. INTERPERSONAL CONTEXT												
A. What are the elements of interpersonal relationship?		II	I		II		I				II	
B. What is the nature of interpersonal perception/attribution?		II	II								II	
C. What are the factors of attraction?			I									
D. What facilitates interpersonal empathy and understanding?		II									II	
E. What factors enter into conflict?			I				I					

DISCIPLINES AND INTERDISCIPLINES

IX. GROUP CONTEXT
A. What distinguishes a small group? — I
B. How do groups affect individuals? — I
C. What factors contribute to task output? — I
D. What motivates group participation? — I
E. What is the nature of interaction in groups? — I
F. What is the nature of decision making in groups? — I

X. ORGANIZATIONAL CONTEXT
A. What is the essence of organization? — II   II   I   II
B. How does authority arise within an organization? — I   II
C. What factors contribute to organizational success? — II   I   I, II
D. What is the nature of decision making in organizations? — II   I   I

XI. MASS CONTEXT
A. What are the functions of mass communication? — II
B. How are information and influence disseminated in mass communication? — I, II
C. What is the impact of media on society? — I   I, II   I

Table 3   CONTRIBUTIONS IN PHILOSOPHY

THEMES	QUESTIONS	REPRESENTATIVE THEORIES	WORLD VIEWS
CODING	What is the nature of the relation between sign and signified?	Semiotic (Morris)	II
		Ordinary Language Philosophy; Speech Acts (Wittgenstein, Austin, Searle)	II
		Symbolic Form (Cassirer, Langer)	II
	How is language structured?	Ordinary Language Philosophy; Speech Acts (Wittgenstein, Austin, Searle)	II
MEANING	What is meaning?	Symbolic Interactionism (Dewey)	II
		Symbolic Forms (Cassirer, Langer)	II
		Phenomenology (Heidegger)	II
		Ordinary Language Philosophy; Speech Acts (Wittgenstein, Austin, Searle)	II
	What conditions give rise to meaning?	Symbolic Forms (Cassirer, Langer)	II
		Ordinary Language Philosophy (Wittgenstein, Austin, Searle)	II
	Where is the locus of meaning?	Symbolic Forms (Cassirer, Langer)	II
		Phenomenology (Heidegger) Ordinary Language Philosophy (Wittgenstein, Austin, Searle)	
THINKING	How do humans solve problems?	Pragmatics (Dewey)	II

people in a culture. Langer dealt more directly with the nature of the symbol-thought relation, furthering our understanding of meaning.

Ordinary language philosophy, developed originally by Wittgenstein (1922, 1953, 1958), spurns traditional linguistic analysis in favor of more holistic, experiential observation of language in use. Later contributors, such as Austin (1962a & b) and Searle (1967, 1969), have furthered this movement by elaborating on speech acts, in which entire discursive meanings or intentions are singled out as units of analysis.

Phenomenology, whose primary spokesperson, Heidegger (1961,

1971), is one of the best-known voices of our time, deals with the first-hand experience of the human being. This experience, which can never be captured in abstract laws or generalizations, is inseparable from language. The person's experience is inseparably wedded to the stream of language into which the person is thrown upon birth, and the individual's definition of experienced events in terms of their potential in his or her life depends greatly upon how those events are symbolized. This view adds an important insight into the theme of meaning.

Pragmatism as a branch of philosophy (James, 1890) evaluates human activity in terms of its utility. The great American pragmatist John Dewey (1910, 1916, 1925, 1929, 1934) had much to say about meaning and thinking. As a symbolic interactionist, he demonstrated how language, including symbols and meanings, is a product of social interaction. His ideas on reflective thinking are well known as a problem-solving attitude and method.

The contributions of philosophy are important but somewhat narrow in the overall picture of communication theory. This work is almost exclusively that of World View II, which treats the person holistically and relies greatly on the experience and interpretation of the individual.

Psychology

Psychology is clearly the biggest discipline dealing with communication. It is a diverse and heterogeneous field, and most of its branches deals in one way or another with communication themes. As a whole, this discipline has produced more theory and research related to communication than any other. Because of its heterogeneous nature, I have divided psychology into three groupings.

Humanistic and clinical psychology have much in common. Many humanists have been or remain clinical psychologists as well. Actually, it would be difficult to separate the literature of these two areas. *Social and behavioral psychology* have been grouped because they share common epistemological assumptions and address similar communication themes. In fact, social psychology has generally been so singular in its attachment to behavioristic methods that it might well be considered a subset of behavioral psychology. The third grouping has been established because it is hard to place with either of the other two. This school deals with human information processing and language. I have labelled it *cognitive psychology.*

Psychology as a whole is not allied with any particular world view. Humanistic psychologists tend to relate more comfortably to World View II, while social psychologists are more often inclined toward World View I. A few social psychologists tend to be more holistic in approach, lying more in the direction of World View II. Cognitive psychology is also mixed, with some researchers holding behavioristic, World View I assumptions. Most cognitive theorists nowadays, however, relate to the second set of assumptions. Let's turn now to a discussion of the major theoretical contributions of these three groups.

• *Humanistic and Clinical Psychology.* No doubt, the primary interest of these theorists is interpersonal communication. It is natural for them to extend their work into organizational communication also, since the organization relies at its base on interpersonal relations. The clinical bent in this body of theory is apparent in the concern for human potential, growth, and change. Interpersonal communication is often viewed as an important vehicle for personal change, and it is also seen as the genesis of various personal disorders. These ideas explain the preoccupation of this subdiscipline with the interpersonal context. They also explain the tendency for these theories to be largely prescriptive, in contrast to the predominantly descriptive theory in the other two areas of psychology.

An excellent, clear overview of the humanistic approach to interpersonal communication is the interaction theory of Luft (1969). This theory centers on a model known as the Johari Window, which illustrates effects of feedback and disclosure, two seminal concepts from this movement. One of the first theorists in this area was Rogers (1942, 1951, 1959, 1961), whose work on client-centered therapy and the encounter group is well known. More recently, Jourard (1968, 1971) has done research on self-disclosure, promoting the idea of transparency or openness in interpersonal relations.

A broader view is provided in Watzlawick, Beavin, and Jackson's (1967) well-known treatment, which centers on the family. Taking a systems view, these theorists define the nature of relationship in terms of communication messages. They note that all interaction involves relationship-defining messages, an idea that has become very popular in recent years (Ellis, 1978; Fitzpatrick, 1977; Parks, 1977).

The humanistic approach on the organizational level is identified with the human relations movement. Here, ideas on interpersonal relations and personal growth are related to organizational goals, such as productivity and decision making. The work of Likert (1961, 1967) and of Argyris (1957, 1959, 1962, 1964, 1971) are examples.

Table 4 summarizes this work from humanistic and clinical psychology.

• *Behavioral and Social Psychology.* This subdivision has addressed just about every theme in our model. Its work is prodigious and broad in scope. It has adapted research methods from the physical sciences to

Table 4 CONTRIBUTIONS IN HUMANISTIC AND CLINICAL
PSYCHOLOGY

THEMES	QUESTIONS	REPRESENTATIVE THEORIES	WORLD VIEW
INTER-PERSONAL	What are the elements of interpersonal relationship?	Congruence Theory (Rogers)	II
		Self-Disclosure (Jourard)	II
		Pragmatics (Watzla-wick, Beavin & Jackson	II
	What is the nature of interpersonal perception/attribution?	Johari Window (Luft)	II
	What facilitates interpersonal empathy and understanding?	Congruence Theory (Rogers)	II
		Self-Disclosure (Jourard)	II
ORGANIZATION	What is the essence of organization?	Human Relations (Likert, Argyris)	II
	What factors contribute to organizational success?	Human Relations (Likert, Argyris)	II
	What is the nature of decision making?	Human Relations (Likert, Argyris)	II

observe a gamut of individual and social behaviors. Some prominent examples of this work appear in Table 5. For purposes of discussion, I divide this work into five parts: learning theory, attitude theory, interpersonal theory, group theory, and others.

Learning theory has been a mainstay of psychology (see Kling, 1971). While many variants have been developed, two broad branches will suffice as overview. Hullian theory (Hull, 1943, 1952) focuses on stimulus and response *associations*. Operant theory, on the other hand, focuses on instrumental or *reinforced* behavior. The two theorists most often associated with these movements in communication circles are Osgood (1963) and Skinner (1957). Both of these men have produced explanations of language behavior. Skinner sees language as reinforced behavior, while Osgood focuses on meaning as internally learned associations of stimuli. Osgood is clearly the most well-known psycholinguist of the behaviorist tradition. He has written widely on language and has provided a foundational theory of meaning through his semantic differential research (Osgood, Suci, and Tannenbaum, 1957; Os-

Table 5   CONTRIBUTIONS IN BEHAVIORAL AND SOCIAL PSYCHOLOGY

THEMES	QUESTIONS	REPRESENTATIVE THEORIES	WORLD VIEW
CODING	What is the relationship between sign and signified?	Learning Theory (Skinner)	I
	How is language produced and understood?	Learning Theory (Skinner, Hull, Osgood)	I
	How is language acquired?	Operant Theory (Skinner)	I
		Mediational Approach (Osgood)	I
	How are nonverbal codes structured?	Communication of Emotion (Ekman & Friesen)	I
	How do nonverbal behaviors function?	Communication of Emotion (Ekman & Friesen)	I
	How are nonverbal codes acquired?	Communication of Emotion (Ekman & Friesen)	I
MEANING	What is meaning?	Mediational Theory (Osgood)	I
	What conditions give rise to meaning?	Mediational Theory (Osgood)	I
	Where is the locus of meaning?	Mediational Theory (Osgood)	I
PERSUASION	What factors in the communication source or message inhibit or facilitate change?	Learning Theory (Hull, Weiss)	I
		Communication Research Tradition (Hovland)	I
	What elements of the person change as a result of communication?	Attitude and Attitude Change (Rokeach, Fishbein)	I
	What elements in the person inhibit or facilitate change?	Learning Theory (Hull, Weiss)	I
		Consistency Theory (Festinger)	I

Table 5 *(Continued)*

THEMES	QUESTIONS	REPRESENTATIVE THEORIES	WORLD VIEW
		Influenceability (McGuire)	I
		Inoculation Theory (McGuire)	I
		Social Judgment Theory (Sherif)	I
INTER-PERSONAL	What are the elements of interpersonal relationship?	FIRO (Schutz)	I
	What is the nature of interpersonal perception/attribution?	Attribution Theory (Heider, Kelley, Jones)	II
	What are the factors of attraction?	Association Theory (Byrne)	I
		Immediacy (Mehrabian)	I
		Balance Theory (Newcomb)	I
GROUP	What distinguishes a small group?	Group Dynamics (Lewin, Cartwright, & Zander)	I, II
	How do groups affect individuals?	Group Dynamics (Lewin)	II
	What factors contribute to task output?	Syntality (Cattell)	I
	What motivates group participation?	Exchange Theory (Thibaut & Kelley)	I
	What is the nature of interaction in groups?	Interaction Process Analysis (Bales)	I
	What is the nature of decision making in groups?	Decision Making and Groupthink (Janis)	II
ORGANIZATION	What is the essence of organization?	Social Psychology of Organizations (Katz & Kahn)	II
MASS	What is the impact of media on society?	Effects Research (Klapper)	I

good & Richards, 1973; Osgood, May & Miron, 1975). Learning theory has been applied to other themes as well. Weiss (1962, 1968) has used learning theory to explain persuasion, and Byrne (1971) developed a learning theory of interpersonal attraction.

Communication research of the 1950s and 1960s was dominated by attitude theory, and this movement lives as a powerful force in our thinking about communication. The Yale Communication Research Program, led by Hovland (Hovland, Janis, & Kelly, 1953), stood as exemplar for many years. It contained the seeds of much theory that bloomed years later. A good deal of research has centered on defining and operationalizing attitude (Fishbein, 1967; Rokeach, 1969). Consistency theories, including Balance Theory (Heider, 1946, 1958), Congruity Theory (Osgood & Tannenbaum, 1955), Dissonance Theory (Festinger, 1957), and Congruence Theory (Rokeach, 1973), provided certain core assumptions about how people behave and why they change. Further explanations were added by Sherif and his associates (Sherif, 1967; Sherif & Cantril, 1947; Sherif & Hovland, 1961; Sherif, Sherif, & Nebergall, 1965) in their social judgment approach. The attitude research tradition also included insights on persuasibility or influenceability (McGuire, 1968), and resistance to persuasion (McGuire, 1964).

Another research area applies behavioristic assumptions to interpersonal communication. Mehrabian (1971), for example, analyzed interactions in terms of power, responsiveness, and immediacy (attraction). Newcomb (1961) applied balance theory to interpersonal attraction, explaining attraction in terms of perceptual consistency. Schutz (1958) produced an explanation of interpersonal behavior in terms of inclusion, control, and affection needs. One tradition from social psychology that bore much fruit in the 1970s is attribution theory, begun by Heider (1958) and continued by several others (e.g., Hastorf, Schneider, & Polefka, 1970; Jones, Kanouse, Kelley, Niskett, Valins, & Weiner, 1971; Kelley, 1971). This approach uses a phenomenological view of interpersonal perception, investigating the processes by which people make inferences about themselves and others. Unlike most of the other theories in this subdivision of psychology, attribution theory takes primarily a World View II stance.

A good deal of social psychology has concerned itself with group processes. Group dynamics, led by Kurt Lewin (1947, 1948), was especially concerned about the relationship of the person to the group. How do groups affect individual behavior, and how does the psychological makeup of the group affect group life? Cattell (1948) created the concept of syntality, or group personality, which included the concept of synergy. Synergy consists of effective and maintenance energy in a group. Thibaut and Kelley (1959) developed their exchange theory, which pictured individual motivation as a function of the costs and rewards of group life. Perhaps the psychological theory most directly related to group communication is the interaction theory of Robert Bales (1950, 1970). Bales developed categories for the analysis of task and socioemotional communication in groups, and later he related these to networks and roles. Networks were the primary focus of a research program led originally by Bavelas (1950). Here, leadership was seen as a function of channel control, which could be highly centralized or dispersed. Finally, we should mention the popular theory of Janis (1967; Janis & Mann, 1977) on groupthink, in which group decision making is evaluated from a critical thinking standpoint. Janis's work on groupthink and decision making, considering his historical and anecdotal methods of research and his treatment of the person as active chooser, is one of the few social psychological theories that takes a World View II stance.

A variety of other work from behavioral and social psychology relates to several themes in our model. The research of Ekman and Friesen (1969, 1972) on the functions of nonverbal behavior helps to enlighten our understanding of coding. So does the work of Dittmann (1972) on the communication of emotion. Katz and Kahn's well known text *The Social Psychology of Organizations* (1966) should also be mentioned. These authors use a systems approach to explain a number of organizational phenomena that bear upon communication. This work is an example of theory that bridges two disciplines: psychology and sociology. Finally, we should mention that a good deal of media effects research takes place within the subdiscipline of social psychology (e.g., Davidson, Boylan, & Yu, 1976; Klapper, 1960).

• *Cognitive Psychology.* This subdiscipline of psychology deals primarily with language and thinking, as indicated in Table 6. Psycholinguistics is the branch of psychology dealing with language, providing an interface with linguistics. Unfortunately, the study of language is difficult to classify in our multidisciplinary schema. Traditionally, linguistics was a branch of anthropology, and many linguists still identify primarily with that field. But linguistics has emerged as a field of its own, which is best classed as an interdiscipline. I have grouped linguistics with anthropology here, since they are closely related and difficult to separate conceptually.

There are two main approaches to psycholinguistics: behavioristic and cognitive. We have already highlighted Osgood as the chief proponent of the behavioristic tradition. Other psycholinguists, who espouse the cognitive notion, tend to follow the work of Noam Chomsky, which is summarized in the section on anthropology and linguistics.

The second theme, thinking, can be approached in a number of

Table 6   CONTRIBUTIONS IN COGNITIVE PSYCHOLOGY

THEMES	QUESTIONS	REPRESENTATIVE THEORIES	WORLD VIEW
CODING	How is language structured?	Psycholinguistics: Behavioristic (Osgood)	I
		Psycholinguistics: Generative (Chomsky)	II
	How is language produced and understood?	Psycholinguistics (as above)	
	How is language acquired?	Psycholinguistics (as above)	
THINKING	By what mechanisms is information processed?	Conceptual Behavior (Bourne)	II
	How does thought develop?	Cognitive Development (Piaget, Bruner)	II
	How do humans solve problems?	Planning (Miller)	II

ways. The work of Bourne (1966) and others investigates the ways in which people form concepts, isolating strategies for seeking out patterns in stimulus events. The theories of developmental psychologists, such as Piaget (1952, 1964, 1971; Piaget & Inhelder, 1958) and Bruner (Bruner, Goodnow, & Austin, 1956) tell a great deal about how people process information. These theories also provide insights into the acquisition and development of conceptual abilities. Finally, I would mention the interesting model of Miller, Galanter, and Pribram (1960), which likens human planning behavior to computer operations.

Cognitive psychology generally assumes that people are active agents with purposeful behavior. They often rely on the self-reports of their subjects, coupled with case observation. For these reasons, most of the contributions from cognitive psychology fit World View II.

Sociology

Table 7 outlines some significant contributions from sociology. As you can see from this table, sociology addresses most of the themes in the model. Basically, there are three broad approaches used in this field. The first looks at societal institutions as entities, deemphasizing interaction. The second is behavior social psychology, which is very similar to its cousin field in psychology. The work summarized in that section a few pages back (Table 5) is also representative of social psychology in sociology. The third approach examines social processes, featuring communication as a primary focus. Most of the work to be summarized in this section comes from this third sociological approach.

Perhaps the major thrust of this social process work stems from symbolic interactionism, a school of thought regarding the person, groups, and institutions (see Littlejohn, 1977a & b). The primary theme of this body of theory is communication, and I draw most of my insights regarding the general nature of communication from symbolic interactionism.

Numerous theorists have contributed, including Mead (1932, 1934, 1936, 1938), Cooley (1930), Blumer (1955, 1969), Kuhn (1956), Duncan (1962), and Denzin (1970). These theorists and others provide their own interpretations and extensions, but the overall framework of symbolic interactionism is rather consistent. Manis and Meltzer (1972) have summarized this movement in the following principles: (1) mind, self, and society are not structures but interactional processes; (2) language is the main tool in this process; (3) the individual's mind is an internal reflection of social processes; (4) behavior is constructed proactively; (5) people behave in accordance with their definitions of situations; and (6) the self consists of both social and unique definitions.

Of particular interest to interpersonal communication is the work of Goffman (1959, 1967, 1971, 1974), who is an interactionist. Goffman has provided interesting analyses of interaction in everyday life, focusing on how people define situations and present the self (see Littlejohn, 1977a, b). Group communication is also addressed by sociologists. Although Table 7 lists symbolic interactionism under coding and meaning, it should be noted that many theorists in this movement discuss language as a group-founded process. The work from social psychology on groups, summarized in the previous section, is quite similar to sociological work in this thematic area.

On the organizational level, Weber's (1947) bureaucratic theory is a landmark. Weber was not an interactionist, and his ideas on organizations subordinate communication to issues of organizational structure and policy. Of more direct interest, perhaps, is Katz and Kahn's (1966) system theory of organizations, which includes communication as one of several organizational processes.

Sociology has been a primary discipline in the study of mass communication. Early on, Lasswell (1948) presented his functional model of mass communication, later elaborated by Wright (1960). Lazarsfeld (Lazarsfeld, Berelson, & Gaudet, 1948), and later Katz (1960, 1968), developed their ideas on the two-step flow hypothesis. This notion, which gives interpersonal channels a central role in the dissemination of influence, has been advanced much further by theorists such as

Rogers (1962; Rogers & Shoemaker, 1971) in their work on the diffusion of innovations. In contrast to these mediational theories, the critics of mass society, summarized by Bell (1956), believe that media and technology have created mass anomie and social distress. This alarmist World View I criticism has been soundly rebuffed by more tempered commentators (Bauer & Bauer, 1960; Bell, 1956).

With the exception of the institutions approach of Weber and mass society theory, most of the work from sociology lies in World View II. This is certainly the case with most symbolic interaction theories, which treat the person as a purposeful actor, relying on participant observation methods.

Anthropology and Linguistics

Although linguistics is generally recognized as a field of its own, it is an interdiscipline whose foundations lie in anthropology. For purposes of discussion, I group these two fields together. By and large, the work in these fields relates to coding and meaning, as indicated in Table 8. These theories address virtually all of the questions related to these themes, but the table isolates the questions emphasized by the selected theories.

Language, of course, is the primary focus of linguistics. Older theories of language structure, such as finite state grammar (Bloomfield, 1933), have given way to the generative approach of Chomsky (1957, 1965, 1972, 1975) and his followers. These theorists view language much more as a process than a structure. For them, language consists of basic, deep, meaningful units; phrase structure rules for building deep structures; and transformation rules for developing utterable, surface sentences. Humans are believed to be born with much more than an advanced ability to learn language; they possess an innate knowledge of universal principles that accelerates language acquisition at a phenomenal rate.

Nonverbal codes have been studied extensively in anthropology. Anthropologists are not only interested in the language patterns of cultures but in their behavioral codes as well. Birdwhistell (1952, 1970) is very well known for his work on kinesics, or the study of bodily activity. In his popular books, Hall (1959, 1966) has elucidated spacial and other codes that make interesting cross-cultural comparisons. Both of these theorists discuss the interrelatedness of all codes and the complexity of messages while maintaining their own foci.

Meaning is addressed by the theory of linguistic relativity, as proposed by Sapir (1921) and Whorf (1956). This well-known theory states that people perceive and think in limited ways, depending upon their culture's language patterns. Relying on research on the Hopi and

Table 7 CONTRIBUTIONS IN SOCIOLOGY

THEMES	QUESTIONS	REPRESENTATIVE THEORIES	WORLD VIEW
SYMBOLIC INTERACTION	How does communication involve symbolic interaction?	Symbolic Interactionism (Mead, Blumer)	II
CODING	What is the nature of the relationship between sign and signified?	Symbolic Interactionism (Mead, Blumer)	II
	How is language acquired?	Symbolic Interactionism (Mead, Blumer)	II
MEANING	What is meaning?	Symbolic Interactionism (Mead, Blumer)	II
	What conditions give rise to meaning?	Symbolic Interactionism (Mead, Blumer)	II
	Where is the locus of meaning?	Symbolic Interactionism (Mead, Blumer)	II
INTER-PERSONAL	What are the elements of relationship?	Presentation of Self (Goffman)	II
ORGANIZATION	What is the essence of organization?	Theory of Bureaucracy (Weber)	I
	How does authority arise within an organization?	Theory of Bureaucracy (Weber)	I
	What factors contribute to organizational success?	Bureaucratic Theory (Weber)	I
	What is the nature of decision making in organizations?	Bureaucratic Theory (Weber)	I
MASS	What are the functions of mass communication?	Functional Theory (Lasswell)	II
	How are information and influence disseminated in mass communication?	Diffusion of Innovations (Rogers)	II
		Multistep Flow (Lazarsfeld)	II
	What is the impact of media on society?	Mass Society (Bell)	I, II
		Symbolic Interactionism (Edelman)	II

other cultures, Whorf found that behavior is based on perception, which in turn is based on grammatical structures. This pattern is believed to limit severely the individual's freedom to act.

Anthropology and linguistics is a mixed bag of world views. The deterministic approaches, such as Whorf's, tend to lie in World View I, while others, such as Chomsky's, take a more flexible stance and relate more completely to the second view.

Other Fields

There is a great deal of work bearing on communication that is rather isolated within a discipline or difficult to place in any traditional category. These contributions are summarized in Table 9 and are discussed below. The following groupings are not presented in any order of importance.

· *Mathematics and Engineering.* No discussion of communication theory is complete without including information theory and cybernetics. Information theory (Shannon & Weaver, 1949) was originally formu-

Table 8 CONTRIBUTIONS IN ANTHROPOLOGY AND LINGUISTICS

THEMES	QUESTIONS	REPRESENTATIVE THEORIES	WORLD VIEW
CODING	How do codes function to create messages?	Kinesics (Birdwhistell)	II
		Proxemics (Hall)	II
	How is language structured?	Finite State Linguistics (Bloomfield)	I
		Generative Grammar (Chomsky)	II
	What nonverbal behaviors function as signs in communication?	Kinesics (Birdwhistell)	I
		Proxemics (Hall)	II
	How are nonverbal codes acquired?	Territorial Imperative (Ardrey)	I
		Proxemics (Hall)	II
MEANING	What is meaning?	Linguistic Relativity (Whorf)	I
	What conditions give rise to meaning?	Linguistic Relativity (Whorf)	I

lated to provide tools for the transmission of information in mechanical and electronic machine systems. It remains an important area in the development of nonhuman systems. Scholars interested in human communication have freely borrowed analogies from information theory to conceptualize communication events. Psychologists interested in sensory perception and cognition (e.g., Miller, 1956) have applied some concepts from information rather directly.

Cybernetics (Wiener, 1948) is the study of self-regulation in human and machine systems. It elaborates feedback and adjustment processes that create system homeostasis. Borrowing as it does from physics, this approach has many World View I elements, but applied to human systems, it is processual and tends toward the other end of the world view spectrum. Cybernetics is an important contributor to general system theory, which is discussed below.

• *English, Literature, and Media Criticism.* This set is merely a convenient category for discussing three otherwise unrelated theorists who originally identified with the field of English and literature. The first is Kenneth Burke (1945, 1950), whose work on symbols is best included with our ideas from symbolic interactionism. Viewing humans as actors, Burke used a dramatistic metaphor to explain communication processes. His work relates most directly to the thematic areas under the general nature of communication, but it relates to meaning as well.

I. A. Richards (Ogden & Richards, 1923; Richards, 1936, 1952) created a theory of meaning and discourse, which has been used as a foundation for many other approaches to these topics. Specifically, Richards identified elements of meaning and applied these to rhetorical clarity in discourse.

Finally, in quite a different vein, we cannot forget the theory of McLuhan (1964), who became quite a pop culture leader in the 1960s and 1970s. Basing his ideas on the work of Innis (1951), McLuhan dwelled on the impact of media upon society.

• *General Semantics.* General semantics was originally developed by Korzybski (1933) as a regimen for the improvement of human thinking. Since its inception, it has been adopted by many scholars and teachers as a model for understanding meaning and language. Basically, it has been used to teach people to be more careful observers of real-world events and to discriminate meanings and perceptions elicited by language from actual symbolized events.

• *General System Theory.* GST, originated by the biologist Bertalanffy (1968), is a true interdiscipline, providing a framework for the unification of scientific and social thought. This framework has been ap-

Table 9 CONTRIBUTIONS IN OTHER AREAS

DISCIPLINE OR AREA	THEMES	QUESTIONS	REPRESENTATIVE THEORIES	WORLD VIEW
	Process	In what ways is communication a process?	Cybernetics (Wiener)	II
MATHE- MATICS AND ENGINEERING	Informa- tion	What is infor- mation?	Information Theory (Shan- non & Weaver)	I
		How is informa- tion trans- mitted?	Information Theory (Shan- non & Weaver)	I
	Inter- personal	What factors enter into conflict?	Game Theory (von Neumann & Morgenstern)	
	Symbolic Interaction	How does com- munication in- volve symbolic interaction?	Rhetoric of Dramatism (Burke)	II
ENGLISH, LITERATURE, AND MEDIA CRITICISM	Meaning	What is mean- ing?	Literary Rhet- oric (Richards)	II
	Mass	What is the im- pact of media on society?	McLuhanism	I
GENERAL SEMANTICS	Meaning	All questions	General Seman- tics (Korzybski)	II
GENERAL SYSTEM THEORY	Process	In what ways is communication processual?	GST (Berta- lanffy)	II
	Informa- tion	In what ways does informa- tion affect peo- ple and systems?	Purposeful Sys- tems (Ackoff & Emery)	I
PSYCHIATRY	Inter- personal	What are the elements of interpersonal relationship?	Metaperception (Laing)	II
		What is the na- ture of inter- personal perception/ attribution?	Metaperception (Laing)	II

Table 9   *(Continued)*

DISCIPLINE OR AREA	THEMES	QUESTIONS	REPRESENTATIVE THEORIES	WORLD VIEW
		What facilitates interpersonal empathy and understanding?	Metaperception (Laing)	II
			Transactional Analysis (Berne)	II
MANAGEMENT	Organization	What is the essence of organization?	Functions (Barnard)	II
			Neo-Weberian (March & Simon)	II
		How does authority arise within the organization?	Functions (Barnard)	II
			Human Relations (Blake & Mouton)	II
		What factors contribute to organizational success?	Scientific Management (Taylor)	I
			Functions (Barnard)	II
			Human Relations	II
		What is the nature of decision making in organizations?	Neo-Weberian (March & Simon)	II

plied to a variety of disciplines and content areas. It seeks to uncover universal principles of order, emphasizing hierarchy, cybernetics, information, and process.

• *Psychiatry.* With its interest in human growth and therapeutic relationships, this field aligns itself with clinical and humanistic psychology in addressing interpersonal communication as a theme. Two psychiatrists have become especially prominent in communication theory. R. D. Laing (Laing, Phillipson, & Lee, 1966; 1967, 1969) has developed a theory of interpersonal perception, applying it specifically to relational health. Eric Berne (1961, 1964) is known for transactional analysis, a very popular model of interpersonal communication and therapy.

· *Management.* This field is especially concerned with organizational communication. A number of traditions have emerged, one of the earliest being scientific management (Taylor, 1919). In contrast to more recent developments, this approach minimizes the importance of communication. On the other hand, Barnard (1938) presented a theory of executive leadership that placed communication at the pinnacle of organizational processes. The human relations movement, spurred by social and humanistic psychology (see, for example, Blake & Mouton, 1964) also emphasized communication but included it as a means for promoting human growth in organizations. A broader, more holistic, approach is the neo-Weberian systems theory of March and Simon (1958), which emphasizes decision-making processes in organizations.

USING A MULTIDISCIPLINARY FRAMEWORK FOR COMPARATIVE EVALUATION

One of the advantages of a multidisciplinary framework such as the one presented here is that it provides a basis for theoretical evaluation. In this section, I will discuss some types of comparative evaluation available to the communication scholar.

Dimensions of Comparative Evaluation

The framework developed in this chapter promotes three dimensions that can guide comparative evaluation. The first of these is *world view,* or the philosophical basis of theories being compared. Our earlier caution bears repeating here: there are numerous world views. Our convenient two-group division is a good general beginning in a treatment such as this, but finer discriminations can be made, and any comparative critic might choose to conceptualize world views somewhat differently than I did here.

The second dimension is *domain,* or theoretical territory. A theory's domain consists of the themes and questions addressed by the theory. A domain may be large, covering several themes, or focused, dealing with only one or two questions within a single-theme category.

The third dimension for comparative evaluation is *field,* consisting of the community or group of scholars producing the theory. A field may be a traditional discipline, such as one of our big four, a subdiscipline, interdiscipline, or a combination of these.

No single multidisciplinary framework is adequate for all comparative evaluations. Each analyst must decide the most useful way to cut the pies of world view, domain, and field in order to accomplish the intended aims.

The comparative critic works with two dimensions at once. The first dimension is the *comparison dimension* and the second, the *evaluation dimension*. The critic makes comparisons between theories varying on the comparison dimension, examining differences within a level on the evaluation dimension. For this reason, the first dimension can also be labeled the *between dimension* and the other the *within dimension*. Table 10 summarizes these dimensions. Examples of evaluations with various between and within dimensions are included in the following section.

Types of Comparative Evaluation

· *Type I.* Here the analyst compares theories with different world views in a single domain. The key question is, To what extent do varying world views apply in this domain? The aim of Type I comparison is

Table 10 DIMENSIONS OF COMPARATIVE EVALUATION

TYPE	COMPARISON DIMENSION (BETWEEN)	EVALUATION DIMENSION (WITHIN)	FOCUS
Type I	World View	Domain	Critic compares theories within a single domain across different world views.
Type II	World View	Field	Critic compares theories within a single field across different world views.
Type III	Domain	Field	Critic compares theories within a single field across different domains.
Type IV	Domain	World View	Critic compares theories within a single world view across different domains.
Type V	Field	World View	Critic compares theories within a single world view across different fields.
Type VI	Field	Domain	Critic compares theories within a single domain across different fields.

to determine the complexity of a particular domain in terms of the various philosophical stances that would be relevant to it.

Consider, for example, the domain of coding. Here we find a variety of theory, with a diversity of world views, offering explanations of coding processes. This widespread interest is an indication that coding is a central communication theme, and that it has been open to widely differing interpretations. It is a philosophically complex domain. This kind of finding may be a clue that careful conceptual analysis is necessary to clarify our understanding of this domain.

· *Type II.* Here the critic compares theories with different world views within a single field. The guiding question in Type II analysis is as follows: to what extent does this field involve varying world views? The aim of this kind of comparison is to cast light on the degree of heterogeneity of thought within a discipline, subdiscipline, or interdiscipline.

Let's take anthropology and linguisitcs as an evaluation field. An examination of the world views behind theories generated in this field reveals that it is very heterogeneous in its approach to communication. This philosophical complexity may be a clue that the study of language is muddled by disagreement over the nature and genesis of knowledge and other philosophical issues.

· *Type III.* Type III comparison is similar to Type II, except that the critic in the later type is comparing theories from the same field dealing with different domains. The critic asks these questions: to what extent does this field address multiple domains? How broad is its interest in communication? Here the aim is to discover the scope of a given field.

If we take mathematics and engineering as an evaluation field, we find that it addresses the theme of information almost exclusively. A search for other themes that have been of interest in this field reveals very little. Game theory and cybernetics are exceptions, but our conclusion here must be that mathematics and engineering are narrow in their approaches to communication. By the way, this is not necessarily a pejorative conclusion. A narrow scope is entirely appropriate considering the nature of these fields.

· *Type IV.* Here the critic looks for the various ways in which theories from a single world view approach different domains. The question is, What are the similarities and differences between the domains addressed by this world view? The aim of such an inquiry is to establish the relevance of a world view for casting light on certain domains.

We find, for example, that the mechanism inherent in the study of information as a domain is highly suited to the assumptions of

World View I, but information theory shares little in common with the domain of meaning, suggesting that World View I may be less relevant than the alternative view in building theory in the latter theme.

• *Type V.* Now the evaluator focuses on a single world view, as it is manifest in different fields, by asking the question, What fields cluster together or share common world views? This question aims at discovering common philosophical bases among various fields. It can also provide a clue as to how to cluster fields of study in seeking knowledge trends. This kind of analysis also helps us discover the prevalence of certain world views.

For example, the tendency of mathematics and behavioral psychology to share World View I reinforces our judgment that behavioral psychology is physicalistic, relying heavily on the assumption that people are like objects in essential respects.

• *Type VI.* While the other five types of comparative evaluation cast interesting light on the status of knowledge about communication, this final type is most relevant for expanding and clarifying this knowledge. In this final type of comparison, the critic examines the ways in which various fields have approached a particular domain, seeking similarities and dissimilarities in their propositional answers to theoretical questions. The guiding question, simply put, is, To what extent do theories within a given domain agree?

This kind of direct theoretical comparison leads to two aims. Where agreement is found, concurrent validity may be inferred. Here the assumption is that concurrence between two or more theories with differing scopes, fields, and methods is evidence that propositions are on the right track. On the other hand, theoretical disagreements may mark important issues for further investigation. Identifying such controversies is extremely important for theory growth.

One example of concurrent validity is found in the domain of source factors affecting persuasion. From rhetoric we learn that good will is an important contribution to ethos (Aristotle, 1932). The communication research tradition in social psychology confirms the same factor in numerous studies, though different terms are used (see Littlejohn, 1971). Unfortunately, such neat agreements are rarely encountered. More often, controversies will be uncovered. One of the most frustrating discoveries in a multidisciplinary analysis is that some domains are almost exclusively covered only by one subdiscipline with a narrow perspective. When this happens, both validity and controversy are impossible to verify.

Perhaps the most obvious barrier to Type VI criticism—and it hinders the other types as well—is semantic differences between fields and subfields. Almost always, different fields use different labels for the same or similar concepts. So the comparative critic must be a flexible reader, who looks beyond traditional disciplinary labels to underlying concepts.

Implications for the Evaluation of Individual Theories

Obviously, no single scholar would normally conduct an independent comparative analysis such as those described above. Usually, such analyses are stepping stones in the evaluation of particular theories or in the process of theory building. Comparing theories in these six ways can provide a great deal of insight into the quality of particular theories. The following are criteria most relevant to comparative analysis:

1. *Scope*—Is this theory comprehensive within its domain? Does it address sufficient questions within its thematic areas? Without looking across disciplines, the critic is blinded to the full depth of possibilities within a thematic area, limiting his or her evaluation of any single theory's scope.

2. *Appropriateness*—Is this theory's world view appropriate to the theoretical questions addressed? This question cannot be answered adequately without examining a range of world views and considering how they apply to various theme areas.

3. *Heuristic value*—Does the theory generate investigations into questions not resolved by other theories, or does it attempt to address established theoretical controversies? The true research-generating value of a theory cannot be validly assessed without a pretty thorough multidisciplinary comparison.

4. *Validity*—To what extent does the theory possess concurrent validity? Here again, cross-disciplinary comparison is essential in identifying points of validity (trends) and controversy.

POSTSCRIPT: THE STUDY OF COMMUNICATION AS INTERDISCIPLINE

Early in this chapter, I mentioned that the study of communication as an interdiscipline of its own is an important endeavor. Communication as a field consists of scholars who have been members of other formal disciplines but who now identify with the study of communication. The International Communication Association is an organization of such scholars. The field also consists of associates in the discipline of Speech Communication, which since its inception in the early part of this century has always made oral communication its focus. This focus is amply clear from the work sponsored by the Speech Communication Association.

The field of communication is very broad in scope, touching upon every theme in our multidisciplinary framework. It is highly eclectic, drawing from insights of the disciplines mentioned in this chapter. It involves ideas backed by a variety of world views. It promotes application, development of skill, research, and new theory.

This book contains the original contributions of a number of the most active scholars in Speech Communication. I hope that this chapter has provided insights into the broad multidisciplinary traditions from which this work has emerged.

References

Ackoff, R. & Emery, F. *On purposeful systems*. Chicago: Aldine, 1972.

Ardrey, R. *The territorial imperative*. New York: Atheneum, 1966.

Argyris, C. *Personality and organization: The conflict between system and the individual*. New York: Harper & Row, 1957.

Argyris, C. Understanding human behavior in organizations. In M. Haire (Ed.), *Modern organization theory*, New York: John Wiley & Sons, 1959.

Argyris, C. *Interpersonal competence and organizational effectiveness*. Homewood, Ill.: Richard D. Irwin, 1962.

Argyris, C. *Integrating the individual and the organization*. New York: John Wiley & Sons, 1964.

Argyris, C. *Management and organizational development*. New York: McGraw-Hill, 1971.

Aristotle. *[The rhetoric]* (L. Cooper, trans.). New York: Appleton-Century, 1932.

Austin, J. L. *How to do things with words*. Cambridge: Harvard University Press, 1962a.

Austin, J. L. *Philosophical papers*. Oxford: Clarendon Press, 1962b.

Bales, R. F. *Interaction process analysis: A method for the study of small groups*. Reading, Mass.: Addison-Wesley, 1950.

Bales, R. F. *Personality and interpersonal behavior*. New York: Holt, Rinehart and Winston, 1970.

Barnard, C. *The functions of the executive*. Cambridge: Harvard University Press, 1938.

Bauer, R., & Bauer, A. H. America, mass society, and mass media. *Journal of Social Issues*, 1960, *16*, 3–66.

Bavelas, A. Communication patterns in task-oriented groups. *Journal of the Acoustical Society of America*, 1950, *22*, 725–730.

Bell, D. The theory of mass society. *Commentary*, July 1956, 75–83.

Berne, E. *Transactional analysis in psychotherapy*. New York: Grove Press, 1961.

Berne, E. *Games people play*. New York: Grove Press, 1964.

Bertalanffy, L. *General system theory: Foundations, development, applications*. New York: George Braziller, 1968.

Birdwhistell, R. *Introduction to kinesics*. Louisville, Ky.: University of Louisville Press, 1952.

Birdwhistell, R. *Kinesics and context*. Philadelphia: University of Pennsylvania Press, 1970.

Black, M. *Models and metaphors*. Ithaca, N.Y.: Cornell University Press, 1962.

Blake, R., & Mouton, J. S. *The managerial grid*. Houston: Gulf Publishing Company, 1964.

Bloomfield, L. *Language*. New York: Holt, 1933.

Blumer, H. Attitudes and the social act. *Social Problems*, 1955, 3, 59–65.

Blumer, H. *Symbolic interactionism: Perspective and method*. Englewood Cliffs, N.J.: Prentice-Hall, 1969.

Bourne, L. *Human conceptual behavior*. Boston: Allyn and Bacon, 1966.

Bruner, J. S., Goodnow, J. J., & Austin, G. A. *A study of thinking*. New York: John Wiley & Sons, 1956.

Budd, R. W., & Ruben, B. D. (Eds.). *Approaches to human communication*. New York: Spartan-Hayden, 1972.

Burke, K. *A grammar of motives*. Englewood Cliffs, N.J.: Prentice-Hall, 1945.

Burke, K. *A rhetoric of motives*. Englewood Cliffs, N.J.: Prentice-Hall, 1950.

Byrne, D. *The attraction paradigm*. New York: Academic Press, 1971.

Cartwright, D. & Zander, A. (eds.) *Group Dynamics: research and theory*. New York: Harper & Row, 1968.

Cassirer, E. *The philosophy of symbolic forms* (3 vols.). (tr. R. Manheim). New Haven: Yale University Press, 1953, 1955, 1957.

Cassirer, E. *An essay on man*. New Haven: Yale University Press, 1944.

Cattell, R. Concepts and methods in the measurement of group syntality. *Psychological Review*, 1948, 55, 48–63.

Chomsky, N. *Syntactic structures*. The Hague: Mouton, 1957.

Chomsky, N. *Aspects of the theory of syntax*. Cambridge: M.I.T. Press, 1965.

Chomsky, N. *Language and mind*. New York: Harcourt Brace Jovanovich, 1972.

Chomsky, N. *Reflections on language*. New York: Pantheon Books, 1975.

Cooley, C. H. *Sociological theory and social research*. New York: Holt, Rinehart and Winston, 1930.

Dance, F. E. X (Ed.). *Human communication theory: original essays*. New York: Holt, Rinehart and Winston, 1967.

Dance, F. E. X. The "concept" of communication. *Journal of Communication*, 1970, 20, 201–210.

Dance, F. E. X., & Larson, C. E. *The functions of human communication: A theoretical approach*. New York: Holt, Rinehart and Winston, 1976.

Davidson, W. P., Boylan, J., & Yu, F. *Mass media: Systems and effects*. New York: Praeger Publications, 1976.

Denzin, N. K. *The research act*. Chicago: Aldine, 1970.

Dewey, J. *How we think*. Boston: D. C. Heath, 1910.

Dewey, J. *Essays in experimental logic.* Chicago: University of Chicago Press, 1916.

Dewey, J. *Experience and nature.* Chicago: Open Court, 1925.

Dewey, J. *The quest for certainty.* New York: Minton, Balch, and Co., 1929.

Dewey, J. *Art as experience.* New York: Minton, Balch, and Co., 1934.

Dittmann, A. T. *Interpersonal messages of emotion.* New York: Springer Publishing, 1972.

Duncan, H. D. *Communication and social order.* New York: The Bedminster Press, 1962.

Edelman, M. *The symbolic uses of politics.* Urbana, Ill.: University of Illinois Press, 1964.

Edelman, M. *Politics as symbolic action.* New York: Academic Press, 1971.

Ekman, P., & Friesen, W. The repertoire of nonverbal behavior: Categories, origins, usage, and coding. *Semiotica,* 1969, *1,* 49–98.

Ekman, P., & Friesen, W. *Emotion in the human face: Guidelines for research and an integration of findings.* New York: Pergamon Press, 1972.

Ellis, D. G. Trait predictors of relational control. In B. D. Ruben (Ed.), *Communication yearbook 2.* New Brunswick, N.J.: Transaction Books, 1978.

Festinger, L. *A theory of cognitive dissonance.* Stanford, Calif.: Stanford University Press, 1957.

Fishbein, M. A behavior theory approach to the relations between beliefs about an object and the attitude toward the object. In M. Fishbein (Ed.), *Readings in attitude theory and measurement.* New York: John Wiley & Sons, 1967.

Fitzpatrick, M. A. A typological approach to communication in relationships. In B. D. Ruben (Ed.), *Communication yearbook 1.* New Brunswick, N.J.: Transaction Books, 1977.

Goffman, E. *The presentation of self in everyday life.* Garden City, N.Y.: Doubleday, 1959.

Goffman, E. *Interaction ritual: essays on face-to-face behavior.* Garden City, N.Y.: Doubleday, 1967.

Goffman, E. *Relations in public.* New York: Basic Books, 1971.

Goffman, E. *Frame analysis: An essay on the organization of experience.* Cambridge: Harvard University Press, 1974.

Grene, M. *The knower and the known.* Berkeley: University of California Press, 1974.

Hall, E. T. *The silent language.* Greenwich, Conn.: Fawcett, 1959.

Hall, E. T. *The hidden dimension.* New York: Random House, 1966.

Hastorf, A. H., Schneider, D. J., & Polefka, J. *Person perception.* Reading, Mass.: Addison-Wesley, 1970.

Heidegger, M. *An introduction to metaphysics.* Garden City, N.Y.: Doubleday, 1961.

Heidegger, M. *On the way to language.* New York: Harper & Row, 1971.

Heider, F. Attitudes and cognitive organization. *Journal of Psychology,* 1946, *21,* 107–112.

Heider, F. *The psychology of interpersonal relations.* New York: John Wiley & Sons, 1958.

Hovland, C. I., Janis, I., & Kelly, H. *Communication and persuasion.* New Haven: Yale Universiy Press, 1953.

Hull, C. L. *Principles of behavior: An introduction to behavior theory.* New York: Appleton, 1943.

Hull, C. L. *A behavior system.* New Haven: Yale University Press, 1952.

Innis, H. A. *The bias of communication.* Toronto: University of Toronto Press, 1951.

James, W. *Principles of psychology.* New York: Holt, Rinehart and Winston, 1980.

Janis, I. *Victims of groupthink: A psychological study of foreign decisions and fiascos.* Boston: Houghton Mifflin, 1967.

Janis, I., & Mann, L. *Decision making: A psychological analysis of conflict, choice, and commitment.* New York: Free Press, 1977.

Jones, E., Kanouse, D. E., Kelley, H. H., Nisbett, R. E., Valins, S., & Weiner, B. *Attribution: Perceiving the causes of behavior.* Morristown, N.J.: General Learning Press, 1971.

Jourard, S. *Disclosing man to himself.* New York: Van Nostrand, 1968.

Jourard, S. *Self-disclosure: an experimental analysis of the transparent self.* New York: John Wiley & Sons, 1971.

Katz, D., & Kahn, D. *The social psychology of organizations.* New York: John Wiley & Sons, 1966.

Katz, E. The two-step flow of communication. In W. Schramm (Ed.), *Mass communications.* Urbana: University of Illinois Press, 1960.

Katz, E. Diffusion III: interpersonal influence. In David Sills (Ed.), *International encyclopedia of the social sciences* (Vol. 4). New York: Macmillan, 1968.

Kelley, H. *Attribution in social interaction.* Morristown, N.J.: General Learning Press, 1971.

Klapper, J. T. *The effects of mass communication.* New York: Free Press, 1960.

Kling, J. W. Learning: introductory survey. In J. W. Kling & L. Riggs (Eds.), *Woodworth and Schlosberg's experimental psychology.* New York: Holt, Rinehart and Winston, 1971.

Knower, F. The development of a sound communicology. Unpublished manuscript.

Korzybski, A. *Science and sanity: An introduction to non-Aristotelian systems and general semantics.* Lancaster, Penn.: International Non-Aristotelian Library Publishing Co., 1933.

Kuhn, M. H., & Hickman, C. A. *Individuals, groups, and economic behavior.* New York: Holt, Rinehart and Winston, 1956.

Laing, R. D. *The politics of experience.* New York: Pantheon Books, 1967.

Laing, R. D. *Self and others.* London: Tavistock Publications, 1969.

Laing, R. D., Phillipson, H., & Lee, A. R. *Interpersonal perception.* New York: Springer Publishing, 1966.

Langer, S. *Philosophy in a new key.* Cambridge: Harvard University Press, 1942.

Langer, S. *Mind: An essay on human feeling.* Baltimore: The Johns Hopkins Press, 3 vols., 1967, 1972, and forthcoming.

Lasswell, H. D. The structure and function of communication in society. In Lyman Bryson (Ed.), *The Communication of ideas.* New York: Institute for Religious and Social Studies, 1948.

Lazarsfeld, P., Berelson, B., & Gaudet, H. *The people's choice.* New York: Columbia University Press, 1948.

Lewin, K. Frontiers in group dynamics: Concept, method, and reality in social science, social equilibria, and social change. *Human Relations,* 1947, *1,* 5–41.

Lewin, K. *Resolving social conflicts: Selected papers on group dynamics.* New York: Harper & Row, 1948.

Likert, R. *New patterns of management.* New York: McGraw-Hill, 1961.

Likert, R. *The human organization.* New York: McGraw-Hill, 1967.

Lin, N. *The study of human communication.* Indianapolis: Bobbs-Merrill, 1973.

Littlejohn, S. W. A bibliography of studies related to variables of source credibility. *Bibliographical Annual in Speech Communication,* 1977, *2,* 1–40.

Littlejohn, S. W. Frame analysis and communication. *Communication Research,* 1977a, *4,* 485–492.

Littlejohn, S. W. Symbolic interactionism as an approach to the study of human communication. *Quarterly Journal of Speech,* 1977b, *63,* 84–90.

Littlejohn, S. W. *Theories of human communication.* Columbus, Ohio. Charles E. Merrill, 1978.

Luft, J. *Of human interaction.* Palo Alto, Calif.: National Press Books, 1969.

Manis, J. G., & Meltzer, B. N. (Eds.). *Symbolic interaction.* Boston: Allyn and Bacon, 1972.

March, J. G., & Simon, H. *Organizations.* New York: John Wiley & Sons, 1958.

McGuire, W. Inducing resistance to persuasion; Some contemporary approaches. In L. Berkowitz (Ed.), *Advances in experimental social psychology.* New York: Academic Press, 1964.

McGuire, W. Personality and susceptibility to social influence. In E. F. Borgatta and W. W. Lambert (Eds.), *Handbook of personality theory and research.* Chicago: Rand McNally, 1968.

McLuhan, M. *Understanding media.* New York: McGraw-Hill, 1964.

Mead, G. H. *The philosophy of the present.* Chicago: Open Court, 1932.

Mead, G. H. *Mind, self, and society.* Chicago: University of Chicago Press, 1934.

Mead, G. H. *Movements of thought in the 19th century.* Chicago: University of Chicago Press, 1936.

Mead, G. H. *The philosophy of the act.* Chicago: University of Chicago, Press, 1938.

Mehrabian, A. *Silent messages.* Belmont, Calif.: Wadsworth, 1971.

Miller, G. A. The magical number seven, plus or minus two: Some limits on our capacity for processing information. *Psychological Review,* 1956, *63,* 81–97.

Miller, G. A., Galanter, E., & Pribram, K. H. *Plans and the structure of behavior*. New York: Holt, Rinehart and Winston, 1960.

Morris, C. *Signs, language, and behavior*. New York: George Braziller, 1946.

Morris, C. Foundations of the theory of signs. In *International encyclopedia of unified science* (Vol 1, Part 1). Chicago: University of Chicago Press, 1955.

Morris, C. *Signification and significance*. Cambridge: M.I.T. Press, 1964.

Newcomb, T. *The acquaintance process*. New York: Holt, Rinehart and Winston, 1961.

Ogden, C. K., & Richards, I. A. *The meaning of meaning*. London: Kegan, Paull Trench, Trubner, and Co., 1923.

Osgood, C. On understanding and creating sentences. *American Psychologist*, 1963, *18*, 735–751.

Osgood, C., May, W. H., & Miron, M. S. *Cross cultural universals of affective meaning*. Urbana: University of Illinois Press, 1975.

Osgood, C., & Richards, M. From yang and yin to *and* or *but*. *Language*, 1973, *49*, 380–412.

Osgood, C., Suci, G., & Tannenbaum, P. H. *The measurement of meaning*. Urbana: University of Illinois Press, 1957.

Osgood, C., & Tannenbaum, P. H. The principle of congruity in the prediction of attitude change. *Psychological Review*, 1955, *62*, 42–55.

Parks, M. Relational communication: Theory and research. *Human Communication Research*, 1977, *3*, 372–381.

Pepper, S. *World hypotheses*. Berkeley: University of California Press, 1942.

Piaget, J. *The origins of intelligence in children*. New York: International University Press, 1952.

Piaget, J. *The early growth of logic in the child*. London: Routledge and Kegan Paul, 1964.

Piaget, J. *Structuralism*. London: Routledge and Kegan Paul, 1971.

Piaget, J., & Inhelder, B. *The growth of logical thinking from childhood to adolescence: An essay on the construction of formal operational structures*. New York: Basic Books, 1958.

Polanyi, M. *Knowing and being*. Chicago: University of Chicago Press, 1969.

Richards, I. A. *The philosophy of rhetoric*. New York: Oxford University Press, 1936.

Richards, I. A. *Principles of literary criticism*. New York: Harcourt, Brace & World, 1952.

Rogers, C. *Counselling and psychotherapy*. Boston: Houghton Mifflin, 1942.

Rogers, C. *Client-centered therapy*. Boston: Houghton Mifflin, 1951.

Rogers, C. A theory of therapy, personality, and interpersonal relationships, as developed in the client centered framework. In S. Koch (Ed.), *Psychology: A study of science* (Vol. 3). New York: McGraw-Hill, 1959.

Rogers, C. *On becoming a person*. Boston: Houghton Mifflin, 1961.

Rogers, E. M. *Diffusion of innovations*. New York: Free Press, 1962.

Rogers, E., & Shoemaker, F. F. *Communication of innovations, a cross-cultural approach*. New York: Free Press, 1971.

Rokeach, M. *Beliefs, attitudes, and values: A theory of organization and change.* San Francisco: Jossey-Bass, 1969.

Rokeach, M. *The nature of human values.* New York: Free Press, 1973.

Sapir, E. *Language: An introduction to the study of speech.* New York: Harcourt, Brace & World, 1921.

Schutz, W. *FIRO: A three-dimensional theory of interpersonal behavior.* New York: Holt, Rinehart and Winston, 1958.

Searle, J. Human communication theory and the philosophy of language: Some remarks. In Frank Dance (Ed.), *Human Communication Theory.* New York: Holt, Rinehart and Winston, 1967.

Searle, J. *Speech acts: An essay in the philosophy of language.* Cambridge: Cambridge University Press, 1969.

Shannon, C., & Weaver, W. *The mathematical theory of communication.* Urbana: University of Illinois Press, 1949.

Sherif, M. *Social interaction—process and products.* Chicago: Aldine, 1967.

Sherif, M., & Cantril, H. *The psychology of ego-involvements.* New York: John Wiley & Sons, 1947.

Sherif, M., & Hovland, C. *Social judgment.* New Haven: Yale University Press, 1961.

Sherif, M., Sherif, C., & Nebergall, R. *Attitude and attitude change: The social judgement-involvement approach.* Philadelphia: Saunders, 1965.

Skinner, B. F. *Verbal behavior.* New York: Appleton-Century-Crofts, 1957.

Taylor, F. *Principles of scientific management.* New York: Harper & Row, 1919.

Thibaut, J. W., & Kelley, H. H. *The social psychology of groups.* New York: John Wiley & Sons, 1959.

von Neumann, J. & Morgenstern, O. *The theory of games and economic behavior.* Princeton, N.J.: Princeton University Press, 1944.

Watzlawick, P., Beavin, J., & Jackson, D. *Pragmatics of communication: A study of interactional patterns, pathologies, and paradoxes.* New York: Norton, 1967.

Weber, M. [*The theory of social and economic organizations*] (A. M. Henderson & T. Parsons, trans.). New York: Oxford University Press, 1947.

Weiss, R. Persuasion and the acquisition of attitudes: Models from conditioning and selective learning. *Psychological Reports,* 1962, *11*, 709–732.

Weiss, R. An extension of Hullian learning theory to persuasive communication. In A. Greenwald, T. Brock, and T. Ostrom (Eds.), *Psychological foundations of attitudes.* New York: Academic Press, 1968.

Whorf, B. L. *Language, thought, and reality.* New York: John Wiley & Sons, 1956.

Wiener, N. *Cybernetics or control and communication in the animal and the machine.* Cambridge: M.I.T. Press, 1948.

Wittgenstein, L. *Tractatus logico-philosophicus.* London: Routledge and Kegan Paul, 1922.

Wittgenstein, L. *Philosophical investigations.* Oxford: Basil Blackwell, 1953.

Wittgenstein, L. *The blue and brown books.* Oxford: Basil Blackwell, 1958.

Wright, C. R. Functional analysis and mass communication. *Public Opinion Quarterly,* 1960, *24,* 605–620.

ESSAYS IN HUMAN COMMUNICATION THEORY:

A Comparative Overview

Frank E. X. Dance

The contributed theoretical essays are herein discussed first from the point of view of certain metatheoretical criteria. The essays are then discussed in terms of the authors' comments on some of the questions about human communication behavior suggested in the authors' protocol and summarized for the readers in the preface. The chapter's purpose is comparative description rather than critical analysis, but some points of judgment will necessarily enter into the descriptive process. Critical analysis of the theoretical contributions is both called for and desirable, but such analysis is the proper domain of reviewers and scholars following their reading of and reflection upon the essays.

Metatheory is the study of the qualities of theory and theory building in general, rather than of any specific subject-matter theory. A metatheoretician comments upon the goals and attributes that should mark any well-formed theory. Metatheoreticians, theorists, and critics disagree on an overall list of the constituent goals and attributes of theory. When lists of goals and attributes appear, the order of importance often varies. Just as there are numerous definitions of theory, there are many points of view on the goals and attributes of theory.

Yet, there is indeed overlap in theory definitions and in theoretical goals and attributes as well.

Definitions of theory are implicit in each of the contributed essays and in a few of the essays are explicitly stated. Here are two additional theory definitions:

> A theory is a set of interrelated constructs (concepts), definitions, and propositions that present a systematic view of phenomena by specifying relations among variables, with the purpose of explaining and predicting the phenomena.
>
> *F. Kerlinger*[1]

> The explanatory power of any scientific theory is the relating of facts that hitherto were thought to be unrelated.
>
> *P. Lieberman*[2]

The most generally agreed upon goals of theory and of theory construction are present in the two definitions given above. The general goals are also probably covertly present all of the time and overtly present some of the time in the mind and behavior of the active theorist. Goals are present, either implicitly or explicitly, in the actual process of theory construction. The goals of theory may then be used as touch points in the process of theory evaluation or analysis.

In addition to goals, which are internal to theory construction, theories have certain attributes. Theory attributes consist of metatheoretical judgments as to how well formed the theory is—judgments that usually refer to the theory's structure rather than to its substance, although it should always be remembered that form and substance are in constant interaction. Theory attributes also differ from theory goals in that the former are usually assessed upon presentation of the theory rather than during the process of theory construction.

Goals and attributes are interrelated and may easily impinge upon one another. In some circumstances, a theorist might elect to approach the theory-building task so as to utilize an attribute as a conscious goal.

Goals are implicit in the act of theory building, and attributes are qualities of the form of the theory usually assessed after the theory has been presented. Theorists and critics are also interested in the outcomes of a theory. Outcomes are embodied in the manner in which a theory is applied, or in the uses to which a theory may be put. Outcomes may be used in the process of falsification. All theories must be open to falsification, to being disproved. If there is no way of testing a theory, of falsifying it, the proposed theory is rejected on its surface as failing an essential test of a well-formed theory.

The majority of metatheoreticians agree that explanation and prediction are two of the major goals of any theory. Control is often considered to be an additional goal of a theory. More metatheoreticians agree upon explanation and prediction as goals than upon control as a goal.

The goals of theory, it is hoped, will culminate in bringing a sense of understanding of the phenomenon or phenomena under examination.

Explanation usually deals with detailing exactly what is involved in, or goes into, making a phenomenon work or happen. How well the theory explains is often considered a measure of its power.

Prediction is usually involved with when the phenomenon will occur, work, or happen. How well the theory predicts is often considered a measure of the theory's precision. Some metatheoreticians also discuss "retrodiction," which refers to the occasions of the phenomenon in the past.

Control is usually concerned with (a) causing the phenomenon to work or happen; (b) preventing the phenomenon from working or happening; (c) aborting the phenomenon once it has begun to occur; or (d) interfering with the normal course of the phenomenon's working or happening.

Among the attributes that may characterize a theory are range, parsimony, and elegance.

Range refers to the number of instances of the subject phenomenon covered by the theory. Does the theory concern itself with all instances of human communication or just with human communication in certain situations? Having made the initial cut, does the theory then deal with all instances of human communication in certain situations or only if certain other conditions are present or absent?

Parsimony refers to the economy of assumptions, concepts, and relationships characterizing the theory. Does the theorist ask the reader to accept as taken for granted a number of assumptions? How many assumptions are taken for granted, and is this reality clearly stated at the outset? Are concepts needlessly fragmented, or when teased apart, are the concepts found to be overlapping, which is ignored by the theorist?

Elegance refers to the simplicity or succinctness of expression of the theory. Is the theory presented understandably, or is the presentation arcane or needlessly opaque? Is the theory clouded by esoteric vocabulary or poor grammatical construction? Is it overelaborated?

When discussing theory assessment, Louis Hjelmslev, in *Prologomena to a Theory of Language,* maintained that "a theory's description shall be free from contradiction (self-consistent), exhaustive, and as simple as possible. The requirement of freedom from contradiction takes precedence over the requirement of exhaustive description; the requirement of exhaustive description takes precedence over the requirement of simplicity."[3] In the remainder of this chapter, the goals of (1) explanation and (2) prediction, and the attributes of (1) range, (2) parsimony, and (3) elegance will be used as comparative points for discussing the various theoretical essays.

Of the seven essays presented, five clearly match the overall criterion of an effort after theory. Two of the essays, thought and talk: "Excuse Me, But Have I Been Talking to Myself?" by Charles R. Berger and William Douglas and "All Is for One but One Is Not for All" by Gerald R. Miller and Michael J. Sunnafrank, seem closer to theoretical speculations or viewpoints rather than to partial or grand-theory construction. As speculative essays, the two are important contributions to the literature but do not easily open themselves to comparative analysis by the criteria with which one assesses theory. These two essays are fine examples of theories "in process," of theories in the prepropositional phase that occupies the theorist who is developing the structure and concepts necessary for a larger theory. The authors do reflect on some of the issues suggested for consideration, and these comments will be treated later in this chapter. Certainly within their restricted range, the essays go far toward offering a description and explanation of the behaviors under scrutiny. The two pieces also bear heavily upon each other in terms of focus and treatment. The position of Miller and Sunnafrank seems to be somewhat at odds with that of Berger and Douglas on the issue of the degree of conscious prediction of communication consequences by participants versus the degree of routinization of spoken language. This difference may relate to a difference between the two essays on the question of the role of intent in human communication. It should also be noted that the two papers certainly assist in the development of an understanding of the human communicative phenomena inasmuch as one prepublication reader found these two pieces to be among the most useful of the essays in terms of the reader's academic interests.

In the next pages, this essay will consider the phenomenon upon which the essays seem to focus; the contributions' attention to explanation and prediction; how the essays bear on the disputed goal of control; the attributes; and the proposed issues pertinent to human communication theory.

Phenomenon

Two of the first questions asked of a theory are: What is it a theory of? and What serves as the data base upon which the theory is predicated? The base phenomenon of each of the contributed essays is implicitly spoken language—most often spoken language for communication among human beings. The reality of the spoken-language base does not mean that the authors have restricted their theories to spoken language, but that spoken language seems to serve as the original base from which the contributed points of view are developed. Each of the essays allows for the theoretical position to be applied with equal force to the expression of spoken language in its alternate forms, such as writing. The titre of focus upon the phenomenon of spoken language varies among the contributions from minimal in Fisher to maximum in Dance.

Explanation (Power) and Prediction (Precision)

These goals are so closely intertwined that they will be treated together. It is also important to note that explanation and prediction also interact with range so that at times, the attribute of range is alluded to in this section.

The two efforts after a rules perspective in theory construction in human communication—Cronen, Pearce, and Harris's "The Coordinated Management of Meaning: A Theory of Communication" and Cushman, Valentinsen, and Dietrich's "A Rules Theory of Interpersonal Relationships"—both provide clear statements of range and, within the boundaries of the indicated range, quite productive, although not entirely complementary, explanations of the phenomena investigated and examined.

Von Wright's practical syllogism, which infuses Cushman, et al. (but not Cronen, et al.), is an *ex post actu* device that explains only after an act has already been performed and thus may well be prone to the fallacy of attributing causality on the basis of temporal sequentiality—the *post hoc, ergo propter hoc* (after this, therefore because of this) fallacy. The rules-perspective essays, perhaps because of data gathering constraints, also tend to fall later in the human developmental chronology than do the considerations of Dance or of Delia, et al. Pushing the rules perspective further and further back developmentally, into childhood, early childhood, and the earliest stages of spoken language acquisition, may prove productive and illuminating. Because of the developmental locus of the data base for the rules perspective, the explanatory power and the predictive precision of the rules chapters seem to be bounded by the interpersonal level and by postchildhood human communicative acts or events. Except for the limitation of the postchildhood boundary, the rules of Cronen, et al., and of Cushman, et al., would apply across the phenomena discussed by the other contributors, thus allowing for a varied arena of testing and speculation.

The emphasis on a "scientific" approach to theory construction, especially noticeable in statements within the essay by Cushman,

Valentinsen, and Dietrich, is laudable. However, what is commonly construed as the "scientific" approach or as the appropriate use of "scientific" methodology is certainly but one among a goodly array of equally valuable paths to knowledge, especially when the "knowledge" being sought is an enlightened understanding of the part played by human communication in the overall human condition.

Delia, O'Keefe, and O'Keefe's "The Constructivist Approach to Communication" provides a substantial body of supporting materials that lend emphasis to the explanatory goal of theory construction. Given the power of the constructivist approach, there seems to be a corresponding predictive strength. The argument made by the authors for concentrated research on a specific theoretical vision is nicely made and quite persuasive. The constructivists are actively pushing their data base closer and closer to the beginnings of individual experience with human communication. This move toward beginnings serves to extend their data base, which is already rooted in adolescent and adult communicative experiences and behaviors. Delia, et al., in their discussion of scripts, organizing schemes, and full awareness, offer observations that might well cause the reader to pose questions for the positions taken by Berger and Douglas, and by Miller and Sunnafrank concerning communicative routinization. The "reflective empiricism" of the constructivist position also bears upon the rules perspective in terms of the constructivist observation concerning negotiation rather than rule-ordained communicative behaviors. It is at this point of meeting between the constructivist perspective and the rules perspective that one might choose to reflect upon exactly how the Cushman, et al. treatment of the constructivist research either supports or contests the rules perspective. The endurance of the contest between the rationalist and the empiricist approaches to knowledge about human behavior, highlighted by the Chomsky/Piaget debate, is also demonstrated in the different starting positions taken by Delia, et al. and by Dance.[4] Whereas the constructivist approach is closely akin to the Piagetian, Dance's approach seems to embody more of the rationalist or Chomskian tradition. However, the "constructivist theory" and the "speech theory" at times make use of both empiricist and rationalist contributions and positions.

Dance also differs from Delia, et al. in the amount of empirical testing of the respective theoretical approaches. Whereas Delia, et al. offer substantial empirical support for many of their constructivist positions, the research support offered by Dance appears relatively meager. What research Dance does cite, with some exceptions, such as J. Johnson, S. H. Johnson, Sharpe, and Zak-Dance, is mostly drawn from outside the speech communication discipline. There is a need for further research on the speech theory of human communication.

Dance aspires to a robust theory characterized by both power and precision, but at this time, his theory is characterized more by explanation than by prediction.

On the surface, at least, there seem to be a number of areas of conceptual confluence among the theories offered by Cronen, et al., Dance, and by Delia, et al. The "constructs" basic to the constructivist approach could readily be interpreted as quite similar to the "contrast" basic to Dance's proposed theory. The manner in which either "contrast" or "constructs" would be articulated or managed in the process of human communication development might well be informed by the rules perspective set forth by Cronen, et al. This brief comment on the possible relationships among three of the essays intimates that whereas none of the present essays may be stating "the" theory, all of them are making contributions to the construction of grand theory in the area of human communication.

Fisher's consideration of general systems theory as it applies to human communication theory is a search after a most fulsome explanation. However the very breadth of the effort makes difficult its realization. Fisher offers an explanatory mind-set important for any theorist to contemplate closely. The predictive goal of Fisher's essay is present in a quite general form but may tend to a loss of precision as it is applied to particular instances.

Control

The theories presented in the contributions, insofar as they have explanatory and predictive qualities, offer the opportunity for control of the behavior or phenomenon under discussion. Miller and Sunnafrank's discussion of "control" within their essay treats control not as a metatheoretical goal but as a primary objective of the phenomenon of human communication from their point of view.

A Sense of Understanding

It would be remarkable were one able to give a close reading to any or all of the contributed essays without developing a corresponding enrichment of one's sense of understanding of human communication.

Range, Parsimony, and Elegance

Range varies widely among the contributions. The narrowest range seems to be that of Berger and Douglas, followed by that of Miller and Sunnafrank. Cronen, et al. and Cushman, et al., although forming their data bases from a relatively bounded range of communicative experiences, offer an extended application range for their theoretical observations. The rules-perspective data base will be considerably extended in range when moved beyond the interpersonal level and to both earlier and later stages of the individual's communicative development. Since range and level interact, it should be mentioned that all four of the essays so far considered under range are almost totally and admittedly limited to the interpersonal level of human communication.

Dance's contribution intends to include all instances of the human use of spoken language from its inception in the individual to the individual's use of spoken language across the entire lifespan. This intent is not fully realized in the present statement of the theory. Dance's applicatory range seems broad, but the data range is at this time focused more on the earliest developmental stages of individual use of spoken language.

Delia, et al. also seem to wish to include the entire developmental range within their theory; however, the constructivist position is consciously interactionist and interpersonal and is thus data-base bound to the range of human interpersonal communication.

Fisher's contribution, edging as it does toward the metatheoretical, has the broadest range of any of the essays.

Again, the fact that the different theoretical contributions have differing ranges may well be a strength rather than a weakness at this stage in the quest for an overall theoretical structure for human communication phenomena.

Parsimony is not an attribute characterizing the theoretical contributions in this volume. Although there are differing degrees of parsimony present—a few of the essays do try to set out their underlying assumptions—generally none of the theories is yet in that stage of development where parsimony has sufficiently been taken into consideration as a theoretical attribute. Perhaps one means of assessing parsimony is by using Professor J. Capella's suggested method of taking two theories that propose to account for the same phenomena and, all other things being equal, choose the theory that requires the fewest assumptions and that proposes the most economical structure for explaining the phenomenon or phenomena under investigation.

Elegance is a singularly elusive attribute to evaluate. Elegance seems to be a combination of taste and artistic judgment. If an essay tends toward obscurantism or is excessively opaque or conceptually inaccessible, then elegance is not that essay's hallmark. Let each reader make the judgment as to each essay's style and whether the reader found that style appealing and elegant.

Other Issues Pertinent to Human Communication Theorizing

In a 1970 study, Dance reported on a thematic and content analysis of 95 published definitions of communication. After partialing out 15 conceptual components, Dance noted that there were three of these conceptual components upon which the definitions of communication critically divided. The three items of critical conceptual differentiation provided points upon which the definitions clearly differed. The three points of differentiation were (1) the level of the observations upon which the definition was based—for example, all animals, just humans, within the individual, between two individuals, among many individuals, and so on; (2) the presence or absence of intent on the part of the sender; and (3) the normative judgment of the communicative act—for example, was the act good or bad, successful or unsuccessful, effective or ineffective, and so on.[5]

As of this writing (1981) it seems that the third point, the normative judgment, is seldom alluded to within the essays in this volume and, in fact, is seldom found in definitions of human communication published in professional journals in recent years.

The other two points, level and intent, are still present and, if judged by the attention given to them, are still quite important.

· Level. If we choose to consider the communication of all animate matter, we accept a task far broader than if we narrow our observational field to include only human beings. If we choose to consider human communication as it occurs within, between, among individuals, from one individual to many, and when mediated by technological extenders such as radio or television, we have a different range from when we restrict our study to one or a few (for example, just intrapersonal or just interpersonal) of these communicative loci.

All of this volume's essays focus primarily upon human communication and treat other places of communication, such as animal communication, indirectly if at all.

The greatest number of the essays focus on the interpersonal level of human communication. Berger and Douglas, for example, center on a relatively narrow area (this judgment of narrowness depends upon whether or not the authors are correct or incorrect in their analysis) of interpersonal communication, even though the reality of intrapersonal communication would seemingly have to be accepted as a given if considering routinization. Miller and Sunnafrank also avowedly focus on the interpersonal level and upon relational development. Cronen, Pearce, and Harris consider their offering to constitute a general theory of interpersonal communication and thus center on the interpersonal level, implicitly and explicitly, throughout their essay. It is worth noting, however, that Cronen, et al. also state that the locus of meaning is intrapersonal, while the locus of action is interpersonal— a statement bringing intrapersonal communication onto center stage when observing and considering interpersonal human communication. An interesting question raised by this statement of Cronen, et al. is the possible relationship between the intrapersonal locus of meaning when considered in the light of Cronen, et al., as well as of Delia, et al., and Fisher's suggestion or implication that meaning may be interpersonally constructed. Cronen, et al. discussion of the individual as a system meshes nicely with Fisher's chapter. Cushman, et al. center their focus on the interpersonal level. Dance's theory developmentally cuts across all levels of human communication. Delia, et al. are almost totally interpersonal, although they do take into consideration the person's biological being, which to some extent forces their theory into the intrapersonal level. In addition, the concern of Delia, et al. with "intent" also causes them to consider seriously the intrapersonal level of human communication. Fisher is not theoretically level-bound, although he focuses more on the interpersonal level since he states that interpersonal communication is by far the most common and most practical of all communication.

The choice of level is no doubt influenced by accessibility—it is very difficult to examine intrapersonal communication—as well as by a theorist's position on the reason for the existence of human communication in the first place.

· *Intent.* The conceptual component of intent may markedly reduce the behavioral field and thus substantially alter a theory's range and power. What is meant by intent? Where does intent situate itself— in the sender, in the receiver, in the message, in the relationship? What about human communicative events marked by accident or deception? On what level does intent have its home? Philosophical considerations of human communication have, in the past decade, raised the questions of intentionality and intent to a new level of visibility and importance.

The two essays in which intent is addressed most directly are those by Dance and by Delia, O'Keefe, and O'Keefe. Delia, et al. consider individual intentionality central to human communication since the constructivists believe communication to be a process in which the communicative intentions of the participants are a focus of interaction. The constructivist's concern for intent is most likely what makes their position contrast to a marked degree with the position of Berger and Douglas, and to a lesser degree, with the position of Miller and Sunnafrank. The constructivist position offers an important treatment of intent, although there are still a number of questions that may be addressed to the constructivist vis-à-vis intentionality and intent. For example, How do communication, spoken language, and intent interact? Does intent lead to communication or flow from communication? Is intent conscious? Is intent structured intrapersonally or interpersonally? These questions aside, it is obvious that the constructivist position holds intent to be central to human communication and thus affords intent close observational and research scrutiny.

Dance believes that spoken language precedes the development of conscious intent and intentionality, and that both intent and intentionality seem to be dependent in their conscious and most human use upon the birth of spoken language. In fact, for Dance, conscious intrapersonal intentionality and intent seem to develop in a direct relationship within the human child. Dance's theory raises choice and intent to a position of great importance within a theory of human communication.

Fisher asserts that intention arises out of interaction and thus effectively dismisses consideration of intrapersonal intent. Meaning, which for some is intimately connected to intent in human communication, for Fisher is retrospectively interpreted or is assigned to the message only by arising out of and after the performance of communicative actions or behaviors. Thus, for Fisher, initial intent is not to be estimated or considered until and unless a communicative action has been performed and then has been confirmed by subsequent actions. Intent seems for Fisher to be somewhat attached to meaning, and both meaning and intent are the result of, rather than prior to, human communication. Here, there seems to be quite a clear difference between Fisher and Dance and Delia, et al.

While an awareness and sensitivity to intent seem to be present both in Cronen, et al. and Cushman, et al., it is difficult to draw to the surface a clear understanding of their view of the role of intentionality and intent in human communication. The comment of Cronen and his colleagues about meaning being located on the intrapersonal level suggests some undeveloped ideas on their part concerning the locus of intent. Cushman, et al. allude directly to intent in a number of instances but never take the further step of defining exactly what it is they mean by the term *intent* or how they are using the term within their theory. Since, at times, it seems that Cushman, et al. are discussing communicative behaviors that obtain within other than specifically human animal behavioral patterns, it is interesting to speculate how this theoretical group might view the part played by common intentions in animal other than human communication. The discussion of standardized usage within the Cushman, et al. essay is also reminiscent of the treatments of automatization and routinization found in Berger and Douglas, and to a lesser extent in Miller and Sunnafrank.

Berger and Douglas's position bears directly but somewhat weakly on the problem of intentionality. A question arises from their treatment as to whether within their thinking intent is unconscious or conscious in the development of routinization. Perhaps intent may be present initially and then fade or become less manifest or conscious as familiarity and routinization take over. In earlier writings, Miller has commented on the place of intent in human communication, but in the piece by Miller and Sunnafrank, there is no centering upon the question of intent. Perhaps Miller and Sunnafrank's discussion of cognitive involvement encompasses their view of intentionality as well.

Intent, intentionality, and meaning are important topics for human communication theory, and it is hoped that the manner in which these topics are treated by the essays in this book may stimulate the interest of the readers concerning the topics as well as intensify the consideration of the topics by human communication scholars.

· *Raison d'Être.* Perhaps a concern with the reason for the existence of human communication seems esoteric. There is, however, an interaction between one's estimate of the basic reason for the existence of human communication and one's choice and performance of research in or on human communication. If, for instance, one views human communication as existing solely or primarily for the purpose of human interaction, as a means of creating and maintaining social relationships and society, then the questions one will be interested in studying and answering will naturally derive from this view and will be interactionist, relational, and mostly interpersonal in nature. There are other possible views than the interactionist view. An argument for an alternate view is that the primary reason for the existence of human communication (spoken language) is mentation, which is then used to inform zoosemiotically present animal communicative behaviors and thus raise those previously present interactive behaviors to a uniquely human form—may be found in Dance's essay in *Communication Yearbook II*.[6] This alternate mentative, or significative, view is also suggested in some of the writings of N. Chomsky, U. Eco, and S. Langer, and is to be the subject of some of the writing in progress by T. Sebeok.

The interactive view of the raison d'être for human communication is certainly the dominant view in the present field of speech communication. With the exception of Dance, each of the present contributors espouses the interactionist view either overtly or by implication.

For Berger and Douglas; Cronen, Pearce, and Harris; Cushman, Valentinsen, and Dietrich; Delia, O'Keefe, and O'Keefe; Fisher; Miller and Sunnafrank; and for Littlejohn as well, the reason for the existence of human communication is interaction. Dance alone argues that the raison d'être of human communication is first, mentation, and second, interaction informed by mentation. Dance suggests that spoken language and human communication allow the individual to take thought and then to inform interaction by that thought.

Since the research and theory-building goals of human communication scholars may be greatly affected by their view of the raison d'être of human communication, perhaps this question needs further investigation, reflection, and discussion.

· *Modal Dominance or Equipotentiality.* The question of the effect of mode (spoken, gestured, etc.) on the birth, development, and manifestation of human communication is studied within a number of disciplines, such as comparative psychology, psycholinguistics, and speech science. Within the field of speech communication, this problem does not seem to concern most current theorists. The only essay in which the issue of the effect of mode upon the acquisition, development, and use of human communication is addressed is Dance's.

· *Falsification.* All theories must be open to falsification if they are to be considered well formed. All of the theories presented in this volume are open to falsification, and all of the theorists herein represented are committed to continued efforts in pursuit of such falsification. It is through efforts after falsification that the theories presented may be tested and refined, or abandoned. Readers with ideas or suggestions for falsification are encouraged to pursue their research interests and to communicate their thoughts and results to the appropriate theorists.

Concluding Comment

The communication of human beings is a complex and involved set of behaviors that comprises a subject the complexity of which engenders a parallel complex and involved search for any underlying theory, theoretical approaches, and understanding. In this volume, we have read a number of theoretical proposals made by theorists from the field of speech communication. There is no strain between theory and research, or between theory and practice. Theory should inform research and be reflected in practice. A number of the contributors, such as Delia, O'Keefe, and O'Keefe, have provided pointed and appropriate commentaries concerning the necessary interpenetration of theory and research.

Theorists are interested in the continued refinement of concepts and of their attendant terms. Theorists continually search for salient variables and for the relationships among them. They try to systematize what we already know so as to better specify our areas of ignorance. Theorists pursue theory and the accompanying research so as to shed light upon the areas of conceptual shadow and to illuminate the dark recesses of our ignorance.

The diligent and continued pursuit of explanation and prediction, leading to a sense of understanding about human communication, is what human communication theory building is all about and is what the essays in this book have as their focus.

Notes

1. Kerlinger, F. *Research methods in the behavioral sciences* (2nd ed.). New York: Holt, Rinehart and Winston, 1973, p. 9.
2. Lieberman, P. *On the origins of language.* New York: Macmillan, 1975, p. 171.
3. Translated by F. J. Whitfield, Madison: University of Wisconsin Press, 1971, p. 11.
4. Piattelli-Palmarini, M. (ed). *Language and learning: The debate between Jean Piaget and Noam Chomsky.* Cambridge: Harvard University Press, 1980, passim.
5. Dance, F. E. X. The "concept" of communication. *Journal of Communication,* 1970, XX, 201–210.
6. Dance, F. E. X. Human communication theory: A highly selective review and two commentaries. In B. Ruben (Ed.), *Communication Yearbook II.* New Brunswick, N.J.: ICA and Transaction Books, 1978, pp. 7–22.